World Cities in History

Joshua Leon explores 6,000 years of urban networks and the politics that drove them, from Uruk in the fourth millennium BCE to Amsterdam's seventeenth-century "golden age." He provides a fresh, interdisciplinary reading of significant periods in history, showing how global networks have shaped everyday life. Alongside grand architecture, art, and literature, these extraordinary places also innovated ways to exert control over far-flung hinterlands, the labor of their citizens, and rigid class, race, and gender divides. Asking what it meant for ordinary people to live in Athens, Rome, Chang'an, or Baghdad – those who built and fed these cities, not just their rulers – he offers one of the few fully rendered applications of world cities theory to historical cases. The result is not only vividly detailed and accessible but an intriguing and theoretically original contribution to urban history.

Joshua K. Leon is professor of political science at Iona University and was the 2022–2023 Robert David Lion Gardiner Fellow at the New-York Historical Society.

World Cities in History

Urban Networks from Ancient Mesopotamia to the Dutch Empire

Joshua K. Leon

Iona University

CAMBRIDGE
UNIVERSITY PRESS

CAMBRIDGE
UNIVERSITY PRESS

Shaftesbury Road, Cambridge CB2 8EA, United Kingdom

One Liberty Plaza, 20th Floor, New York, NY 10006, USA

477 Williamstown Road, Port Melbourne, VIC 3207, Australia

314–321, 3rd Floor, Plot 3, Splendor Forum, Jasola District Centre, New Delhi – 110025, India

103 Penang Road, #05-06/07, Visioncrest Commercial, Singapore 238467

Cambridge University Press is part of Cambridge University Press & Assessment, a department of the University of Cambridge.

We share the University's mission to contribute to society through the pursuit of education, learning and research at the highest international levels of excellence.

www.cambridge.org
Information on this title: www.cambridge.org/9781009444972

DOI: 10.1017/9781009444958

First published 2025

A catalogue record for this publication is available from the British Library

Library of Congress Cataloging-in-Publication Data
Names: Leon, Joshua K., 1980- author.
Title: World cities in history : urban networks from ancient Mesopotamia to the Dutch Empire / Joshua K. Leon, Iona College, New York.
Description: Cambridge, United Kingdom ; New York, NY : Cambridge University Press, 2024. | Includes bibliographical references and index.
Identifiers: LCCN 2023059508 (print) | LCCN 2023059509 (ebook) | ISBN 9781009444972 (hardback) | ISBN 9781009444996 (paperback) | ISBN 9781009444958 (ebook)
Subjects: LCSH: Cities and towns–History.
Classification: LCC HT111 .L46 2024 (print) | LCC HT111 (ebook) | DDC 909/.09732–dc23/eng/20240102
LC record available at https://lccn.loc.gov/2023059508
LC ebook record available at https://lccn.loc.gov/2023059509

ISBN 978-1-009-44497-2 Hardback
ISBN 978-1-009-44499-6 Paperback

For my wife, Erin L. Leon

Contents

Figures

Acknowledgments

This project began when my then-department chair Robert J. Lacey encouraged me to apply for sabbatical in 2018–2019. I was in residence at the New York Historical Society (NYHS) when I completed revisions for this book, with generous support from the Robert David Lion Gardiner Foundation.

Owen Temby offered encouraging feedback to an early chapter draft at the 2019 New England Political Science Association (NEPSA) conference in Portland, Maine. James Busumtwi-Sam encouraged me to address the non-western cities more fully at the 2019 International Studies Association (ISA) conference in Accra, Ghana. Zachary Shirkey, a fellow enthusiast of ancient world politics, read a draft of Chapter 1 at the 2022 NEPSA in Bretton Woods, New Hampshire. Mats Berglund led a lively discussion in response to Chapter 11 at the 2022 European Association of Urban History (EUAH) in Antwerp, Belgium. Alison Suen offered detailed responses to Chapter 6. I took most of their advice, and value their unique perspectives.

A very special thank you to Lucy Rhymer, Rosa Martin, and the team at Cambridge University Press, along with three anonymous reviewers for their detailed insights.

I was delighted at William A. Dorman's vocal encouragement midway through the project. Sadly, Bill passed away in 2022. As he would say, keep on keeping on. My mentors Orfeo Fioretos, Patrick Cannon, Mark A. Pollack, and Bahman Fozouni continue to influence my thinking in anything I write. This book attempts to follow their lofty examples.

My departmental colleagues – Robert J. Lacey, Jeanne Sheehan Zaino, Mary Hagerty, Ceceli Chadwick, and Jeff Sherman – are simply the best. The same goes for my campus colleagues Bhaswati Sengupta, Alison Suen, Joshua R. Klein, and Alice Kelly, my colleague at NYHS. All of them endured countless conversations about pre-modern cities, responding with ideas, moral support, and unwavering positivity. A reading group organized by the artist collective Archeology of the Frivolous kept discussion alive during the pandemic shutdowns.

The New York Public Library's (NYPL) Marli program offered special access to the NYPL's vast research collection, as well as the main libraries at NYU and Columbia University. Iona University's small but excellent library was tremendously helpful. Special thanks to the many librarians at these institutions whose work made this research possible.

Café Ines on the Upper East Side offered a welcoming space to work.

Several friends and family read drafts, responding with lively conversations. My wife, Erin L. Leon, read every word of every draft, copy reading and offering valuable suggestions from the beginning. Together we explored archeological sites and museums all over the world, to see and feel the lost worlds that inhabit this book.

1 Introduction

Captives sustained the population of Babylon. Its towering walls limited escape. Athens was powerful because of seafaring prowess, not local abundance. Venice had a small population but was a major force in the Mediterranean. Hanseatic Lübeck was even smaller but dominated the Baltics, a security threat to large kingdoms. Amsterdam's influence accelerated on the backs of slaves, distant growing areas, and mineral extraction along an intricate network of towns.

Tenochtitlan used diplomacy and alliances to exploit territories, not direct authority. Ancient Rome was the core in a web of peripheral cities, a vacuum for foreign goods. Ptolemaic Alexandria brutally dominated its producing hinterlands in a veritable police state system of land management. These cities were not self-sufficient. Their leaders designed them to take control over resources from elsewhere, much as primary goods producers in the modern world's poorest regions routinely work for prices set by investors in New York, London or Chicago.

This book is about the politics of pre-modern city networks and the cities at the centers of them. It enters a sustained conversation about cities as drivers of globalization and shapers of social and geographic division. World cities studies – explained and critiqued in this chapter – helped put cities at the center of popular and scholarly discussion. We live in a seemingly terminal urban age, what Brenner and Schmid call planetary urbanization, with an expansion of cities at unprecedented physical scales and ecological impacts.[1] This book is for any reader looking to engage with historic precedents to this. On an elemental level, it is for anyone interested in the urban politics of expansionist states in as vivid and precise detail as possible. Hopefully it encourages world cities scholars to fully engage with important social histories. It spells out the case for more inclusive approaches to the study of urban networks.

1 Neil Brenner and Christian Schmid, "Planetary Urbanization," in Mathew Gandy (ed.), *Urban Constellations* (Berlin: Jovis, 2012), 10–13, 11.

Ten empirical chapters form the heart of the book. Each is a case study of an important urban age. Chapter 2 explores networks in Mesopotamia, especially those of Uruk, Ur, and Babylon. Chapters 3 and 4 survey Classical and Hellenistic Greek cities, with substantial discussion of Athens and Alexandria. Chapter 5 connects the ancient city of Rome to its empire and hinterlands. Chapter 6 explores the modular walled ancient and medieval Chinese capital of Chang'an. Chapter 7 is about the Mesoamerican urban revolutions in Teotihuacan, Tikal, and Tenochtitlan. Chapter 8 explores Islamic city networks leading up to Baghdad's founding during the Abbasid period. Chapter 9 is about Italian communes, with an emphasis on Venice. Chapters 10 and 11 shift to the Baltics and Atlantic, scrutinizing the Hanseatic League of trading cities and the "hegemonic" Dutch Empire in turn.

These places leveraged architecture and planning to assume seminal roles in *intercity relations*, the formal and informal engagement between cities, including diplomacy and statecraft by city leaders. Except for Amsterdam, these cities are not literally "world cities" in the sense that they influenced every inhabited continent. In reality they had limited to no knowledge of whole zones of civilization, let alone the logistical reach to dominate them. Instead they occupied central places in their own worlds: the Fertile Crescent, the Yellow River Basin, the Mediterranean, Mesoamerica, the Baltics, and so on. The inhabitants of these cities knew of worlds beyond, frequently engaging them. The Silk Roads resoundingly expanded contacts, firing geographic imaginations across Eurasia in antiquity. Some urban spheres of influence were near universal in pre-modern notions of time and space. Baghdad resided at the center of *Dar al Islam*, the boundaries of Islamic territory. Rome was the microcosm of the *orbis terrarum*, the expanse of the world as the Romans understood it. Their architectural symbols spoke of their cities as seats of world dominion. Their respective worlds excluded India and China, from which luxury goods regularly arrived. Given constraints, the reach of these cities was nothing short of remarkable. Their exertions forged expansive networks that carried trade, diplomacy, radical notions, and assertions of power. They set the precedent for modern world cities – today's New Yorks, Londons, and Hong Kongs – whose impacts are planetary in scale.

Each chapter hinges on the following themes:

> *Environmental preconditions for city networks.* The world cities under study did not project power on the basis of resource superiority over other places. In a recurrent theme throughout history, the leading centers of power suffered some form of environmental *scarcity* rather than any special abundance. This goes part way to explaining why the first cities emerged in the southern part of the Fertile Crescent rather than the north, where agriculture could be

rain fed, not necessitating massive irrigation systems. The leading power centers overcame enormous challenges, having to manage resources over longer distances than places of abundance. Remarkably, Mayans forged large cities in dense tropically forested areas. This challenge in turn required city builders to develop complex systems of administration and hierarchy, themselves a kind of power. However the leading cities did have decisive environmental advantages, most importantly riverine or oceanic sea routes that allowed them to establish linkages with other places.

Population politics: Forced resettlement, expulsions, and childbirths. Pre-modern cities, without vaccines, without antibiotics and other basic public health measures, were population sinks with higher death rates than in rural or nomadic settings. Population was power. Maintaining it in cities required migration – frequently involuntary. Greek city founding entailed mergers of older cities, and Mesopotamian cities abducted populations in episodes including the Babylonian captivity (see Chapter 2). There was tremendous pressure on women to bear large numbers of children until their bodies gave out in their mid-twenties, as was the case in ancient Athens. Labor demands required forcibly stationary populations in and out of the city. City leaders locked gates at night, with architectural features in ancient and medieval cities serving the purposes of surveillance and control. An extreme case of this was in Ptolemaic Egypt, which met environmental challenges and labor shortages by erecting what must be considered one of the most totalitarian labor systems in history. This was central to the politics of the ancient world, where desertion was the most potent weapon of the lower orders. No less grotesque was the transatlantic slave trade run between Amsterdam and Dutch holdings in West Africa, the Caribbean, and the Americas. There too, desertion was the most potent resistance, as slaves and even terrified mercenaries fled and formed colonies. Their branding of slaves to aid recapture harkens back to severe regulatory measures in other eras.

The domination of the hinterlands by cities. Ptolemaic Egypt's repressive system of agriculture and hydrological construction is an extreme example, but in each of the cases under study, the power of cities over rural spaces expanded. Italian city-states called their spheres of influence *contados*, a concept widely in evidence elsewhere. In ages where nomadic existences were common, cities sought control over stationary populations outside their walls. Golden ages for cities tended to be disastrous for those living in their hinterlands, as Rome's latifundia suggest. The latifundia were large slaveholding plantations owned by wealthy patricians from the cities who used them as retreats. They entail extensive land management from urban cores that used them as sources of income to support idle patrician lifestyles. Centralizing states denounced pastoralism and nomadism, movements outside administrative control. Cities also extracted massive surpluses from growing regions, leaving actual growers in destitution. The lack of automated technology meant that the only way to increase output was to work labor harder. Rome's fall may well have been a good thing for rural Italy.

Menageries of state-types. The city-state figures heavily in the history of city networks, but cities themselves have autonomous or semi-autonomous roles in establishing linkages under a variety of settings. City networks form the foundations of some territorial empires, as was the case with the Hellenistic satrapies left over in the wake of Alexander the Great's conquests. In other instances, city-states make for potent adversaries to large populous empires. Athens was swamped by Macedonian and then Roman power, while Venice retained independence for centuries. The history of city networks shows the indeterminacy of statecraft, spanning time periods in which city-states, territorial empires, nomadic societies, feudal orders, and religious authority all comingled. Today's codified nation-state system is an exception to civilized history. Moreover, urban ages have come and gone, interrupted by so-called dark ages where non-urban systems prevailed. In some cases the urban ages were the interruptions, as dark ages lasted considerably longer. "Dark age" is a subjective term, given that such periods arguably offered respite for peasantries otherwise dominated by cities. Scholars are challenging the pejorative phrase.[2] What we today call civil liberties, especially freedom of migration, may well have been greater in the absence of central states emanating from cities regulating population movements. These were by definition extended periods of deurbanization, usually with recessions in the knowledge production sustaining cities, such as written language. Ancient Mesopotamian history featured centuries-long dark ages, as did that of Ancient Greece and medieval Europe.

[2] For example, Matthew Gabriele and David M. Perry, *The Bright Ages: A New History of Medieval Europe* (New York: Harper Collins, 2021), 2.

Urban experiences in city networks were distinctive. As with today's world cities, everyday life in ancient, medieval, and pre-modern cities was shaped by extremes. Inequality tended to worsen in these places during their golden ages, evidenced in built environments, especially by increased differentiation in housing conditions. As global connectivity sustained larger populations, conditions consequentially deteriorated. The extreme case is Rome, in which housing conditions for the poor were so dire that many slept in graveyards or top floor units prone to collapse and tragic holocausts. City networks also homogenized experiences, creating proto-international styles that gave linked cities a sense of familiarity for mobile populations. This was in evidence far outside core cities, shaping life on the periphery as well. A traveler in the Hellenistic period arriving at a new city would know to visit the gymnasiums and agoras that were focal points of social activity. These elements are found as far afield as present day Afghanistan. Teotihuacan apartments housed a cosmopolitan cacophony of languages and customs. A traveler in the Roman Empire, from Palestine to Britain, would head straight for the baths. Architectural styles traveled alongside literature, political dissent, languages, news, manufactured goods, religions, and so on. Mesoamerican style horizons proliferated in art and architecture. City building in city networks was outward looking. Ports such as Rome's Ostia and Athens's Piraeus grew. The concept of inns evolved. Grand boulevards and showy architecture from Nebuchadnezzar II's Processional Way to the Athenian Acropolis projected power to visitors as well as restive populations. Baghdad's exotic markets, its Chinese junks at port, its litany of languages and religions helped establish the city as a preeminent cosmopolis of the early ninth century CE.

What all of these city networks have in common is that the management of labor, physical resources, and production is the reason for their existence. They were linked physically in terms of regional or global contacts, even if indirectly. They were linked metaphysically in the realms of ideas, aesthetics, and culture. From the step gabled houses in the Baltics, to Greek and Roman city planning and architecture, city networks tend toward stylistic homogenization or oft-bemoaned international styles of the times. Within these criteria is a great deal of variation. Population distributions and patterns differ widely. City networks existed across a number of economic systems and state types before capitalism and the sovereign state. The internet is the most important metaphysical linkage today, but ancient cities expressed soft power through informational storage means of their own: cuneiform, linear A, linear B, tablature, and papyrus. Venice and Amsterdam were printing powerhouses. Bodies of water were the most important linkages between cities until the 1800s. Pre-modern networks saw growth in waterborne long distance trading in a diversity of goods as shipping became more efficient. Each city studied here asserted its own remarkable innovative and adaptive approach to city building. Some, like Venice and Tikal, were astonishing in their persistence and capacities for resurgence.

Fascinating and impactful on their own, these case selections derive from a search for analogies to the present-day world city network. Today's world cities are connected at a planetary scale. They are not places but "processes," by one definition, constantly reinventing themselves around financial flows in an age of capitalism.[3] The leading cities in earlier urban networks operated under different social logics than today but show striking similarities. They had dense concentrations in knowledge capital, administrative capability, long distance trade, financial mechanisms, and migration. They were heavily altered by their positions in world networks, building and rebuilding in response to far flung contacts. The negative byproducts of this are also in evidence. Cities became more crowded, expensive, and prone to steepening social hierarchies. Contexts may change dramatically, but these human experiences will be familiar. Survival in these cities was as daunting as any nonurban settings. We will nevertheless see a great deal of variance. Different things have moved from place to place via differing mechanisms, creating unique iterations of the world city across time.

A persistent assertion of this book is that the city as theorized by modern urbanists was realized long ago, starting with Uruk from the fourth millennium BCE.[4] Cities are not simply large settlements, which existed with populations in the thousands during the Neolithic period. All cities have large populations and contiguous built-up areas. These are prerequisite conditions. Cities are by definition not self-sufficient, relying on trade or a hinterland for resources. They entail the elaborate management of internal spaces, and of their essential supply zones. Unlike egalitarian Neolithic villages, cities established class categories, specialized labor, and property regimes that limited access to goods. Writing emerged to facilitate this differentiation. World cities are central to the most elaborate regional networks linking multiple urban areas.

Each chapter centers on a world city and its network with as much geographic and structural variation as possible while retaining explanatory depth.

[3] Manuel Castells, "The Space of Flows," in Ida Susser (ed.), *The Castells Reader on Cities and Social Theory* (Oxford: Blackwell, 2002), 314–366, 322.

[4] For an elaborate discussion on the definition of early cities in historic context, see Edward W. Soja, *Postmetropolis: Critical Studies of Cities and Regions* (Oxford: Blackwell, 2000), 19.

For example, Lübeck, a leader in the medieval Hanseatic League, had a population of 28,000, about one-seventieth the size of Tang Chang'an. The Hanse network required intense negotiation between relatively equal cities across boundaries. Chang'an and Rome existed in the context of unified territorial empires. Where Rome's urban network enabled a degree of local autonomy, its contemporary Han Chang'an went further with bureaucratic control. Some of our cases explore independent city-states such as classical Athens or medieval Venice. Others, like Lübeck, made decisions in the context of multiple layers of overarching imperial and ecclesiastical authority. Mesoamerica, China, and the Fertile Crescent were pristine sites of urbanization, where cities and their aesthetics emerged without prior knowledge of urbanisms elsewhere. Cities like Rome and Tenochtitlan were apotheoses of what came before, and what had been learned from elsewhere. None of this is to say that these are the only city networks that existed. Indeed, a key principle of this book is that the similarities across time and place are uncanny, right up to the present. Taylor recently referred to studies that traverse temporal boundaries as undertakings in "city generics."[5]

The network concept is subject to voluminous discussion by social scientists amidst globalization. These fields have often couched networks in terms of intercity business relations in order to map the world economy, though they are more varied than this.[6] Further, urban theorists have closely studied the role of instant communications technologies in fostering commercial relationships between cities. Networks can be defined as physical and metaphysical flows through places, aided by social contacts. As a leading scholar of world cities has asserted, urban populations are especially adept at organizing networks, and have been for a long time.[7]

Networks have flowed through cities throughout their six millennia of existence. The first cities were components of city networks, pushing the limits of time and space. Greg Woolf defines the ancient Mediterranean network simply as "a loose web across which people, goods, and ideas moved back and forth."[8] City networks were densest at their cores, imbricated within one another, as in Greece circa 500 BCE, Italy at the start of the Common Era and around 1300 CE, or the Netherlands at 1650. Vast territorial empires bound some urban networks, such as the Roman Empire and Abbasid Caliphate. Others, like the Hanseatic League, Venetian *Stato da Mar*, and the Dutch world network, relied

5 Peter J. Taylor, "City Generics: External Urban Relations in Ancient Mesopotamian and Modern Global City Networks," *Urban Geography* 40, no. 8 (2019), 2010–2030.

6 Peter J. Taylor, *Extraordinary Cities: Millennia of Moral Syndromes, World-Systems and City-State Relations* (Northampton: Edward Elgar, 2013), 21; Taylor, "City Generics."

7 Taylor, *Extraordinary Cities*, 79.

8 Greg Woolf, *The Life and Death of Ancient Cities: A Natural History* (Oxford: Oxford University Press, 2020), 209.

on intricate social ties. The Hanse merchants elevated their informal network to an art form, a source of power designed to create in groups and out groups.[9] Networks were evidenced inside cities themselves, in the tightly regulated *emporia* of Greek city-states, the walled markets of Chang'an, in the canals plied by the merchants of Holland and Venice, and in the sequestered barracks of Hanse traders based in London, Bergen, and Bruges.

Larger populations over time thickened connectivity in these regions while innovations in seafaring accelerated human flows.[10] "People moved, things moved, ideas moved," as Woolf put it.[11] These physical and ideational flows included architectural knowledge and building materials, connecting visual cultures across long distances.[12] Travelers from Spain to Central Asia during the Hellenistic period would easily recognize the central components of Greek urbanism. Weary merchants journeying to any large Abbasid city would know there was a bathhouse waiting.

Just as only a fraction of the world population flies today, voluntary mobility was limited to an elite few (slaves and subaltern classes were often forced to migrate). For Woolf and other specialists, this was more than enough to create far ranging cultural singularity.[13] Even minor cities used their surpluses to barter along trading circuits. "The network connected many small worlds, in which power and authority was fundamentally based in small polities," according to Woolf's description of the ancient Mediterranean.[14] Elite travel required systems of transportation and hospitality. Variations on these themes were clear in non-Mediterranean regions as well. The *caravanserai* network stretched from North Africa, Arabia, Iraq, Iran, to Central Asia, providing lodging where travelers could rest and bathe during long journeys. This system overlapped with similar networks reaching China. Few individuals went the distance, making explorers such as Xuanzang, Marco Polo, and Ibn Battuta all the more important.

At the very outermost extension of city networks, goods rather than people made first contacts. Ancient cities did not exist in isolation, even across extreme distances. Luxury goods flowed between Chang'an and Rome, changing hands repeatedly along the Silk Roads. There was little if any proven direct human contact between the world's largest contemporary empires or many major cities between them. The points of origin of these traveling goods

[9] For examples of this extensive literature, see Andrea Caracausi and Christof Jeggle (eds.), *Commercial Networks and European Cities, 1400–1800* (London: Pickering and Chatto, 2014); Ulf Christian Ewert and Stephan Selzer, *Institutions of Hanseatic Trade: Studies on the Political Economy of a Medieval Network Organization* (Frankfurt: Peter Lang, 2016); Sunhild Kleingärtner and Gabriel Zeilinger (eds.), *Raumbildung Durch Netzwerke?* (Bonn: Habelt, 2012).

[10] Woolf, *The Life and Death of Ancient Cities*, 223. [11] Ibid., 214. [12] Ibid., 224.

[13] Ibid., 215. [14] Ibid., 221.

remained misunderstood at their Eurasian antipodes. Herodotus' *Histories*, written in the fifth century BCE, repeated stories claiming that giant ants harvested gold from India, which was collected by Indian merchants who barely escaped with their lives attempting to abscond with the valuable export.[15] Pliny the Elder mentions the same story nearly five centuries later.[16]

Historic analogy entails limits. These cities were not linked digitally, leaving a much different sense of time and space. They did not exist under an overarching nation-state system, making these cities by definition more "global" than "international." They didn't exist under dense global governance arrangements set by national leaders. Cities were often empowered to conduct their own diplomacy. These limitations are significant as history trends backward to an age when "mayors rule the world," as Benjamin Barber phrased it.[17] Eroding boundaries leave cities with greater decision-making latitude. If true, the nation-state era will be a blip in the long history of civilization, which looks more like it once did, with complicated varieties of authority.

World Cities Studies in a New Age of Capital

Fernand Braudel, Peter Hall, and Immanuel Wallerstein explored city networks in detail from the early 1970s onward. They placed urban hierarchies at the heart of world economic systems across a litany of times and places.[18] World cities studies emerged only later, a research program deeply rooted in the neoliberal turn of the 1980s and 1990s. Though the history of city networks dates from 3200 BCE in Mesopotamia, world cities studies portray them as something uniquely modern in postindustrial capitalist times, or even futurist in orientation.[19] This is in marked contrast with the earlier studies of city networks, led by historians such as Braudel, and in big histories such as Wallerstein's *The Modern World System* trilogy.

The late city planner and philosopher John Friedmann directed the attention of urbanists toward a hypothesized network of what he called "world cities"

15 Herodotus, *The Histories* (New York: Penguin, 2003), 215.

16 Pliny the Elder, *Natural History* (New York: Penguin, 1991), 296.

17 Benjamin Barber, *If Mayors Ruled the World: Dysfunctional Nations, Rising Cities* (New Haven: Yale University Press, 2014).

18 Fernand Braudel, *The Mediterranean: And the Mediterranean World in the Age of Phillip II Volume II* (Berkeley: University of California Press, 1995), 680; Fernand Braudel, *The Wheels of Commerce* (Berkeley: University of California Press, 1992), 104; Peter Hall, "The Metropolitan Explosion," in Neil Brenner and Roger Keil (eds.), *The Global Cities Reader* (London: Routledge, 2006), 23–24; Immanuel Wallerstein, *The Modern World System I: Capitalist Agriculture and the Origins of the European World Economy in the Sixteenth Century* (Berkeley: University of California Press, 2011), 349.

19 For example, even Greg Clark's 2016 *Global Cities: A Short History* (Washington, DC: Brookings Institute), devotes roughly the same amount of space to speculating on the future of global cities as it does to explaining five millennia of their history.

that were ascending in a denationalizing world economy. World cities developed command functions in the globalizing economy as hierarchies formed between primary and secondary cities. These urban networks transcended boundaries, attracting immigration as well as financial capital.[20] His prescient research in the 1980s tried to make sense of conservative historic shifts that academia was just beginning to grapple with as economic inequality trended upward. As Friedmann later remembered in an autobiographical chapter in his book, *The Prospect of Cities*:

> By the early 1980s, it was evident that a period of major upheavals was at hand. It would take decades to work through their full implications: the deindustrialization of the industrialized world, the rise of the global economy, the triumph of neoliberal ideology, the end of the Cold War, the collapse of the Soviet Union, the end of the Third World, the new information technologies – all these would require a rethinking of theoretical positions, my own along with everyone else's. The lifeways to which all of us had become accustomed would never return. We were living at the beginning of a new age.[21]

Friedmann hypothesized that intercity relations were crucial to these trends as world production became definitively transnational. Friedmann's landmark 1982 essay co-authored with a graduate student posited that newly unleashed multinational corporations had taken "control of economic space."[22] This research was avowedly a product of a new era of market triumphalism. Communications technology allowed greater connectivity between cities, irrespective of national boundaries. Lax financial regulations empowered corporations to redirect investments almost at will.[23] This is the same problem analyzed by much world cities research today, making it a kind of dismal science. As public financing dried up amidst austerity, cities in fiscal crises competed for private capital, setting off an arms race of corporate appeasement.[24]

Though these themes inform Friedmann's later work in urban planning and ethics, he left it to other scholars to systematically carry out his proposed agenda in the 1990s and 2000s.[25] It is Saskia Sassen whose name is most

[20] John Friedmann, "The World City Hypothesis," *Development and Change* 17, no. 1 (1986), 69–83, 74.
[21] John Friedmann, *The Prospect of Cities* (Minneapolis: University of Minnesota Press, 2002), 144.
[22] John Friedmann and Goetz Wolff, "World City Formation: An Agenda for Research and Action," *International Journal for Urban and Regional Research* 6, no. 3 (1982), 309–344, 310.
[23] Ibid., 315; also see Friedmann, "World City Hypothesis."
[24] For elaboration on this idea, called "municipal mercantilism," see Joshua K. Leon, "Global Cities at Any Cost: Resisting Municipal Mercantilism," *City* 21, no. 1 (2017), 1–21.
[25] John Friedmann, *Planning in the Public Domain: From Knowledge to Action* (Princeton: Princeton University Press, 1987), 382.

associated with the term "global city," owing to her 1991 classic *The Global City: New York, London, Tokyo*. Sassen's global city archetype is a variation on the world city concept. She resorted to the updated term to signify a break from previous eras, explaining the latest iteration of the world city. For Sassen, the economic system moved toward a fully realized era of global capitalism, with cities changing along with it. The global city produces the hard and soft infrastructure needed to manage post-national economies. Global cities produced the means to manage world resources, and rapidly expanded their financial sectors. They didn't simply coordinate preexisting functions.[26]

Sassen's voluminous explorations of "producer services" concentrating in New York, London, and Tokyo operationalized the global city.[27] These include finance, insurance, and real estate ("FIRE") industries, and legal sectors to manage the thicket of complications surrounding global transactions. The more business networks grew in geographic complexity, the more they required central management.[28] As we will see in these chapters, cities throughout history expand by extracting and managing external resources. They become "global" as they exert power elsewhere. Global cities are, by Sassen's definition, the places with the highest transnational connectivity via the circuitry of producer services with command functions.[29] They have the deepest agglomerations of firms capable of managing networks and navigating a thicket of international legal environments.[30] As capital mobility grew, Sassen predicted the city network to enlarge, form hierarchies, and establish specializations in a positive sum playing field.[31] These cities offer firms critical masses of high end, knowledge-oriented sectors.[32]

At the same time, this high wage labor force carries with it a yawning demand for low wage services.[33] This entails the undocumented kitchen workers in Manhattan's glamorous restaurants, the cleaning staff at business hotels, textile homeworkers producing custom clothing, and so on.[34] As Sassen frames it, the major nodes in the world economy concentrate "top level transnational managers" alongside their "secretaries" and "the janitors

[26] Sassen takes pains to distinguish the global city from previous world cities concepts. See Saskia Sassen, *The Global City: New York, London, Tokyo* (Princeton: Princeton University Press, 2001), 349.

[27] Peter J. Taylor, *World City Network: A Global Urban Analysis* (London: Routledge, 2004), 33.

[28] Sassen, *Global City*, 127.

[29] Saskia Sassen, "Locating Cities on Global Circuits," in Saskia Sassen (ed.), *Global Network, Linked Cities* (London: Routledge, 2002), 1–33, 3.

[30] Saskia Sassen, *Losing Control? Sovereignty in an Age of Globalization* (New York: Columbia University Press, 1996), 11.

[31] Sassen, *Global City*, 173. [32] Ibid., 32. [33] Ibid., 11, 227, 244.

[34] More than half of New York City's dishwashers are undocumented. Fiscal Policy Institute, *Working for a Better Life: A Profile of Immigrants in the New York State Economy* (New York: Fiscal Policy Institute, 2007), 21.

cleaning the buildings where the new professional class works."[35] Put bluntly, wealth thrives on poverty. This too is consistent with the history of global cities, not unique to the modern capitalist period.

Sassen identified these dystopian trends early, developing her analysis of them ever since. Her work is essential to understanding the global dimensions of displacement at the local level. Like Friedmann, she sees the rise of neoliberal capitalism as a critical juncture and historic dividing line. "The end of the Cold War launched one of the most brutal economic phases of the modern era," she asserted in her 2014 book *Expulsions*, in a sense identifying the crystallization of the trends taking form at the time Friedmann took up the issue of intercity relations.[36] Methodologically she distinguishes these macro-global trends from national action.[37] The leading global cities gentrified, as Sassen predicted, reaching extreme levels of division, exclusion, and displacement through real estate inflation.[38] They attained through market manipulation what would otherwise require distasteful segregation laws, an irony implicit in *Expulsions*. Sassen's research speaks, in various ways, to the human and capital flows linking cities in a digital age. If Sassen's major work *Territory, Authority, Rights* is correct, we're living in a pivotal juncture in state development, with national sovereignty eroding, its candle burning at both ends by unaccountable business networks and their antipodes in activism.[39] Though the nation-state is the primary form of social organization, "we are living through an epochal transformation," she predicts.[40] Because her term global city has become so firmly associated with these components of modern capitalism, this book uses the longer-standing term "world city" to describe its premodern cases. The world city, as conceptualized here, also has command functions but operates according to precapitalistic logics in their own unique contexts.[41]

Sassen's emphasis on the urban experiences in cities impacted by global forces has gone less discussed by the many overviews of her work. In the tradition of Dickens, Engels, and Mike Davis, Sassen is attuned to physical changes happening in cities in tandem with the global political forces she

35 Saskia Sassen, *Cities in a World Economy* (Thousand Oaks, CA: Sage, 2018), 2.

36 Saskia Sassen, *Expulsions: Brutality and Complexity in the Global Economy* (Cambridge, MA: Harvard University Press, 2014), 18.

37 Saskia Sassen, "Deciphering the Global," in Saskia Sassen (ed.), *Deciphering the Global: Its Scales, Spaces and Subjects* (New York: Routledge, 2007), 1–18, 7.

38 Sassen, *Global City*, 190.

39 Sassen, *Territory, Authority, Rights: From Medieval to Global Assemblages* (Princeton: Princeton University Press, 2008), 328, 330.

40 Ibid., 1.

41 For the same reasons I use the term "world cities studies" to define the field, a change from my previous article that referred to this literature as "global cities studies." The longer standing scholarly term is more appropriate for this book. I should add that the term "world city" remains in wide use, including by the GaWC, the leading think tank in this area. See Leon, "Global Cities at Any Cost."

theorizes. Like those figures, she visits the dystopian spaces in global cities, a method that enables vivid analysis of the shifting lived experiences in these places.[42] This is an under-discussed strength of *The Global City*, which offers lucid accounts of social inequalities in New York, London, and Tokyo as they unfolded, connecting them to the theory.

As she recounts:

> I spent many hours speaking with illegal immigrants in Tokyo and in Yokohama in an attempt to learn how and why they decided to migrate to Japan, given its reputation as a closed society. It is impossible to do justice to their answers here, but the main points were as follows: First, they were individuals who had, in one way or another, become mobilized into labor migrations before coming; second, Japan's growing role in their countries, together with the consequent availability of information about Japan, had created linkages and made Japan emerge in their minds as an option for emigration.[43]

With this, we can see the impacts of intercity relations in urban experiences. Migrants and their unseemly, unregulated workspaces formed the underbelly of a glamorizing economy of consumption, two sides of cities that are explicitly linked.[44] In London: "New, elegant shops and restaurants – and sharp increases in the prices of housing – manifest the new lifestyle."[45] Here she adds visual nuance to what would otherwise be distant bird's eye processes. In her words:

> Walking though those streets [in working class Hackney] in the summer of 1987 offered what is probably one of the most stunning instances of how landlords will let row after row of what had once been elegant cream-colored facades fall into dark grey disrepair for decades, only to be quickly restored to their old splendor in a few months when the market calls.[46]

But for all this centralized control over resources, she sees a growth of ungovernable spaces. This includes digital space where power is now expressed.[47] It entails the proliferation of informal work and living spaces as a structural fact of post-Cold War capitalism. The global city is a zone of concentrated power where displacement is a constant threat, a force beyond individual control. The long history of world cities is, as we will see, also a history of expulsions. In fact some cities consisted almost entirely of displaced populations. In tandem with this, the world city has long struggled to control ungovernable spaces. The need to assert authority over digital space is the latest manifestation of a broader project to regulate human activity.

*****

42 Sassen, *Territory, Authority, Rights*, 273. 43 Sassen, *The Global City*, 320.
44 Ibid., 323. 45 Ibid., 273. 46 Ibid.
47 Saskia Sassen, "Electronic Space and Power," in Saskia Sassen (ed.), *Globalization and its Discontents: Essays on the New Mobility of People and Money* (New York: New Press, 1998), 177–194, 188.

The Geographer Peter J. Taylor is the scholar most responsible for the "relational turn" in global cities studies, which emphasizes quantitative data to understand the city network as a whole rather than relying on singular case studies, as Sassen does.[48] In 1998, he became the founding director of Loughborough University's Globalization and World Cities Research Network (GaWC), a massive repository of research in intercity relations. Here, argues Taylor, lies the evidential crisis. Sassen, he notes, "makes a major contribution to comparative studies but says little on relations between these cities."[49] Does a world city network exist at all? If so, how should the world city be defined and categorized? To address this, GaWC began as what he called a "taxonomic exercise," he explained to me in an interview, growing into a substantial generative research program.[50] What GaWC is most famous for is its occasional indexes ranking the leading world cities on the basis of global business connections.[51] They have inspired a litany of imitators in the corporate and think tank worlds, kicking off the league table phenomenon Taylor himself lamented to me. GaWC is heavily influenced by Sassen's earlier focus on producer services.[52] The field became, at its worst, a study of the game of capitalism that challenged none of its rules, encouraging the gentrified dystopias Sassen warned about.[53] Yet, of major global cities scholars, Taylor shows the greatest interest in situating the world city network in historic context.[54] His 2013 book *Extraordinary Cities* argues that networked cities played pivotal roles in shaping history during uncommon yet

48 Allan Watson and Jonathan V. Beaverstock, "World City Network Research at a Theoretical Impasse: On the Need to Reestablish Qualitative Approaches to Understanding Agency in World City Networks," *Tijdschrift Voor Economische en Sociale Geographie* 105, no. 4 (2014), 412–426, 416.

49 Taylor, *World City Network*, 33.

50 Peter J. Taylor, personal interview, June 20, 2016.

51 Peter J. Taylor, "The GUCP/GaWC Project," in Peter J. Taylor, Pengfei Ni, Ben Derudder, Michael Hoyler, Jin Huang, and Frank Witlox (eds.), *Global Urban Analysis: A Survey of Cities in Globalization* (London: Earthscan, 2011), 1–11, 2; Peter J. Taylor, "The Interlocking Network Model," in Ben Derudder, Michael Hoyler, Peter J. Taylor, and Frank Witlox (eds.), *International Handbook of Globalization and World Cities* (Northampton: Edward Elgar, 2011), 51–62, 51; Peter J. Taylor, "Urbanization," in Mark Juergensmeyer, Saskia Sassen, Manfred B. Steger, and Victor Faessel (eds.), *The Oxford Handbook of Global Studies* (Oxford: Oxford University Press, 2018), 513–527, 518.

52 Peter J. Taylor, "Advanced Producer Service Centres in the World Economy," in Peter J. Taylor, Pengfei Ni, Ben Derudder, Michael Hoyler, Jin Huang, and Frank Witlox (eds.), *Global Urban Analysis: A Survey of Cities in Globalization* (London: Earthscan, 2011), 22–55, 22.

53 Leon, "Global Cities at Any Cost," 1.

54 P. J. Taylor, "Homo Geographicus: A Geohistorical Manifesto for Cities," GaWC Research Bulletin 107 (October 18, 2014), available at www.lboro.ac.uk/gawc/rb/rb107.html, accessed January 27, 2020; Peter J. Taylor, "Problematizing City/State Relations: Towards a Geohistorical Understanding of Contemporary Globalization," *Transactions of the Institute of British Geographers* 32, no. 2 (2007), 133–150, 142; Taylor, "Urbanization," 516.

sustained creative flourishes.[55] His oeuvre returns in fits and starts to premodern city networks such as the Hanseatic League, and the roles of Venice, Genoa, and Bruges as core cities.[56]

Influenced by Sassen, Manuel Castells' *The Rise of the Network Society* sees technological developments as provoking irreversible changes in intercity relations. Tectonic shifts in time and space bridging innovations are the most consequential of revolutions. The industrial revolution starting in Britain rapidly reconfigured the global economy, providing a precedent to the pace of change in the present-day.[57] The maturation of digital networking technology by the 1990s was no less transformative than nineteenth century industrialization.[58] Castells' much discussed "space of flows" linking cities are digitally facilitated exchanges in "crystallized time."[59] More than anyone, Castells framed the global city concept as part of a novel capitalist revolution unique to a reconfigured world economy. This is consistent with the broader intellectual commentary on capitalism's ascendance by the twenty-first century. But where Francis Fukuyama proffered a triumphalist "end of history," Friedmann, Sassen, and Castells clearly understood neoliberal capitalism's dystopian social consequences for cities.

Though largely ignored by global cities studies, the most thorough history of intercity relations to date consists of two edited volumes from the Copenhagen Polis Centre on thirty-six "city-state cultures." Their editor, Mogens Herman Hansen, argues that "urbanization and state formation go hand in hand."[60] Urbanization was a relational process involving regional interactions. This includes high periods of commerce, which is why city networks tend to overlap with so-called golden ages.[61] They share language, culture, aesthetics, and political ideas.[62] If core cities decline, city-state culture disintegrates with them.[63] In short, history is loaded with periods of

55 Taylor, *Extraordinary Cities*, 4.

56 For example, Taylor, *World City Network*, 11, 13; and Taylor, "Problematizing City/State Relations," 140, 142.

57 Manuel Castells, *The Rise of the Network Society* (Oxford: Blackwell, 2000), 33; Also see Manuel Castells and Pekka Himanen, "Models of Development in the Global Information Age: Constructing an Analytical Framework," in Manuel Castells and Pekka Himanen (eds.), *Reconceptualizing Development in the Global Information Age* (Oxford: Oxford University Press, 2014), 7–25, 11.

58 Castells, *Rise of the Network Society*, 51.

59 Ibid., 441.

60 Mogens Herman Hansen, "The Concepts of City-State and City-State Culture," in Mogens Herman Hansen (ed.), *A Comparative Study of Thirty City-State Cultures* (Copenhagen: The Royal Danish Academy of Arts and Letters, 2000), 11–34, 15.

61 Ibid., 17.

62 Ibid.

63 Ibid.; Mogens Herman Hansen, "Introduction," in Mogens Herman Hansen (ed.), *A Comparative Study of Six City-State Cultures* (Copenhagen: The Royal Danish Academy of Arts and Letters, 2002), 7–21, 12.

dense intercity relations on all continents, foreshadowing urban interactions today.[64]

In rare two-way dialogue between global cities theorists and scholars of antiquity, Castells wrote the conclusion to the edited volume *Connectivity in Antiquity*, in which anthropologists and archeologists applied his theory in *The Rise of the Network Society* to ancient regional networks. The general consensus among the authors was that there were previous technological revolutions that transformed power relations irreversibly, establishing new class and labor hierarchies in punctuated equilibrium.[65] Then, as now, there was an ebb and flow to globalization, as guises of state authority assemble and disassemble to accommodate these fluctuations.[66] Serving as a respondent, Castells was apprehensive if not hostile to the enterprise of retroactively applying a self-consciously modern theory to the distant past.[67] Yet he concedes, as the volume argues, that networks were fundamental to political development, going as far back as the age of cities, and even to the Neolithic period, notions long held by antiquarians from a variety of disciplines.[68] He was struck by the many analogous political situations in light of archeological discoveries pointing toward distinctive associations between dense settlement, invention, and inequality:

> [W]hen, in my own research, I limited the validity of my analysis of the social structure that I theorized as network society to our contemporary society, tentatively identified as the Information Age, I was wrong both empirically and theoretically. Empirically: networks seem to have always been at the heart of the social structure and social change, as the impressive body of archeological and historical evidence . . . seems to

64 Mogens Herman Hansen, "The Impact of City-State Cultures in World History," in Mogens Herman Hansen (ed.), *A Comparative Study of Thirty City-State Cultures* (Copenhagen: The Royal Danish Academy of Arts and Letters, 2000), 597–623, 605.

65 Thomas E. Levy, "Grand Narratives, Technological Revolutions and the Past: Deep Time Studies of Metallurgy and Social Evolution in the Eastern Mediterranean," in Øystein S. LaBianca and Arnold Scham (eds.), *Connectivity in Antiquity: Globalization as a Long-Term Historical Process* (London: Equinox, 2006), 10–25, 13.

66 William R. Thompson, "Trade Pulsations, Collapse and Reorientation in the Ancient World," in Øystein S. LaBianca and Arnold Scham (eds.), *Connectivity in Antiquity: Globalization as a Long-Term Historical Process* (London: Equinox, 2006), 32–58, 34.

67 Manuel Castells, "Nothing New under the Sun?" in Øystein S. LaBianca and Arnold Scham (eds.), *Connectivity in Antiquity: Globalization as a Long-Term Historical Process* (London: Equinox, 2006), 158–167, 159.

68 Philip D. Curtin, *Cross Cultural Trade in World History* (Cambridge: Cambridge University Press, 1984), 1, 61; A. G. Hopkins, "Globalization: An Agenda for Historians," in A. G. Hopkins (ed.), *Globalization in World History* (London: Pimlico, 2002), 1–10, 3; Peter N. Stearns, *Globalization in World History* (New York: Routledge, 2017), 4; Ad van der Woude, Jan de Vries, Akira Hayami, "The Hierarchies, Provisioning, and Demographic Patterns of Cities," in Ad van der Woude, Jan de Vries, and Akira Hayami (eds.), *Urbanization in History: A Process of Dynamic Interactions* (Oxford: Oxford University Press, 1990), 1–19, 2.

indicate. Networks did not have to wait for microelectronics to be a decisive tool in organizing production, trade, power and communication.[69]

Castells conceded there is "nothing new under the sun" in the annals of city networks, but reasserted that, as he saw it, information technology was a clear historic dividing line.[70] As with other technological revolutions, life in today's network is changing in ways that are distinctive.[71] Technology is the critical variable, the context in which "people live, love, fight, and die."[72]

End of History, Start of Amnesia

There are problems with disconnecting from the past. The emphasis of global cities studies on late twentieth century developments gives the post-Cold War era a year zero feel. First, global cities studies risk omitting important links that left path-dependent legacies if they overemphasize digital ties between cities. The abundance of littoral cities in today's urban archipelago is one, deriving from the extended period in which sea travel was the most important means of shipping and transport. There are also links whose analog forms were similar in principle to today's digital networks, writing, printing, and mapping to name a few.

In fact a consciousness of world city hierarchies in the popular discourse has been evident since the early nineteenth century as railways reinforced land-based intercity linkage.[73] As Youssef Cassis frames it in his study of financial centers from the late 1700s onward:

> The existence of a hierarchy of international financial centers was clearly in contemporaries' minds. In Britain, in particular, there was a keen awareness from the turn of the century of the City's newly acquired role as the centre of European and even world trade – less thought was given to finance as such.[74]

Against the backdrop of rapid twentieth-century urbanization, Max Weber's 1921 study *The City* focused on ancient and medieval cities in the West in a seminal attempt at classification. There are references to networking between cities and their hinterlands.[75]

Second, missing from this dialogue is the *political* history of city networks – a gap in the global cities literature that this book addresses. Scholarly work that leaves out the myriad patterns of oppression and dissent related to intercity relations can create the false impression of apolitical times. In our age of

[69] Castells, "Nothing New under the Sun?," 158. [70] Ibid., 166. [71] Ibid., 161.
[72] Ibid.
[73] Youssef Cassis, *Capitals of Capital: A History of International Financial Centers, 1780–2005* (Cambridge: Cambridge University Press, 2006), 63.
[74] Ibid., 37. [75] Max Weber, *The City* (Toronto: Free Press, 1966), 66.

immigrant rights and anti-gentrification movements that are byproducts of intercity relations, it's increasingly important to explore previous high periods of globalization in politicized terms. Secular political ideology as we know it was largely absent for most of pre-modern times, especially in ancient cities. Politics as a response to human conditions was not. City walls were intended to prevent captive laborers from deserting their harsh stations in life, just as they kept invaders out. As in today's city network, the city was not just an empowering tool designed to foster human mobility. It was also designed to *regulate* mobility and monopolize resources.

Some global cities theorists may object to the application of the field's hypotheses on previous periods. For Castells and Sassen, the internet is a critical variable obviously not present in previous eras. Castells has noted that spaces of flows have existed in multitudes of historic contexts.[76] Moreover, it is important to note that world cities hypotheses are being applied in numerous questionable directions. The emphasis on digital technologies has directed the application of global cities research toward the potentially limiting study of new media trends.[77] Global cities theorists may also point out that the ethos of capitalism arguably did not exist in most of the cases under study in this book, and that world cities can only operate by capitalist logics. This line of argument is problematic and capable of leading the field astray. The emphasis on corporate capital and knowledge accumulation has led global cities studies away from its critical roots, toward apolitical, decontextualized business studies. Using global cities theorists as consultants, ethically questionable institutions borrow from the scholarly literature, including the work of the GaWC essentially to inform business location strategy.[78] *This book by contrast situates world cities in their latest guise as part of a long history of class struggle and survival.*

Others may object to engaging with history on methodological grounds. The field has taken a data-driven turn away from Sassen's vivid, multifaceted descriptive approaches.[79] Flows – the movement of people, information, and

76 Castells, "Nothing New under the Sun?," 159.

77 For an overview of the growing study of networks in politics, see Jennifer Nicholl Victor, Alexander H. Montgomery, and Mark Lubell, "The Emergence of the Study of Networks in Politics," in Jennifer Nicholl Victor, Alexander H. Montgomery, and Mark Lubell (eds.), *The Oxford Handbook of Political Networks* (Oxford: Oxford University Press, 2017), 3–58.

78 Sponsors of such research include Z/Yen, the state of Qatar, PriceWaterhouseCoopers, Partnership for New York City (a business association), MasterCard, the Mori Foundation (named after the powerful developer), Citi, A. T. Kearney, and other organizations representing corporate, financial, and state interests. For more detail, see Leon, "Global Cities at Any Cost," 6.

79 This turn in global cities studies is critiqued in Michiel van Meeteren, Ben Derudder, and David Bassens, "Can the Straw Man Speak? An Engagement with Postcolonial Critiques of 'Global Cities Research'," *Dialogues in Human Geography* 6, no. 3 (2016), 247–267; and Watson and Beaverstock, "World City Network Research at a Theoretical Impasse."

materials between cities – are hard to measure. This is particularly the case across city networks in history, occurring in varying contexts of space and time. Taylor laments the absence of firm data on trade and adds the problem of "no comprehensive information on the agents, people in the city, doing the inter-city networking."[80] Looking into the past to analyze flows offers its own problems. Selective survival in built, artistic, and written records greatly compounds this problem when we try to make sense of city networks. There is inevitable approximation and guesswork, even as specialists across fields find new artifacts and develop more precise methods. For example, archeologists often estimate ancient urban population sizes based on the built footprints of as yet uncovered cities. Containers found in ancient shipwrecks are useful measures for trade, but some goods perish. In reality, trade in perishable goods is almost impossible to calculate, leading to an undercount of trade as a whole. This does not mean global cities studies should avoid times and places of profound importance.

*****

A consistent critique of global cities studies is that it does not apply broadly enough. By this argument, the research program restricts its focus to a few corporate clusters, leaving out other categories of cities that are important artifacts of globalization. Critics have argued that small population centers are omitted from this discussion.[81] More distressingly, many of the same critics argue that non-Western cities are systematically, disproportionately ignored by global cities studies.[82] For example, Lagos is only a "beta" city in the GaWC's most recent index from 2020, ranked in the second tier below "alpha cities" with the most discernable global connectivity. That puts this vast metropolis teeming with concentrated interpersonal and global exchange well behind Brisbane, Boston, and Houston.[83] Global forces undoubtedly shape Lagos, Nairobi, and cities like them. They are also active influencers of global processes shaping other places, even if their strengths cannot be measured in terms of concentrated corporate capital.

[80] Peter J. Taylor, "Historical World City Networks," in Ben Derudder, Michael Hoyler, Peter J. Taylor, and Frank Witlox eds., *International Handbook of Globalization and World Cities* (Northampton: Edward Elgar, 2011), 9–21, 12.

[81] David Bell and Mark Jayne, "Conceptualizing Small Cities," in David Bell and Mark Jayne (eds.), *Small Cities: Urbanization beyond the Metropolis* (London: Routledge, 2006), 3–18, 5.

[82] Tim Edensor and Mark Jayne, "Urban Theory beyond the West," in Tim Edensor and Mark Jayne (eds.), *Urban Theory beyond the West: A World of Cities* (London: Routledge, 2012), 1–27, 5.

[83] Globalization and World Cities Research Network, "The World According to GaWC" (November 13, 2018), available at www.lboro.ac.uk/gawc/world2018t.html, last accessed February 12, 2020.

Jennifer Robinson's *Ordinary Cities* galvanized much of this countermovement in academia, calling for a post-colonial turn in urban studies that places so-called Third World cities on the scholarly map.[84] Though they may not be central to the world economy in terms of power projection, poor cities are highly relevant to it as suppliers of raw goods and labor.[85] This recalls the core–periphery model to which the periphery is every bit as essential to the world economy as the core it enriches.[86] Engaging with history broadens the scope of cities that matter, not just *where* but *when*. Limiting the field to the neoliberal era leaves out five millennia of urban history. Implicit in this book is the notion that previous iterations of city networks warrant exploration in order to better understand the evolution of power relations. This entails the centers of power as well as their exploited populations and peripheries. Historic centers are in effect "ordinary cities." To leave them out of the discourse is to invite amnesia toward centuries of political precedent, to concede there was little relevant history before digitally aided capitalism.

Another central claim of global cities research, that the digitally infused capitalist age is fundamentally different than previous periods, also warrants reconsidering. The differences between the post-Cold War world and previous eras are startling at a glance. We see the expansion of global governance over a singular economy, most notably with the World Trade Organization culminating from the Uruguay Round of trade negotiations in 1995. Capital crosses borders at greater speeds and volumes than at any comparable time. This enabled increasingly complex transnational production while creating dense sets of rules locking in the privileges of the global core over the periphery.[87] This breathed new life into core capitals, especially New York and London, as centers of power in the world economy and managers of dispersed production.[88] In an ironic sense, these unprecedented changes cemented after the Cold War are keeping the North–South divide around for a little while longer. As Vijay Prashad shows thoroughly in *The Poorer Nations*, today's system of free trade capitalism is a revanchist movement. It is a pushback against decades of promising decolonization by the former colonial capitals that are now described as the leading global cities. Chapter 11 of this book explores the role of Dutch cities in engineering this divide, now centuries old. In historic

84 Jennifer Robinson, *Ordinary Cities: Between Modernity and Development* (London: Routledge, 2006), 102.

85 Ibid., 101.

86 Ibid., 95.

87 See John H. Barton, Judith L. Goldstein, Timothy E. Josling, and Richard E. Steinberg, *The Evolution of the Trade Regime: Politics, Law, and Economics of the GATT and WTO* (Princeton: Princeton University Press, 2006); and Robert Wade, "What Strategies Are Viable for Developing Countries Today? The World Trade Organization and the Shrinking of 'Development Space'," *Review of International Political Economy* 10, no. 4 (2003): 621–644.

88 Vijay Prashad, *The Poorer Nations: A Possible History of the Global South* (London: Verso, 2013), 23.

light, the transition from colonialism to neocolonialism, on principles established in the 1600s, was evolutionary, not revolutionary. Absent Soviet opposition, the other imperial powers in Europe and North America retrenched. A real revolution would genuinely upend North–South power relations sculpted over time. That would make this period look less immutable in retrospect than it now seems to us.

Chapter 2 takes us to the Fertile Crescent, arguably the first core–periphery world system. How and why were cities invented?

2 Origins of Urbanization

Mesopotamian City Networks

Babylon was a city constructed from mud. It was also the biggest city that had ever existed, or ever would exist until the rise of Rome roughly half a millennium later. From the vantage point of approaching trading caravans, cargo ships, Egyptian diplomats, stateless nomadic populations, or Greek tourists such as Herodotus and Aristotle, it would have literally been a city upon a hill. It was visible for miles over a flat plain. This was already an ancient city, built atop previous versions of itself. It was the ultimate "manufactured landscape," to use the modern urbanist phrase, a vast artificially constructed zone. Put simply, it sat on the world's biggest landfill. Instead of clearing debris from destroyed buildings and garbage in the streets, Babylonian planners built new structures over it during the summer construction months. Summer was the only time the one load-bearing building material in abundance, clay, reliably baked in the sun to make bricks without rain to destroy them. The Euphrates River flowed through the city, enabling efficient contacts with other places.

Babylon at the time of Nebuchadnezzar II (630–562 BCE) in the sixth century BCE came when the concept of city building had ample known precedent.[1] Great cities had existed in southern Mesopotamia since the fourth millennium, vying for control of far-flung trading networks, building to reflect their places in the system. Despite the ebb and flow of conquest and collapse, interrupted by long so-called dark periods where no great cities existed, Mesopotamia retained its identity as a singular "cuneiform culture" aware of a history that began with a mythical flood.[2] Yet Nebuchadnezzar II's city was an outlier in a world with a highly decentralized population. For starters, his city was all out of proportion with the scale of human settlements at the time.

[1] Dates for historic figures in parentheses are birth and death dates, unless noted otherwise.

[2] The term is admittedly fluid, but best encapsulates the context for the series of city networks that centered on Mesopotamia and used this style of writing. For a full discussion see, Karen Radner and Eleanor Robson, "Introduction," in Karen Radner and Eleanor Robson (eds.), *The Oxford Handbook of Cuneiform Culture* (Oxford: Oxford University Press, 2011), xvii–xxxii, xvii.

Its main ziggurat was one of the tallest structures in the world, at 300 feet, with a base of 300 feet at each side.[3] It was possibly the "tower of babel" that the Book of Genesis describes ominously:

> They said to one another, "Come, let us mold bricks and harden them with fire." They used bricks for stone, and bitumen for mortar. Then they said, "Come, let us build ourselves a city and a tower with its top in the sky, and so make a name for ourselves; otherwise we shall be scattered all over the earth."[4]

The Old Testament was partly written in Nebuchadnezzar II's Babylon by Jews deported there after his military campaign against Egypt. Literary accounts of the Babylonian captivity interspersed throughout the biblical texts provide evidence that urbanization during this time was not voluntary, but a symptom of centralized power that may have been reviled by people forced to live in cities at a time when humankind was "scattered all over the earth." The city's military power was described by the Old Testament as a punishment from God whose "onset is that of a storm wind that heaps up captives like sand."[5] Many of them would have settled in the city's cavernous unplanned residential streets like the other denizens of this cosmopolitan city. Elevated ziggurats were designed to house the city gods as ethereally as possible. Even kings could not ignore the god Marduk's command to "let the mud bricks be molded, and build high the shrine!"[6] The first cities had divine orientation.

Nebuchadnezzar II's core districts also showed evidence of central planning, a departure from the norm in the history of Mesopotamian city building. The famed blue Ishtar Gate opened to the broad Processional Way, an early precedent for grand boulevards. Broadened streets emerged in some leading cities despite the searing hot sun that left most other streets in the city deliberately shaded. If Nebuchadnezzar II was Babylon's Napoleon III, the Haussmann(s) who did the actual planning of new construction remain anonymous, as do the laborers, architects, and other skilled artisans. Mesopotamian kings tended to present construction feats as their own, right down to the bricklaying. But there is ample evidence that such specialists worked in cities.

The architecture of Babylon had foreign and domestic implications. It would have towered over city-dwellers, reifying dominant state ideologies. As one leading archeologist noted, urban forms in Babylonia reflected "pervasive, long term conservatism and the high degree of resistance to change."[7]

[3] Steven Bertman, *Handbook to Life in Ancient Mesopotamia* (New York: Facts on File 2003), 12.

[4] *Genesis* 11:3–4. [5] *Habakkuk* 1:9.

[6] Stephanie Dalley (ed.), *Myths from Mesopotamia* (Oxford: Oxford University Press, 2008), 262

[7] Heather D. Baker, "Urban Form in the First Millennium BC," in Gwendolyn Leick (ed.), *The Babylonian World* (New York: Routledge, 2007), 66–77, 74.

During periods of intensive international relations, Babylon placed itself at the center of the universe. Its built environment enthralled outsiders. The fifth-century Greek historian Herodotus, who may have seen it firsthand, offered exaggerated superlatives that are nonetheless indicative of the city's sheer size. He claimed Babylon was so large that people living in its inner city were not immediately aware of its conquest by the Persian king Cyrus the Great (c. 600–530 BCE).[8] Aristotle said this information took three days to reach every inhabitant. By his reckoning Babylon was too large to be classified as a city by the Greek understanding. As with today's alpha cities, Babylon was meant to leave a panoply of finely targeted impressions for diverse audiences.

Mesopotamia is a term coined by ancient Greek historians meaning "land between the two rivers," referring to the Tigris and Euphrates waterways in modern day Iraq. (Sumerians and Akkadians simply referred to their own territory as "The Land.") Its political boundaries are inexact, complicated by centuries of nomadic migrations and extensive intercity relations stretching across the Near East. What V. Gordon Childe called "the urban revolution" in the 1930s occurred in the fourth millennium BCE in its southern region near the Persian Gulf. For Childe, true cities were distinct from mere large settlements by their ability to foster artistic culture, complex administration, writing, and long distance trade.[9] These were not self-sufficient economies expanding in vacuums on the sole basis of agricultural surplus. Rather they traded their own excess production for the materials essential to make stratified urban life possible. As we will see, southern Mesopotamia lacked important resources. Yet it was the site of the first great city, Uruk, which came to dominate the more self-sufficient northern region. The invention of cities coincided with the emergence of a city network partly motivated by scarcity.

The term "urban revolution" implies a terminal arrival based on the organizational superiority of cities over decentralized modes of living. In reality, city networks emerge in fits and starts. Far from an evolutionary stage of progress, urbanization receded for centuries-long periods in ancient Mesopotamia, only to return again. Significant swaths of territory went ungoverned when city-states were the predominate form of social organization. In some events, dominant cities held other cities in subordinate positions. In others, cities needed cooperative governance arrangements. Spaces between cities were under constant threat. This included even the most well-trodden overland trading routes. Conversely, cities threatened their nomadic and village-based neighbors, subjecting them to captivity, extracting tributes, or enslavement. The high periods of urban administrative, architectural, and artistic innovations

8 For an analysis of his account, see Marc van de Mieroop, "Reading Babylon," *American Journal of Archeology* 107, no. 2 (2003), 257–275, 261.

9 V. Gordon Childe, "The Urban Revolution," *Town Planning Review* 12, no. 1 (1950), 3–17, 9.

that are the subject of this chapter would not have been high periods for them. The political contests of the time revolve around spatial domination brought about by unprecedented centralized authority.

A variety of city networks emerged in this context. The Sumerians established the Uruk system along with new towns in the north. They were intended to expand trade relations with the resource rich hinterlands. Later the Akkadian Empire incubated important trading systems, as did the meticulously bureaucratic Third Dynasty of Ur (Ur III) in the third millennium. Bitter wars between urban empires did not preclude city networks. Control over the links between cities was as valuable as direct plunder. Written records are subject to selective survival, leaving gaps in scholarly understanding. Archeological records are also incomplete. No major city is completely excavated. Most not even close. Sargon the Great's third millennium capital city of Akkad remains undiscovered. Housing for the lower classes was often constructed from perishable reeds and has now vanished, dampening historians' understandings of how nonelites lived. What's certain is that highly interdependent networks repeatedly originated in Mesopotamia from 3200 BCE until Cyrus' conquest of Babylon in the sixth century BCE. Why did city networks emerge there and then?

Environmental Conditions for Network Emergence: The Advantage of Scarcity

The urban revolution was more of an evolution. Settlements with some elements of Childe's criteria date back to the Neolithic period. In 6850 BCE, Jericho had the city walls that would be the hallmark of future cities. Its fortifications reached 9 meters high. The site in present-day Palestine had sedentary living replete with irrigated agriculture alongside domesticated animals. Its population of perhaps 2,000 lived in stone homes. It appears to have survived for millennia due to a fortuitous location near a spring-fed oasis.[10] Çatalhüyük in Anatolia had densely packed housing in 6500 BCE, albeit without doors or windows. There was ceiling entry only.[11] Such settlements appear in India as early as 2500 BCE and in China about a millennium later.[12] Until then humankind lived approximately 190,000 years without permanent towns or governments.

The southern alluvium would seem an unlikely geographic candidate for the emergence of such astonishingly complex phenomena as cities and states, coterminous at this time.[13] This section of the Fertile Crescent did have arable

[10] Paul Bairoch, *Cities and Economic Development: From the Dawn of History to the Present* (Chicago: University of Chicago Press, 1988), 10.
[11] Ibid. [12] Ibid. [13] Alluviums are river basins that deposit fertile soil.

plains around the rivers capable of supporting sedentary villages. Agriculture was the core of the Mesopotamian economy in every era. But, as we have seen, these already existed for millennia. What made these new settlements unprecedented was their place as world trading powers with advanced state development. Political scientist James C. Scott put things succinctly: "no alluvium, no state."[14] At the same time he suggests water transport for trade was nearly as important of a precondition for state development.[15]

Mesopotamia had both ingredients, starting with deep fertile soil ripe for agriculture, provided water could reach it. Rain fed agriculture was impossible, unlike in the northern tier of the Fertile Crescent.[16] Farming in the south was much more labor intensive. There was no summer rainfall. Yet the rivers flooded unpredictably. This necessitated elaborate irrigation systems even to support prehistoric villages.[17] *The Epic of Creation* embodies these realities in an origin myth etched into history by urban scribes.[18] The god Enbilulu of rivers and canals personifies the immense vigilance required to produce the prerequisite surpluses for city life:

> He is Enbilulu, the lord, their enricher;
> Their deity is mighty, responsible for sacrificial omens,
> Who looks after pasturage and watering places, establishes them for land,
> Who opens up wells and apportions the waters of abundance.
> Secondly, let them address Enbilulu as Epadun, lord of the countryside and . . .,
> Canal controller of heaven and earth, establisher of the furrow,
> Who maintains the ploughland in the countryside,
> Who directs ditches and canals and marks out the furrows.
> Thirdly, let them praise Enbilulu as Gugal ("canal-controller") of the gods' irrigated land.
> Lord of abundance and the luxuriance of great grain-piles.
> Responsible for riches, who gives surplus to homes,
> Giver of cereals, producer of grain.
> Fourthly, he is Enbilulu as Hegal ("abundance"), who heaps up a surplus for people,
> Who brings rain of abundance over the broad earth, and makes vegetation grow profusely.

Leaders in these highly religious societies wanted to keep the gods happy in the precarious environment of the first cities. The swelling of the rivers inspired a flood myth in *The Epic of Gilgamesh* analogous to the one told in

[14] James C. Scott, *Against the Grain: A Deep History of the Earliest States* (New Haven: Yale University Press, 2017), 124.
[15] Ibid., 125.
[16] Amélie Kuhrt, *The Ancient Near East c. 3000–330 BC Vol. I* (New York: Routledge, 1995), 21.
[17] J. N. Postgate, *Early Mesopotamia: Society and Economy at the Dawn of History* (New York: Routledge, 1994), 18.
[18] This is thought to have been written in the late second millennium BCE.

Genesis. There were searing summers requiring significant adaptation in city building. Days long sandstorms ground construction to a halt.[19]

Complicating matters further, inhospitable mountains, marshlands, and deserts hemmed in the Fertile Crescent. Relative isolation helped maintain a coherent cultural identity. It also led to critical scarcity in the raw materials required for city building. This forced interaction with faraway places in Eurasia, setting the conditions for the core–periphery trading network of Uruk that we will explore further in this chapter. Consider what the inventors of cities did *not* have in their immediate environs: important domesticated animals; stone; abundant forests for timber; papyrus for future writing (cuneiform was etched into clay tablets); and precious materials for luxury goods to delineate hierarchy. The Sumerians made creative use of what they had. This included barley, which could grow in potentially salty soil. It also included bitumen to fasten and waterproof sunbaked clay. Lacking horses for riding or hauling until perhaps 2500 BCE, they used mules to pull the first chariots.[20]

In sum, the largest cities were far from self-sufficient. They exchanged agricultural surplus for vital imports. Caravan trading dates to prehistory. Longstanding land routes stretched thousands of miles.[21] Lapis lazuli was culturally significant to Mesopotamian cities, repeatedly mentioned in literature. Its closest source was in the mountainous present-day Afghan–Pakistani border. The Fertile Crescent consumer market was the heart of a lapis lazuli network that reached the eastern Mediterranean in the third millennium.[22] The lapis lazuli trails utilized the rivers and Persian Gulf shipping lanes. Given the working hypothesis that environmental conditions underpin city networks, the nonlittoral rise of linked cities is unusual. There is a longstanding argument that Ur was a port city in the third millennium. The Persian Gulf may have reached hundreds of miles further afield before receding. This thesis is hotly contested.[23] In either case, cities always located alongside the rivers. In addition to their mercurial irrigation potential, the Tigris and Euphrates were trading superhighways. Cities had tightly regulated quays that received foreign goods transported by boat. Waterborne shipments enabled an exponentially greater volume of trade. Ur III accounts claim the state could transport half its barley harvest via barges.[24] Import-reliant metropolises in the southern alluvium benefited from the south flowing rivers. Ur III's leaders put

19 Aage Westenholz, "The Sumerian City-State," in Mogens Herman Hansen (ed.), *A Comparative Study of Six City-State Cultures* (Copenhagen: Royal Danish Academy of Arts and Letters, 2002), 23–42, 24.

20 Ronald M. Glassman, *The Origins of Democracy in Tribes, City States and Nation-States* (Cham, Switzerland: Springer, 2017), 853; David W. Anthony, *The Horse, the Wheel, and Language: How Bronze-Age Riders from the Eurasian Steppes Shaped the Modern World* (Princeton: Princeton University Press, 2010), 203, 222.

21 David Wengrow, *What Makes Civilization? The Ancient Near East and the Future of the West* (Oxford: Oxford University Press, 2010), 28.

22 Ibid., 35.

23 Most scholars accept the theory, but it has been challenged. For an overview of this debate, see Susan Pollack, *Ancient Mesopotamia: The Eden That Never Was* (Cambridge: Cambridge University Press, 1999), 34.

24 Scott, *Against the Grain*, 134.

the weight of the state behind the shipbuilding industry.[25] Moreover, even the most powerful cities could not prevent overland raids. Shipping was safer.

At its simplest, agricultural surplus and trading networks were the basic ingredients of the first cities. What the portions of these ingredients were remains a highly contested question across disciplines. Older theories emphasizing agricultural surplus convey the narrative that higher yields and greater efficiencies could support larger, denser populations.[26] This enabled specialization, encouraging social hierarchies, freeing labor for the complex production of manufactured goods, and ushering in the expansion of skilled artisanal classes. Jane Jacobs upended this dialogue in *The Economy of Cities*, arguing that "cities must have preceded agriculture."[27] Jacobs hypothesizes that advanced farming methods were urban inventions, required of cities finding new forms of labor by way of import substitution. The most competitive settlement populations became exporters. As exports grow, cities grow, she contended.[28] New methods, new tools, and the like created the potential for increased food production. What is clear in her estimation is that trade is the predominate factor fueling urbanization then and now. If this is true, then the first city networks are as old as the first cities. Neolithic villages could not make the transition to cities without one another. Her thesis, expounded in the hypothetical example of "New Obsidian" (based on Çatalhüyük), is hard to prove.[29] It has been challenged from the "stages of agriculture" perspective reflective of the older theories.[30] However, her thesis does extrapolate from important realities. First, urban elites dominated rural land markets, often directly managing these producing territories. Second, no city was autarkic. Nearly every city had shipyards that would reflect mercantilist policies. Since commerce included untraceable perishable goods, there may have been voluminous "invisible" intercity trade lost to history.[31]

Also lost to history are the plausible laments of peripheral populations who were in myriad ways subordinated to concentrated power in cities.

Cities of Mud: Politics in Urban Networks

The Book of Revelation does not presage a future apocalypse. It more likely described a current one for persecuted Christians. "Babylon the great, mother

[25] Postgate, *Early Mesopotamia*, 230.
[26] Childe, "The Urban Revolution," 11; Henri Frankfort, *The Birth of Civilization in the Near East* (London: Ernest Benn, 1951), 63.
[27] Jane Jacobs, *The Economy of Cities* (New York: Vintage Books, 1969), 18. [28] Ibid., 139.
[29] Ibid., 18. [30] Bairoch, *Cities and Economic Development*, 5.
[31] Audrey Bossuyt, Laurence Broze, and Victor Ginsburgh, "On Invisible Trade Relations between Mesopotamian Cities during the Third Millennium B.C.," *The Professional Geographer* 53, no. 3 (2001), 374–383, 375.

of harlots and of the abominations of the earth," symbolized Rome, the alpha city of that age (see Chapter 5).[32] The emergence of city networks in Mesopotamia meant new forms of spatial domination. Intercity relations could be extractive. Paltry gains in labor productivity in preindustrial economies incentivized zero-sum games – for example, plundering rival cities. Relations with the hinterlands could be equally exploitive. The theme of urban decadence was also present in Mesopotamian literature, though it does not present radical alternatives to the purported iniquities of city life as the Bible does. In fact, religion was imbued in the urban form. For example, the poem *Erra and Ishum* describes Uruk as a "city of prostitutes, courtesans and call girls" where men "changed their masculinity into femininity."[33] The temptations brought about by urban abundance threatened so-called masculine warrior qualities associated with the moral vitality of the city-state:

> City food, however fancy, cannot compare with what is cooked on the embers
> Best beer, however sweet, cannot compare with water from a water skin.
> A palace built on a platform cannot compare with the shelters of a camp.
> Go out to the battlefield, warrior Erra, make your weapons resound![34]

The city-state was coterminous with civilization, while the countryside fostered ungoverned, chaotic, definitively lower modes of nomadic living. One Sumerian poem couches the archetypal nomad in chauvinistic precivilized stereotypes:

> He is dressed in sheepskins;
> He lives in tents in wind and rain;
> He doesn't offer sacrifices.
> Armed vagabond in the steppe,
> He digs up truffles and is restless.
> He eats raw meat,
> lives his life without a home,
> and, when he dies, he is not buried according to the proper rituals.[35]

Urban elite classes produced all known Mesopotamian literature. The superiority of city life was critical to their propaganda. This reinforced social hierarchies within the city, presupposing an improved quality-of-life in dense settlements. It justified the power of urban land masters over distant environs. Because no cuneiform scribes worked out of rural societies, nomads got to offer no rebuttals for posterity. Meanwhile, the poems of the urban elite extol city life. The names of the authors are almost always unknown. They are tied to the temple and palace, institutions at the top of the spatial hierarchies

32 *Revelation* 17:5. 33 *Myths from Mesopotamia*, 305. 34 Ibid., 287.
35 Cited in Marc van de Mieroop, *The Ancient Mesopotamian City* (Oxford: Oxford University Press, 1999), 43.

characterized by the dominance of city over country. Contrast this Akkadian account of Babylon with the Book of Revelation lament earlier in this section:

> Babylon is such that one is filled with joy looking at it.
> He who lives in Babylon his life will be prolonged.
> Babylon is like a Dilmun date whose fruit is uniquely sweet.[36]

Or this account of the Assyrian city of Arbela:

> Arbela, Arbela!
> Heaven without rival, Arbela!
> City of joyful music, Arbela!
> City of festivals, Arbela!
> City of happy households, Arbela![37]

These official narratives made forceful note of their places in a network of cities bringing access to foreign goods. Luxury imports were a significant trading market that the elite considered essential. Without fineries the Mesopotamian royal and religious classes would not have been able to maintain visual distinction over the subaltern strata. The city is portrayed lovingly as a hub of world commerce capable of amassing surpluses. As one Sumerian poem puts it:

> In those days, she (Innana) filled Akkade's stores for emmer wheat with gold,
> Filled its stores for white emmer with wheat and silver,
> copper, tin, and blocks of lapis lazuli were regularly delivered in its granaries,
> the outside of its grain silos she plastered over with mud.
> Its old women were given counsel,
> its old men were given eloquence,
> its maidens were given playgrounds,
> its young men were given the strength of weapons,
> its little ones were given happiness.
> Nursemaids holding the children of generals,
> played the *algasurrû*-lyre;
> Inside the city was the *tigi*-drum, outside were the reed pipes and tambourines.
> Its harbor, where the ships moored, was full of joy.[38]

The absent referent in these verses is the sparse nomadically inhabited desert that surrounded the cornucopian city. Walled fortifications surrounding cities were the boundaries between urban order and rural chaos. So went the constant refrain of the literate classes who monopolized the power of tablature. The transformation of the outdoorsman Enkidu in *The Epic of Gilgamesh* from a stereotypical wanderer capable of beastly behavior to a member of urban society provides another case in point. A full male life could be hardened by the harsh trials of the hinterlands, including possibly the battlefield, becoming civilized by the city without becoming soft.

[36] Ibid. [37] Ibid. [38] Ibid., 42.

James C. Scott's recent book *Against the Grain* challenges the conventional association between the rise of the city-state and human progress. This discourse, he argues, reflects deeply ingrained value judgments. These are the same judgments inherent in the passages we have just seen, foreshadowing Europeans' self-justifying "civilizing" missions. Scott is not the first social scientist to make this case but *Against the Grain* is perhaps the most strident book on early state development to do so. In this recasting of the urban revolution, city walls are just as necessary to keep captive populations trapped as they are to prevent sieges. This may have been one reason for locking the city gates each night with or without the presence of marauders. By one prayer:

> The countryside is quiet, the land is totally still,
> the cattle lie down, the people are asleep,
> the doors are fastened, the city gates closed.[39]

Far from provisioning greater physical security, daily life inside the walls may well have been nastier, shorter, and more brutish than preexisting modes of living. Scott makes the case that the rise of cities constituted a *decline* in the quality of life in the southern alluvium. Neolithic communities before the advent of state control were hardly stagnant innovators. They cultivated land through the use of fire.[40] The Neolithic combination of hunting, gathering, and farming led to more nutritious diets than those of the first urbanites whose food sources were limited by grain-based monocultures. Infant survival and other basic indicators of wellbeing probably deteriorated with city life. Bones recovered from archeological sites show greater evidence of stunting, disease, and malnourishment in large cities.[41] Concentrating populations in dense built environments was a dangerous undertaking in an age before preventive medicines like antibiotics and vaccines, conducive to plagues. These are persistent themes in cities even today.[42]

Demographics were destiny in ancient cities. The size of the population under centralized control was the most significant indicator of relative power within early city networks. City leaders faced constant manual labor shortages. For this reason the property holding nobility terminally feared desertion, the most potent form of political expression available to ordinary residents. "The slave must not go out of the gate," is the advice contained in an Old Babylonian letter between members of the literate class. "Keep an eye on him, and don't let him get upset."[43] The threat of desertion applied to free or

[39] Ibid., 76. [40] Scott, *Against the Grain*, 37. [41] Ibid., 82.

[42] For example, Mumbai is the most economically productive space in India by any measure, yet well into this century, life expectancy there was significantly less than in India's famously decentralized population. See Chittaranjan Tembhekar, "Mumbaikars Die Younger than Other Indians," *Times of India* (November 3, 2009).

[43] Postgate, *Early Mesopotamia*, 107.

quasi-free citizens as well as slaves. A broader concern among the elite is evident in an Assyrian letter chronicling dire water shortages:

> The king should write to Ubar, the commander of Babylon, that he should grant us an outlet from the Banītu canal, so that we can drink water with them and not have to desert the king because of lack of water. All countries should not say: "The people of Nippur, who submitted to Assyria, became fed up with the lack of water and deserted."[44]

Population imperatives had major implications for the status of women. They appear to have been pressured into childbearing much more often than in hunter-gatherer societies.[45] This lessened their range of potential participation in society, reinforcing increasingly severe patriarchal norms. Worse still, the bodily strain of childbirth greatly abbreviated women's lives in ancient cities. The state subjected female slaves to enforced breeding for the sake of maintaining productive labor power. As a result, enslaved woman of reproductive age carried higher exchange value. The personal emotions this aroused in these entrapped women may have been no less painful than they would be for anyone repeatedly raped in today's society. Such was the extreme cost administrators were willing to extract from the lower ranks. This to maintain fragile city-state populations in city networks with unstable balances of power, the dangers mortal. Cities that lost control of human and physical capital were subject to complete destruction by their rivals. Conquering kings made this outcome clear enough in inscriptions detailing these brazen events. "The city and its houses, from its foundations to its parapets, I swept away, I demolished, I burned with fire," boasted the Neo-Assyrian king Sennacherib (c. 745–681 BCE) after defeating Babylon.[46]

For all these sacrifices, Scott points out that early cities were more labor intensive than hunter-gatherer economies. Maintaining permanent crop fields required constant attention. Irrigation earthworks, manufacturing industries, and monumental structures necessitated never-quite-large-enough armies of slave and *corvée* labor. Increased production constituting an urban "surplus" would not have led to much leisure time for the strained lower classes. Only patricians (*awilum*) controlled the means of production, thereby enjoying the surplus of their properties – assuming disgruntled laborers did not vote with their feet and revert to nomadic life. The Codex Hammurabi defines the rest of society as either slaves (*wardum*) or a murkier classification denoting something between enslaved and free (*mushkenum*).[47] Hammurabi's laws required

[44] van de Mieroop, *The Ancient Mesopotamian City*, 159. [45] Scott, *Against the Grain*, 114.

[46] Mark W. Chavalas (ed.), *The Ancient Near East: Historic Sources in Translation* (Oxford: Blackwell Publishing, 2006), 349.

[47] There is a great deal of scholarly debate over how directly these laws were enforced. Hammurabi's codes were not the first written laws, contrary to popular belief. However, they are exceptionally well preserved and offer insight into the value systems of city leaders at the very least.

vigilance in preventing slave desertions. Harboring runaway slaves was a capital crime.[48] This suggests how important slaves must have been to the Old Babylonian economy Hammurabi presided over between c. 1810 and 1750 BCE, although the precise centrality of chattel slavery in cities is ambiguous.[49] The Neo-Babylonian captivity of the Judeans was one episode in the longstanding practice of forced resettlement. Managers in city administrations oversaw deportations numbering in the hundreds of thousands.[50] This underpinned the romantic, multi-ethnic, anachronistic veneer of the earliest cities that is evocative of today's world cities, where migration is at least nominally voluntary.

When given the choice, ordinary people may have done the opposite: reverted back to decentralized community life when power in cities was no longer sufficient to hold them. Cities dominate the modern discussion of thousands of years of history in the southern alluvium. Part of this is because of their justifiably important scientific, cultural, and institutional achievements.[51] Another reason is the inordinate record cities left behind. It's easy to forget that city-states' high periods were comparatively brief, bookended by centuries of deurbanization. As one historian put it, "we must recognize that the 250 years of central-state dominance (or 291 years, counting Babylon's brief hegemony) stand out as anomalous within the thousand years of recorded political history between *c.* 2600 and 1600; for 709 of those years, division was the norm."[52]

City-states had forms of political accountability other than desertion, starting with quasi-pluralistic governance structures. Kings nominally worked for the gods who formally owned cities, only rarely deifying themselves. Mesopotamia's pervasive state religions had democratic sensibilities evident in literature. Here is how the poem "Etana" sanctifies city building:

> The great gods, the Igigi designed a city,
> The Igigi laid its foundation,
> The Anunnaki designed the city of Kish,
> The Anunnaki laid its foundation,
> The Igigi made its brickwork firm . . .
> Let Etana be their builder . . .[53]

[48] *The Code of Hammurabi*, trans. L. W. King (1915), 7. [49] Ibid., 6.

[50] Scott, *Against the Grain*, 177.

[51] There is also an ideological justification for Assyriology, which has its roots in a Western-led race to excavate the first cities in search of antecedents to their own "civilizing" expansionist tendencies.

[52] Seth Richardson, "Early Mesopotamia: The Presumptive State," *Past and Present* no. 215 (2012), 3–49, 16.

[53] *Myths from Mesopotamia*, 190.

Etana is possibly a real Sumerian ruler. Kish had enduring symbolic significance (later conquerors frequently granted themselves the title "King of Kish").[54] The Anunnaki and Igigi were the assemblies of the older underworld gods and the youthful deities, respectively. The gods seem to operate by deliberation and consensus. Here they form a layer of authority over the king who executes their decrees. Early Mesopotamian cities correspondingly had various deliberative bodies. Kings sat at the head of assemblies while splitting duties with councils on judicial rulings.[55] Thorkild Jacobsen went as far as to call this "primitive democracy," although scholars have debated just how democratic the Mesopotamian city-states were since his thesis emerged in the 1940s.[56] City-states appear to have become more authoritarian over time as dominant cities formed large empires. This trajectory too is debated.[57] Kings certainly had expansive foreign policymaking powers, thereby making them the architects of the extensive intercity relations required to establish city networks. On the other hand, politics within the city walls – the territory most subject to direct governance – may have benefitted from these relatively small polities conducive to direct participation by elder councils and groups of professionals.[58]

The prologue of the Codex Hammurabi (1754 BCE) asserts that "the strong should not harm the weak."[59] Cities had redistributive mechanisms for protecting orphans and widows. There were price controls for essential goods and services. Debt to urban land masters – lenders from the nobility or temple – was a constant threat to tenant farmers and smallholders working the land. Even locally born free members of society were at risk of total household collapse and temporary enslavement if they could not pay off loans. Tributes required by the city also placed heavy burdens on families. The Codex Hammurabi devotes considerable attention to lending conditions. This includes the possibility of debt forgiveness if bad circumstances such as natural disasters damaged the harvests. That provided a modicum of protection for the working classes that went against the interests of elite lenders.[60] This indicates that the king had to be receptive to debt strains facing the laborers on which urban surpluses depended, given the threat of desertion.

[54] This is because it was thought to be the first city to reconstitute itself after the mythical flood that wiped out much of human existence. It is the starting place for the Kings List chronicling lines of succession.

[55] Westenholz, "The Sumerian City-State," 31.

[56] Thorkild Jacobsen, "Primitive Democracy in Ancient Mesopotamia," *Journal of Near Eastern Studies* 2, no. 3 (1943), 159–172.

[57] Marc van de Mieroop challenges this position in van de Mieroop, *The Ancient Mesopotamian City*, 118.

[58] Ibid., 123. [59] *The Code of Hammurabi*, 3. [60] Ibid., 11.

This review of these persistent political problems facing the earliest city networks casts doubt on the rationalist view of time presupposing urbanization as a form of linear progress. To reiterate, the invention of the city and the global trading networks that enabled it seem to have been more labor intensive than the systems they replaced. Cities were not exercises in problem solving operating on the logic of what political scientists call an "efficiency of history."[61] A narrow elite passed inherent inefficiencies on to "unfree labor" (see Chapter 3) that had to bear the rising costs of city building. Periods of deurbanization may not have been setbacks on the path to progress, instead reflecting resistance to the emergent hierarchies. Cities were effectively collections of social power brought about by new institutional capabilities, as will be seen in the next section.

City Networks, Alpha Cities: Uruk, Ur, and Babylon

The rest of this chapter looks at three cities that flourished in Mesopotamia: Uruk at the turn of the fourth millennium, Ur III in the third millennium, and Babylon's incarnations in the second and first millenniums BCE. These cities stood at the center of global networks in trade, politics, and diplomacy. They were built, engineered, and socially ordered to maintain these positions.

Uruk City Network

Southern Mesopotamia was possibly half urbanized in the third millennium.[62] Another estimate places this figure much higher, at 90 percent.[63] These ballpark figures suggest the region could have been at least as urbanized as the planetary population is today. Perhaps these societies were as urbanized as fully industrialized northern countries, at roughly 80 percent.[64] It is all the more remarkable that this was a case of pristine urbanization, meaning that it happened without influence from any other place. Uruk is, by Childe's criteria, ground zero for the urban revolution. By the time the Sumerian city network ruptured under the weight of Akkadian king Sargon the Great's invasions in the 2300s BCE, the core city of Uruk had perhaps fifty city-states in its orbit

[61] James G. Marsh and Johann P. Olsen, "The Institutional Dynamics of International Political Orders," *International Organization* 52, no. 4 (1998), 943–969, 956.

[62] Westenholz, "The Sumerian City-State," 26.

[63] Gwendolyn Leick, *Mesopotamia: The Invention of the City* (New York: Penguin, 2001), xviii; Guillermo Algaze, *Ancient Mesopotamia at the Dawn of Civilization: The Evolution of an Urban Landscape* (Chicago: University of Chicago Press, 2008), 102.

[64] If this sounds implausible, it is important to remember that the hinterlands were largely governed by administrations from inside the city walls. Portions of the agricultural workforce reverse commuted from the city.

according to the literary record.[65] A network of small trading towns extended this reach.

The city of Uruk, located at Warka in southern Iraq, was the stuff of fables. The scale of the city was unprecedented, an incredible site in the ancient world. *The Epic of Gilgamesh* chronicles the adventures of a swashbuckling third millennium king of Uruk, whose actual existence is listed on the Mesopotamian "Kings List."[66] It opens with a remarkable account of Gilgamesh's city:

> He had the wall of Uruk built, the sheepfold
> Of holiest Eanna, the pure treasury.
> See its wall, which is like a copper band,
> Survey its battlements, which nobody else can match,
> Take the threshold, which is from time immemorial,
> Approach Eanna, the home of Ishtar,
> Which no future king nor any man will ever match!
> Go up on the wall of Uruk and walk around!
> Inspect the foundation platform and scrutinize the brickwork!
> Testify that its bricks are baked bricks,
> And that the Seven Counselors must have laid its foundations!
> One square mile is city, one square mile is orchards, one square mile is clay pits, as well as the open ground of Ishtar's temple.
> Three square miles and the open ground comprise Uruk.[67]

This was not wholly out of line with the city's actual appearances, which archeologists have gleaned from the excavation site at Warka. The walled city comprised about two square miles. There was additional settlement outside the city walls. Estimates based on a site of that geographic size would put the population in the range of 40,000–50,000 inhabitants. It was likely the largest city in the world by a wide margin at the turn of the third millennium.[68] More importantly, there were no comparably populated cities in the rank-size distribution of Mesopotamian archeological sites.[69] Intercity relations were evidently hierarchal even though city-states were nominally independent. That said, Uruk appears not to have directly controlled neighboring city-states as would territorial empires. Rather it inordinately influenced them through an

65 Westenholz, "The Sumerian City-State," 26.

66 The famed Kings List is a running record of rulers that the Mesopotamians maintained throughout their history. It is impressively thorough, despite invasions and language changes.

67 The "Seven Counselors" were mythical craftsmen sages. Dalley, *Myths from Mesopotamia*, 50.

68 Granted, population estimates for cities at the time are highly inexact, although there is widespread agreement that Uruk was in fact the world's largest city.

69 Hans J. Nissen, "Cultural and Political Networks in the Ancient Near East during the Fourth and Third Millennia B.C.," in Mitchell S. Rothman (ed.), *Uruk Mesopotamia & Its Neighbors: Cross Cultural Interactions in the Era of State Formation* (Santa Fe: School of American Research Press, 2001), 149–180, 157.

elaborate system of hard economic power and soft cultural power. Its dominance is evident in population distributions that mirror the "primate city" pattern, in which one leading city is by far larger than the next largest urban centers.[70] Uruk's growth may have come at the expense of would-be rivals.[71] By one widely cited analysis, there were four settlements in the Uruk sphere of influence large enough to constitute cities. There were six "large towns," complemented by a vast network of 122 small towns, villages and hamlets.[72]

A seminal undertaking, Uruk certainly met the eye test for an alpha city. Uruk had architecture on a scale to match its urban footprint. There was a frenetic pace of building, tearing down, and rebuilding at even larger sizes. Its walls were 7 meters tall, interspersed with gates and towers.[73] There were planned public spaces, although archeologists struggle to determine the uses of construction. This could have included gardens if the account in *Epic of Gilgamesh* is accurate. Temples dominated the urban landscapes of Mesopotamian cities, owing to the importance of religion in city management. Uruk's skyline featured an 11-meters-high ziggurat with a temple that measured an additional 6 meters. One of the city's two religious districts, called "Eanna," had multiple buildings of at least 10 meters tall.[74] This district also had economic functions as the site of workshops, trade, warehouses for stored goods, and economic administration.[75] These structures were effectively a central business district intended to secure control over economic transactions. This was in addition to serving the city's patron god, Inanna.

Uruk was an inventive society whose credits included wheeled carts, rotary power, and bulk packaging.[76] This reduced time and space constraints on trade. It exported food products, alcoholic beverages, and textiles. These goods required processing and timely delivery.[77] It may well be that the network of smaller settlements were economic monocultures exporting raw goods to the core city. These were then assembled, consumed, or re-exported at higher value. The textile manufacturing industry that emerged during this time most likely depended on substantial wool imports from grazing pasturelands.[78] Uruk is believed to have employed at least 5,000 workers in textile factories – 10 percent of its population – processing this wool into finished garments that

70 The primate city distribution is common today, evident most notably with the population dominance of London in the United Kingdom. We also see it with Buenos Aires relative to the rest of Argentina. By contrast, China and Australia have more even population distributions, particularly at the high end.

71 For example, as Uruk expanded over the course of the fourth millennium, population estimates for the large city of Nippur shrank. See the chart in Algaze, *Ancient Mesopotamia at the Dawn of Civilization*, 110.

72 Ibid., 113. 73 Pollack, *Ancient Mesopotamia*, 47.

74 Measurement figures cited in Nissen, "Cultural and Political Networks," 154. 75 Ibid.

76 Wengrow, *What Makes Civilization?*, 77. 77 Ibid., 79.

78 Algaze, *Ancient Mesopotamia at the Dawn of Civilization*, 94.

distinguished the elite.[79] Urban capital financed these ventures, foreshadowing the explosion of textile manufacturing in the city of Ur.

Beyond that, the city depended on a multitude of imports to produce itself. Cities with concentrations of urban elites in ancient times constituted strong consumption markets for long distance trading. They controlled the surpluses that could be bartered for new expressions of wealth in a pre-monetary economy. Leading Uruk specialist Guillermo Algaze implores us to consider the breadth and scope of imports evident in the archeological record:

> ... (1) pine used as roofing timber; (2) copper, silver, lead, and gold used as tools, weapons, vessels, jewelry, and other objects of personal adornment and, more rarely, as architectural accents in elite buildings; (3) precious stones such as lapis, carnelian, agate, chalcedony, amazonite, amethyst, aragonite, and jasper for use in jewelry, occasionally, as architectural decoration in public buildings; (4) semiprecious stones such as chlorite, obsidian, rock crystal, quartz, alabaster, gypsum, marble, diorite, serpentine, and bituminous limestone used for statuary, ritual and utilitarian vessels, and implements; (5) common stones such as basalt, flint, and obsidian, used for agricultural and household implements, and limestone, which uniquely in the Uruk period, was occasionally used in the foundation of important buildings and platforms; (6) bitumen, which was used as a general purpose adhesive and waterproofing substance, for caulking boats, and, again uniquely in Uruk times, for flooring and even as brick mortar in some public buildings; and finally (7) valuable liquids such as wine.[80]

The cornucopian city described in literature did not draw exclusively on its own environmental abundance. It drew on the abundance of resource-rich places such as the northern tier of the Fertile Crescent, where it established colonies, and beyond. Notably urbanism did not take off in Upper Mesopotamia until much later, despite its surplus potential. The most significant ecological benefit may have been Uruk's place further downstream, with greater transport and communication access to other places.[81] Algaze meticulously describes Uruk's critical mass of knowledge, achieved by having large, concentrated populations capable of sharing ideas.[82] From there it developed new ways to overcome environmental deficits, particularly in the form of irrigation techniques to *emulate* surplus conditions. Algaze's emphasis on "technologies of the intellect" transcends the terms of physicality on which ancient cities are understood.[83] There is a "human capital" component analogous to modern global cities, which evolves beyond initial environmental advantages to become a self-sustaining site of knowledge production.

Uruk is significant in the history of world cities because it develops the first information storage. Ingenious administrative innovations were arguably more important than physical inventions in cementing Uruk's place as an alpha city. For starters, intricate cylinder heads were a significant scribal innovation. They

[79] Ibid., 84. [80] Ibid., 95. [81] Ibid., 116. [82] Ibid., 127. [83] Ibid., 128.

sealed shipments in its network, distinguishing their origins and perhaps institutionalizing trade agreements.[84] The Eanna temple district was the site of the first known writing, dating as far back as 3200.[85] The ability to store information was a milestone in statecraft, enabling the temple to record ever increasing volumes of resources, formalize transactions, and manage land. This gave the state a monopoly on the means of production, suggesting a kind of command economy. Only trained scribes working for the nobility could execute and read these public documents, which were for commercial purposes (the use of cuneiform writing for literature did not happen for another five centuries). Even most kings were illiterate. This power grew as etched pictographs evolved into ever more elaborate cuneiform. Uruk scribes developed scripts that would be understood in other city-states to facilitate trade, eventually corresponding with the Sumerian language – in effect a soft power projection.[86] The Uruk city-state also used the first writing to establish "Lexical Lists," formalizing professional titles and cementing ranks within its hierarchy.[87] In other words, the first writing commodified people as well as products, including recorded slave transactions. Claude Lévi-Strauss understood the implication for labor relations, asserting that "the primary function of writing, as a means of communication, is to facilitate the enslavement of other human beings."[88] To this we can add that writing enabled interurban hierarchies dependent on "unfree labor."

Guillermo Algaze greatly influenced Mesopotamian studies with his 1993 book *The Uruk World System.*[89] The book calls attention to smaller settlements in the city network, drawing on archeological evidence to ascertain their relationship to the core city. Algaze's thesis is that the Uruk city network resembled Immanuel Wallerstein's "world systems" analysis.[90] In Wallerstein's modern construct, a northern core absorbs resources from postcolonial places in the southern periphery, assembling them at higher value. These advantages can be locked in politically and culturally. Algaze reiterates that Mesopotamia was "a land devoid of most resources other than the basic ones provided by agriculture and animal husbandry," where "a substantial proportion of the material

84 Kuhrt, *The Ancient Near East c. 3000-330BC Vol. I*, 40.
85 Postgate, *Early Mesopotamia*, 66.
86 Karen Rhea Nemet-Nejat, *Daily Life in Ancient Mesopotamia* (Westport, CT: Greenwood, 1998), 49.
87 Nissen, "Cultural and Political Networks," 156.
88 Claude Lévi-Strauss, *Tristes Tropiques* (New York: Atheneum, 1964), 292.
89 Guillermo Algaze, *The Uruk World System: The Dynamics of Expansion of Early Mesopotamian Civilization*, 2nd ed. (Chicago: University of Chicago Press, 2005).
90 For elaboration on Wallerstein's thesis in relation to the modern world, see Immanuel Wallerstein, *World Systems Analysis: An Introduction* (Durham, NC: Duke University Press, 2004).

requirements needed to sustain highly stratified social systems had to be imported."[91] Scarcity motivated Uruk's regional expansion.

The spread of "Uruk culture" across Mesopotamia happened in concert with the city's external expansion. New towns emerged that evince more master planning than with the improvisational growth of older cities. City builders constructed them in Uruk fashion, evidently replicating the core city's administrative characteristics in their built environments.[92] They were positioned near access points to resources, rather than for their proximity to agriculturally productive spaces.[93] Strategic access to northward trading routes was particularly important in determining locations for new settlements.[94] Some of them had large populations and sizeable architectural proportions.[95] These outposts also traded with other regions, suggestive of even broader interdependence, even if indigenous inhabitants objected to Uruk colonists.[96] Uruk artistic styles were heavily present in these towns – in fact artifacts sharing the Uruk aesthetic have been found as far away as Syria, Iran, and Turkey. The peripheral towns were not as economically diversified as Uruk. These cities were likely self-governing, but dependent on the central market. Recalling Jacobs, economic monocultures are bound to struggle. That reality may have weakened smaller towns before Sargon's invasions, even as Uruk appears to have grown.[97]

Ur III: Seeing Like a State

In the 1920s, British archeologist Charles Leonard Woolley unearthed the Sumerian city of Ur, which enjoyed an imperial heyday during its Third Dynasty period *c.* 2113 and 2029 BCE. The largely undisturbed burial he found was a tell-all on the magnitude of Tutankhamen's tomb in Egypt. It told of opulent wealth by the standards of any time period. For our purposes, it told of complex trading networks capable of putting processed materials from the Indus Valley and Afghanistan all in one place. These were the fineries that more than a dozen nobles, possibly kings and queens, took with them to the afterlife. They brought their retinues of servants as well, proof of human sacrifice. Woolley thought they may have voluntarily allowed themselves to be killed. More recent evidence shows that less cooperative attendants had their skulls bludgeoned. Either way "the great death pit" told the story of immense social control in city-states, through the soft power of language and religion – or simply through the ability to marshal force.[98]

[91] Algaze, *The Uruk World System*, 1. [92] Ibid., 25. [93] Ibid., 61. [94] Ibid., 69.
[95] Ibid., 38. [96] Ibid., 84. [97] Ibid., 114.
[98] Bertman, *Handbook to Life in Ancient Mesopotamia*, 36; Leick, *Mesopotamia*, 112.

Perhaps more notable to posterity than Ur's relatively short-lived hegemony was the record the city left behind under Third Dynasty rule. Thousands of Ur III tablets make the city's name forever synonymous with the concept of centralized government. The bulk of these tablets recorded economic transactions, even the most mundane. In one case the death of a sheep was noted in three tablets.[99] The lived experiences of some transactions would not have been mundane for those involved. For example the record of "two female slaves at two-thirds output for seven days" evinces the hierarchy required to maintain Ur III's command economy.[100] (The tablets also document private transactions, but the powerful manufacturing sector was firmly under state authority.) The Ur III tablets are not a simple case of selective survival. Scholars agree that the city-state's meticulous documentation reflects an extraordinary period of bureaucratic power that stood out in a region that was a veritable laboratory for state building.

The bureaucratization program during king Shulgi's long reign from 2094 to 2047 BCE evokes the "technology of the intellect" developed during the Uruk period. The physical city was underpinned by an informational component capable of managing increasingly complex production. Shulgi's predecessor Ur-Nammu, the dynasty's founder, had already engaged in extensive city building worthy of the new regime. Visitors would have seen a dense, bustling city with named streets flanked by tightly packed housing whose designs expertly managed the region's scorching sunlight.[101] A massive ziggurat was the city's centerpiece.[102] Shulgi effectively instituted the proverbial software of the world city to complement this mud brick hardware. Bureaucratization was in reality a power grab over the means of production, using early language to reinforce state ideology. This included self-deification, propagandistic hymnals, and the use of curriculum to indoctrinate the educated scribal class.[103] This class staffed a greatly expanded civil service capable of implementing state regulations.[104] Ur III records show that large swaths of the city's assets were under palace control, including real estate holdings.[105] For all its overarching authority, the state eased the flow of many kinds of transactions through the implementation of standard weights and measures. It also codified the use of silver as a means of exchange.[106]

[99] Postgate, *Early Mesopotamia*, 42. [100] Chavalas (ed.), *The Ancient Near East*, 66.

[101] Mary Shepperson, "Planning for the Sun: Urban Forms as a Mesopotamian Response to the Sun," *World Archeology* 41, no. 3 (2009), 363–378, 369.

[102] Kuhrt, *The Ancient Near East c. 3000–330BC Vol. I*, 64.

[103] Robert McCormick Adams, "Old Babylonian Networks of Urban Notables," *Cuneiform Digital Library Journal* 7 (2009), 1–14, 2.

[104] Leick, *Mesopotamia*, 123.

[105] McCormick Adams, "Old Babylonian Networks of Urban Notables," 2.

[106] Leick, *Mesopotamia*, 125.

Concerning the hardware of global connectivity, Ur III maintained a capital-intensive shipbuilding center producing unusually high capacity trading vessels.[107] One of Shulgi's hymns boasts of creating land-based sinews of regional linkage to complement waterborne travel:

> I enlarged the footpaths, straightened the highways of the land,
> I made secure travel, built there "big houses,"
> Planted gardens alongside of them, establishing resting places,
> Settled there friendly folk,
> So that who comes from below, who comes from above,
> Might refresh themselves in its cool shade,
> The wayfarer who travels the highway at night,
> Might find refuge there as well as in a built city.[108]

This description of "secure travel" replete with rest stops is probably idealistic in the context of Ur III. Marauders increasingly pressured the city during Shulgi's reign. It does, however, reflect the city's investment in distance-bridging infrastructure in order to foster intercity interactions.

Ur III textile manufacturing employed an estimated 50,000–60,000 workers, far surpassing the textile industry concentrated in Uruk nearly a millennium earlier.[109] The industry relied on millions of sheep, with 500,000 of them owned by the capital city.[110] Another six city-states contributed to the textile economy. Ur produced 24,000 garments annually.[111] This form of production required specialization in a division of labor between managerial, artisanal, and rote unskilled labor.[112] The tremendous amount of labor hours required to maintain this volume of wool processing led to a flow of workers from the countryside into metropolitan areas.[113] Ur employed an estimated 13,200 weavers, who were mostly woman and children.[114] This was categorically semi-captive "unfree labor" working on subsistence rations provided by the state. They lived *by your leave* as subalterns in work gangs headed by either men or women.

An analysis of the Ur III tablets makes the case that this system was far too extractive to sustain, particularly on the hinterlands.[115] State survival depended on extracting ever-increasing values from its own population and from

[107] Postgate, *Early Mesopotamia*, 230.
[108] Kuhrt, *The Ancient Near East c. 3000–330BC Vol. I*, 69.
[109] Algaze, *Ancient Mesopotamia at the Dawn of Civilization*, 83. [110] Ibid., 82.
[111] Ibid., 91.
[112] For an overview of how this process might have worked, see Richard Firth and Mary-Louise Nosch, "Spinning and Weaving Wool in Ur III Administrative Texts," *Journal of Cuneiform Studies* 64 (2012), 65–82.
[113] Algaze, *Ancient Mesopotamia at the Dawn of Civilization*, 91.
[114] van de Mieroop, *The Ancient Mesopotamian City*, 186.
[115] McCormick Adams, "Old Babylonian Networks of Urban Notables," 3.

surrounding villages. These actors were better off not shelling out exorbitant tributes to the city in various guises. They were likely looking for any sign of weakness in city power. "Civilizations are built upon the systematic exploitation of major portions of their populations," concluded Susan Pollack, "who till the fields, weave the cloth, build the monuments, and fund the lifestyles of the wealthy and powerful."[116] The collapse of Ur III at the hands of invading nomadic Amorites was followed by a period of population dispersal where burdensome tributes and forced labor may have been curtailed.[117]

The famished, pestilent city's hopeless resistance to the Amorite onslaught was captured in a lament to its departing god: "My Nanna, do not grow tired yourself but leave your city!"[118]

Babylon: Urbanism and Interdependence

Akhenaten ruled over a resurgent Egypt in a shrinking world. A web of marriages, including one of his own, signaled a growing diplomatic thicket in which great powers forged agreements. His mother-in-law was the daughter of a king in a distant but powerful major city: Babylon. No cities on Babylon's order of magnitude existed in Egypt. Its population was decentralized and its economy was traditionally more self-sufficient than Babylon's, owing to a superior ecological support system. Egyptian settlements emerged along the Nile, or temporarily near monumental construction sites in so-called pyramid cities. Kings could move court, as Akhenaten did when he established Amarna in 1346 BCE. He brought with him a series of diplomatic letters, a valuable record of early international relations. Increasingly rapid horse drawn transport enabled more contact between the first rate powers. Alas, faster moving armies led to wars over control of their peripheries, necessitating delicate negotiations.[119] Notably the letters discovered in Egypt were not written in the Egyptian language or in hieroglyphics. They were cuneiform documents in Akkadian, the Mesopotamian language at this time, and the diplomatic *lingua franca*.[120]

Much of this correspondence concerned trade. Egypt was Mesopotamia's sole gold supplier. It also exported ivory, ebony, and alabaster, importing copper and precious stones.[121] This is hardly new. Long distance trade had

[116] Pollack, *Ancient Mesopotamia*, 218. [117] Scott, *Against the Grain*, 214.
[118] Chavalas (ed.), *The Ancient Near East*, 71. [119] Leick, *Mesopotamia*, 250.
[120] Raymond Cohen and Raymond Westbrook, "Introduction: The Amarna System," in Raymond Cohen and Raymond Westbrook (eds.), *Amarna Diplomacy: The Beginnings of International Relations* (Baltimore: The Johns Hopkins University Press, 1992), 1–14, 1.
[121] Carlo Zaccagnini, "The Interdependence of Great Powers," in Raymond Cohen and Raymond Westbrook (eds.), *Amarna Diplomacy: The Beginnings of International Relations* (Baltimore: The Johns Hopkins University Press, 1992), 141–153, 141.

by then existed for millennia. But the Amarna letters communicate much more. The letters indicate that Babylon was a force to be reckoned with, consistent with scriptural accounts of its swift military might. Egyptian kings referred to the city-state's kings on equal terms as "brother."[122] They also indicate more elaborate global governance arrangements with complex political dimensions, such as protocols for visiting dignitaries.[123] The city, its environs, and professional classes needed to be capable of pulling off visits by important emissaries. Babylon's urban form projected the images of power and stability.

No doubt it did so quite well. As we have seen, it had dense concentrations of outsized buildings. The wealthiest residents lived nearest the temple and palaces, evidenced by larger housing stock in these areas.[124] As in previous high periods for cities, these were the sites of the most prestigious roles in society. It shared the same basic architectural features with its predecessors, except it was much larger. In terms of scale, Babylon was roughly twice the size of Uruk.[125] An increasingly integrated agricultural system in the southern alluvium may have made it possible to sustain an extraordinarily large sedentary population unlike any before it.[126]

Finally, the urban experience in Babylon informs scholarly understanding of social relations in this world system. Granted, this was much different for individuals in a society with deeply ingrained stratification. For everyone the visual experience at the culmination of Nebuchadnezzar II's building spree would have included impressive symbolic adornments: Ishtar Gate, Processional Way, the ziggurat, Nebuchadnezzar II's three palaces, the massive city walls, and temples throughout the city (Figure 2.1). Monumental structures intentionally towered over residential districts. Their builders meant them to be visible. However the distance with which one could approach such buildings varied based on status. Access to them was limited to the public. There is little knowledge of open spaces that may have been gardens or parks, but these could well have been exclusive.[127] Haphazard residential streets are thought to have been gated in places, limiting access by clan or profession. Housing size varied greatly. This is a standard way researchers guess at social disparities. The average size of excavated homes seems to have increased between the Old Babylonian period of the second millennium and the

[122] Kuhrt, *The Ancient Near East c. 3000–330BC Vol. I*, 339. [123] Ibid., 347.

[124] Heather D. Baker, "From Street Alter to Palace: Reading the Built Environment of Early Babylonia," in Karen Radner and Eleanor Robson (eds.), *The Oxford Handbook of Cuneiform Culture* (Oxford: Oxford University Press, 2011), 533–552, 542.

[125] van de Mieroop, *The Ancient Mesopotamian City*, 94. [126] Ibid., 30.

[127] The "Hanging Gardens of Babylon" would definitely have been exclusive. Greek accounts from ancient times say that Nebuchadnezzar II built them. However, there is as yet no archeological proof of this. It has also been posited that they existed in Nineveh and were built by Sennacherib. For a broader discussion on green spaces in the city, see Baker, "Urban Form in the First Millennium BC," 72.

Figure 2.1 A piece of the Ishtar Gate, along Babylon's Processional Way, constructed by Nebuchadnezzar II around 575 BCE.
Courtesy of the Metropolitan Museum of Art, New York, Fletcher Fund, 1931.

Neo-Babylonian period of the first millennium. By one estimate this figure more than doubled to 417 square meters.[128] This possibly means that there was economic growth. However differentiation in the size of homes indicates what a leading scholar of Mesopotamian cityscapes thinks is "an unprecedented degree of social inequality."[129]

Conclusion: Menageries of Statecraft

It is useful to remember that the Uruk, Ur III, and Babylonian high periods are rare golden ages of intercity relations. Most Mesopotamians across history knew these places in myths, if they knew them at all. In addition to a selective survival bias, these societies lend themselves to modern fascination because they bear uncanny resemblances to present-day modes of living.

And why not?

What dedicated *flâneur* would not time travel back to the corridors of these multicultural cities, to witness the crowded, frenetic pace of street life? Likewise, the energy would have been palpable for those privileged enough to enjoy this extremely unusual use of space. They may have seen the drudgery of rural life as an inferior alternative, perhaps not seeing the existence of the city as a cause of that drudgery. This theme, captured in admittedly propagandistic literature, must have spoken to genuine emotions. Equally real must have been the awe at the unearthly sizes of the buildings by both admirers and detractors.

[128] Baker, "From Street Alter to Palace," 541. [129] Ibid., 541.

It is tempting to look at city-states in evolutionary terms. That is, with the presumption that cities were organizationally superior to their less-complex neighbors, thereby subsuming them. However tribes such as the Amorites routinely defeated cities. Captives, subalterns, and workers disgruntled by heavy tribute all seem to have regularly opted out of city life.

By this logic we could infer apparent superiority in territorial empires such as Achaemenid Persia, which overtook Babylon. But this was the same empire the small Greek city-states triumphed over, as we will discuss in Chapter 3. In short, the world was a menagerie of different kinds of states, in addition to nonstate societies. Their lifespans offer insufficient clarity on a process of natural selection. Extinct species regularly come back to life. City networks in their purest forms interact with each other, but city-states like Babylon achieved sufficient primacy to engage on equal terms with empires, establishing their own quasi-empires. This despite that fact that their truest sovereignty was within their walls.

These city networks went far beyond physical expressions of power. Certainly there was ample warfare during these times, but these cities stood out in their ability to marshal nonmilitary forms of coercion. State development in cities deployed "technologies of the intellect" to cement inequality, establishing the economic dependencies that fueled these golden ages. What is chilling is that innovative minds using writing for "Lexical Lists" conscientiously devised social hierarchies from scratch. Then, as now, knowledge is a potent weapon.

Despite their stunning continuities, there are significant distinctions between the three networks discussed here, which span nearly three millennia of evolution, collapse, and change. The Uruk network dominated northern territories. Later, the northern hinterlands once influenced by Uruk grew dominant. Geographic horizons expanded. Babylon came into dense diplomatic, military, and economic contact with distant power centers such as Egypt. Some city-states experimented with pluralistic forms of government while others, like Ur III, presaged bureaucratic authoritarianism. In the annals of city networks, extreme top-down governance often engenders pushback, as we will explore further in subsequent chapters.

After Mesopotamian cities lost independence, one of the most remarkably inventive city networks in history took form in mainland Greece.

3 *Agora* and *Emporia*

The Greek City-States

It was winter, 430/431 BCE, when Pericles delivered his famous oration honoring Athenians who died in the Peloponnesian War's first year. The de facto – though not absolute – Athenian leader asked mourners to gaze at the Parthenon each day as a reminder of their city's greatness.[1] The temple is the centerpiece of an astonishing construction spree in Periclean Athens. Pericles (495–425 BCE), known for his military command, was a zealous city builder. The Parthenon's vast architecture dominated a burgeoning city center that symbolized Athens' core status in the Mediterranean. Dues from 330 tributary cities helped finance it.[2] On top of that, the Parthenon was a bank as well as a religious site. This was where those tributes ended up as the cooperative Delian League became the Athenian Empire, moving its treasury from Delos to Athens.

Pericles' oration was less a eulogy than an argument for his planned war of attrition against Sparta, an ancient *Why We Fight.* Where Sparta shunned nonresidents, Athenians "throw open our city to the world, and never by alien acts exclude foreigners from any opportunity of learning or observing."[3] Where Sparta was a highly conservative oligarchy fearful of democracy, Pericles praised the dominant pluralistic traditions in Athens. He stridently reminded his audience of the city's high living standards. Base as this material appeal sounds to modern ears, in his mind it justified protracted sacrifice in a war that lasted a generation. Athens was fighting for a regional trading system and its central place in it. Sparta was an autarky unusually landlocked in

1 "Art Humanities: Primary Source Reader, The Parthenon," Columbia University. Available at https://arthum.college.columbia.edu/sites/default/files/PDFs/arthum_parthenon_reader.pdf, last accessed August 26, 2018.

2 Mogens Herman Hansen and Thomas Heine Nielsen, *An Inventory of Archaic and Classical Poleis* (Oxford: Oxford University Press, 2004), 1356.

3 "Ancient History Sourcebook: Thucydides, Pericles Funeral Oration from the Peloponnesian War," Fordham University. Available at https://sourcebooks.fordham.edu/ancient/pericles-funeralspeech.asp, last accessed August 26, 2018.

seafaring Hellas. Most of its city-state neighbors were littoral.[4] Athenian scholars studied Sparta's severe regimentation as an outlier, even an oddity, among Greek *poleis*. Athens, Pericles argued, was a seminal innovator in an established city network: "our city draws the produce of the world into our harbor, so that to the Athenian the fruits of other countries are as familiar a luxury as those of his own."[5] This system reduced poverty, increased consumption, and led to more comfortable housing, he argued. All supported claims.[6]

Sparta used its superior ground forces to invade Attica, ravaging the city's farming hinterlands in an attempt to draw Athens into direct land battle with its *hoplite* army. As per Pericles' defensive-minded strategy, the whole population of Attica instead retreated behind the city's miles-long circuit wall. As Aristotle later pointed out in *Politics*, city walls could deter available siege technology.[7] Athenian leaders had successfully used diplomatic subterfuge to expand the barrier over Spartan objection, according to Thucydides' contemporary telling.[8] The Athenian Long Wall, with seventeen gates, defined boundaries for the sprawling haphazardly constructed city enveloping the majestic Acropolis where the Parthenon stands.[9] Crucially, the Long Wall reached the port city of Piraeus, the most important commercial harbor in Classical Hellas. This fortification protected the source of Athenian power: Its trading routes. Evidence suggests Athenian dietary need exceeded what Attica's thin topsoil would bear, invasion or not. The city relied on overseas imports for its staples.[10] As G. E. M. de Ste. Croix points out, "Athens was altogether exceptional in needing to import the greater part of her food supply, as well as all her timber and metals."[11] A dominant navy preserved this lifeline.

A protracted plague devastated the city in the war's second year, exacerbated by crowded conditions created by the rural evacuation. The epidemic claimed one-third of the population, including Pericles himself.[12] This basic war strategy nevertheless enabled continued power over the Athenian sphere of influence until the collapse of its empire a quarter century later. City life

4 Hansen and Nielsen, *Inventory of Archaic and Classical Poleis*, 23.
5 "Ancient History Sourcebook."
6 Josiah Ober, *The Rise and Fall of Classical Greece* (Princeton: Princeton University Press, 2015), 2.
7 Aristotle, *Politics* (Oxford: Oxford University Press, 1995), 277.
8 Thucydides, *The Peloponnesian War* (Oxford: Oxford University Press, 2009), 44.
9 Robert Garland, *Daily Life of the Ancient Greeks* (Indianapolis: Hackett, 1998), 24.
10 Ober, *Rise and Fall of Classical Greece*, 23.
11 G. E. M. de Ste. Croix, *The Class Struggle in the Ancient Greek World: From the Archaic Age to the Arab Conquests* (Ithaca: Cornell University Press, 1981), 294.
12 Anton Powell, *Athens and Sparta: Constructing Greek Political and Social History From 478 B.C.*, 2nd ed. (New York: Routledge, 2001), 159.

went on even during the war, sometimes with Spartan armies encamped in the countryside. The Theater of Dionysus debuted plays by Sophocles, Euripides, and Aristophanes in front of 20,000 spectators.[13] The Athenian *agora* still functioned as a space for leisure, shopping, and politics while the legally designated *emporion* at Piraeus fostered foreign exchange. A shipbuilding facility in the latter city was the most expensive project initiated by Pericles, not the Parthenon.[14]

A contemporary movement within classical scholarship presses the argument that the Greek city-state system is a great anachronism in history, well ahead of its time. Keep in mind this is a society that is casually incomprehensible to a modern worldview. Classical Greeks did not value wage labor, valorizing leisure and political engagement instead. (This norm came to fascinate Marxists). Macroeconomics as a concept did not exist. The Greek understanding of *oikonomia* – from which the word "economics" derives – referred to *oikos*, the family estate. There was no protestant ethic. Ideally slaves did bootstraps labor. Foreign migrants (*metics*) conducted intercity trade in Piraeus and at lesser *emporia*. Successful household heads (always men) were then freed for the activities that mattered. They performed public duties (*liturgies*), assigned by lottery, and manned the warrior *hoplite* ranks at personal expense. Along the way they innovated political structures that were startlingly pluralistic in a despotic world. In this chapter we will explore how city builders tried to cement these priorities, projecting dyed-in-the-wool prejudices as well as radical ideals.

Hindsight on ancient Greece is fluid. Scholars have little direct knowledge about the majority of the perhaps 1,500 autonomous city-states that came in and out of existence, despite valuable efforts addressing this methodological challenge.[15] The largest city was probably Athens, with a population thought to reach 250,000 inclusive of its hinterlands.[16] Typical "cities" resembled villages. They had populations of a few thousand, sometimes less.[17] Of the three most important city-states in the Classical Age – Athens, Sparta, and Syracuse – records are by far the most abundant for Athens. There are fewer records on the smaller cities. Literary accounts from which we might make inferences about Greek life are disproportionately from Athenian philosophers, historians, poets, and playwrights. This includes their impressions of other

13 Garland, *Daily Life of the Ancient Greeks*, 183.

14 Hansen and Nielsen, *Inventory of Archaic and Classical Poleis*, 183.

15 For valiant efforts to quantify and offer perspective on ancient Greece, see especially Hansen and Nielsen, *Inventory of Archaic and Classical Poleis*, and the POLIS repository of data maintained by Stanford University, freely available at http://polis.stanford.edu. Figures cited here are from the former, on p. 54.

16 Ober, *Rise and Fall of Classical Greece*, 7.

17 Hansen and Nielsen, *Inventory of Archaic and Classical Poleis*, 139.

cities. At the same time, dramatic cultural, political, and economic innovations in Athens inform scholarly generalizations about the city-state system as a whole.

Hendrik Spruyt applies evolutionary biology to show that the city-state as a form of social organization could not meet the competitive demands of world trade by the middle ages.[18] For Spruyt, the modern nation-state emerged from a process of natural selection. If so, Greek city-states were prescient dinosaurs, establishing complex regional trading systems that prefigured human flows in today's urban century. Spruyt's treatment of city-states explains neither their resemblance to present urban networks nor helps us understand the longevity of this remarkable period in the history of the city-state. By one estimate, the Greek *poleis* endured for 1,200 years, roughly four-times the age of the modern nation-state system.[19] Revisionist scholarship in recent years emphasizes their advanced aspects. For example, about half of ancient Greece lived in cities, a share not reached on a planetary scale until this century.[20] By M. I. Finley's estimate, "the Greco-Roman world was more urbanized than *any other society before the modern era*."[21] Greek "efflorescence" entailed economic growth unequaled before Britain and Holland emerged as world powers.[22] In one economic history, Hellenic growth remained "unprecedented" until early modern times, making "remarkable" use of technological innovation in what bears uncanny resemblance to a modern rules-based society.[23]

The remainder of this chapter explains this exceptional epoch in urban history from its origins. The positions of the Greek *poleis* in a well-defined city network by the age of Pericles formed a backdrop for their endemic social struggles. City building in these places meant efforts to resolve, to accommodate, or to simply sequester these struggles as situations demanded.

Applying the hypothesis of this book, this chapter argues that global interactions influenced the physical form of the Greek city-state, culminating in distinctive sets of urban experiences. The city network incubated the spread of a dangerous class-conscious political innovation called *dēmokratia*, an

18 Hendrik Spruyt, *The Sovereign State and Its Competitors: An Analysis of Systems Change* (Princeton: Princeton University Press, 1994), 186.
19 Mogens Herman Hansen, "The Hellenistic *Polis*," in Mogens Herman Hansen (ed.), *A Comparative Study of Thirty City-State Cultures* (Copenhagen: The Royal Danish Academy of Arts and Letters, 2000), 141–187, 141.
20 Ober, *Rise and Fall of Classical Greece*, 7.
21 M. I. Finley, "The Ancient City: From Fustel de Coulanges to Max Weber and Beyond," in Brian D. Shaw and Richard P. Saller (eds.), *Economy and Society in Ancient Greece* (London: Chatto and Windus, 1981), 2–23, 20, emphasis mine.
22 Ober, *Rise and Fall of Classical Greece*, 81.
23 Alain Bresson, *The Making of the Ancient Greek Economy: Institutions, Markets, and Growth in the City-States* (Princeton: Princeton University Press, 2016), xxii.

Athenian export. But first things first. When did this city network come about, and why? How did the Greek *poleis* emerge as sovereign cities?

Their defining struggle was environmental.

Emergence of a City Network

Mainland Greece's hostile physical geography made it inevitably decentralized.[24] Only about one-quarter of the land was arable.[25] Soil wasn't rich enough to grow wheat in abundance, so farmers settled on less desirable barley. Much of the rest of this territory consists of mountains against jagged coastline. Cities were isolated from each other by land.[26] Roads were rudimentary where they existed at all. Only the very rich had horses. Land travel meant traversing long distances on foot for most. No rivers could support transport and communication networks.

The transportation of goods and people had to happen by sea. This too was treacherous. By Hesoid's eighth century account of merchant sailing during the Archaic Period in *Works and Days*, "an income means life to wretched mortals, but it is a terrible fate to die among the waves."[27] Shipping traffic halted in winter due to dangerous storms. An omnipresent specter of shipwrecks spurred a brisk insurance market that incentivized commercial voyages. Shipping circuits hewed close to the coasts, avoiding the open ocean. Routes were short. Merchant vessels sailed between nearby ports by day rather than risk night sailing. As William Bell Dinsmoor noted, mainland Greece is smaller than Scotland, but has more coastline than the entire UK. For all these risks, an abundance of natural harbors and islands enabled this "stepping stone" pattern of sailing.[28] Greek cities owed much to overseas contact with other Bronze Age societies, most importantly Minoa.

Retroactively named after King Minos, this Aegean civilization located on the island of Crete was a hub of trans-Mediterranean contact starting from the 2000s BCE onward, exposing Greeks to Egyptian cultural aesthetics.[29] Cretan script known as linear A (still indecipherable) documented accounting figures, inventory, and land holdings. Like other innovations in writing, it served commercial purposes. Mixed-use palaces dominated Europe's first truly urban

24 I define "mainland" Greece in accordance with modern national boundaries.

25 Thomas R. Martin, *Ancient Greece: From Prehistoric to Hellenistic Times* (New Haven: Yale University Press, 2000), 2.

26 A. Andrews, "The Growth of the City-State," in Hugh Lloyd Jones (ed.), *The Greek World* (Middlesex: Penguin, 1962), 26–65, 27.

27 Cited in Martin, *Ancient Greece*, 2.

28 William Bell Dinsmoor, *The Architecture of Ancient Greece* (New York: W. W. Norton, 1975), xvii.

29 Martin, *Ancient Greece*, 24.

scenes. In addition to royal residences, the palace at Knossos stored goods earmarked for trade, had an *agora*, and by extension a theater. Construction began around 1,700 BCE following a devastating earthquake, culminating in a five-floor, thousand-room mega-structure at the core of a city with a population in excess of 80,000.[30] Mycenaean Greeks learned from Cretan shipbuilding. What became known as linear B clay tablets on the mainland used the same script, which were in the Greek language as seafaring Mycenaean armies came to dominate regional trading. This is the period orally mythologized by Homer's *Iliad* and *Odyssey*, composed after outside invasions ended Mycenaean palace society and written language along with it.

In sum, a period of significant intercity relations ended due to warfare. This typifies the ebb and flow of interdependence in the history of city networks – provided we take the long view. It is important to remember that palace society lasted until 1,000 BCE, the equivalent of thirteen modern lifetimes.[31] The ensuing "Dark Age," entailing deurbanization and a hiatus in written language, also showed a telltale decline in sea travel that marked a reversion away from global interaction. Vital indicators like population also collapsed. The extended, relatively prosperous palace era remained a lacuna in the historic memories of Classical Greeks.

A comprehensive project on what it calls city-state cultures by the Copenhagen Polis Centre (CPC) dates the emergence of the *poleis* system from the 600s BCE, the start of the Archaic Period.[32] The Greek world reconstituted itself via an intense period of urbanization, crystalizing in the emergence of autonomous city-states with a shared Hellenic identity. The extensive CPC study defines the *polis* as an independent centralized settlement, consistent of a "political community."[33] The *asty* was the built environment, corresponding to the standard notion of a physical city. The *polis* could be synonymous with an *acropolis* (a defensible settlement carrying out administrative functions) and a *politai* (the citizen body).[34] While a *polis* could comprise many towns, there was always only one dominant *asty*, which was the site of the most important decision-making. The *chôra* was territory under the control of the *polis*. This referred to the countryside whose resources the city could draw from directly.[35]

Poleis developed independently unless subjected to dominant neighbors. Despite persistent violent political fragmentation, cities shared unifying markers, most notably language, religion, festivals, and sporting events.

[30] Figures cited in Dinsmoor, *Architecture of Ancient Greece*, 11; Martin, *Ancient Greece*, 26; and Steven Mithen, *Thirst: Water and Power in the Ancient World* (Cambridge: Harvard University Press, 2012), 77.

[31] Just as remarkably, Cretan cities weren't walled. Intercity invasions must have been an afterthought.

[32] Hansen, "The Hellenistic *Polis*," 147. [33] Ibid., 152. [34] Ibid. [35] Ibid.

Greeks famously distinguished themselves from non-Greek speaking "barbarians." The Panhellenic Games initiated in 776 BCE brought tens of thousands of spectators every four years. City leaders from across the Greek world consulted the oracle at Delphi, making it a significant factor in international affairs. Individuals consulted the oracle on personal matters. Delos housed intercity wealth for a time. All of these undertakings required traversing long distances, evidence that travel was ubiquitous in the Greek world.

Historians frequently note that Hellas comprised tiny polities sandwiched between great empires, punching above its weight to achieve "immortality" through outsized cultural, political, and military achievements.[36] In one of Plato's narratives, Socrates describes Hellas as but one "hallow" in a vast world, "living around the sea like ants or frogs around a marsh."[37] While there is certainly truth to this narrative, it obscures the fact that the Greek city-network occurred on a vast scale. Starting in the eighth century, Greek colonization established new *poleis* from Spain to the far reaches of the Black Sea. Some of these colonies eventually forged colonies of their own. There were major Greek settlements in North Africa and the Middle East.[38] By the third century CE, an estimated thirty million people lived across this expanse.[39] Greek colonies were largely independent of their parent cities. For example, Syracuse, founded by a Corinthian expedition to the island of Sicily, became a major power in its own right. In fact, Syracuse defeated the Athenian navy in a battle that turned the Peloponnesian War decisively. So what drove colonization? "When the people of Thera consulted the oracle [at Delphi], the priestess reminded them of the colony they were to found in Libya," according to Herodotus. This after the city faced a seven-year drought.[40] Superstitious as it was, the anecdote speaks to resource-scarce ecologies driving people out of overpopulated cities.

This was a time of high geographic mobility, reflected in cities' citizenship structures. Every city had a contingent of *metics*, free foreigners who had the right to live permanently in their destination cities. They lacked citizenship rights and were required to register with the state, provided they had, in the case of Athens, citizen sponsorship. *Metics* were required to perform public duties including military service during emergencies. They had only limited rights to land ownership, the primary source of wealth in ancient Greece, but

36 In the words of political scientist Josiah Ober, in Ober, *Rise and Fall of Classical Greece*, 293.

37 Plato, *Phaedo* (Oxford: Oxford University Press, 2009), 109a.

38 George Forrest, "Greece: The History of the Archaic Period," in John Boardman, Jasper Griffin, and Oswyn Murray (eds.), *The Oxford History of Greece and the Hellenistic World* (Oxford: Oxford University Press, 2001), 13–46, 18.

39 Hansen, "The Hellenistic *Polis*," 141.

40 Cited in P. J. Rhodes, *The Greek City States: A Source Book*, 2nd ed (Cambridge: Cambridge University Press, 2007), 32.

served entrepreneurial functions.[41] The modern narrative of migrants occupying roles in the labor market at the expense of citizens never arose in ancient Greece, which equated wage labor with slavery. Pericles extolled Athens' exceptional openness. By one count there were 30,000 foreigners, comprising 10 percent of the Athenian population, representing sixty states, some of which were non-Greek.[42] Large numbers of them lived in the harbor city of Piraeus, which conducted the bulk of trade.

Sparta provides a useful antipode. Its oligarchic leadership discouraged foreign stays. The city extracted labor from *helots*, war captives relegated to state property. Slavery thus freed citizens for Sparta's regimented military lifestyle. Its governing body annually renewed a declaration of war against *helots*, enabling Spartan citizens to murder them without penalty. Such was the threat of revolt, a danger preventing the city's superior land armies from venturing too far from home. Spartan self-sufficiency never formed a powerful alternative to the dominant interdependent economic model. On the political side of things, it engaged in extensive intercity governance by necessity. It never achieved sufficient military hegemony to fully assert its will unilaterally. The Spartan-led Peloponnesian League endured in various guises for centuries. The league achieved monumental military victories, including in the Persian Wars (Athens was an ally) and against the Athenian Empire in the Peloponnesian War by 404. Notably Sparta resisted allied calls to destroy Athens after victory for fear of a power vacuum. This highlights an important reality. The inability of any single power to establish unipolar hegemony enabled the system of sovereign cities to continue for centuries.

Athens by contrast deployed its navy to project strength, dictating economic policies to cities within its sphere of influence. Piraeus was the site of the massive naval depot constructed by Pericles. Its shipyards rapidly manufactured *triremes*, the multistory warships that patrolled trade routes, prevented piracy, and fought large scale battles. Though Pericles' funeral oration idealized the city's cosmopolitanism as an example of magnanimous vulnerability in Athens, sounding almost altruistic, trade was in reality a source of power. According to pseudo-Xenophon's *Athenian Constitution*,

> The Athenians have first of all discovered forms of luxury foodstuffs by mingling with different people in different places: What is pleasant in Sicily or Italy or Cyprus or Lydia or the Black Sea or the Peloponnese or anywhere else, all these are collected together in one place through their control of the sea.[43]

Athens could embargo uncooperative cities; thus, prohibiting access to essential goods. In one critical case Thucydides relays the city of Megara's

41 Garland, *Daily Life of the Ancient Greeks*, 74.
42 Ibid., 75.
43 Cited in Rhodes, *Greek City States*, 192.

complaint "that they were being excluded from the harbors in the Athenian Empire and from trade with Athens."[44] Issued by the Athenian government at the behest of Pericles in 432, it was effectively a death threat against a disobedient city.[45] This incident helped set off the Peloponnesian War. Fear of Athenian power led several cities to side with Sparta, including Megara after the embargo. The loss of allies enabled Pericles' to portray Athens as a solitary resister against Sparta, which was able to "bring with them all their confederates, while we Athenians advance unsupported into the territory of a neighbor."[46] Conservative Sparta, for its part, feared an Athenian rise entailing the imposition of democracy on smaller cities.

The Delian League reflected the power shift from Sparta to Athens, due originally to widespread dissatisfaction toward Spartan leadership under a rogue commander.[47] This was nominally a defensive alliance to preempt Persian incursions, but extended to trade and finance on Athenian terms. Delos was the site of cooperative meetings (*synods*) among nominally equal partners and a shared treasury, until the latter function moved to Athens and the former ceased altogether. This was due in part to collective action problems. Members had the incentive to free ride.[48] At any rate the end result was a coercive arrangement. Thucydides depicts the city of Melos attempting to take a neutral position between Athens and Sparta.[49] His ensuing dialogue is required reading in international relations courses to this day, a classic example of political realism. At its end, an Athenian army massacred and enslaved the Melian citizenry as punishment for defecting. At the same time, weaker cities at least indirectly financed the architecture that came to symbolize the Athenian golden age. Plutarch believed Pericles pilfered the League treasury to pay for the Parthenon, initiated in 447.[50] If so, his gambit would have entailed a great deal of irony as the temple later housed the strongbox containing the treasury.

Historians lament the lack of technological progress in Hellas. "Even such devices as the windmill and the screw were invented late," one standard history points out.[51] Recent writing by social scientists challenges this notion. In fact the Greeks heavily utilized wind power early on to address time and space challenges – for sailing. In this maritime society it was shipbuilding that

44 Ibid., 193.
45 Bresson, *Making of the Ancient Greek Economy*, 358.
46 "Ancient History Sourcebook."
47 "Delian League" is what modern scholars call the alliance, after the city of Delos, where it was based.
48 Ober, *Rise and Fall of Classical Greece*, 67.
49 Thucydides, *Peloponnesian War*, 302.
50 Powell, *Athens and Sparta*, 60.
51 Jasper Griffin, "Introduction," in John Boardman, Jasper Griffin, and Oswyn Murray (eds.), *The Oxford History of Greece and the Hellenistic World* (Oxford: Oxford University Press, 2001), 1–12, 7.

underwent substantial innovation over time, according to Alain Bresson's extensive economic study.[52] By the high Classical Period, the Greeks either developed their own innovations to accommodate highly sophisticated trade networks or adapted them from the ancient Near East. Written language reemerged to facilitate commerce, this time most likely derivative of the Phoenician alphabet. Lydia invented coinage in the seventh century BCE. The concept diffused across the Greek world, culminating in Athens' gradual monetization of the bartering economy. Athenian coins, stamped with the goddess Athena's ubiquitous owl symbol, were the region's dominant currency. Not always by choice. In the 440s Athens formally declared, "if anyone mints silver coinage in the cities, and does not use Athenian coinage, weights and measures but uses foreign coinage, weights and measures, [the Athenian council] shall punish and penalize him."[53] It was a decree to the League that harmonized these elemental aspects of trade in an attempt to cement a favorable position. It also underscored the coercion underlying Athenian designs that otherwise resemble proto-global governance schemes. Smaller states nevertheless benefited as the Athenian navy neutralized Persian maritime power as well as piracy.

Drawing on abundant Athenian records it is possible to overstate interdependence – just as researchers working 2,500 years from now may distort reality by relying on records from, say, New York City. This warrants two points: First, smaller *poleis* were import-dependent, as de Ste. Croix acknowledges, despite a largely primitivist view of ancient economies.[54] Second, Athens had a unique position, true, but in a trading system actively involving hundreds of *poleis*. They developed specialization according to natural resource advantages or manufacturing prowess.[55] "The country not self-sufficing in respect to every commodity, but deficient in some, while in others producing more than enough," wrote Isocrates, could establish importation markets with the "superabundant" Piraeus as an ideal.[56] In one political scientist's estimation, Hellas traded relatively high value goods and services for lower margin raw materials and, alas, slaves.[57] A major economic study hypothesizes a core–periphery model where cities imported raw goods from abroad, reassembling them at higher value in a virtuous cycle that sustained growth.[58]

[52] Bresson, *Making of the Ancient Greek Economy*, xxiv.
[53] Formal inscription cited in Rhodes, *Greek City States*, 259.
[54] de Ste. Croix, *Class Struggle in the Ancient Greek World*, 294.
[55] Ober, *Rise and Fall of Classical Greece*, 12.
[56] Isocrates, *The Panegyricus of Isocrates* (New Haven: Storer and Morehouse, 1851), 9.
[57] Ober, *Rise and Fall of Classical Greece*, 120.
[58] Bresson, *Making of the Ancient Greek Economy*, 416.

The main limitation was technological. Hellas lacked innovations like the steam engine.[59] Still, self-sufficiency problems stemming from Greece's hostile ecology led to experimentations in seafaring. On the other hand, constant fears of scarcity led the state to ban some forms of trade, particularly the exportation of vital goods such as grain and corn, on severe penalty. One law called for the death of the exporter "along with his family."[60] Athens forbade financing trading voyages that excluded the city-state, also by capital punishment.[61] These cases certainly curtailed intercity commerce. Yet, their severity speaks to how externally dependent cities must have been. Greek elites may have further expanded regional commerce had they not been culturally averse to business activity. Cities sequestered foreign trade to the *emporion* while the *agora* was a site of domestic transactions.[62]

The reachable presence of large empires further encouraged human flows, especially Persia, Egypt, Etruria, Carthage, and eventually Rome (see Chapter 5). Despite high costs, Greek sailors managed long distance trading profitably, according to evidence from shipwrecks containing cargo amphorae.[63] What Held et al. call the *extensity* of globalization reached well into Eurasia and Africa.[64] This included special trading zones. According to Herodotus:

> Among [the king of Egypt's] favors to certain of the Greeks he granted permission to those who arrived in Egypt to occupy the city of Naucratis, and those who did not want to settle there but came on voyages he granted sites where they could set up alters and sanctuaries to the gods. The largest, most famous and best-used sanctuary is the one known as Hellenium, founded jointly by Chios, Teos, Phocaea and Clazomenae of the Ionians, Cnidus, Halicarnassus and Phaselis of the Dorians, and Mytilene alone of the Aeolians. The sanctuary belongs to these cities, and these cities provide the overseers of the market.[65]

What did city life feel like during this high period of global interactions?

The Urban Experience

Greek *poleis* valued public over private construction. Housing stock was poor. Male citizens spent typical days outdoors, including long hours in the *agora*, the center of city life. Although there is no modern equivalent to *agoras*, they resembled main squares or plazas. These were physically open public spaces

[59] A deficiency more than one historian has pointed out.
[60] Bresson, *Making of the Ancient Greek Economy*, 393. [61] Ibid., 404.
[62] Rhodes, *Greek City States*, 108. [63] Bresson, *Making of the Ancient Greek Economy*, 378.
[64] David Held, Anthony McGrew, David Goldblatt, and Jonathan Perraton, *Global Transformations: Politics, Economics, and Culture* (Stanford: Stanford University Press, 1999), 49.
[65] Rhodes, *Greek City States*, 36.

commonly complemented by covered stoas. They were regulated to foster market exchange and boisterous political dialogue. The name derives from a Greek word meaning "loaf about."[66] Various civic buildings lined it, where democratic societies staffed them by lottery. Socrates famously spent each day in the *agora* espousing subversive anti-democratic philosophy until a large citizen jury sentenced him to death for it a few feet away.

His student's student, Aristotle (384–322 BCE), outlined essential elements of a city. Aristotle asserts that cities should be neither too large nor too small – justifying the city-state system – and that they should be linked to the sea. A later section of *Politics* establishes health as the foremost concern for cities. In a challenge familiar to today's megacities trying to isolate sewage, Aristotle notes that "the drinking water ought to be separated from the water used for other purposes."[67] This reflects an enduring overlap between city planning and public health discourses. Hippodamus (498–408 BCE), the master planner of the time, was a physician. Public bathrooms were nonexistent. As were hospitals. Drinking water came out of simple public fountains fed mainly by natural streams. Waste collectors disposed of dung at a presumably safe distance from the city, subject to municipal enforcement.[68] Varying scholarly evidence shows that men typically died during their thirties, with woman dying from childbirth and work-related hardships by their twenties.[69] The urban condition likely worsened human development for city dwellers, despite greater affluence than the hinterlands.

Next, Aristotle recommends heavy fortifications "if a city is to avoid destruction, and to escape from suffering and humiliation."[70] Walls defined the limits of the *asty*, most famously the Long Walls, the first massive piece of architecture that visitors to Athens would have seen up close. The main entryway was its Double Gate, so named because it was designed to trap invaders. His ideal city had the ability to dispatch armies while retaining functionality under siege. As we've seen, this meant maintaining extensive trade ties, not simple self-sufficiency. Aristotle cites the "Hippodamian" grids popular in his time as an ideal arrangement of buildings in peacetime, but their straight streets were security liabilities. He recommended retaining older unplanned residential streets in some neighborhoods to frustrate invasion forces.[71] (Athens, where Aristotle studied at Plato's academy, wasn't master planned, growing via unpaved meandering streets). From there, his ideal city preserved its highest function: Politics. The right planning depended on the type of government: "A citadel [or *acropolis*] suits oligarchies and

[66] Garland, *Daily Life of the Ancient Greeks*, 26. [67] Aristotle, *Politics*, 276.
[68] Garland, *Daily Life of the Ancient Greeks*, 24.
[69] Ober, *Rise and Fall of Classical Greece*, 88. [70] Aristotle, *Politics*, 277. [71] Ibid.

monarchies; a level plain suits democracy; neither suits an aristocracy for which a number of strongholds is preferable."[72]

Indeed travelers between cities would have noticed important visual contrasts. Greek city-states varied in scale but were hardly villages. The smallest *poleis* still had thousands of inhabitants.[73] These were not places where everyone knew one another, a reality that belies myths of face-to-face direct democracy. Being from different classes or genders would also limit interaction. The scale of public buildings tended to vary according to the size of *poleis*. For all these potential variations, visitors to any Hellenic cities would immediately notice the similarities in their built environments. The post and lintel form was ubiquitous along with familiar stone building materials. Most Greek cities took Aristotle's advice and built walls through which citizens could pass freely during peacetime.[74] From there, cities centered public life on the *agora*, from which no private buildings could be built. The *agora* evolved toward market functions by the Classical Age in lieu of formal political assembly.[75] Temporary stalls would evoke today's pop-up markets. By that time, temples had long replaced palaces as the architectural centerpieces of Hellenic cities. Central cities housed entertainment venues for theater and sports, ranging from basic dugouts to the Theater of Dionysus at Athens, which attracted visitors throughout the Greek world when permitted.[76] *Gymnasia* were the sites of sports, military training, and education, making them among the most utilized buildings.[77]

Athens stood out mainly for the scale of this construction. For example, the Parthenon was a conservative design. It is an apotheosis of Greek styles rather than a departure from them. Where the iconic Athenian *acropolis* (elevated fortification) stands is where we find the remarkable buildings for which Athens is known today, featuring Doric and Ionic schemes.[78] Yet the *acropolis* was a common component of Greek cities. In Athens it was once synonymous with the *polis*, its walls having defined the city until it expanded to encompass more territory marked by the Long Walls.[79] The structures built by Pericles on this large overlook would have been visible from miles away. Primarily a temple dedicated to the city's patron goddess Athena, containing her treasures, the Parthenon is at its highest point (Figure 3.1). In Classical Athens it would have been crowded by a multitude of buildings and statues competing for attention.[80] These structures replaced buildings destroyed by Persian armies a

72 Ibid., 276. Brackets are from the text. Italics are mine.
73 Hansen and Nielsen, *Inventory of Archaic and Classical Poleis*, 141.
74 This according to archeological and written evidence. Ibid., 137. 75 Ibid., 141. 76 Ibid.
77 Ibid.
78 The colonnaded Parthenon is primarily in the Doric style, ironic as Athens has Ionian origins. Ionic columns feature prominently in the nearby Erechtheion.
79 Hansen, "The Hellenistic *Polis*," 152. 80 Garland, *Daily Life of the Ancient Greeks*, 23.

Figure 3.1 The Parthenon, commissioned by Pericles, still towers over Athens. Its conservative design prominently features Doric styles brought to Athens from the Peloponnese.
Photo by the author.

generation earlier. The Proplyaia, also built by Pericles, was the main gateway to the *acropolis* atop a grand staircase. The theater at Athens expanded in the fifth century as plays grew more complicated thanks to theatrical innovations by Aeschylus and Sophocles. Construction halted on numerous projects during the Peloponnesian War. Yet the theater underwent a massive conversion from wood to stone.[81]

The immensity of Athenian construction is typical of alpha cities in history. Some of this is readily explainable place maintenance. Construction in Piraeus relates directly to trade. Beyond this, Athenian motivations look more idiosyncratic. The Periclean building program reifies the dominant ideology, yet it's an ideology that was radical in its time. Athenian building plans seemed not to represent the interests of the elite, meeting with conservative criticism. There was apparently opposition to the Long Walls. They protected the core city but left large swaths of land (the primary source of elite wealth) vulnerable to the Peloponnesian invasions.[82] Pericles faced criticism for costs at the *acropolis*. These public works appear to have been viewed as redistribution to the city's citizen poor rather than methods of extraction. Work would have

[81] Dinsmoor, *Architecture of Ancient Greece*, 208.

[82] Powell, *Athens and Sparta*, 64.

been shared among citizens too poor to lead lives of leisure, alongside *metics*, and slaves. Still, the ancient Greeks didn't justify construction on macroeconomic grounds as with today's alpha cities. They did not value what we would call modern capitalist principles. Nor did they consider construction a means of bolstering productivity or cultivating "human capital." Thucydides suggests that buildings reflect the intent to deceive, offering a thought experiment:

> If the city of Sparta were to become deserted, with only temples and the foundations of buildings left to view, I imagine that with the passage of time future generations would find it very hard to credit its reputed power ... If the same happened to Athens, people would assume from the overt appearance that the city's power was twice what it is.[83]

Sparta's urban tableau coincided with it's opt-out positions on migration and trade. Thucydides describes this large city as a "dispersed settlement, devoid of temples or expensive buildings, more a collection of villages in the old Greek way."[84] It famously lacked a city wall.[85]

Architectural motifs diffused across the Hellenic world. They fostered distinctively Greek cities, much as international styles homogenized twentieth century skylines. Ionic design principles emerged from Asia Minor, influenced by Egypt and Mesopotamia. They predominated wherever Ionians settled.[86] In their standardized form, Ionic columns were tall and narrow, emerging from a base. They have sets of volutes at their tops. Ionic columns support continuous friezes. Doric forms emerged from the Dorian migrations, emanating from the Peloponnese. They lack the bases and volutes that characterize Ionic columns, projecting a more austere look, topped by metopes separated by triglyphs. In practice these styles often mixed.

Athens was a center of achievement in these derivative styles. The "Periclean architects" flourished thanks to new commissions in the Athenian Empire.[87] These include Ictinus, the Parthenon's lead architect. His writings were also influential in the ancient world, studied by Vitruvius centuries later. The co-architect of the Parthenon, Callicrates, operated in the Ionic style. He is credited with designing the all-Ionic Temple of Athena Nike at the *acropolis*, likely designing several more prominent buildings.[88] Sculpture was the most revered art. Phidias' "Phidian school" rebuilt monumental statues, gaining fame in his own time. The Classical form in Greek art matured, its architecture, sculpture, and decorative arts subject to eternal revival.[89] The Mediterranean world sought out Athenian decorative pottery, an important city export.

83 Thucydides, *Peloponnesian War*, 7. 84 Ibid.
85 Equally famously asserting that its soldiers were its walls.
86 Dinsmoor, *Architecture of Ancient Greece*, 60. 87 Ibid., 148. 88 Ibid.
89 John Boardman, "Greek Art and Architecture," in John Boardman, Jasper Griffin, and Oswyn Murray (eds.), *The Oxford History of Greece and the Hellenistic World* (Oxford: Oxford University Press, 2001), 330–360, 344.

Urban planning matured later. Rationalist arrangements with streets crossing at right angles replaced the disorganized, incremental growth of the Archaic period. Politically speaking, a street grid enabled standardized equally sized plots for housing.[90] This was clearly evident by the fifth century, with gridiron streets mirroring Egyptian cemeteries and pyramid cities.[91] The idea spread in popularity during the Classical Age.[92] The exact time of its emergence is debated, however. Modern scholarship finds evidence of central planning from as far back as eighth century colonization.[93] Cities built from scratch were more likely to adopt systematic planning. The rebuilding of Miletus after its destruction in 494 BCE was an example associated with Hippodamus. The Hellenistic period, spurred by the founding of new cities in the wake of Alexander the Great's conquests, was a heyday of rationalist planning along Hippodamian lines.

Pericles commissioned Hippodamus to lay out the city center at Piraeus, site of all three Athenian harbors, shipbuilding, and the *emporion*.[94] Before the Romans destroyed it, Piraeus' residential streets were regimented at right angles with equal-sized plots. This was the most important port in the Eastern Mediterranean. The costs prioritized there owed much to Athens' reliance on foodstuffs like corn from the Black Sea region, and exports such as silver. Athens imported nearly all shipbuilding materials for its fleet. In addition, Piraeus was a middle market for goods that were neither from nor destined for Athens. The port city maintained this position in part because of its advanced system of loading and unloading ships, aided by slave labor.[95] The *emporion* was tightly regulated, carrying its own special set of rules. As with the *agora*, these places were subject to special governance. Markers notified passersby with the message "boundary stone of the *emporion* and the street."[96] Cities tightly controlled the terms of trade, including the prices of many goods. Officials closely monitored the activities of foreigners. Taxes on trade were light. Still, constraints defined commerce as much as the free market.

Poor temporary lodging presented another barrier. Aristophanes' *Frogs* depicts hotels as insect infested dens of prostitution.[97] Hotels only come into existence by the fifth century. Before that, aristocrats customarily lodged members of their own class.[98] Xenophon's *Revenues* recommended fresh hotel construction near harbors as part of a program to attract foreigners.[99]

[90] Hansen, "The Hellenistic *Polis*," 162. [91] Dinsmoor, *Architecture of Ancient Greece*, 212.

[92] Ibid. [93] Hansen, "The Hellenistic *Polis*," 162.

[94] Mogens Herman Hansen, "Attika," in Mogens Herman Hansen (ed.), *A Comparative Study of Thirty City-State Cultures* (Copenhagen: The Royal Danish Academy of Arts and Letters, 2000), 624–639, 636.

[95] Garland, *Daily Life of the Ancient Greeks*, 157.

[96] Bresson, *Making of the Ancient Greek Economy*, 306.

[97] Aristophanes, *Frogs and Other Plays* (Oxford: Oxford University Press, 2015), 176.

[98] Garland, *Daily Life of the Ancient Greeks*, 158.

[99] Ober, *Rise and Fall of Classical Greece*, 248.

Athens' magnificence extended only to its public buildings, as the Greeks devalued private construction. City streets beyond the *agora* and *acropolis* were narrow, squalid, and sparse. "Most of the houses are mean, the pleasant ones few," wrote one observer. "A stranger would doubt, on first acquaintance that this was really the renowned city of the Athenians."[100] Building materials were rudimentary. The walls so flimsy that the politician Demosthenes (382–322 BCE) rhetorically asked Athenian men why they were surprised at burglaries when "thieves are bold and walls are made of merely mud.'[101] Robbers could simply punch holes through them. Houses had dirt floors and most had only one poorly lit room with makeshift partitioning.

In these extremely patriarchal societies, men strove to add rooms for the purpose of keeping their wives further out of public view. The wealthy had rooms for formal drinking parties called *symposiums* involving intellectual repartee, exclusionary of women save for hired prostitutes.[102] This served in the absence of anything resembling a modern nightlife. For women, the *polis* offered little beyond tightly regimented, suffocating lives requiring them to suffer through arranged marriages starting in their mid-teens to men twice their age. They were expected to maximize the number of risky childbirths. Ruling patriarchies pressured them to maintain population size, a source of military power in intercity relations.[103] In a constellation of cities where built environments were expressions of public values over private, the *agora* over home construction, Classical Greece subjected women to its most barebones spaces. "There is one prime source of a scandal for a woman," wrote Euripides, "that she won't stay at home." There were far fewer opportunities for women to appear in public. Respectable women needed accompaniment to avoid shaming, leading to scenes on the city streets that would have recalled Margaret Atwood's dystopian novel *The Handmaid's Tale*. By contrast, citizen men in the upper income tiers had the freest reign over the public spaces where power was expressed.[104] Correspondingly women had no formal legal rights. The curious exception was in Sparta, where woman controlled a sizeable minority of estate property, to the expressed concern of its leaders.

Economic Roots of Revolution

Xenophon (430–c. 355 BCE) wrote the best-known economic tract from the time. "It must, I should think, be the business of the good economist at any rate to manage his own house or estate well," he wrote in his Socratic dialogue

[100] Cited in Garland, *Daily Life of the Ancient Greeks*, 83. [101] Ibid., 84. [102] Ibid., 96.
[103] Ibid., 51. [104] Ibid., 53.

Oikonomikos.[105] As we've seen, the Greek term *oikos* related to private estate management, not systemic production. Xenophon spoke to male estate holders. The main thrust was how to get others to do the work, namely slaves and women. Stark cultural differences between then and now led classicists to reject modern comparisons. M. I. Finley's classic study *The Ancient Economy* asserts that per capita growth was negligible for centuries. It was never intended to begin with.[106] The Greeks didn't value productivity increases, the modern world's obsession. "Technological progress, economic growth, productivity, even efficiency have not been significant goals since the beginning of time," states Finley.[107] M. M. Austin and P. Vidal-Naquet's widely cited volume *Economic and Social History of Ancient Greece* clarifies early on that "what we call the productive spirit was unknown to the Greeks."[108] Socialist political economist Karl Polanyi influenced this thinking by contending that nonmarket relations subsumed market exchange, while modern planners take market independence for granted.[109]

de Ste. Croix laid the groundwork for his astonishingly detailed *The Class Struggle in the Ancient Greek World* by underscoring fundamental differences. "The Greek world, compared with the modern one," he iterates, "was very underdeveloped technologically, and therefore infinitely less productive."[110] Ancient societies lagged well behind the medieval "dark ages" in terms of invention. The wheelbarrow came about in Europe roughly a millennium after the Classical Age. The Greeks had animal power, but not the tools to fully utilize it. Greek ships ran on inefficient rudder systems, he contends, undercutting a lauded aspect of Greek adaptation.[111] For de Ste. Croix this justifies a Marxist analysis, a modernist application if there ever was one. Absent per capita productivity growth, the elite extracted increased value via "unfree labor."[112]

"Modernists" couch Classical studies in language akin to that of the current economic system. They retroactively apply economic concepts like GDP and Gini coefficients in ways that make the ancient world readily comparable to the present-day. Political scientist Josiah Ober exemplifies this approach in an essay called "Wealthy Hellas," also a presidential address to the American

105 Xenophon, *The Economist: A Treatise on the Science of the Household in the Form of a Dialogue* (Adelaide: University of Adelaide, 2014), Book I, available at www.gutenberg.org/files/1173/1173-h/1173-h.htm, last accessed February 24, 2024..

106 M. I. Finley, *The Ancient Economy* (Berkeley: University of California Press, 1999), 182.

107 Ibid., 147.

108 M. M. Austin and P. Vidal-Naquet, *Economic and Social History of Ancient Greece: An Introduction* (Berkeley: University of California Press, 1977), 15.

109 Matthijs Krul, "Markets in Ancient Greece: The Challenge of the New Institutionalism," in Gareth Dale (ed.), *Reconstructing Karl Polanyi: Excavation and Critique* (London: Pluto Press, 2016), 178–201, 182.

110 de Ste. Croix, *Class Struggle in the Ancient Greek World*, 38. 111 Ibid. 112 Ibid., 113.

Philological Association in 2010.[113] He describes the Greek economy as highly diversified and specialized, much as Pericles did in his oration, living well above subsistence. The whole of mainland Greece, not just Athens, could sustain growing populations from the Archaic Period onward by feeding themselves through an elaborate trading system. A very large share of the citizen population, perhaps half, worked in nonagricultural sectors.[114] Population growth and high rates of urbanization suggest the Greek economy was high performing. Private construction saw steady improvement, with archeological evidence showing increasingly large, sturdier housing stock. That Greek home construction was fairly uniform in size suggests surprisingly low levels of inequality for a society with such ingrained stratification.[115] Counting slaves, economists estimate Gini coefficient levels comparable to today's United States.[116] This was possible because of what present-day analysts would call good governance. That is, evenly applied sets of rules regulating markets alongside fair competition forcing adaptation.[117] Alain Bresson echoes this assessment, saying – contra de Ste. Croix – that the Greeks were "incomparably better integrated into the networks of foreign markets than their medieval and early modern counterparts."[118] By his reckoning they established a level of integration not matched until the emergence of Venice, Genoa (see Chapter 9), and the Hanseatic League (see Chapter 10).[119]

de Ste. Croix describes the Greco-Roman periods as "essentially urban, a civilization of cities."[120] Of the four most traded goods – grain, wine, oil, and slaves – three are agricultural products.[121] From their primitivist foundations the two rival scholars, Finley and de Ste. Croix, departed from each other on the question of social hierarchy. For Finley, class relations were rooted in social status. For de Ste. Croix, they derived from control over the land and labor that endowed these resources. This lent itself to the domination of the *asty* over the agricultural *chôra*. There was no real estate industry allocating resources on market principles. Property changed hands largely through inheritances and dowries, excluding noncitizens.[122] City-dwelling elite classes were predominately landowners with estates outside the walls. For de Ste Croix, this urban–rural divide incentivized what he estimated to be a peasant society

[113] Josiah Ober, "Wealthy Hellas," *Transactions of the American Philological Association* 140, no. 2 (2010), 241–286. It was adapted as the fourth chapter in his book *The Rise and Fall of Classical Greece.*

[114] Ober, *Rise and Fall of Classical Greece*, 102. [115] Ibid., 88.

[116] According to one estimate, the worst case is 0.45, identical to the latest figure for the United States cited in the CIA World Factbook. Ibid., 93.

[117] Ibid., 103. [118] Bresson, *Making of the Ancient Greek Economy*, 437.

[119] These cases, for Bresson, were the noteworthy pre-modern exceptions.

[120] de Ste. Croix, *Class Struggle in the Ancient Greek World*, 10.

[121] Finley, *Ancient Economy*, 33. [122] Ibid., 116.

heavily reliant on exploited "unfree" labor including large amounts of slavery. This is not too far from Frederick Engels' appraisal in his *Origins of the Family, Private Property, and the State*:

> All the fields of Attica were thick with mortgage columns bearing inscriptions stating that the land on which they stood was mortgaged to such and such for so and so much. The fields not so marked had for the most part already been sold on account of unpaid mortgages or interest, and had passed into the ownership of the noble usurer; the peasant could count himself lucky if he was allowed to remain as a tenant and live on one-sixth of the produce of his labor, while he paid five-sixths to his new master as rent.[123]

Scholars debate how much the Greek economy depended on slavery.[124] Engels estimated that most of Attica's population consisted of formal slaves, which contemporary scholars say is a drastic overestimation. Still, there were likely tens of thousands of slaves in Attica alone.[125] They were foreigners acquired in slave markets or raised in captivity. (Solon's sixth century reforms forbade the enslavement of citizens). Their labor varied. For modernists this reflected the unusually specialized nature of the Greek economy.[126] Some were state functionaries such as clerks and accountants, making them relatively well-off compared with other slaves. Others did the gamut of domestic housework. Wealthy owners leased off gangs of mostly barbarian slaves en-masse for the most dangerous mining and industrial labor.[127] Slaves extracted silver from the Laurion mines, a critical source of wealth for the Athenian Empire. The slave population was divided by origin as well, lessening the possibility for organized revolt. Who, then, were the proletariat?

de Ste. Croix holds that landlord–tenant and lender–debtor relationships fostered a permanent peasantry that "may not only have formed the actual majority of the population but may also have had a larger share (usually a much larger share) in production than slaves and other unfree workers."[128] He describes rural landscapes subject to heavy penalties, populations of "poor rustics" removed from the core cities even by language.[129] There was a partial exception. Athenian democracy, in which the lowest class citizens had rights, offered protections against a predatory elite. Here de Ste. Croix does two things. First, he establishes the existence of an underclass. Second, he frames democracy as a revolutionary counterpunch that was radical enough to scare

[123] Fredrick Engels, *Origins of the Family, Private Property, and the State*, chap. V, available at www.marxists.org/archive/marx/works/1884/origin-family/, last accessed February 13, 2024.
[124] Sparta was a clearer case. It entirely relied on *helot* slaves for the everyday functioning of the city.
[125] Garland, *Daily Life of the Ancient Greeks*, 70.
[126] Ober, *Rise and Fall of Classical Greece*, 113.
[127] Garland, *Daily Life of the Ancient Greeks*, 72.
[128] de Ste. Croix, *Class Struggle in the Ancient Greek World*, 209.
[129] Ibid., 216. Also see p. 65.

the oligarchs. Like few times in history up to this point, there had to be compromises across classes. Tenant farmers were the primary beneficiaries.

*****

The Spartans won the Peloponnesian War in 404 BCE after forging an alliance with Persia that enabled them to counter Athens at sea. Athenian capitulation resulted in the reign of the Thirty Tyrants. This lasted all of eight months. The wealthy Thirty lost Spartan support and were promptly overthrown by democratic forces in 403 after a notorious series of executions and expulsions turned the public against them. Longstanding democratic norms in Athens persisted even if the Athenian Empire didn't. That many of the Thirty were Socrates' students did not help his cause leading up to his execution in 399. Channeling Socrates' voice, Plato's conservative *Republic* imagines a highly stratified city ideally managed by expert bureaucrats, analogized to gold (rulers), silver (militia), and iron (workers).[130] This is a far cry from a city where citizens performed public duties by lottery.

Athens before the reforms of Solon (c. 630–560 BCE) did not yet have a large empire. It was not an alpha city at the heart of a vast network. This was not the maritime power that could cover its social contracts by extracting tributes from rival cities, dominating Aegean trade or importing slaves and *metics* to make time for the good life. Resultantly, Athens had an intensifying reliance on land production in Attica. Increased demands incurred by a growing population exacerbated this problem, resulting in the worsening inequality that drew Engels' attention. Here is where we see rising debt bondage among the agricultural citizen population.[131] The wealthy, by contrast, acquired Athenian slaves, confiscated land, and extracted rents from exhausted farmers.

These were the conditions for a political moment of truth. Historians are not sure what flashpoint crisis precipitated Solon's reforms in 594 BCE, his year as *archon*. In what the rich surely saw as a defeat, Solon cancelled all debts, a radical proposition for any time and place. He outlawed the enslavement of any Athenian citizen. This freed them with no record of compensation to their owners.[132] However, he stopped short of land redistribution to the poor as a compromise. This left the real possibility of mass exploitation, prompting Solon to ban acts of "intimidation or humiliation" (*hubris*) by Athenians

130 Plato, *Republic* (Oxford: Oxford University Press, 1993), 115.

131 Ober, *Rise and Fall of Classical Greece*, 147.

132 For discussion from multiple perspectives on Solonian reforms, see Ober, *Rise and Fall of Classical Greece*, 144–153; de Ste. Croix, *Class Struggle in the Ancient Greek World*, 137, 282; and Plutarch, "The Life of Solon," in *The Parallel Lives*, available at http://penelope.uchicago.edu/Thayer/E/Roman/Texts/Plutarch/Lives/Solon*.html, last accessed February 13, 2024.

against one another, a theoretical protection for the poor.[133] He further defined citizenship rights according to income levels. The wealthiest class had access to the most important offices, while the poorest could vote in the assembly and serve as jurors. In Aristotle's view, this gave "the people only the necessary minimum of power."[134] For Marxist intellectuals it was a "radical reform" that defied elite class interests.[135] For modernists it was a moderate series of compromises intended to create a middle class, a kind of ancient New Deal. Either way it placed the city on a path toward democracy. The city's high visibility in the years to come made it a model for other *poleis*.

Cleisthenes created a representative system in 507, dividing society according to new political tribes.[136] His ten new tribes broke the aristocratic hold on the *genos*, the family groups of the nobility. By now Athens had a sovereign assembly in which all male citizens voted on policy if they chose to participate. As with citizen juries, majority votes decided outcomes. This included citizens who had little if any property. Ostracisms put the most prominent statesmen at risk of expulsion for ten years. This was by citizen vote, another check on power. At this point it is important to remember that these bodies excluded women, *metics*, and slaves. They can hardly be called democratic in any modern sense.[137] There is evidence that these excluded groups knew their interests and where possible pushed back against the hierarchy – no less than the male smallholders whose positions improved in Greek democracy. When in a position to organize, *helots* revolted on multiple occasions, even as the Greek upper classes viewed slavery as part of a natural order of things. For what it is worth, we can say that Greek democracy responded to the interests of poor men while remaining exclusionary. It was a revolution *for some*. The aristocracies by and large preferred oligarchy, viewing democracy as "in effect the domination of the poor over the rich."[138] The diffusion of power within the Greek city-states was unique to anything that occurred before it.

All of the surviving written record comes from the literate affluent, hence the upper class anti-democratic tilt evident in classical writing. At their highest minded, the intellectuals argued that democracy was a flawed system because it kept the best people from being in power. "Among the people there is the greatest ignorance, disorder, and wretchedness," wrote pseudo-Xenophon.

133 Ober, *Rise and Fall of Classical Greece*, 150. 134 Aristotle, *Politics*, 81.

135 de Ste. Croix, *Class Struggle in the Ancient Greek World*, 137. Also see Engels, *Origins of the Family, Private Property, and the State*, chap. IV–V.

136 Ober, *Rise and Fall of Classical Greece*, 162.

137 Here it's important to remember that Solon's reforms could have also solidified the positions of the elite. As Finley remarks, "even in Athens it is almost impossible to find a man of modest means, let alone a really poor man, in a position of leadership." Finley, *Ancient Economy*, 37.

138 de Ste. Croix, *Class Struggle in the Ancient Greek World*, 284.

"They are led more and more in the direction of badness by poverty, and by the lack of refinement and the ignorance which lack of money brings some men."[139] Plato's *Republic* is a well-constructed remedy for this perceived problem. He outlines a caste system in a society that would instill order. This from childhoods inculcated with "stories which are designed to make them fear death as little as possible."[140] The leadership class would be correspondingly dispassionate, while the rest would know their places. His strict regimentation of social structures has shades of the Spartan *polis*. Other complaints are more base, falling back on predictable tropes that may or may not be grounded in reality. In the words of Isocrates:

> When I was a boy, being rich was considered so secure and honorable that almost everyone pretended he owned more property than he actually did possess, because he wanted the prestige it gave. Now, on the other hand, one has to defend oneself against being rich as if it were the worst of crimes.[141]

The rich nonetheless profited handsomely from Athenian commercial hegemony, which was partially restored in the years after its defeat. Taxation was low under normal circumstances and democracy never became confiscatory. This meant grudging acceptance of democracy as a source of influence in the world, not to mention the absence of any practical alternatives after centuries of reforms. Aristotle, in characteristic moderation, recommended steering a path between "extreme democracy or an unmixed oligarchy."[142] A poor citizenry would give itself over to tyranny, he asserts. Successful democracy needs middle class citizens who are modest property holders. This, for Aristotle, was the most stable, lasting type of *polis*.

Conservatives in the Athenian nobility still expressed resentments along the lines of Isocrates, frequently expressing admiration for Spartan order, hierarchy, and discipline. Their counterparts in other *poleis* feared the Athenian Empire because of its propensity for installing democratic regimes. Xenophon pointed out that the rich in divided cities turned to Sparta in crisis, while the *demos* (citizenry) idealized Athens.[143] In de Ste. Croix's telling, "oligarchic and democratic leaders had no hesitation in calling in outside powers to help them gain the upper hand over their adversaries."[144] For our purposes, democracy was salient in the flow of ideas across interconnected cities. The concentration of political power called "oligarchy" was the unspoken political state of things up until this point in history. In the trans-Hellenic discourse it crystallizes as a competing ideology up for debate rather

[139] Cited in Rhodes, *Greek City States*, 39. [140] Plato, *Republic*, 80.
[141] Cited in de Ste. Croix, *Class Struggle in the Ancient Greek World*, 297.
[142] Aristotle, *Politics*, 159. [143] de Ste. Croix, *Class Struggle in the Ancient Greek World*, 296.
[144] Ibid., 295.

than a given. In sum, the Classical Age was a high period for democracy. The kingships that ran *poleis* in previous centuries largely disappeared. Democracy was the typical form of local government until the Hellenistic Age.[145]

Conclusion: A World Run on Coins

Thebes defeated Sparta not long after the Spartan victory over Athens. The Thebans freed Sparta's *helots*, thus ending the underlying source of Spartan hegemony. From there, mainland Greece saw continual shifts in the balance of power until Philip II of Macedon solidified his conquests over the region. This ended the formal autonomy of the city-states after protracted resistance led by Athens. The Classical Age closed with the Macedonian conquests, although the *poleis* retained considerable self-governance under Philip.

Until then, Hellas persisted for centuries under what political realists call *anarchic* conditions, with no central authority to enforce rules over cities. The Greeks were noted military innovators. Arms were important Athenian exports. Well-trained Greek soldiers were in demand as mercenaries across the ancient world. The trouble was that Greek methods of warfare resulted in mostly indecisive battles. No Greek city could establish authority over all of the other cities. There was constant preparation for warfare, impacting the Greek social hierarchy. The more affluent citizens acquired armor at their own expenses, serving in the *hoplite* ranks. The lowest class citizens (*thetes*) increased their value to society by serving as rowers in Greek *triremes*.

Classical scholarship rightly laments the persistent emphasis on Athens, owing to the survival of its records. Books routinely caution that the study of Classical Hellas occurs through an Athenian lens. Athens was an outlier, they note. Yet the existence of an alpha city is typical of city networks which rely on a few places conducive to political, cultural, and economic flows. Athens was meaningful to the existence of other cities, expressing power beyond force. Alpha cities are not synonymous with imperial capitals. Macedon had superior military strength but as yet no city with comparable sophistication. Philip invaded a world run on Athenian coins.

This was a high period for city networks. Cities were the central political units, adaptive and innovative when it came to survival. If we take the modernist view, they did far more than survive. Cities in our other city networks under study for this book usually lacked such persistent autonomy.

[145] Hansen and Nielsen, *Inventory of Archaic and Classical Poleis*, 20.

Spruyt is right to use evolutionary thinking to point out that they never exercised central control, making them vulnerable.[146] But this obscures the duration of city-state independence in Greece. Given the actual time horizons, we can play with the analogy: The poignant thing about dinosaurs was how inconceivably long they lasted as the dominant species.

Cities were small and nimble. They experimented with systems that larger rivals couldn't. This changed. Cities under imperial control marshaled resources on a scale not seen in world history. Enter the namesake of Philip's successor, Alexander the Great. One of his numerous Alexandrias rose to become the most prominent commercial city of ancient times – a new kind of alpha city for a new kind of city network.

[146] Spruyt, *Sovereign State and Its Competitors*, 186.

4 Alexandria, Alpha City

His biography is stranger than fiction. He marched into Asia at the head of 50,000 soldiers, with a penchant for personally charging into enemy lines ahead of them. Before long, Alexander swiftly conquered the Achaemenid "Persian" Empire with population estimates in the tens of millions.[1] In 336 BCE, Alexander had assumed the Macedonian kingship, subduing the restive *poleis* effectively conquered by his father, Philip II (c. 382–336 BCE), along the way leveling the Greek city-state of Thebes in 335. In 334, he invaded Persian-controlled Asia, ceremoniously declaring the whole expanse "spear won."

Two years later, Alexander the Great (356–323 BCE) was in northern Egypt founding what he expressly intended to be a significant global *entrepôt*. Alexander involved himself in the city's planning, including a Hippodamian street grid and public building locations. Alexandria was master planned, characteristic of this heavy-handed new wave of Greek colonization. Alexander forcibly relocated nearby Egyptian villagers to comprise the city's first settlers. By the time of his death in 323, Alexander's conquests reached as far as India. They left a vast network of cities in their wake, provided the new imperial commanders could keep settlers from deserting. Cities in this archipelago ranged from reconstituted older towns, to new metropolises built from scratch, to garrisoned outposts intended to keep trading routes safe from ungoverned nomads. Urbanization was key to Alexander's vision of cultural hybridization and global interaction that moved populations – not always voluntarily – across Europe and Asia. Like many ancient state-builders, Alexander saw his subjects as better off ruled by the concentrated authority represented by cities. In words ascribed to him by Arrian, the Macedonians had been "vagabonds and poor" pastoralists roaming the mountains "clothed in sheepskins." Alexander reminded his troops (and potential settlers) that Philip

[1] F. W. Walbank, *The Hellenistic World* (Sussex: The Harvester Press, 1981), 30.

had "turned you into city-dwellers and civilized you by the gift of good laws."[2] Their preference for cities in scarcely known parts of the world was at best mixed. Abandonment was common.

As we will see in this chapter, Alexandria was a prototypical world city in the eastern Mediterranean, with trade links reaching well into Asia and Europe. Like all ancient experiments in statecraft, the city defied easy categorization. It was the capital of a territorial empire, the very political form that was overtaking the *polis* as the primary mode of Greek social organization. Yet it was modeled on the *polis*, replete with important architectural elements and civic bodies in the image of Athens.[3] The familiar Greek elements are in Arrian's description of Alexander vigorously planning out "the location of the *agora*" and "of course the city wall."[4]

Complicating definitions further, Alexandria-by-Egypt (the city's full name) was not formally in what Ptolemaic rulers deemed the country of Egypt, making it a hybrid city-state and imperial capital in one breath. The Hellenistic age, as historians have retroactively called the period from the death of Alexander to the conquest of Egypt by Rome in 31 BCE, coincided with the rise of territorial empires and the decline of city-state autonomy.[5] The politics of the time shifted from a Classical epoch that was conducive to potentially revolutionary regimes, such as Solon's Athens, toward an age of kings. Democracy didn't quite die, but its possibilities were tightly circumscribed by the royal regimes. Riots and desertion tended to be the main political weapons of the *demos* in Ptolemaic Egypt, rather than the democratic mechanisms used in Athens.[6] Inequality worsened, evident in the palatial built environments of Hellenistic metropolises. Radical ideas did not spread across the Hellenistic city network as they had in Classical times. The city-states under Macedonian influence were less disposed to democracy. In G. E. M. de Ste. Croix's mind the social system was conductive to class inequality. "[Macedonia's city leagues] explicitly guaranteed the social order: city constitutions were 'frozen,' and there was an express prohibition of the redistribution

[2] Cited in ibid., 29. For full context, see Arrian, *Anabasis of Alexander* (London: Hodder and Staughton, 1884), available at https://en.wikisource.org/wiki/The_Anabasis_of_Alexander, last accessed February 15, 2024.

[3] R. E. Wycherley, *How the Greeks Built Cities* (London: Macmillan, 1962), 27.

[4] Graham Shipley, *The Greek World after Alexander: 323–330 BC* (New York: Routledge, 2000), 214.

[5] At least a decline in the autonomy of major city-states such as Athens and Sparta. Smaller *poleis* in the Classical Period tended to be under the influence of the major cities, which were effectively mini-empires.

[6] Peter Green, *The Hellenistic Age: A Short History* (New York: Modern Library, 2008), 76.

of land, the cancellation of debts, the confiscation of property, and the freeing of slaves with a view to revolution," noted St. Croix[7]

Yet this was an age of cities, which grew in scale, number, and connectivity – trade between them increased markedly. Large cities fed off of the logic of territorial empires. Though less clearly bounded than walled cities and decentralized, the Hellenistic successor empires favored concentrations of capital and power. Cities were useful in projecting power across open spaces, the better to extract resources for the royal coffers. Dispersed non-sedentary tribes were largely ungovernable. Isocrates urged Philip to invade Persia, to "found cities in this region and settle in them there those men who are now wandering around through lack of their everyday needs, and doing outrage to whoever they fall in with."[8] In other words, the advice of this conservative figure in Greek politics was to cloister populations in the city or the *chôra*, where their activities could be monitored and taxed.

Significantly, the Macedonians expropriated the entire Achaemenid treasury, including at least 10,350,000 pounds of gold.[9] This massive capital infusion fueled a construction boom in the successor kingdoms. Nowhere was this more the case than in Ptolemaic Alexandria, the leading commercial center at this time. Some brief superlatives: The city's population reached a half-million.[10] Its lighthouse was one of the ancient world's seven wonders. Strabo (c. 64–c. 87 BCE) describes the sea and lake harbors as hubs of maritime activity. Ships carried merchandise of "great value" in and out of the city. His *Geography* notes the environmental conditions for ancient iterations of the world city, in an age where sea travel was by far the most efficient vehicle for trade:

> The advantages of the city's site are various; for, first, the place is washed by two seas, on the north by the [Egyptian] Sea, as it is called, and on the south by Lake Mareia, also called Mareotis. This is filled by many canals from the Nile, both from above and on the sides.[11]

Moreover, Alexandria's library was a hub of information storage. It was also a proto-university, attracting intellectuals from across the Greek world, surpassing Athens in most scientific fields.

The city's prominence drew from two basic factors. One was the simultaneous emergence of a network of new towns reproduced in the Greek mold. This went well beyond trade, constituting established political, linguistic,

[7] Here de Ste. Croix is channeling pseudo-Demosthenes. de Ste. Croix, *Class Struggle in the Ancient Greek World*, 299.

[8] Walbank, *Hellenistic World*, 30.

[9] Figures extrapolated from Green, *Hellenistic Age*, 10.

[10] Shipley, *Greek World after Alexander*, 215.

[11] Strabo, *Geography* (Cambridge: Loeb Classical Library, 1932), book xvii. Spelling change by the author. Also note that "Egyptian sea" refers to the Mediterranean.

cultural, and aesthetic ties. The other was Alexandria's hyper-bureaucratic system of agricultural extraction in its hinterlands.

Hellenistic World System(s)

Alexander's empire splintered quickly after his death. From the wars of the *diádochoi*, or successors, crystalized several large empires. The Ptolemaic line ruled over Egypt. The Seleucid dynasty occupied the Near East and Mesopotamia. The Attalid kings became the major force in Asia Minor, ruling from the great city of Pergamon. Macedonian successors also controlled mainland Greece, although the city-states remained formidable. The island-based city-state of Rhodes notably retained its independence, becoming a major maritime power.

The nineteenth century historian Johann Gustav Droysen was the first to label this period "Hellenistic," distinguished in his mind by unprecedented globalization:

> East and West were ripe for fusion, and on both sides fermentation and transformation quickly followed. The new awakening of popular life led to ever more novel developments in the state and the intellectual sphere, in commerce and art, in religion and morality. Let us describe this new world-historical principle with the word "Hellenistic." Greek culture, in dominating the life of the world of the East, also fertilized it, and so created that Hellenism in which the paganism of Asia and Greece – indeed all antiquity itself – was destined to culminate.[12]

A common visual style existed from the Western Mediterranean to Afghanistan.[13] Alexandria, for its part, was not solely an imposition of Greek culture on Egypt. It was a syncretism of Greek, Egyptian, Italian, and Near Eastern aesthetics.[14] Evidence based on recovered coinage suggests a "big" Hellenistic world "stretching from the Atlantic to the Indian subcontinent."[15] The *koine*, a modified version of the Greek language, emerged as a *lingua franca* spoken across this expanse. This common language overcame differences in Greek dialects. As one annual report from the University of Aarhus' Center for the Study of Antiquity – which has contributed a great deal to contemporary Hellenistic studies – put it, "[t]he Hellenistic Age led to an

12 Translated from German in Peter Thonemann, *The Hellenistic Age: A Very Short Introduction* (Oxford: Oxford University Press, 2018), 5.

13 The Afghani ruin at Ai-Khanoum evinces a large Greek city possibly also named after Alexander, replete with all the familiar architectural elements, including a theater, palace, and gymnasium.

14 Miguel John Versluys, *Visual Style and Constructing Identity in the Hellenistic World: Nemrud Dağ and Commagene Under Antiochos I* (Cambridge: Cambridge University Press, 2017), 3.

15 Peter Thonemann, *The Hellenistic World: Using Coins as Sources* (Cambridge: Cambridge University Press, 2015), 25.

intensification of koineisation. Greeks coming from different regions of the Greek world were integrated into new societies together with non-Greeks. An important example is the city of Alexandria."[16]

Cities linked by trade routes enabled this fusion. Their creations were deliberate policy. Macedonian kings in effect constructed a city network with sheer top down power, purposefully hastening urbanization. There may have been population pressures leading to this. There appears to have been sustained growth in the generations leading up to Alexander's invasion, with little space in the traditional locations of Greek colonization.[17] Excess population had motivated Greek emigration in the past, but there is much more to this. Cities did not simply exist to house their residents. Ryan Boehm's study of the role of cities in the successor empires refers to the expansion of Hellenistic cities as "structural urbanization."[18] For Boehm, the "focus was not just the selective augmentation of specific sites, but also on constructing a nodal framework, linking and interconnecting cities and regions in a way that mapped out the infrastructural power of these nascent kingdoms."[19] He asserts that urban networks helped empires concentrate administration, conduct speedy diplomacy, and marshal resources.[20] A case in point, Hellenistic kings fielded armies on the order of 80,000 troops, more than double the size of the largest armies in the age of sovereign city-states.[21] In sum, networked cities were effective power bases.[22] Rather than wait for their formation, states forced the issue using administrative prowess.

This began with Philip, a relentless founder of cities. Initiating settlements in places that lacked overarching authority gave him full control. New cities had no dangerous traditions of independence as with rebellious Athens and Sparta. They exercised only the local decision making powers that royal authorities granted them, leaving most foreign policy to the king.[23] This starkly contrasts with earlier Greek migrations (see Chapter 3) where new *poleis* were always autonomous. It was Philip who experimented with the "name cities" (e.g.

[16] George Hinge, "Language and Race: Theocritus and the Koine Identity of Ptolemaic Egypt," in George Hinge and Jens A. Krasilnikoff (eds.), *Alexandria: A Cultural and Religious Melting Pot* (Aarhus: Aarhus University Press, 2009), 66–79, 70.

[17] Richard Billows, "Cities," in Andrew Erskine (ed.), *A Companion to the Hellenistic World* (Oxford: Blackwell Publishing, 2003), 196–215, 197.

[18] Ryan Boehm, *City and Empire in the Age of Successors: Urbanization and Social Response in the Making of Hellenistic Kingdoms* (Oakland: University of California Press, 2018), 18.

[19] Ibid. [20] Ibid.

[21] Simon Price, "The History of the Hellenistic Period," in John Boardman, Jasper Griffin, and Oswyn Murray (eds.), *The Oxford History of Greece and the Hellenistic World* (Oxford: Oxford University Press, 2001), 364–389, 376.

[22] This contrasts with the Achaemenid elite preference for governing dispersed populations.

[23] John D. Grainger, *Great Power Diplomacy in the Hellenistic World* (New York: Routledge, 2017), 56.

Alexandria), a nomenclature that indicates the Greek shift toward dictatorial power.[24]

This informed Alexander's desire to continue urbanization policies, albeit on a global scale. Before his death he planned the mass relocation of populations between Europe and Asia, starting with soldiers placed in new towns.[25] Troops were granted land in these towns, serving as on-notice garrisons to protect trade routes from piracy or to fight in the successors' endless conflicts. Put mildly, his cosmopolitan vision was not the free market vote-with-their-feet portrait of globalization idealized today. Arrian (c. 86–c. 160) noted that settlers in Alexander's cities did "not all remain there willingly."[26] Hellenistic kings transferred populations with impunity. Josephus (37–c. 100 CE) records that Antiochus III removed "two-thousand Jewish families with their effects from Mesopotamia and Babylonia to the forts and most essential places."[27] The successors went as far as to slaughter settlers trying to return to Greece from sites as far away as Iran. Desertion from new settlements was tantamount to military mutiny and treated accordingly.[28] In Diodorus' first-century CE telling, settlers who "longed for the Greek customs and manner of life" stayed put on the threat of fearsome reprisal from Alexander. "But when he was dead they rose in revolt."[29]

For many, urbanization was a brutal process entailing the destruction of restive cities. This, ironically, as monarchies engaged in building programs. Populations could be expelled or enslaved (the fate of Thebes). The main objective for the Hellenistic kings was a favorable settlement pattern. There were coerced mergers between cities, a process called *synoikism*. Whole buildings were dismantled, sometimes physically carted to new locations. Some *synoikisms* were voluntary, or at the king's request, coupled with positive inducements. Others were purely coercive.[30] They often created lasting power centers including Ephesus, Antioch, and Rhodes. At other times these attempts at social engineering badly flopped.[31] Strabo describes the creation of the new capital of Thessalonica by Cassander (c. 355–297 BCE), the successor who ruled Macedonia:

[24] R. Malcolm Errington, *A History of the Hellenistic World: 323–30 BC* (Oxford: Blackwell Publishing, 2008), 69.

[25] Green, *Hellenistic Age*, 22. [26] Cited in Walbank, *Hellenistic World*, 44.

[27] Flavius Josephus, *The Antiquities of the Jews*, book xii, available at www.gutenberg.org/cache/epub/2848/pg2848-images.html, last accessed February 15, 2024.

[28] Errington, *History of the Hellenistic World*, 69.

[29] Diodorus, *The Library of History* (Cambridge: Loeb Classical Library, 1947), book xviii.

[30] Boehm, *City and Empire in the Age of Successors*, 20.

[31] Gary Reger, "Hellenistic Greece and Western Asia Minor," in Walter Scheidel, Ian Morris, and Richard Saller (eds.), *The Cambridge Economic History of the Greco-Roman World* (Cambridge: Cambridge University Press, 2007), 460–483, 463.

> Cassander named the city after his wife Thessalonice, daughter of Philip son of Amyntas, after he had *razed to the ground the towns in Crusis and those on the Thermaean Gulf, about twenty-six in number*, and had settled all the inhabitants together in one city; and this city is the metropolis of what is now Macedonia.[32]

Notably, the slave trade accounted for the largest share of long distance migration.[33] The number of slaves entering mainland Greece offset population loss from emigration. Egypt, like other core areas, was a net importer of slaves put to domestic labor for urban elites under Ptolemaic rule.[34]

Enhanced by unbridled state power, cities in the successor kingdoms dwarfed the Classical city-states. The largest Classical core cities – Athens and Syracuse – had population sizes of approximately 100,000 by the most liberal estimates.[35] Cities of this size became commonplace. At the largest scale, Seleucia-on-the-Tigris may have had 600,000 inhabitants.[36] Antioch had a half-million. The highest population estimates for Alexandria reach a full million.[37] Administration grew more complex within cities. Interdependence *between* cities also became denser. Nominally voluntary migration increased, although the details behind the migration waves fueling urban growth are murky to modern historians. In the broadest sense, the *koine*, alongside familiar Greek-style built environments, made relocation easier. Commercial, diplomatic, and social ties created opportunities for migration. Patronage by urban elites attracted intellectuals and artists.[38] "For Greeks it was one world," according to a classic study, "easy to move in and one which offered high status and wealth if one was prepared to take a chance."[39] One thing is certain: As "population sinks" with higher death rates than births, cities could not maintain these sizes without migration, whether by push or pull factors.[40] To put it in perspective, the sum total of migration across the Greco-Roman periods is an estimated twenty to forty million. This figure includes slaves, forcibly relocated by the millions.[41]

32 Strabo, *Geography*, book vii, emphasis mine.
33 Walter Scheidel, "Demography," in Walter Scheidel, Ian Morris, and Richard Saller (eds.), *The Cambridge Economic History of the Greco-Roman World* (Cambridge: Cambridge University Press, 2007), 38–86, 49.
34 Ibid., 64.
35 Walter Scheidel, "Creating a Metropolis: A Comparative Demographic Perspective," in W. V. Harris and Giovanni Ruffini (eds.), *Ancient Alexandria between Egypt and Greece* (Boston: Brill, 2004), 1–32, 1.
36 This was another "name city," founded by Seleucus I Nicator, the biggest of several eponymous cities.
37 Keep in mind that population estimates for ancient cities are inherently inexact and that Athens likely had a population of 250,000, including its *chôra* (see Chapter 3). Billows, "Cities," 199.
38 Green, *Hellenistic Age*, 48.
39 Walbank, *Hellenistic World*, 78.
40 Scheidel, "Creating a Metropolis," 18.
41 Ibid., 49.

A number of scholars couch this era in terms of world systems analysis (see Chapter 2).[42] This is foreshadowed by the perpetual need for Greek cities to engage in trade, driven by the environmental deficits that we saw in Chapter 3. There was, as one study of intercity mobility put it, a "redistributive process by which the ecologies of other regions are brought in to play to remedy local dearth."[43] The urgency grew with increasingly large cities, often foisted on uprooted populations through *synoikisms*. Evidence on the basis of shipwreck analysis shows international commerce intensified, including with so-called barbarian zones.[44] Who benefited? Was the Hellenistic city network a conduit for the exploitation of a "barbarian" periphery? Modernists see a core–periphery pattern, but soft-pedal the notion that these relationships were necessarily zero-sum.[45] Living standards improved, at least in mainland Greece, between the Archaic and Hellenistic periods according to longitudinal studies.[46] The historic waters are muddy here. Despite the harsh practices inherent in population politics, monarchs frequently granted the proudest city-states protections from forms of exploitation such as heavy taxation and garrisoning.

Hellenistic leaders outside Greece, however, notably dominated local populations. Particularly those of their rural hinterlands. Hellenistic migration was strictly hierarchal, with Macedonians self-cast as "the new master race."[47] Greeks ran Hellenistic cities to the summary exclusion of native inhabitants. To offer context, the Seleucid Empire's Greek population never exceeded 2.5 percent, a kind of minority-rule analogous to modern colonial and postcolonial systems.[48] The local populations were a ready workforce the heavily armed Macedonians could press into agricultural labor.[49] This workforce was essential to an elite that could not increase production via automation – which

[42] For perspectives that grapple with the application of world systems approaches to Hellenistic economies, see Zofia Archibald, John Davies, Vincent Gabrielsen, and G. J. Oliver (eds.), *Hellenistic Economies* (New York: Routledge, 2001); and Per Bilde, Troels Engberg-Pedersen, Lise Hannestad, Jan Zahle, and Klavs Randsborg (eds.), *Centre and Periphery in the Hellenistic World* (Aarhus: Aarhus University Press, 1993).

[43] Nicholas Purcell, "Mobility and the Polis," in Oswyn Murray and Simon Price, *The Greek City: From Homer to Alexander* (Oxford: Clarendon Press, 1990), 29–58, 50.

[44] Simply put, Hellenistic commercial vessels were larger than their Classical predecessors, and there were more of them. David Gibbons, "Shipwrecks and Hellenistic Trade," in Zofia Archibald, John Davies, Vincent Gabrielsen, and G. J. Oliver (eds.), *Hellenistic Economies* (New York: Routledge, 2001), 273–312, 288.

[45] Bresson, *Making of the Ancient Greek Economy*, 416.

[46] For this perspective, see, especially Josiah Ober, "Greek Economic Performance, 800–300 BCE: A Comparison Case," in François de Callataÿ (ed.), *Quantifying the Greco Roman Economy and Beyond* (Bari: Edipuglia, 2014), 103–122; and Geoffrey Kron, "Comparative Evidence and the Reconstruction of the Ancient Economy: Greco-Roman Housing and the Level and Distribution of Wealth and Income," in François de Callataÿ (ed.), *Quantifying the Greco Roman Economy and Beyond* (Bari: Edipuglia, 2014), 123–146.

[47] Walbank, *Hellenistic World*, 62. [48] Ibid., 67. [49] Ibid., 43.

Aristotle scoffed was the only alternative to slavery.[50] This is the inherent problem with applying measures of economic growth in the ancient world. Increased output depended on getting laborers to work harder, which the Ptolemies had down to a science.

In an important essay, Graham Shipley applies the world systems model to the Hellenistic economy, arguing that there is evidence of exploitive core–periphery economic relations.[51] This was the case even though the economic policies of the successors were hardly deliberate, in Shipley's view. Recall that the ancient Greek concern for economics extended no further than household management. The successor dynasties – especially the Ptolemies – were in effect vast estate managers extracting as much tribute as possible from local labor and from royal land. Their ability to extract surpluses from peasant populations, Shipley postulates, is evident in the monumental gigantism of Hellenistic architecture.[52] As we will see in the next section, much about Greek-built environments remained the same as in previous periods, differing primarily in scale. This was the result of costly building sprees, visual proof of heavily concentrated capital. There is consensus, even among modernist scholars, that this period saw growing polarization.[53] Concentrated resettled populations placed additional burdens on farming regions.[54] Years of warfare had further made Greece "poor and miserable," in Diodorus' words. Peripheral towns struggled to retain population, encouraging more resettlements.[55] The cynic poet Circidas laments "swinish wealth" offering a "perishing handout to the fellow eating bare minimum."[56]

Granting that geographic dependencies intensified, scholars struggle to define just where the cores and peripheries were. The Western Mediterranean could be put forward as a global core, from which Alexandria benefited. As one economist suggested, the central economic region ran "from Byzantion through the Aegean past Rhodes and Cyprus to Antioch and Alexandria and back, which fed and was fed by peripheral areas."[57] This reflects an emphasis on long-distance trade, a bread and butter application of Wallerstein's model. There were also identifiable cores and peripheries within each kingdom.[58] Alexandria absorbed Egyptian surplus.

[50] Aristotle, *Politics*, 14.

[51] Graham Shipley, "Distance, Development and Decline? World Systems Analysis and the 'Hellenistic' World," in Per Bilde, Troels Engberg-Pedersen, Lise Hannestad, Jan Zahle, and Klavs Randsborg (eds.), *Centre and Periphery in the Hellenistic World* (Aarhus: Aarhus University Press, 1993), 271–284, 275.

[52] Ibid., 276. [53] Ibid., 277. [54] Walbank, *Hellenistic World*, 161. [55] Ibid., 167.

[56] Cited in ibid., 168.

[57] John K. Davies, "Hellenistic Economies in the Post-Finley Era," Zofia Archibald, John Davies, Vincent Gabrielsen, and G. J. Oliver (eds.), *Hellenistic Economies* (New York: Routledge, 2001), 11–62, 41.

[58] Shipley, "Distance, Development and Decline?," 283.

There was inevitably intense class conflict, but the Greek city network was not a conduit for radical ideologies the way it had been during the Delian League's hegemony. Political globalization in the realm of ideas – class-conscious democracy – declined. Athens could not marshal the resources to defeat the Macedonian kings, not for lack of trying.[59] Athens remained democratic at home but could no longer project (or impose) the idea across the Aegean. As we have seen, the revolutionary third rails in the ancient world were land redistribution, debt cancellation, and slave emancipation. Ironically it was Sparta that tried all three, its leaders' hands forced into such policies by a local economy that reached combustible levels of inequality. The successors ruthlessly put down this rebellion, even – especially – as it gained traction in other cities. Beleaguered lower classes heralded Spartan king Cleomenes III (260–219 BCE) as a savior. He was killed trying to foment revolt in Egypt.[60] Monarchism itself had no organized opposition.

Though constantly at war, Macedonian kings shared an innate fear of revolution by the lower classes. They actively stifled any source of class foment real or perceived.[61] To wit, de Ste. Croix contends that the Hellenistic age entailed "the destruction of Greek democracy."[62] The landed elite held political power in cities, regardless of the nominal system of government. Assemblies took a backseat to patronage. The urban-based rich monopolized policy initiatives through liturgies – self-financed public service – circumventing democratic mechanisms and lasting reforms. (This was Circidas' "perishing handout" to the starving). Liturgies softened the stresses of extreme inequality but sidelined the *demos*. Mobile mercenaries replaced citizen armies, effectively creating employment for the roving dispossessed lamented by Isocrates.

Revisions to the Urban Form

Drastic changes to the social fabric caused only subtle changes in urban forms, if we can accept as subtle the tremendous increase in scale by Hellenistic times. The *poleis* had invented most of the kinds of spaces needed for a sea-linked society. The basic elements of the Greek city had already crystallized by the Classical Age. "The culture of the Greek East may have been banal," suggests A. H. M. Jones' landmark study of post-Classical Greek cities. 'It

[59] An Athenian alliance stubbornly resisted Philip in the Battle of Chaeronea in 338 BCE and revolted again against Macedonia in the Lamian War after Alexander's death. The city-states were defeated both times.

[60] Walbank, *Hellenistic World*, 170.

[61] Green, *Hellenistic Age*, 76.

[62] de Ste. Croix, *Class Struggle in the Ancient Greek World*, 300.

may have lacked originality and venerated too obsequiously the classical past."[63]

To briefly reiterate, *agoras* were still there. However, they had long ago transitioned from political to market functions.[64] They became more enclosed. Even Athens underwent such modifications in the Hellenistic period. This coincided with the decline in radical democracy there as elsewhere.[65] The *emporion* remained a designated zone for foreign commerce. It marked an important delineation in a culture that devalued market activity more than ever. Major cities were crowded with religious monuments and shrines of all kinds. They reflected imperial narratives and impressed foreign eyes. Theaters and stadiums were hallmarks of a complete city. (Performances would be less accessible to non-Greek speaking majorities, however). City walls remained a common feature. Every city had a *gymnasion*. Recall their varied uses, from exercise to schooling to military education. *Gymnasia* became more important as purveyors of Greek culture for children of the elite growing up in what were technically foreign lands. As a result, civic leaders invested greater funds into them, building them larger and more opulently.[66]

What truly changed? Cities were far more centrally planned in the Hellenistic period. Variations on the Hippodamian form became popular from the fourth century onward, amplified by Alexander's spree of city foundations. Their simultaneous creation at a time when this design was popular contributed to this homogeneity. Gridiron streets at right angles were grafted onto natural environments across the transcontinental Greek world. These have been variously regarded as utilitarian, with function militantly outranking form.[67] There may have been social engineering at play, as the Hippodamian grid could separate out functions, as well as residents. Such segregation was important to Aristotle.[68] Hippodamian layouts drew laments common from travelers in any high period of globalization. Every place looks the same!

In short, the common aesthetic reflected the internationalization of the time. The Doric, Ionic, and Corinthian architectural styles adorned the colonnaded buildings that sat impressively at the heart of every large city. A prominent Hellenistic architect codified the major Greek forms, later written into history by Vitruvius in the first century BCE.[69] Planners, architects, and engineers versed in Greek styles worked across the city network. Sostratos, the architect

63 A. H. M. Jones, *The Greek City: From Alexander to Justinian* (Oxford: Oxford University Press, 1940), 284.

64 Wycherley, *How the Greeks Built Cities*, 82.

65 Shipley, *Greek World after Alexander*, 89.

66 Ibid., 87; see also Jones, *Greek City*, 236.

67 Shipley, *Greek World after Alexander*, 91.

68 Robin Osborn, "Urban Landscape and Architecture," in George Boys-Stones, Barbara Graziosi, and Phiroze Vasunia (eds.), *The Oxford Handbook of Hellenic Studies* (Oxford: Oxford University Press, 2009), 238–246, 239.

69 Dinsmoor, *Architecture of Ancient Greece*, 273.

thought to have designed the lighthouse at Pharos in the third century BCE, also appears to have worked and received awards across the Greek world.[70] The early Hellenistic period saw a massive building boom, with ever more numerous and larger buildings. It's plausible that aristocrats financed them in part to create employment, thereby addressing the social byproduct of over-population that was the rationale prefiguring Alexander's conquests.[71]

Thus far, we have discussed changes mainly in degree, but new kinds of construction were invented – and marveled at in Alexandria. Broad, colonnaded streets appeared in Greek cities for the first time, expansive enough to accommodate the grandiosity of kingships. Alexandria's Canopic Way played host to many of history's most dazzling royal triumphs. Its lighthouse was likely among the first buildings of its kind, certainly the most ambitious. Among other things, the colossal structure at Pharos helped manage the city's dense shipping traffic. Libraries were also a recent innovation, particularly those at Alexandria, Pergamon, and Ephesus.

The geographic placement of cities was distinctive in Hellenistic times. The number of Alexandrias founded by Alexander himself varies from approximately a dozen to Plutarch's less likely estimate of "over seventy."[72] Alexandria-by-Egypt is an outlier for several reasons. It was the only such named city located on the Mediterranean along preexisting Greek shipping lanes.[73] Most Greek cities had naturally located near the sea, including colonies. Other than Alexandria-by-Egypt, most of the cities founded by Alexander were located east of the Fertile Crescent. Their locations reflected Alexander's political will as much as environmental determinants. Granted, they were located near rivers, fertile lands, and other accessible points, mirroring Achaemenid settlement patterns.[74]

Key here was Alexander's desire to centralize nomadic populations in these vast expanses. This way they were governable, living under the rules of a social order. Settled nomads would not disrupt agriculture and commerce through raids. Local labor – like the unemployed Greek emigrants – could staff an army and profitably exploit the land.[75] Alexander's army, which averaged roughly 100,000 troops, relied on local populations for soldiers.

[70] Alexander Meeus, "The Career of Sostratos of Knidos: Politics, Diplomacy and the Alexandrian Building Programme in the Early Hellenistic Period," in Timothy Howe, E. Edward Garvin, and Graham Wrightson (eds.), *Greece, Macedon, and Persia* (Oxford: Oxbow Books, 2015), 143–171, 154.

[71] Jones, *Greek City*, 277.

[72] P. M. Fraser, *The Cities of Alexander the Great* (Oxford: Oxford University Press, 1996), 7.

[73] As we have seen, the Greeks had traded with Egypt for centuries. The Pharaohs even allowed the permanent settlement of Naucratis for Greek merchants.

[74] Fraser, *Cities of Alexander the Great*, 172. [75] Ibid., 185.

Strategic town locations near former Achaemenid fortresses enabled protection against remaining nomads.

In any case, Hellenization was a definitively urban phenomenon that would not have occurred without cities. The *asty* and *chôra* were islands, Hellenism an archipelago. Greek cultural influence waned the further one strayed from cities.[76] There were ample tribal lands that were never truly regulated by state administrations. This fact underpinned territorial empires generally. The clean and neat maps showing their territories in history books were more claims than reality.[77] This is most certainly the case in successor states and in the Roman Empire, which we will explore further in Chapter 5. Suffice to say at this stage that the question of how best to extract resources from potentially hostile areas "within" empires remained open.

As a result, city placements fostered a kind of frontier dynamic where city and country tensely interacted. This reflects Alexander's grand cosmopolitan vision. Cities were designed to foster flows of people who would intermingle – and intermarry – across all backgrounds, even as they spread Greek culture. This, in his mind, would create a larger syncretism consisting of European and Asian cultures on equal terms.[78] Urban linkages were critical to this task.

In reality, the urban experiences within these cities would have entailed yawning cultural divides. To start with, Alexander's successors shared neither his cosmopolitan vision nor his desire for additional conquests that would have extended linkages further. They quietly abandoned both after his death. The mass of urban laborers had limited access to public services. They may have become accustomed to Greek amenities, such as fountains and drainage. They could frequent the same bathhouses as the Greek-speaking elite for tiny fees. The liturgical system afforded them free meals, games, and gifts.[79] Grandly scaled architecture may have had the intended unifying effect. Shrines paid homage to local gods. Then again, the average citizens may have lacked the literacy to read the inscriptions notably abundant on Hellenistic buildings.[80] Upward mobility was difficult to pursue, as they most likely did not speak the language of the nobility. The urban masses could not attend Greek schools. Furthermore, the authorities provided few services to those living outside city walls despite their integral place in the urban economy.[81]

Constructing an Alpha City

Alexandria was by far the most incredible centrifuge of Hellenistic globalization. Its large polyglot population was the closest thing to a realization of Alexander's cosmopolitan dream. He predicted it would become "large

[76] Jones, *Greek City*, 31. [77] Ibid., 44. [78] Fraser, *Cities of Alexander the Great*, 189.
[79] Jones, *Greek City*, 285. [80] Ibid. [81] Ibid., 286.

and populous."[82] His advisors assured him the city "would abound in resources and would sustain men from every nation."[83] Its otherworldly skyline inspired travel writing for millennia. All of this is fitting, as tourists flocked there to see Alexander's embalmed body in its gilded mausoleum. Ptolemy I Soter ("savior," c. 367–282 BCE), the city's royal booster, hijacked the body for (ironically) a symbolic legitimation of the new dynasty.

Alexandria was considered the greater city over Rome, well into the latter city's expansion. It has been called a precursor to modernity. In terms of commerce and culture, one Hellenistic scholar called it "more like London or Paris or New York today than were Periclean Athens or even Knossos at the height of its glory."[84] True, it was the preeminent world city of its time. But its early phases were more comparable to statist, rootless downtown Dubai than those comparatively organic cities. Even its population was imported, its buildings willed into form by top down authority. Hippodamian was the oft-copied style. As with present-day world cities, Alexandria had the biggest and best of what was commonplace. "The whole city is crisscrossed with streets suitable for the traffic of horses and carriages, and by two that are very wide, being more than [30 meters] in breadth; these intersect each other at right angles," according to Strabo.[85] Beyond bricks and mortar, Alexandria was, as we will see, the world's leading knowledge center. The remainder of this chapter addresses the city's planning and architecture, its relationship to the hinterlands, and its intercity relations in turn.

The City

Alexandria was founded primarily for the sake of commerce. Like every interconnected city its position required environmental foundations. Hence its placement at a stretch of northern Egypt surrounded by bodies of water. With an architect at his side, Alexander personally decided the placement of the *agora*, the city walls, and temples. The sparsely inhabited stretch of land made for a desirable location, in his mind, because of its series of deep-water harbors and a presumably healthy climate.[86] He purportedly adjusted the street grid to capture the cooling prevailing winds.[87] As Strabo described, the city took full advantage of the Mediterranean Sea to the north, and lake Mareotis to its south. Its location in the Nile Delta gave it ready access to trade routes in

[82] Cited in Shipley, *Greek World after Alexander*, 214. [83] Cited in ibid.

[84] Peter Green, *Alexander to Actium: The Historic Evolution of the Hellenistic Age* (Berkeley: University of California Press, 1990), 80.

[85] Strabo, *Geography*, book xvii. [86] Green, *Alexander to Actium*, 83.

[87] Judith McKenzie, *The Architecture of Alexandria and Egypt, c. 300 BC to AD 700* (New Haven: Yale University Press, 2007), 38.

Africa and the Red Sea, where the Ptolemaic Empire extended its trading outposts. The city, in his telling, also had sophisticated canal systems.

Ancient historians made much out of the city's unique location enabling trade. Vitruvius extols "a harbor rendered safe by nature, an excellent center for trade, corn fields throughout all Egypt, and the greater usefulness of the mighty river Nile."[88] The advantages of this location had been long known to Greeks. According to Homer, there was "an island out in the ocean's heavy surge, well off the Egyptian coast – they call it Pharos . . . there's a snug harbor there."[89] That island was incorporated into the city by a massive bridge, and became the site of the lighthouse. It offered a natural buffer against rough seas. Likewise, the Nile cannot be underestimated as a facilitator of regional commerce. In Strabo's telling, the river enabled far ranging land-based trade, making the city "the greatest trading center of the inhabited world."[90] The city's lake harbors, in his estimation, carried a greater volume of trade than its seaports.

The new city incorporated the nearby villages of Rhakotis, Canopis, and perhaps dozens more – including one on Pharos – and nomadic populations. Macedonian soldiers may have settled there.[91] These settlements were probably mostly compulsory, with the typical medley of punitive and positive inducements. According to the *Alexander Romance*, Alexander "ordered all those who lived within thirty miles of the city to leave their villages and move to the city; he presented them with parcels of land and called them Alexandrians."[92] He ordered them to pay tribute at similar levels to those levied by their previous Achaemenid rulers, for the purpose of constructing the city. It appears some nomads managed to refuse settlement, continuing their pastoral modes of living to the east of Alexandria.[93] Within a generation Alexandria surpassed Athens as the most important commercial and cultural Greek city, and in population. This despite the fact that much of it was of non-Greek origin. It had no time-honored Greek identity. It was multilingual, multiethnic, and multinational at the start. Diodorus put this population at 300,000 "free" inhabitants in the first century BCE. Modern scholars surmise another 200,000 slaves.[94]

Beyond the well-documented resettlements at Alexandria's outset, most of the details of this remarkable growth are unknown. What is certain is that the

88 Vitruvius, *The Ten Books on Architecture* (New York: Dover, 1960), 36.
89 Homer, *The Odyssey* (New York: Penguin, 1996), 135.
90 Cited in P. M. Fraser, *Ptolemaic Alexandria: I* (Oxford: Oxford University Press, 1972), 132.
91 Scheidel, "Creating a Metropolis," 22.
92 *The Greek Alexander Romance* (New York: Penguin, 1991), 64.
93 Scheidel, "Creating a Metropolis," 22.
94 Jane Rowlandson, "Town and Country in Ptolemaic Egypt," in Andrew Erskine (ed.), *A Companion to the Hellenistic World* (Oxford: Blackwell Publishing, 2003), 249–263, 253.

city was extraordinarily diverse. Egyptian, Jewish, Gallic, Italian, Greek, and Arab migrants rubbed shoulders in the city's crowded public spaces, all of these groups profoundly shaping the city's culture. They resided in their own quarters, preserving their identities. For those with freedom of movement, Alexandria was for much of its history an "open city" uniquely capable of integrating diverse backgrounds.

That said, non-Greeks had no formal status. Informally, Greeks saw them as barbarian if they did not share their language. In the purported words of one woman, Praxinoa the "racist":

> Heavens, what a crowd! How and when are we to get through this plague? They're like ants – there's no numbering or countering them. You've done us a good turn, Ptolemy, since your father was in heaven. Nowadays no ruffian slips up to you in the street Egyptian-fashion and does you a mischief – the trick those packets of rascality used to play, one as bad as another with their nasty tricks, a cursed lot.[95]

Not all of the Greek population was privileged. An underclass of Greek noncitizens outnumbered citizens in a steep categorical caste system reflective of Greek city-states.[96] The masses of impoverished, underrepresented cross-sections of society made for a combustible brew. Of all the potential cleavages – there were currents of Egyptian nationalism – class inequality rather than ethnicity was the driving force behind social conflict.[97] This was a crowded city whose urban footprint was up to one-third covered by its palace district.[98] For Greek males the city was a democracy organized into *demes*. But assembly politics dissolved over time and in any case it was tightly circumscribed by a dictatorial monarchy residing in the city.[99] Politics devolved into a violent dialogue between kings and the sundry underclasses, with riots the only available form of collective expression. "For the inhabitants of Egypt are capable of terrible violence," Polybius (c. 200–c. 118 BCE) breathlessly remarked.[100]

The Ptolemies were responsible for city-building in Alexandria. They seized power – of course, violently – after Alexander's death. Ptolemy I built the city walls, also completing a number of religious sites. Ptolemy II Philadelphus ("brother loving") oversaw a massive construction program during his reign from 285 to 246 BCE. He is arguably the city's primary master builder figure, although his predecessor initiated much of the ambitious Ptolemaic projects. Ptolemy II finished the city's agora and its vast entertainment venues: The stadium, hippodrome, and theater. He also assembled a zoo. Exotic animals symbolized globalism.

95 Hinge, "Language and Race," 75. 96 Fraser, *Ptolemaic Alexandria*, 51.
97 Ibid., 71. 98 Rowlandson, "Town and Country in Ptolemaic Egypt," 252.
99 Ibid., 253. 100 Cited in Fraser, *Ptolemaic Alexandria*, 82.

More importantly, Ptolemy II completed the legendary Pharos lighthouse, which was a true skyscraper even by modern standards. In a prime era for vanity projects, it had practical uses belying its monumentality. The prototype for all future lighthouses, Sostratos designed it to maximize harbor capacity. He justified its astronomical height by the need to aid navigation, absent natural pedestals. According to an epigram that was etched in the tower:

> As a savior of the Greeks, this watchman of Pharos, was set up, lord Proteus
> by Sostratos the Knidian, son of Dexiphanes.
> Since in Egypt there are no lookout-points or mountains as on islands,
> but low lies the breakwater where ships take harbor,
> for that reason, cleaving the air sheer and steep,
> this tower shines forth across countless leagues
> by day, and all night long quickly a sailor on the waves
> will see the great fire blazing from its peak
> and though he may run to the Bull's Horn itself, he would not miss
> Zeus Soter, o Proteus, in sailing hither.[101]

The Pharos had military uses as a watchtower. It could have communicated with the Egyptian *chôra*.[102] The lower levels had a barracks alongside government offices.[103] A landmark in mixed-use construction, the lighthouse attracted droves of tourists. They would have traversed the water on the Heptastadion, an extended long causeway linking the island with the city that was possibly built by Sostratos (it ingeniously sheltered the inner harbors).[104] From inside they climbed a wide spiral ramp to an observation deck with ethereal views of the urban landscape, passing concession stands with snacks and drinks along the way.[105]

The Pharos, its formal name, was about 110 meters tall with a 30-meter base.[106] Its mirror-amplified beacon was visible for 100 miles offshore, resembling a bright star by night to approaching sailors.[107] By day the tower is thought to have appeared glowing white. It was constructed with stone, although the exact materials are unknown.[108] As the epigram describes, the tower had a large statue of Zeus at its peak. From here we can glean insights into the physical economy of a first rate Hellenistic core city. The Pharos was extraordinarily costly, likely paid for by riches Ptolemy II gained from long distance trade via royal monopolies. This was a de facto corporate city-state with dense commerce as far away as India. Funds would also have derived from the city's highly extractive relationship with the *chôra*. The seminal

[101] Meeus, "Career of Sostratos of Knidos," 149. [102] Ibid., 152.
[103] Theodore Vrettos, *Alexandria: City of the Western Mind* (New York: The Free Press, 2001), 32.
[104] McKenzie, *Architecture of Alexandria and Egypt*, 45. [105] Vrettos, *Alexandria*, 32.
[106] McKenzie, *Architecture of Alexandria and Egypt*, 42. [107] Vrettos, *Alexandria*, 32.
[108] McKenzie, *Architecture of Alexandria and Egypt*, 42.

concept, its design, its engineering, show that Hellenistic exchange went well beyond physical goods. Its core cities featured the knowledge economy that incubated Sostratos' international career. Though obscure to history, he was famous in his time. To Greco-Roman writers he was the acknowledged equal to Archimedes.[109] Pharos represents the "technology of the intellect" made possible in the context of city networks connecting concentrated populations (see Chapter 2).

The Museum and Library complex situated in the palace district emblematized this. One of its missions was to preserve all Greek literature ever published. There is considerable debate over how many neatly rolled papyrus scrolls the royal library owned. Scholars put the figure, variously, at between 200,000 and 700,000.[110] Alexandrian head librarians, a significant title, categorized and organized works acquired (at times stolen) by the Ptolemaic kings.[111] Libraries were a novel idea at this time. Book collections were privately held, with the closest precedent being Aristotle's collection at the Lyceum.[112] Though the product of royal patronage, the library was accessible to literate Greeks. This is the Alexandrian version of the "open city." The political system was closed off, but there was ample intellectual foment. This is a key distinction from the politically boisterous intellectual milieu in Athens. More than just a series of holdings, the complex gained prestige across the Hellenistic world for its scholarship. It was a site of scientific advancements that had famous philosophers, astronomers, theologians, and other experts in residence. The library recruited them from across the city network. It offered "free meals, high salaries, no taxes to pay, very pleasant surroundings, good lodgings and servants."[113]

In sum, human flows in ancient world cities were complex. There were good reasons for voluntary migration, but the Hellenistic states assembled populations coercively. The largest deportations uprooted hundreds of thousands of people in connection with city planning.[114] One problem was convincing them to take the risk of urban life. Alexandria had more deaths than births. Though relatively healthier than most ancient cities, Alexandria had chronic epidemics such as leprosy.[115] Excessive childbearing expectations still endangered urban women, despite Alexandria's improved gender relations.[116] (Women in

109 Ibid.

110 Minna Skafte Jensen, "Homeric Scholarship in Alexandria," in George Hinge and Jens A. Krasilnikoff (eds.), *Alexandria: A Cultural and Religious Melting Pot* (Aarhus: Aarhus University Press, 2009), 80–93, 80.

111 Green, *Alexander to Actium*, 89.

112 Fraser, *Ptolemaic Alexandria*, 320.

113 Cited in Green, *Alexander to Actium*, 87.

114 One notorious transfer involved twelve Greek cities deported to the city of Tigranocerta. Appian said this comprised 300,000 deportees, although the figure may be symbolic. Scheidel, "Creating a Metropolis," 26.

115 Ibid., 18.

116 Scheidel, "Demography," 41.

Ptolemaic Alexandria had property rights, could initiate divorce without personal devastation, and were powerful in the ruling dynasty). Poor harvests meant widespread malnutrition. Still, its population growth was considerable, possibly passing the 100,000 mark by 300 BCE, and the half-million plateau a century later.[117] Overcoming excess mortality to maintain high growth rates required estimated annual immigration of nearly 9000 people.[118] Being governed remained a dangerous proposition. This was even more the case in the city's rural *chôra*.

The Egyptian Hinterlands

Oddly enough, the Ptolemies were not big on founding large cities. Within their empire, Alexandria was a classic primate city in the rank–size distribution, out of proportion with anything else in the empire. It was tenfold larger than Memphis, Ptolemaic Egypt's second city and Egypt's former capital. Thebes and Ptolomais were similarly sized.[119] Alexandria dealt on more equal terms with the leading cities outside its borders while having at times predatory relations with its own broader region.

Egypt was one of the most densely populated areas in the Mediterranean world, with perhaps 4.5 million people.[120] Rather than marshal this human capital toward new grand cities, the Ptolemies embarked on a massive villagization effort. Greeks intensively settled the fertile northern Nile, recreating much of their way of life uneasily alongside native Egyptians. Military settlers called *kleruchs* managed land, leaving labor to hired hands or leasing it out to local peasants.[121] Visible changes included extensive irrigation projects, reclaiming vast tracts of land.[122] Greeks comprised 16 percent of the population in the Egyptian Fayum, according to census figures.[123] Most settlers, however, lived in Alexandria or other nearby cities – absentee management from afar. They imported their most beloved staples: Vines and olives. For the state, the goal was maximal governance from Alexandria. For starters, there was a rural belt called the "land of the Alexandrians" controlled by urban estates.[124] It appears to have been used to bring the Greeks' favorite foods to city markets. But the ruling authorities went much further.

117 Scheidel, "Creating a Metropolis," 15. 118 Ibid., 20.
119 Joseph G. Manning, "Hellenistic Egypt," in Walter Scheidel, Ian Morris, and Richard Saller (eds.), *The Cambridge Economic History of the Greco-Roman World* (Cambridge: Cambridge University Press, 2007), 434–483, 442.
120 Ibid., 441. 121 Rowlandson, "Town and Country in Ptolemaic Egypt," 256.
122 Manning, "Hellenistic Egypt," 441.
123 Rowlandson, "Town and Country in Ptolemaic Egypt," 256.
124 Livia Capponi, "The *Oikos* of Alexandria," in W. V. Harris and Giovanni Ruffini (eds.), *Ancient Alexandria between Egypt and Greece* (Boston: Brill, 2004), 115–124, 115.

Alexandria's relationships with the Egyptian growing lands reveal the Ptolemaic Empire to be a strict command economy. It relied on innovations in administrative bureaucracy and authoritarian monitoring to maximize the revenues that built and revitalized the city. The monarchy headed this exercise in spatial domination, regulating rural output from the cloistered palace district. There is clear evidence of an increasingly impoverished rural population toiling to create surpluses for an urban elite. Virtually all the land in Egypt belonged to the state. The state imposed a dizzying array of rents and taxes on peasants. Papyrus scrolls detailing punitive revenues derived from farming were long and byzantine.[125] Tax collectors were trained to boost morale by simply encouraging laborers not to give up, lest they become "so discouraged that (as sometimes happened) they abandoned their holdings and fled."[126] A missive to collectors instructs them "to put a stop to such things" should "any of them complain." If peasants were "hard pressed because of their rents or completely exhausted," the letter iterates, "you must not let this pass without investigation."[127]

The royal house tightly managed agricultural production from start to finish. The state supplied peasants with seeds, which they agreed to cultivate by oath. Breaking that vow by growing different crops was a serious crime. Peasants toiled under the surveillance of guards representing the interests of the royal family. "They shall compel the oil-makers to work everyday and shall stay beside them," the law in that trade stated.[128] Though not legally slaves, they were effectively captives until the end of the season. Simply put, "any oil-maker who goes elsewhere shall be subject to arrest."[129] This headed off what the Greeks called *anachôrêsis*. It was a kind of mass strike in which peasants deserted en-masse to become nomads or defect to other countries.[130] Real or not, this was not a risk the Ptolemies were willing to take. Alexandria's wealth depended on agricultural output. It imported mountains of grain daily via specialized ships. A decline could destabilize the whole realm. For this reason, there were mercenary garrisons strategically placed in Egypt's administrative districts (*nomes*).

The Nile had fertilized empires for millennia by this point but presented extreme challenges to ancient administrations. Its mercurial water levels necessitated elaborate irrigation systems for mass agriculture. Rostovtzeff's magisterial *The Social & Economic History of the Hellenistic World* offers a

125 See, for example, Roger S. Bagnall and Peter Derow, *The Hellenistic Period: Historical Sources in Translation* (Oxford: Blackwell Publishing, 2004), 181.
126 Walbank, *Hellenistic World*, 106. 127 Cited in ibid.
128 Bagnall and Derow, *Hellenistic Period*, 190. 129 Ibid.
130 Shipley, *Greek World after Alexander*, 195; Walbank, *Hellenistic World*, 116.

glimpse of the virtual conscription required to construct and maintain these massive earthworks absent automated technology:

> Organized work, of course, means compulsory work, and such it has been in Egypt for the purposes of irrigation system[s] from time immemorial, *the whole of the population* with their draught-animals being mobilized at certain times for the common task. So it was in Pharaonic Egypt and so it remained under the Ptolemies.[131]

The need for mass mobilization was compounded by a chronic shortage of labor power for construction, agriculture, and the military.[132] As in core cities, population was power.

This heavy-handedness made for combustible situations. The most ferocious dissent in Egypt was from the countryside. Outside Alexandria there appears to have been no veneer of democracy to channel grievances, although peasants had legal rights. In bad times, Greek land managers – the closest thing to a middle class – took their lives into their own hands when venturing "into" Egypt from Alexandria. One complaint indicative of these dangers alleges attacks by non-Greeks in the city of Memphis: "Some of them had stones in their hands and others sticks, and they tried to force their way in, in order to seize the opportunity to plunder the temple and put me to death because I am a Greek."[133] These tensions were not necessarily from existential racial animosity. In many cases ancient populations tended to accept benevolent outsiders.[134] Class unrest, on the other hand, appears to have grown over time, an apparent inevitability in the Ptolemaic system. Historians contend that these fissures hastened Egypt's decline, as it took a geopolitical backseat to rapidly rising Rome in the second century BCE.[135]

Intercity Relations

The Ptolemies tightly controlled economic activity through a closed currency system and monopolies on the most lucrative goods in the domestic market. They levied heavy customs duties on foreign trade, exports as well as imports. This statism probably stifled many forms of transaction, particularly private exchange. It was less conscientious macroeconomic policy than an all-out

131 M. Rostovtzeff, *The Social & Economic History of the Hellenistic World* (Oxford: Oxford University Press, 1941), 275. Emphasis mine.

132 Dorothy J. Thompson, "The Ptolemies and Egypt," in Andrew Erskine (ed.), *A Companion to the Hellenistic World* (Oxford: Blackwell Publishing, 2003), 105–120, 108.

133 Cited in Shipley, *Greek World after Alexander*, 221.

134 At first, the Macedonian takeover seemed to Egyptians a welcome respite from Achaemenid rule. For much of Asia, life did not change much under the Hellenistic kings. What Alexander's great battles implied for the rank and file was a mere swapping of nobility at the reins. Much of the Persian political system stayed the same.

135 Thompson, "Ptolemies and Egypt," 115.

effort to skim the most possible revenues for the royal coffers.[136] Still, Egypt's immense production potential gave the Ptolemies leverage in global governance.

Rhodes was the most important maritime power among the independent city-states. It retained a critical alliance with the Ptolemies, who helped finance its security as it resisted attacks from imperial commanders. Later, as the Ptolemaic navy weakened, Rhodes in turn patrolled the Aegean, guaranteeing a modicum of mercantile security.[137] These were two core cities benefiting from positive sum economic relations. This is analogous to dyadic relations between the world's leading modern cities. As with the "NyLon" transatlantic relationship between New York and London, what we may call "RHALEX" exemplified intercity interdependence.[138] Rhodes was notable as the only city-state of considerable geopolitical influence in an age of territorial empires. It achieved this through inordinate wealth as a center of commerce. It had a formidable, technologically advanced navy that for a time held hegemony at sea. Just as importantly, Rhodes forged a web of diplomatic agreements with imperial neighbors. It had an additional thicket of private associations across cities that solidified its commercial ties.[139] The archeological evidence for a dyadic "RHALEX" centers on recovered *amphorae* from Hellenistic shipwrecks. Of the 120,000 known Greek *amphorae* stamps, about 80,000 were marked as traveling between Alexandria and Rhodes.[140] This also speaks to the commercial preponderance shared by these cities during their ascendancies. Not much is known about the specific goods traded between these two leading cities, although it is unlikely that Rhodes was self-sufficient in grain, which the Egyptian *chôra* produced in abundance.[141] It is possible, conversely, that goods reached Alexandria from Asia by way of Rhodes.[142]

Slavery was a valuable "commodity" in intercity trade, which wealthy Alexandria had a large market for. Every port had a slave market. The largest was at Delos. In Strabo's words (though his figure is certainly exaggerated), the Delos slave market was "large and wealthy, it could have a turnover of ten thousand slaves a day. From where comes the proverb, 'Merchant, sail in, unload, everything has been sold'."[143]

[136] Fraser, *Ptolemaic Alexandria*, 148. [137] Ibid., 162.

[138] This nomenclature, alongside similar mash ups, is deployed by the Globalization and World Cities (GaWC) project to describe dyadic connectivity between cities.

[139] Vincent Gabrielsen, "The Rhodian Associations and Economic Activity," in Zofia Archibald, John Davies, Vincent Gabrielsen, and G. J. Oliver (eds.), *Hellenistic Economies* (New York: Routledge, 2001), 215–244, 219.

[140] Gibbons, "Shipwrecks and Hellenistic Trade," 292. Since Rhodian amphorae often had two stamps, this could be as low as 40,000, still dwarfing trade elsewhere.

[141] Fraser, *Ptolemaic Alexandria*, 164. [142] Ibid., 168.

[143] Cited in Vincent Gabrielsen, "Piracy and the Slave Trade," in Andrew Erskine (ed.), *A Companion to the Hellenistic World* (Oxford: Blackwell Publishing, 2003), 389–404, 391.

Economic relations were guided by diplomacy, which grew more elaborate. City-states granted awards to citizens of other *poleis*. These could come with material benefits. Private individuals, as well as cities, could enjoy special trading rights. They granted citizenship to one another, as well as sanctuary.[144] City-states typically had these powers available to them despite existing layers of imperial control. *Poleis* took advantage of what freedoms kings offered. Some levels of autonomy always existed, as successor kings engaged in the never-ending rhetoric of restoring the independence of venerable Greek cities from their rivals. Hellenistic kings outwardly supported what the Greeks called *autonomia* for the mainland *poleis*, the Ptolemies included. In practice, these were the successor kings' Monroe Doctrines, meaning no one shall violate the sanctity of smaller states *but us*.[145] Kings did not typically govern the daily activities of cities. Moreover, they counted on city leagues to establish agreements on economic matters. Although none was the geopolitical force of the Delian League, this made them important in setting the rules for trade and finance. In this sense, the *polis* continued into the Roman Empire. Territorial empires grafted themselves on to city structures. They did not replace them.

Conclusion: Spear Won Cities

The cavalier way the Hellenistic kings moved resources around large swaths of the world was justified on Alexander's legacy. Macedonian successors believed in their right to do what they wished in "spear won" territories – even mass deportation. They built a city network partly by force, which was prerequisite as the ancient populous often resisted relocating to population sinks where city life increased their risk of premature death.

When Alexander cast a spear onto the shore in Turkey, he did not have precise knowledge of the territories he was to conquer. Mapping was in its infancy, despite laudatory efforts by geographers and explorers. The things Greeks thought they knew about the Eurasian landmass were continually amended as soldiers marched fretfully forward toward the "end of the world and the great outer sea." There was still the belief that the planet terminated abruptly, though intellectuals posited that it was spherical. The source of the Nile was very much unknown. Alexander thought Africa and Asia comprised one continent.[146] Ancient city networks still lacked innovations in navigation and mapping that later accelerated globalization in the Middle Ages. This makes these high periods of interdependence all the more remarkable for their ability to overcome time and space constraints in a mysterious world.

[144] Gary Reger, "The Economy," in Andrew Erskine (ed.), *A Companion to the Hellenistic World* (Oxford: Blackwell Publishing, 2003), 331–353, 345.

[145] Shipley, *Greek World after Alexander*, 73.

[146] Green, *Hellenistic Age*, 62.

Zuiderhoek conceptualizes the ancient Greco-Roman city as its own category of settlement with analytically distinctive characteristics.[147] The definition for what constitutes an ancient city is fluid, usually falling back on the you-know-it-when-you-see-it eye test. They seem to grow in tandem with their hinterlands and with other cities. The city was an invention that spread around a world that was nomadic. It was the chosen mode of living for those capable of controlling the behavior of others. Greek cities grew with the advent of territorial empires, a relatively novel form of state in Hellenic culture in Alexander's time. "Alexandria-by-Egypt" was a singularly powerful "consumer city" capable of extracting resources from other places. Greek empires' urban roots underpinned waves of urbanization. As we've seen, the number of large cities multiplied, their peak sizes on freakish scales. Those larger cities were in effect empires unto themselves with enhanced spheres of influence. As Zuiderhoek explains:

> Their rise roughly coincided with that of the Hellenistic kingdoms and Carthage and Rome as Mediterranean superpowers. "Top-heavy" urban networks, characterized by a few very large cities next to numerous much smaller ones, are in fact characteristic of pre-modern territorial empires, in which the spending power of rent-seeking political elites encouraged large concentrations of people and resources, leading to the formation of administrative urban giants.[148]

A new type of city emerged in the Greco-Roman world – arguably borrowed from Asia and Mesopotamia. Cities became assemblages of power in international relations. Consumer cities absorbed surpluses from far-flung geographies. Of the aforementioned cities we turn attention to Rome, which in the first century BCE reduced Egypt to a vassal state, and ultimately a province.

Polybius' *Histories* documents this swift rise, asserting that "in less than fifty-three years nearly the whole world was overcome and fell under the single dominion of Rome, a thing the like of which had never happened before."[149] Rome was the ultimate consumer city, the heart of an urban network that absorbed world resources on unprecedented scale and scope.

[147] Arjan Zuiderhoek, *The Ancient City* (Cambridge: Cambridge University Press, 2017), 4.
[148] Ibid., 35. [149] Polybius, *The Histories* (Cambridge: Loeb Classical Library, 1922), book vi.

5 City Networks in the Roman Empire

Rome's was a politics of all five senses. At the end of the first century BCE it was the world's unrivaled "maximum city." The city's ferocity mirrored the collapsing Republic, in the midst of two centuries of ceaseless civil wars and untenable expansion. It was the palpitating heart of a state bursting at the seams in its last decades. The city inhaled and exhaled to the rhythm of far-flung Mediterranean geopolitics. Generations of economic dislocation left the hinterlands with little recourse but to migrate en-masse to the city, its population peaking at one million. Violent political factions left some contemplating evacuation. Early death from disease negated the choice for others. Conquests abroad formed the context for the city's crowded multistory warrens, its narrow filth-drenched streets, haphazardly crisscrossed by wooden buttresses used to keep its infested fire-prone tenements upright.[1] Juvenal's *Satire*, written in the early second century, constructs a scene of what walking through the city might have felt like from the perspective of a friend:

> If social duty calls, the rich man will be carried above the heads of the crowd by his tall Ligurian litter bearers. As the people give way he will be swiftly transported to his destination, and, inside the litter, he will read or write or sleep, for the litter with the windows closed induces sleep. Without any personal strain, he will arrive before us. Whereas we, although we hurry, are blocked by a wave of people in front of us. And the great crowd behind crushes us. One man hits me with his elbow, another with a hard pole; one man strikes me on the head with a wood beam, another with a wine jar. My legs are covered with thick mud. Then, on all sides, big feet step on me, and a nail from a soldier's boot pierces my toe.[2]

Republican Rome lacked most of the over-scaled buildings associated with the Principate founded by Augustus (63 BCE–14 CE). Even the city's core temples suffered neglect, owing to civil unrest and resources diverted to

[1] Diane Favro, *The Urban Image of Augustan Rome* (Cambridge: Cambridge University Press, 1996), 46.

[2] Cited in Jo-Ann Shelton (ed.), *As the Romans Did: A Sourcebook in Roman Social History*, 2nd ed. (Oxford: Oxford University Press, 1998), 69.

conflicts. Facades flaked off of sacred spaces. Its state-sponsored gardens went unattended. Population growth strained the city's vaunted aqueducts and much revered *cloaca maxima* (the "great sewer"). The muddy unpaved streets, choked with refuse and feces tossed from upper floor apartments (*insulae*), were extremely dangerous. Muggers haunted the streets at night. Though few pedestrians ventured out after dark, horse-drawn commercial traffic made the streets so noisy that it was impossible to rest. By day, malnourished people lingered in the heat along public benches. Sparse restaurants lining the streets, which fed the proletariat, had less food to sell in wartime. The urban working classes hard won grain distribution program, to which 300,000 free citizen men were entitled, was also under stress. Rome was not self-sufficient, relying on imports from around the war-torn Mediterranean. There were riots in response to conditions. Street violence between the factions supporting rival noble warlords heightened the tensions.[3]

The city in the late Republic probably housed 750,000 people.[4] Scholars widely agree that the peak population exceeded one million in the early Principate (the first century CE), based on extrapolations from the number of grain recipients, and on the scale of its archeological footprint. It may have been twice the size of any other city in its network.[5] To reiterate, population estimates for ancient cities are inexact, but what's certain is that the city grew largely in tandem with its expanding empire. For starters, the city could not have existed on this scale without massive seaborne imports, starting with grain, but entailing varied nonfood items. Put bluntly, live bodies were a crucial resource that the city had to import. Rome was a definitive "population sink," with high death rates requiring constant migration, voluntary or otherwise.[6] Migration into unhealthy cities halted broader population growth in Italy.[7] Literary records attest to influxes of people speaking myriad languages – a true world city. Growing linguistic diversity may even explain a decline in the popularity of spoken plays in favor of theatrical miming.

The Roman Empire's population peaked at the same time as the city, reaching between sixty and seventy million people, an estimated quarter of

3 This account of street life was pieced together with the help of two vivid books in this area, Favro, *Urban Image of Augustan Rome*, ch. 2 and Jeremy Hartnett, *The Roman Street: Urban Life and Society in Pompeii, Herculaneum, and Rome* (Cambridge: Cambridge University Press, 2017), ch. 1.

4 O. F. Robinson, *Ancient Rome: City Planning and Administration* (New York: Routledge, 1992), 8.

5 Gregory S. Aldrete, *Daily Life in the Roman City: Rome, Pompeii, and Ostia* (Norman: University of Oklahoma Press, 2008), 21.

6 Scheidel, "Demography," 49.

7 Saskia Hin, "Population," in Harriet I. Flower (ed.), *The Cambridge Companion to the Roman Republic* (Cambridge: Cambridge University Press, 2004), 149–166, 156.

the world's population.[8] The Romans didn't have anything resembling modern cartography. They never saw proportionate spatial representations of their territory, stretching at times from Britain to Iraq. Most importantly they had full control of the territories surrounding the Mediterranean. A large public illustration displayed in the heart of the city during Augustus' reign appears to have depicted the sea as a riverine highway.[9] They referred to it as "our sea" (*Mare Nostrum*), a more or less accurate designation after significant victories over pirates by Pompey (106–48 BCE). This ambitious depiction of the *orbis terrarum* (the inhabited landmass) featured hundreds of cities connected by roads, with Rome prominently displayed near the center. Its intent was to give the Roman public a sense of the city's place in the world, a remarkable piece of Augustan propaganda.[10] The map extended to India and the China Sea, societies with which Rome had trading contacts.

Rome did not govern this territory through intensive bureaucracy in the Ur III mold (see Chapter 2). Its central administration was one-twentieth the size of Han China's, a contemporary empire of comparable size.[11] As we will see, Rome's was an urban empire, reliant on a network of existing and newly created cities to carry out the task of governing. Cities collected its taxes and recruited its soldiers.[12] They managed commerce along the Empire's land and sea networks, extracting resources from their hinterlands. They were the incubators of "Romanization," a form of soft power that was vital to maintaining class rigidity and preventing rebellions. There were no fully independent city-states in the Roman world – other than perhaps Rome itself – but cities were self-governing in local matters beyond their critical role in managing the Empire.[13]

As in all other ancient high periods, agriculture formed the basis of the Roman economy. Land formed the basis of elite wealth. The intensification of agriculture in slave-driven *latifundia* corresponded with the demands of sedentary living on unprecedented scales. Cities grew much larger than they had during the heyday of the Greek *poleis*, exceeding even Hellenistic cities in scale.[14] The empire-wide population possibly approached a 20 percent

[8] Scheidel, "Demography," 47.

[9] The map does not survive, but a thirteenth century copy is likely based on it. See Mary Beard, *SPQR: A History of Ancient Rome* (New York: W. W. Norton, 2015), 364.

[10] Claude Nicolet, *Space, Geography, and Politics in the Early Roman Empire* (Ann Arbor: University of Michigan Press, 1991), 96.

[11] Peter Garnsey and Richard Saller, *The Roman Empire: Economy, Society, and Culture*, 2nd ed. (Oakland: University of California Press, 2015), 35.

[12] Ibid., 45. [13] Ibid., 42.

[14] Alan Bowman and Andrew Wilson, "Introduction," in Alan Bowman and Andrew Wilson (eds.), *Settlement, Urbanization, and Population* (Oxford: Oxford University Press, 2012), 1–14, 13.

urbanization rate, though estimates vary widely.[15] Between seven and ten million people likely lived in cities, though peasants outside of cities labored under urban elites.[16] There were over 1,800 cities by the second century CE, most with populations in the low thousands, with several exceeding 100,000. Alexandria persisted as a major world city through this period, shipping Egyptian foodstuffs to Rome following much the same exploitive process as the Ptolemies. Cities, including smaller ones, christened more and larger buildings than in eras past using the *liturgy* system, committing noble wealth to public undertakings.[17]

All of this helped maintain Rome's "consumer city" status in the early Principate, but another question precedes it. How did Rome, of all places, emerge as the center of an empire with global reach? The answer lies in its ability to do what Athens could not: Forge a durable alliance of cities capable of projecting unmatched military manpower. To this we turn.

Italian City Network

According to state-sponsored myth, the Romans were the descendants of Trojan warriors under the leadership of Aeneas, seeking refuge after the fall of Troy. Romulus, the city's founder, killed his brother in a dispute over where to locate the new settlement and became the first city builder to whom Julius Caesar (abortively) and Augustus would liken themselves.

From there came a series of bloody power struggles analogous to those of the late Republic, not coincidently as Virgil and Livy elaborated on Rome's history in the *Aeneid* and the *History of Rome*, respectively. Women were integral to this precarious early state building. They populated the new city-state through their mass abduction from rival tribes. They stoically accepted forcible marriages to Rome's male settlers and negotiated mergers with the other Italian tribes. The suicide of Lucretia after her assault by a member of the ruling family sparked the rebellion that led to the Republic. These unverified myths emerged centuries after they supposedly occurred, just as Rome became a major force in the Mediterranean. They conjure simpler times of agrarian values and female piety. These narratives were bound up in the legal and built environments carefully constructed by Augustus along the lines of "restoration."[18]

What is certain about the emergence of Rome? There was a settlement in Rome's location by the end of the eleventh century, well before the time of

[15] Andrew Wilson, "City Sizes and Urbanization in the Roman Empire," in Alan Bowman and Andrew Wilson (eds.), *Settlement, Urbanization, and Population* (Oxford: Oxford University Press, 2012), 161–195, 191.

[16] Ibid. [17] Ibid., 177. [18] Beard, *SPQR*, 100.

Rome's mythological founding in 753 BCE.[19] This was just one of many emerging city-states in its vicinity which were in regular skirmishes. By the fourth century, Rome was a heavyweight among Mediterranean city-states, with a size and capability on par with the larger *poleis* in the Greek world.

Given harsh local conditions, it seems unlikely that a city of unprecedented size would take root in Rome's location. The agricultural capacity of its hinterlands were, at best, no better than other cities in the Mediterranean that did not achieve hegemony.[20] Irregular rainfall severely undermined crop production. Agricultural areas suffered from summer droughts, with the hope of sufficient rains in the autumn.[21] Elevated areas in Italy limited the amount of flatlands available for large-scale agriculture.[22] The distribution of this finite amount of land was central to class conflict in the late Republic, and to the vexing question of troop resettlement after Rome's major wars.[23] There was a massive overuse of the natural resources in the city's vicinity. This caused deforestation and drastic soil erosion.[24] Mountains disrupted land-based communication and exchange. Making matters worse, the climate was highly malarial, contributing to Rome's horrid urban "population sink." The Tiber's flooding was frequently disastrous. Summer was the peak death season for rich and poor alike. Life expectancy from birth was as low as twenty years.[25]

This exacerbated the need for migration that shaped Rome's cosmopolitan character.[26] Many migrants were forcibly resettled in the city as slaves abducted in Rome's overseas conquests. Others came voluntarily seeking economic opportunity or access to grain distribution. Still others were displaced by the devalorization of peasant farming.[27] In this light, environmental scarcity forced this former backwater to look reluctantly outward throughout its history. Waterborne travel was the most significant long-term environmental advantage that Rome had over neighboring cities. Scholars of Italy's physical geography find a correlation between the scale of river systems and

19 Aldrete, *Daily Life in the Roman City*, 9.
20 Nicholas Purcell, "Urbanism," in Alessandro Barchiesi and Walter Scheidel (eds.), *The Oxford Handbook of Roman Studies* (Oxford: Oxford University Press, 2010), 579–591, 581.
21 Garnsey and Saller, *Roman Empire*, 20.
22 Simon Stoddart, "The Physical Geography of Republican Italy," in Nathan Rosenstein and Robert Morstein-Marx (eds.), *A Companion to the Roman Republic* (Oxford: Blackwell Publishing, 2006), 102–119, 110.
23 Jochen Bleicken, *Augustus: The Biography* (New York: Penguin, 2016), 264.
24 Robert Sallares, "Ecology," in Walter Scheidel, Ian Morris, and Richard Saller (eds.), *The Cambridge Economic History of the Greco-Roman World* (Cambridge: Cambridge University Press, 2007), 15–37, 24.
25 John R. Patterson, "The City of Rome," in Nathan Rosenstein and Robert Morstein-Marx (eds.), *A Companion to the Roman Republic* (Oxford: Blackwell Publishing, 2006), 345–361, 351.
26 Stoddart, "Physical Geography of Republican Italy," 114.
27 Patterson, "City of Rome," 351.

the size of the accompanying ancient settlements.[28] The Tiber was landlocked Rome's global gateway. In founding the city near a broad bend in the river, on a defensible inland hill, our mythical Romulus was on to something. This gave the city harbor access even without a seaport.[29] In the words of Livy's *History of Rome*:

> Not without cause did gods and men select this place for establishing our City – with its healthful hills; its convenient river, by which crops may be floated down from the midland regions and foreign commodities brought up; its sea, near enough for use, yet not exposing us, by too great propinquity, to peril from foreign fleets; a situation in the heart of Italy – a spot, in short, of a nature uniquely adapted for the expansion of a city.[30]

Rome was a fully formed city-state by the seventh century BCE, a relative latecomer among Latin cities. Although details are murky, it was eventually able to deal on equal terms with its city-state neighbors through a combination of force and diplomacy. There is extensive research suggesting that a mature "city-state culture" emerged in Latium (Central Italy), with Rome in a dominant position.[31] There was fierce resistance to this, with the Latin League of cities organized by rival Tusculum to counter Roman power in the 400s. A series of wars led to an alliance in 338 that is reminiscent of the Delian League (see Chapter 3), with Rome as first among equals in a peace agreement that was not entirely punitive. Rome did not enslave or destroy neighboring cities as it would outside Latium. Numerous Latin cities were restricted in their activities but, consequentially, their residents received Roman citizenship.[32] Put in perspective, Rome had a population of perhaps 35,000, while the typical Latin city numbered 5,000.[33] These cities had defined urban centers with recognized hinterlands within their spheres of influence. Rome's territory was by far the largest in Latium, stretching to the Tyrrhenian Sea. In ancient time and space, this must have felt something like the United States controlling the Atlantic seaboard with gradual westward aims.

Rome's population advantage was put to use in the Latin Wars. It is impossible to know for sure what considerations underscored Rome's decision to extend citizenship across Latium. The profound effect was to take the alliance structure further than anything that occurred in mainland Greece, creating binding intercity governance arrangements. Cities were self-governing but

28 Stoddart, "Physical Geography of Republican Italy," 113.
29 Aldrete, *Daily Life in the Roman City*, 12.
30 Livy, *The History of Rome* (Cambridge: Harvard University Press, 1924), book v.
31 See Tim J. Cornell, "The City-States in Latium," in Mogens Herman Hansen (ed.), *A Comparative Study of Thirty City-State Cultures* (Copenhagen: The Royal Danish Academy of Arts and Letters, 2000), 207–228.
32 Ibid., 213. 33 Ibid., 215.

had to provide soldiers. This sidestepped the infighting that occurred among Greek *poleis*, increasing Rome's manpower advantage. Italian allies provided three-fifths of Rome's soldiers by the second century BCE.[34] "So," notes Purcell, "between 340 and 180 BCE Rome became a single state with numerous urban centers."[35] The Italian city network crystallized.

These cities retained most of their city-state characteristics. Rome led nominally by agreement. It did not impose building schemes on the cities in its network. However, there was considerable aesthetic regionalization, and even nascent globalization via long distance networking.[36] Archeological evidence suggests these cities shared building styles, planning features, preferred materials, languages, and administrative approaches.[37] Rome had rudimentary elements of its future self, such as the Forum, first paved around 650.[38] Similar features were also evident in the Latin cities of Gabii and Ardea, among others, and the Etruscan cities of Caere, Tarquinii, and Veii.[39] Roman colonization facilitated this transference of ideas, additionally conferring Roman laws on cities in its orbit. Latin, Etruscan, and Italic cultures intermingled in cities under Roman hegemony, creating what one scholar described as a "melting pot" of "open cities," to apply modern parlance.[40] Critically, Rome's alliance enabled it to repel invading tribes. Regional integration in Latium took hold more or less independently of outside coercion.[41] By the 500s the city had substantial monumental construction. This was coupled with economic sophistication comparable to other leading Mediterranean centers.[42]

None of this is to say that lasting Latin alliances reduced warfare.[43] Instead they projected conflict outward, setting the conditions for battles of historic magnitude. This was an extremely warlike culture, encouraging competition between nobles for *virtus* (manhood) and *dignitas* (achievement). More Roman citizens meant larger armies. More city-state protectorates meant more pretexts for "defensive" wars.[44] In short, Rome's expanding network of cities formed the basis for its ability to project power. The Battle of Cannae in the

[34] Keith Hopkins, *Conqueror and Slaves* (Cambridge: Cambridge University Press, 1978), 31.
[35] Purcell, "Urbanism," 584. [36] Cornell, "City-States in Latium," 211. [37] Ibid., 212.
[38] John E. Stambaugh, *The Ancient Roman City* (Baltimore: Johns Hopkins University Press, 1988), 14.
[39] Cornell, "City-States in Latium," 212. [40] Ibid., 223.
[41] A glaring potential exception was the Gallic sack of 390 BCE, but the Romans notably rebuilt the city quickly after paying a ransom, resuming hegemony. In general, Rome had relative security in its neighborhood.
[42] Purcell, "Urbanism," 581.
[43] The last major conflict between Italian cities, the Social Wars in the early first century BCE, cost perhaps 300,000 lives according to Roman sources. The result was the mass extension of Roman citizenship to the defeated Italian allies. This suggests that these cities retained independent interests yet seem to have sought greater integration with Rome by this time as opposed to separatism.
[44] The Romans viewed all their wars as defensive, no matter how farfetched.

second Punic War in 216 BCE resulted in 40,000 to 70,000 Romans dead at the hands of Hannibal's invading army in one afternoon.[45] The Roman legions at this stage were less notable for decisive victories than for their ability to sustain losses. Rome expelled Hannibal from Italy in a war of attrition, and successfully invaded Africa. It assumed hegemony in the Mediterranean with Carthage's defeat.

This was not master planned. Roman commanders competed for short-term glory. There was no blueprint for Mediterranean dominance. Rather it was achieved through a series of wars whose circumstances were rarely under Roman control. It is worth reminding ourselves that this occurred over centuries. In that light there is a pattern visible over the *longue durée*.

Now that Rome was in this position, environmental conditions again came to the fore. Horden and Purcell's magisterial book *The Corrupting Sea* conceives of the Mediterranean as a social entity whose ecology fostered the connectivity needed for mass urbanization:

> Carthage, Athens, Rome, Alexandria, Antioch, Constantinople, Marseille, Cordoba, Barcelona, Pisa, Florence, Venice … the list could be extended a long way, and its items could be so ordered as to stand for a quite effective summary of many aspects of the Mediterranean past. After all, the Mediterranean has probably been the most durably and densely urbanized region in world history. No other comparable area can boast so many towns and cities of such antiquity.[46]

They go on to highlight the importance of seaborne trade in making early megacities possible, which require "essential supplies from far afield and from a number of different directions."[47] They note that Rome's grain supply came from "Gaul, Spain, North Africa, Sicily, Sardinia, Egypt, Cyprus and the Chersonese, as well as Italy."[48] Their nuanced history of the Mediterranean explores its series of readily navigable shipping lanes in which coastlines were visible for sailors with limited technology.[49] This enabled seafarers to reach secluded microclimates like "frogs around a marsh," recalling Plato's words. Seaborne transit seldom required venturing beyond sight of the coast for very long. When it did happen, this terrified crews. Instead ships tended to hug the shore, making do with simple lists (*periplus*) of way stations with estimated distances measured in time. It was cheaper for Rome to import grain from the aforementioned places than it was to transport it by cart from beyond a hundred mile radius.[50] This produced a distorted but logical meaning of proximity for Roman intellectuals. Strabo's *Geography* couches Rome's

[45] Mary Beard asserts that this figure entailed "something at the level of a hundred deaths a minute." Beard, *SPQR*, 180.

[46] Peregrine Horden and Nicholas Purcell, *The Corrupting Sea: A Study of Mediterranean History* (Oxford: Blackwell, 2000), 90. Ellipsis theirs.

[47] Ibid., 112. [48] Ibid. [49] Ibid., 137. [50] Scott, *Against the Grain*, 134.

location in more expansive terms than Livy. The city was "naturally well suited to hegemony, because it surpasses the countries that surround it in both the valor of its people and in its size, but it can also easily avail itself of their services *because it is close to them*."[51] By "close" he is referring to Greece and Libya. Over time Romans developed far-ranging social and regional consciousness.

This process culminated with the founding of cities outside Italy. Characteristic of ancient cities, these were painful undertakings. They required the deportation of Romans, the expulsion of existing inhabitants, or mergers reminiscent of *synoikisms* – forced population transfers. Native property was frequently parceled out to new colonists.[52] Julius Caesar's (100–44 CE) plan to deport 80,000 people from Rome to overseas colonies demonstrates both Rome's vociferous effort to expand its urban network and the state's powers of displacement.[53] It also reflected overpopulation after generations of haphazard expansion. Rome was a distinctly urban society early on, associating cities with civilization. During the Latin expansion the Romans were leery of leaving tribes like the mountain dwelling Samnites beyond administrative control.[54] This reflects a pattern of organizing defeated populations into consolidated settlements.[55] From there, the state could carry out the two most important functions demanded of cities: Tax collection and army recruitment. Colonists deserted if the lands in new settlements were inadequate. These towns resultantly struggled to maintain population. Some Roman colonies were completely abandoned.[56]

From here it is important to distinguish between the two main types of cities. First, *coloniae* were towns settled originally by Roman citizens. They lived under municipal laws modeled after Rome. *Municipia* had greater local autonomy, replete with local magistrates. *Municipia* in Italy after the Social Wars (91–88 BCE) enjoyed the best of both worlds, local autonomy with full citizenship. Beyond Italy the Romans were highly selective in awarding citizenship, creating a privileged elite across the Empire. *Municipia* were organized as a source of Roman power. These statuses eventually became blurred, with provincials preferring *municipia* status. Cities had legally designated territory (*pomerium*) beyond their urban limits, analogous to the Greek *chôra*. Although the lived experiences were decidedly rural in the Roman Empire, the city dominated the countryside by design. As much as Roman literature could lionize agrarian self-sufficiency, urban elites pitilessly

51 Strabo, *Geography*, book vi. Emphasis mine.
52 Purcell, "Urbanism," 583.
53 As with much of Julius Caesar's plans for Rome, they were halted by his assassination.
54 Stambaugh, *Ancient Roman City*, 19.
55 Ray Laurence, Simon Esmonde Cleary, and Gareth Sears, *The City in the Roman West c. 250 BC–c. AD 250* (Cambridge: Cambridge University Press, 2011), 25.
56 Ibid., 38.

extracted surpluses from the hinterlands. Cities "taught the more savage how to live under forms of government," according to Strabo.[57]

Notably the radical reformer Gaius Gracchus proposed the first *colonia* outside Italy – over the rubble of Carthage – as the peasantry faced unprecedented economic stress.[58]

Conquerors and Slaves: The Agrarian Crisis

"The nobles began to be alarmed," wrote Plutarch in his matter-of-fact biography on Gaius and Tiberius Gracchus.[59] The lives of the famed reformist siblings of the late Republic ended in rapacious murders. Julius Caesar, like the Gracchi, proposed land redistribution – meeting a similar fate. Through the eyes of the urban nobility this was as close as it got to revolution, in theory upending class relations in a society where land was the ultimate source of propertied wealth.

Rome's conquests changed the Italian economy drastically.

Consider the policy changes that gained traction for Gaius Gracchus (c. 154–121 BCE), which would have significantly restructured the ossified social order of the Republic. In the words of Plutarch:

> Of the laws which he proposed by way of gratifying the people and overthrowing the Senate, one was agrarian, and divided public land among the poor citizens . . . another concerned the allies, and gave the Italians equal suffrage rights with Roman citizens; another related to the supplies of grain, and lowered the market price to the poor.[60]

This alludes to the bleak conditions in a society where 80 percent of the population merely subsisted.[61] There is evidence that the allied cities in Italy sought greater inclusion. The big picture is that the forced migration of slaves into Italy displaced the free Italian peasantry. The number of enslaved captives grew with the scale of warfare. The Romans took 25,000 slaves in the first Punic War, 85,000 in the second. Aemelius Paullus' destructive Greek conquests took 150,000 from Epirus alone in 167.[62] Combined with other methods of acquiring slaves – such as recovering exposed infants in Rome's streets or forced breeding – it is certain that the slave trade was much expanded in the late Republic. Its wars enriched the elite but harmed the free poor.

Statistics corroborate the Gracchi's anecdotal experiences. Rich and poor alike understood the crisis in the countryside. Tiberius Gracchus' (163–133 BCE) pro-poor fervor reportedly derived from a trip through the Tuscan

57 Strabo, *Geography*, book ii. 58 Purcell, "Urbanism," 585.

59 Plutarch, *Parallel Lives* (Cambridge: Loeb Classical Library, 1921), vol. x. 60 Ibid.

61 Mary T. Boatwright, *Hadrian and the Cities of the Roman Empire* (Princeton: Princeton University Press, 2000), 3.

62 Philip Kay, *Rome's Economic Revolution* (Oxford: Oxford University Press, 2014), 178.

countryside, which the peasantry had deserted. He found "barbarian slaves" tilling the soil in their place.[63] The former were left "houseless and homeless" to "wander about with their wives and children."[64] For Tiberius, Rome's overseas conquests generated vast wealth that enriched the senatorial strata at the expense of "the men who fight and die for Italy."[65] In sum, the question for Tiberius was how to equitably distribute the resources Rome expropriated in its expansionist wars.

Class conflict was permanently endemic to Rome's social fabric. Plebeians staged mass walkouts from the city in 494 BCE under stress from debt servitude. The Twelve Tables laws – an effort to make the rules transparent – were one result of the centuries-long Conflict of the Orders. Another result was the creation of tribunes to represent the people in government. Tribunes carried significant enough power that patricians renounced their noble status to run for this office. Plebeians eventually became eligible for consulships in the Senate. Walkouts were a constant threat for two centuries, leading to expanded suffrage. By the late Republic, patrician status amounted to "the right to hold a few ancient priesthoods and to wear a particular form of fancy footwear" as Mary Beard put it.[66] However, there remained astonishingly high wealth requirements to enter the Senate: One million sesterces in Augustus' time. This was more than a thousand fold above a typical soldier's annual salary, which itself was substantial at the time. Members of the equestrian order, the next rung down, had to have 400,000 sesterces.

Keith Hopkins' classic *Conquerors and Slaves* captures just how dramatically class tensions worsened by the Gracchi's time in the second century BCE. Perpetual warfare called rural smallholders away from their land for extended tours. They frequently returned to find their farms confiscated by creditors in what amounted to massive land acquisitions from the urban elite in Rome.[67] It was an ancient form of what David Harvey calls "accumulation by dispossession." Liturgical building projects in cities were financed from rural surpluses squeezed out of newly formed *latifundia*, the large-scale plantations that harnessed the power of "unfree labor."[68] This exacerbated the predatory relations between city and country upon which the urban archipelago thrived. Hopkins describes the shift from peasantry to slavery in bold terms:

> Only a handful of human societies can properly be called "slave societies", if by slave society we mean a society in which slaves play an important part in production and

[63] Plutarch, *Parallel Lives*, vol. x. [64] Ibid. [65] Ibid. [66] Beard, *SPQR*, 147.

[67] Hopkins, *Conqueror and Slaves*, 4.

[68] As Kehoe points out, "much of the wealth gained from agriculture was spent on public building." Dennis P. Kehoe, "The Early Roman Empire: Production," in Walter Scheidel, Ian Morris, and Richard Saller (eds.), *The Cambridge Economic History of the Greco-Roman World* (Cambridge: Cambridge University Press, 2007), 543–591, 550.

form a high proportion (say over twenty percent) of the population. There are only two well established cases from antiquity: classical Athens and Roman Italy.[69]

The importation of slaves abducted in conquests increased markedly in the first and second century. There may have been an influx of four million slaves during these centuries. Slaves accounted for perhaps one-third of Italy's population.[70] This displaced 1.5 million peasants over just one 8-year span from 88 to 80 BCE, half their total population.[71] Roman leaders resettled landless farmers in new colonies in attempts to tidily deal with unemployment while freeing up land for acquisition.[72] The mass enlistment of peasants in the army served these ends as well.[73]

Conditions in *latifundia* were particularly hard on the slaves forced to replace evicted peasants. Apuleius' novel *The Golden Ass* describes mill slaves in the countryside:

> Their skins were seamed all over with the marks of old floggings, as you could see through the holes in their ragged shirts that shaded rather than covered their backs; but some wore only loin cloths. They had letters marked on their foreheads, and half-shaved heads and irons on their legs.[74]

Slaves had high upfront costs, but, in Hopkins' words, "were forcibly imported aliens who were exploited to a degree and in a way in which citizens would not allow."[75] Some cases in point: Columella's writing for aristocratic consumption asserts that "there is no better method of maintaining control over even the most worthless of men than demanding hard labor."[76] Columella recommended personal inspections to make sure "they are securely chained," rather than trusting foremen to do the job of fastening them to secure quarters after hours.[77] Slaves were routinely flogged. Male owners raped women slaves. In one macabre instance a friend of Augustus fed his slave to eels for the sake of enjoyment.[78] This horrified the emperor but even he felt legally powerless to punish the killing. Beyond these perverse expressions of power relations, the economics of slave dependence led to poor conditions. The potentially high cost of slaves incentivized their captors to force them to work longer hours with fewer days off to rest.[79] Imported slaves were smaller in number than the emigrating peasants they replaced, requiring more labor to maximize profitability. Slaves took part in the politics of desertion despite tight monitoring. For example, the "rebellion" led by Spartacus began as an attempt among

[69] Hopkins, *Conqueror and Slaves*, 99.
[70] Walter Scheidel, "Human Mobility in Italy, II: The Slave Population," *The Journal of Roman Studies* 95 (2005), 64–79, 64.
[71] Hopkins, *Conqueror and Slaves*, 16. [72] Ibid., 36. [73] Ibid., 30.
[74] Apuleius, *The Golden Ass* (New York: Farrar, Straus, and Giroux, 1979), 202.
[75] Hopkins, *Conqueror and Slaves*, 112. [76] Cited in Shelton, *As the Romans Did*, 169.
[77] Cited in ibid. [78] Ibid., 175. [79] Hopkins, *Conqueror and Slaves*, 111.

slaves in Italy to return to their home countries rather than change the Italian power structure.

The central feature of the Gracchan reforms was to distribute the unused state lands (*ager publicus*) to the poor. This as rich landlords expanded their holdings by rapidly acquiring these spaces. In response, the Gracchi sought to enforce limits on estate sizes.[80] Their message notably resonated in the Roman metropolis, the only site of electoral politics on matters affecting all Italy. This suggests that the lower classes were aware of what was happening in the countryside and felt connected to it. A case in point, the Gracchi faced the masses during their public speeches rather than addressing the assembled senators, as was tradition in Roman politics.[81] The end result was that the well-positioned urban elite took possession of most *ager publicus* in what amounts to a wave of privatization.[82] This was an age of gigantism in villa architecture, where the nobility temporarily retreated from Rome to manage the rural sources of their wealth. The Gracchi did succeed in cementing the grain distribution program in Rome.[83] Their remarkable achievement wrought important changes in the city. Dispossessed farmers fled to Rome in large numbers, drawn in part by the promise of free grain. This placed further stress on the hinterlands as large numbers of farmers went from producers to consumers of grain.

There are no precise annual censuses for Rome, but Julius Caesar and Augustus were clearly worried about overpopulation, evidenced in their efforts to create colonies and reduce the grain rolls. What's clear is that unimaginably bad conditions forced farmers to abandon their land for cities, mostly Rome itself. Peasantries living in specialized "agro-towns" abandoned these settlements for larger cities. Leaders in smaller towns appealed to the Senate to stop this outmigration, lest they become entirely deserted. Colonization efforts created dozens of new towns to moderate the flow of urban migration.[84] This uprooting could be harsh. Hopkins reminds us that "peasants were unlikely to walk three hundred or more kilometers from their ancestral homes in central Italy, into new and often hostile territory, unless they were pushed hard."[85] None of this countered the prevailing trends. Modern population estimates suggest that Rome grew rapidly during the agrarian crisis, increasing four-fold from 150,000 to 600,000.[86]

80 Kay, *Rome's Economic Revolution*, 163.
81 Plutarch, *Parallel Lives*, vol. x.
82 Kay, *Rome's Economic Revolution*, 187.
83 For the sake of brevity I mention the Gracchi in tandem. It is worth clarifying that their careers in power did not overlap. The younger Gaius took over as leader for the reform agenda after his brother's assassination.
84 Hopkins, *Conqueror and Slaves*, 57.
85 Ibid.
86 Kay, *Rome's Economic Revolution*, 182.

To summarize, we see a chain reaction of interrelated global forces (conquest, migration, inequality) shaping local ones (rural dispossession), conspiring to place enormous stress on the city. This was the political-economic context for the rise of warlords competing for power – for example, Sulla, Crassus, Pompey, Caesar, Antony, and Octavian (later Augustus). For our purposes, global forces set the stage for the squalid, entropic, deteriorating city that was late Republican Rome. Livy records that Hellenistic kings reveled in mocking the capital city of their future conquerors, which "was not yet beautified in either its public places or its private districts."[87] Rome's Republican elite lamented their city's condition as their global consciousness grew. Rome built haphazardly, lacking the rational Hippodamian street plan of Hellenistic cities and its own colonies. Cicero (106–43 BCE) compared Rome unfavorably to the large city of Capua. "When they consider Rome," he opined, "placed on hills and valleys, and with its balcony's and overhangs, its streets which aren't the best, its alleys which are really narrow – they will laugh and disparage us."[88]

Refugees from the agrarian crisis had more serious problems. There were too few jobs for the growing poor population. This prompted the literate elite to lament the influx of "the idle, the impoverished and the reckless of all Italy" seeking handouts.[89] Once respectable working class Romans turned to thievery, joining the growing numbers of muggers on the streets.[90] Rising housing demand prompted more shoddily constructed *insulae*, often exceeding seven floors in height, despite the safety risks. Rents soared, further devouring the limited wages of the city's laboring classes.[91] A case in point, Cicero was a leading slumlord. "Two of my buildings have fallen down, and the rest have large cracks," he quipped, seemingly unbothered. "Not only the tenants, but even the mice have moved out!"[92] The tremendous concentration of late Republican wealth became apparent in the city's first outsized monumental construction. The lesser nobility owned mansions rivaling the leading houses of previous generations. Warlords carried out their rivalries with namesake public construction, for example the Theater of Pompey and Caesar's Forum Iulium. However, Rome's most iconic construction occurred under the Principate.

[87] Cited in Diane Favro, "Making Rome a World City," in Karl Galinsky (ed.), *The Cambridge Companion to the Age of Augustus* (Cambridge: Cambridge University Press, 2005), 234–263, 234.
[88] Cited in Hartnett, *Roman Street*, 27. [89] Patterson, "City of Rome," 351.
[90] Favro, *Urban Image of Augustan Rome*, 29. [91] Ibid.
[92] Shelton, *As the Romans Did*, 64.

Augustus the City Builder: Revolution and Restoration

"I found Rome of mud brick," said Augustus, "I leave you a city of marble."[93] Augustus was Rome's most important city builder. Not simply for the structures he commissioned, but for ushering in the Principate that fostered a building spree across the Mediterranean world for generations. His enigmatic political career entailed many layers of reinvention. It was a personal reinvention, moderating his spree of political murders – "proscriptions" – in the Republic's violent last days. It was a global reinvention, seeking out a *modus vivendi* between the Empire, cities, and the army. For Rome it was a physical reconstruction to reflect the new political order that did away with the fractured Republican oligarchy, a marble microcosm of a new world.

Augustus' famous boast might have referred to the newly exploitable marble quarries available to Roman builders.[94] His structures reinvented the heart of the city but probably didn't change neighborhood aesthetics much. Slums ran right up to new buildings made of sturdier materials in larger scales. The Forum Augustum and its dramatic Temple of Mars Ultor ("Mars the Avenger") were, like all of this new construction, designed to instill a sense of community based on conservative values.[95] Statues of famous Romans referenced an austere past, an ode to *mos maiorum* or "the way our ancestors did things."[96] It is important to remember the official make believe that the Republic had not just fallen. Augustus had merely restored the dignity of the old oligarchy, returning the state to more virtuous times. The old political offices remained. Augustus and his loyalists assumed them at will while retaining control of the legions. His palace was small in relation to the absolute authority he assumed. His wife Livia sat on its veranda spinning wool as the virtuous Lucretia had done. A woman sitting quietly in her place was an idealized use of private space in this vision, a reassertion of supposed early Republican patriarchy. Diane Favro's vivid studies of Augustan Rome describe his architecture as "conservative, refined, and unthreatening."[97] This "sedate" aesthetic reflected the *modus vivendi* he reached between traditional factions.[98] The outsized new forum concealed nearby slums, but the *princeps* ("first man") did not demolish them (Figure 5.1).[99] This avoided Julius Caesar's conspicuously dictatorial heavy handedness.[100]

Augustus' second motive was to project a cosmopolitan image in line with a matured geographic consciousness. The Roman public was made to

[93] Cited in Favro, "Making Rome a World City," 254.
[94] At any rate, most buildings were constructed by stone, with the exception of the completely marble-walled *Ara Pacis*. Marble was mainly decorative.
[95] Favro, *Urban Image of Augustan Rome*, 96. [96] Stambaugh, *Ancient Roman City*, 53.
[97] Favro, "Making Rome a World City," 248. [98] Ibid. [99] Ibid., 251.
[100] Favro, *Urban Image of Augustan Rome*, 144.

Figure 5.1 The Roman Forum, the scale of which still dwarfs visitors. Photo by the author.

understand that Augustus was "Father of the World," not just the leader of a city-state, large as it was. As Cassius Dio explains:

Adorn this capital with utter disregard of expense and make it magnificent with festivals of every kind. For it is fitting that we who rule over many people should surpass all men in all things, and brilliance of this sort also tends in a way to inspire our allies with respect for us and our enemies with terror.[101]

The giant map in the Porticus Vipsania, the map mentioned in the introduction, was overseen by Augustus' loyal co-leader Marcus Agrippa (c. 63 BCE–12 CE) with the aim of conveying the extent of the Empire to the public. A bronze marker in the Forum symbolized Rome's place at the center of a universal built network in which "all roads lead to Rome."[102] The Mausoleum of Augustus, commissioned in 28 BCE – taking at least five years to complete – was in Favro's words "a monument for the world, not a city."[103] The structure had a base of 85 meters and stood 45 meters high. Its adoptive pan-Mediterranean history referenced Alexander the Great and the Greek East.[104] The Campus Martius was the only Haussmannesque site Augustus had room to overhaul, incorporating it into the otherwise cramped haphazard city. It merged

[101] Cassius Dio, *Roman History* (London: Loeb Classical Library, 1917), 151.
[102] Favro, "Making Rome a World City," 244. [103] Ibid., 245. [104] Ibid..

triumphal architecture staged to expansive, dramatic lines of sight. A large pyramid tied Rome's history to Egypt's, a reminder of the conquest over Antony and Cleopatra in 31 BCE that ended in Augustus' sole rule of the Empire. This juxtaposed with the pious *Ara Pacis* whose reliefs tell Augustus' family story, making for a stunning visit to this day. This and the expanded Forum brought welcome relief from Rome's cramped conditions. They instilled a metaphysical sense of order to its chaos.

To wit, the quality of life was superior to the city of the late Republic. Augustus did not allow rivals, instead encouraging the aristocracy to finance the prosaic projects the Romans prided themselves on. "The Romans had the best foresight in those markets the Greeks made but little account of," wrote Strabo in praise of Roman practicality, "such as the construction of the roads and aqueducts, and of sewers that could wash out the filth of the city into the Tiber."[105] Strabo lauded Agrippa's active infrastructure management in his role as aedile responsible for public works, an oddly unglamorous job for Rome's most decorated general.[106] To aid in Rome's refurbishment, Augustus divided the sprawling city into fourteen districts. The city's appearance improved in minute ways, such as with the restoration of eighty-two smaller temples in one year.[107]

These were significant developments as the Romans utilized their masterful engineering prowess on projects other than lofty palaces and villas. Indeed, Augustus' anti-sumptuary laws discouraged these things. Not so much reducing inequality as masking it. In a sense, Augustus' regime partially fulfilled the Gracchi's promise of channeling newfound imperial wealth into public goods. Augustus created the office of *curator aquarum* to oversee the city's remarkable collection of aqueducts. Frontinus (c. 40–103 CE), who held this position, wrote a manual that demonstrates the seriousness of the effort, so "that the water may flow to the reservoirs and public fountains without interruption day and night."[108] Augustus built three new aqueducts, ranging between 20 and 30 kilometers in length, delivering about 150,000 cubic meters of water daily.[109] Pliny the Elder gushed that "nothing more remarkable has ever existed in all the world."[110]

There was an antipodal de-emphasis on private construction. Economic planning went no further than the Greek *oikos*, a matter relegated to individual estate management. This left no room for social housing programs to match Rome's public works. There was no serious effort to bring running water to the city's upper floor *insulae* where the poor precariously resided. "We live in a

105 Strabo, *Geography*, book v. 106 Ibid. 107 Favro, "Making Rome a World City," 242.
108 Frontinus, *Complete Works of Frontinus* (Hastings: Delphi, 2015), 103.
109 Aldrete, *Daily Life in the Roman City*, 29.
110 Pliny the Elder, *Natural History*, book xxxvi.

city which is, to a great extent, propped up by flimsy boards," remarked Juvenal in a counterpoint to Augustus' marble city.[111] He recalls trying to sleep in an apartment in terminal risk of collapse, the ever-present fire danger, and shady landlords (not unlike Cicero) nonplussed by it all. "I live in a little cell," remarked the first century poet Martial, "with one window that doesn't even fit properly."[112] He added dryly that "Novius is my neighbor; we can reach out of our windows and touch hands."[113] None of this made housing any cheaper. Juvenal lamented that "the finest home . . . can be bought outright for as much as you pay in a year's rent for your dark hovel."[114] Augustus garrisoned the city with soldiers who theoretically could police crime. Burglaries occurred with little recourse as laws emphasized personal retribution over formal policing.

*****

Augustan Rome reinforced a nuclear family unit in which fathers ruled over daughters, wives, sons, and slaves. Women wedded much younger than men, making marriages effectively parent–child relationships. Traditionalist narratives blamed women for civic misfortune. Vestal Virgin priestesses were beaten or killed (by live burial) in crises.[115] This on the grounds that they must surely have invited catastrophe on the city by violating sacred chastity vows.[116] More broadly, female virtue signaled the health of the state. "In the good old days, poverty made our Latin women chaste," wrote Juvenal. "Luxury, more destructive than war, threatens the city and takes revenge for the lands we have conquered." Wealth, he said, "brought with it foreign customs."[117] Rome's global ties meant "unmanly luxuries" and "ugly affluence" that mocked tradition.

Strict rules stipulated women's modest appearances and policed their engagement in so-called vice. Husbands had far ranging powers to kill their wives in events such as adultery. The ancient Latin word *domus* refers to this power structure as well as the physical home.[118] The Romans departed from the gender segregation built into Greek upper class housing designs. Women were visible in these households, but in servile roles. The typical home layout

111 Cited in Shelton, *As the Romans Did*, 63. Juvenal's exact years of birth and death are uncertain, but he describes the city as it was during the first and second centuries CE.
112 Cited in ibid. 113 Cited in ibid., 71. 114 Cited in ibid., 64.
115 Phyllis Culham, "Woman in the Roman Republic," in Harriet I. Flower (ed.), *The Cambridge Companion to the Roman Republic* (Cambridge: Cambridge University Press, 2004), 127–148, 134.
116 Ibid., 130. 117 Cited in Shelton, *As the Romans Did*, 300.
118 Karl-Joachim Hölkeskamp, "Under Roman Roofs: Family, House, and Household," in Harriet I. Flower (ed.), *The Cambridge Companion to the Roman Republic* (Cambridge: Cambridge University Press, 2004), 101–126, 107.

encouraged this, intended to foster public as well as private activity.[119] However, noble women were generally confined to the home, never leaving without accompaniment.[120] Behind closed doors, husbands punished wives for minor transgressions. In one instance a man beat his wife to death with a club for drinking, "but no one even reproached him, for all the best men thought she deserved the punishment."[121] Augustus vigorously sought to regulate gender norms, including punishments for remaining unmarried past certain ages. He set timetables for remarriage if marriages ended.[122] These laws aimed to maximize procreation through dangerous childbirths. They must have instilled psychological distress, in addition to shortening lives.

This harsh set of norms was rooted in "the ideal of an original state of uncorrupted innocence, when blissful simplicity, self-sufficiency, and austere frugality were the hallmark of life," in the words of a detailed study of Rome's private sphere.[123] Mediterranean integration was a far cry from this ideal, forming the context for anti-global reactions in Roman society. As the archetypal consumer city the Romans were fully dependent on their provinces for imports while almost certainly failing to reciprocate the imbalance in trade. Far from "self-sufficient," Rome required 200,000 tons of wheat per year to survive, most of which was imported from abroad.[124] All provinces supplied the city in some form.[125] Urban slaves constituted a large source of labor within the city, both skilled and unskilled. For example, Rome altogether lacked an education system before importing Greek slaves to tutor boys. Perhaps one-third of the city was enslaved, carrying out a litany of functions essential to managing the government and the large estates of the wealthy. Slaves performed much of the hard labor involved in maintaining the city and worked in factories. Finally, the costs of Augustus' city building came in large part from the mass plunder of foreign treasuries, most importantly that of Alexandria after Egypt's annexation. Overall, Italy used its wealth to swallow up luxuries. Morality laws notwithstanding, Italy was the primary market for luxury products in a vast trading network, changing its aesthetic.[126]

Vitruvius addressed *The Ten Books on Architecture* directly to Augustus. He apparently did not design many well-known buildings (serving as a military engineer for Julius Caesar).[127] However, his *Ten Books* is the only surviving ancient treatise on architecture. The work is detailed and

[119] Ibid., 109. [120] Aldrete, *Daily Life in the Roman City*, 58.
[121] Shelton, *As the Romans Did*, 46. [122] Aldrete, *Daily Life in the Roman City*, 61.
[123] Hölkeskamp, "Under Roman Roofs," 103. [124] Garnsey and Saller, *Roman Empire*, 110.
[125] Ibid., 120.
[126] M. Rostovtzeff, *The Social and Economic History of the Roman Empire*, 2nd ed. (Oxford: Oxford University Press, 1957), 69.
[127] Edmund Thomas, "Architecture," in Alessandro Barchiesi and Walter Scheidel (eds.), *The Oxford Handbook of Roman Studies* (Oxford: Oxford University Press, 2010), 838–854, 844.

workmanlike in the ideological mold of Augustan conservatism. In keeping with urban prejudices, he sees a world divided between "a rude and barbarous mode of life" and "civilization and refinement."[128] There remains the danger of becoming "softened by the charm of civilization."[129] Reflecting gendered overtones, architecture should avoid Greek "unchastity" while holding the line between urbanity and "savagery."[130] Vitruvius meticulously lays out materials and methods for the elemental features of a city: Temples, bathhouses, forums (analogous to the Greek *agora*), city walls, harbors, statehouses, and theaters. Though steeped in Hellenistic forms, *The Ten Books on Architecture* emphasized Roman elements. Bathhouses served important sanitary functions. Like the Greek *gymnasia* they fostered cross-class interaction.[131] They marked "Romanized" cities across the Empire. In total these elements comprised an international style in urban planning, including widespread architectural mimicry. Vitruvius' *Ten Books* was a handbook for cities around the world, not just Rome.[132] In his mind Rome was distinctive in terms of scale. Its "unlimited" population required increases in "the number of dwelling places indefinitely," at greater heights. This sounds almost like the housing policy that never occurred in Rome.[133] Still, he thought floor plans should be distinctive between classes. The affluent needed higher functionality to carry out public obligations.[134]

In terms of urban planning, Vitruvius viewed cities in relational terms. Their siting was important for climatic reasons – he believed ideal weather bolstered intelligence – and networking capacity near "rivers or seaports affording easy means of transport."[135] For this, Rome was the cardinal alpha city at the world's center, a geographic and cosmological ideal. It was "the truly perfect territory . . . having on each side the entire extent of the world."[136] In turn, it had "the right to command" its empire. This brings us to the question of Roman universalism.

Rise to Globalism

The *Res Gestae Divi Augusti* ("acts of the deified Augustus") spelled out what Agrippa's map conveyed visually. Rome was as limitless as the *orbis terrarum*. Inscribed on the Mausoleum of Augustus in 13 CE it portrayed the *princeps* as a Roosevelt-esque figure, presiding over a world transformed by vigorous military and diplomatic achievements. Some of which were

128 Vitruvius, *Ten Books on Architecture*, 40. 129 Ibid., 55. 130 Ibid.
131 To clarify, bathhouses promoted public bathing, although the sanitation benefits could be offset by contaminated water.
132 Thomas, "Architecture," 844. 133 Vitruvius, *Ten Books on Architecture*, 56.
134 Ibid., 16. 135 Ibid., 21. 136 Ibid., 173.

exaggerated. It extolled the city's refurbishment and architectural achievements, and newly founded cities. This narrative had vast geographic range, listing dozens of locations from around the world. This is an indicator of global awareness among literate Romans.[137] Augustus officially "placed the whole world under the sovereignty of the Roman people."[138] What was the Empire really?

Rostovtzeff's classic study *The Social and Economic History of the Roman Empire* sees the beginnings of an elaborate single market:

> Apart from agriculture, the chief factor in the economic life of the early Roman Empire was certainly commerce. Wide opportunities were opened to the people of the Empire after the end of the civil wars. The unification of the civilized world; its transformation practically into [a] one world state; peace within and without; complete safety on the seas, protected by the Roman navy, now a standing force; the increasing numbers of well paved roads, built for military purposes but also used for commercial intercourse.[139]

Yet Rostovtzeff implies something more limited than this when he defines the early Principate as "a commonwealth of self-governing cities" and an "aggregate of city-states."[140] Augustus forged social contracts with Roman citizens and the urban population in the Empire, Rostovtzeff noted, leaving those living in the spaces between under cities' brutal control or disassociated altogether.[141] Eighty to ninety percent of the population would fall under the latter categories. A truer map of the Roman Empire would resemble "frogs around a marsh" as opposed to the clear shaded territories running up to the *limes* that the Romans themselves never saw.

Within the linked urban network we see unprecedented integration, evidenced most strongly by the Roman grain market, which needed a fleet of 2,000 ships to feed the city.[142] It is possible that the food system in Europe was less integrated in early modern times.[143] Modernists see the Principate in the first and second centuries CE as a high period for economic growth in the ancient world.[144] They revise common historical claims about the slowness of land-based travel, arguing that the Roman road network added significant efficiency to trade. This enabled specialized forms of production resembling a market economy.[145] Shipwreck evidence suggests Mediterranean Sea traffic

137 Nicolet, *Space, Geography, and Politics*, 20.
138 Augustus, *Res Gestae Divi Augusti* (Cambridge: Loeb Classical Library, 1924), ch. 1.
139 Rostovtzeff, *Social and Economic History of the Roman Empire*, 66.
140 Ibid., 49 and 51, respectively. 141 Ibid., 51.
142 Peter Temin, *The Roman Market Economy* (Princeton: Princeton University Press, 2012), 31.
143 Ibid., 30. 144 Ibid., 222. 145 Ibid., 223.

peaked in antiquity during this time.[146] Pricing was Mediterranean-wide rather than localized, meaning cities consumed commodities far from where they were produced – agricultural products (not just grain), metals, textiles, manufactures, and building materials. The experience in Rome changed. Aelius Aristides reported in the second century:

> The city appears a kind of common emporium of the world. Cargoes from India and, if you will, even Arabia the Blessed, one can see in such numbers as to surmise that in those lands the trees will have been stripped bare and that the inhabitants of those lands, if they need anything, must come here and beg for a share of their own. Your farmlands are Egypt, Sicily and all of cultivated Africa.[147]

Aristides' rich, widely cited text speaks to the scope of migration that existed in ancient Rome. It evokes Rome's corresponding place as a core city extracting resources from a vast periphery.

On the issue of migration, a leading authority on Greco-Roman demographics describes "population movements on an unprecedented scale."[148] As we have seen, Italy was the center of a far ranging slave market, and the Romans organized colonial outmigration.[149] Large numbers of Roman citizens moved (or were transferred) to the provinces.[150] Settlers abroad numbered 750,000.[151] Here it is important to remember that migration was mostly state organized – put bluntly, forced – in the ancient world. The Roman Empire was no different. Individuated social and economic forces resembling those of modern globalization were secondary. A case in point, the military was an important source of frontier settlement and cultural interaction.[152] On the other hand, environmental push and pull factors in Mediterranean microclimates might have led to regular shifts in short distance flows. By contrast, voluntary long-distance travel was limited to the urban elite, our proverbial frogs hopping from city to city. There were an estimated 60,000 long-range sea passengers per year, a small percentage of the imperial population.[153] This set lived untied

146 Neville Morley, "The Early Roman Empire: Distribution," Walter Scheidel, Ian Morris, and Richard Saller (eds.), *The Cambridge Economic History of the Greco-Roman World* (Cambridge: Cambridge University Press, 2007), 570–591, 572.

147 Cited in Neville Morley, "Globalization and the Roman Economy," in Martin Pitts and Miguel John Versluys (eds.), *Globalisation and the Roman World: World History, Connectivity, and Material Culture* (Cambridge: Cambridge University Press, 2015), 49–68, 55.

148 Walter Scheidel, "Human Mobility in Roman Italy, I: The Free Population," *The Journal of Roman Studies* 94 (2004), 1–26, 1.

149 Ibid., 11. 150 Ibid., 13.

151 This contributed to declines in the Italian population. Ibid., 20.

152 Saskia T. Roselaar, "State-Organized Mobility in the Roman Empire: Legionaries and Auxiliaries," in Luuk de Ligt and Laurens E. Tacoma (eds.), *Migration and Mobility in the Early Roman Empire* (Boston: Brill, 2016), 138–157, 143.

153 Greg Woolf, "Movers and Stayers," in Luuk de Ligt and Laurens E. Tacoma (eds.), *Migration and Mobility in the Early Roman Empire* (Boston: Brill, 2016), 439–461, 460.

Figure 5.2 Interior of upper class apartment in Roman Ephesus, present-day Turkey.
Photo by Erin L. Leon.

to the land or to any personal labor at all. They had a top-down influence on a globalizing culture, economy, and governmental structures. All sizeable towns had facilities for travelers and hospitality protocols for the nobility, whether traveling on business or tourism.

Rome was of course the most important center of this high period of globalization in antiquity, but liturgical construction boomed in the provinces as cities strove for Romanization. Imperial funds also contributed to building commissions in provincial cities in the early Principate. There were marked increases in construction in the first and second centuries, mirroring that of trade patterns. As with estimates of trade, studies of building inscriptions show construction tapering off as the Roman "one world state" began to fragment in the third and fourth centuries.[154] Cities of all sizes were more visually impressive in the early Principate than in times past. New capital allowed cities to construct the infrastructure needed to support larger populations.[155] Rather than building to stand out in their visual styles, cities in the Empire differentiated in terms of the scale and quantity of the typical elements elucidated by Vitruvius. Buildings, then, were artifacts of globalization but also reinforced it (Figure 5.2). Construction was an important source of employment, as the

[154] Wilson, "City Sizes and Urbanization," 167. [155] Ibid., 177.

emperor Vespasian (9–79 CE) notably opted for more expensive construction contracts over efficiency in order to have work on hand for laborers. Rome had a ready army of at least 25,000 seasonal migrant laborers in its construction industry.[156] Imported materials for public construction were signs of prestige. The colossal columns for Hadrian's reconstructed Pantheon – the one still intact today – were quarried, crafted, and shipped from Egypt in a year-long effort requiring immense cost and labor.

By Hadrian's time, Roman universalism ran up against limits. The public may have been force-fed universalist propaganda, but Roman expansion stopped. Hadrian ceded territory won by his predecessor Trajan, the only Roman emperor with a long record of conquests. As Mary T. Boatwright shows, he turned to cities as the source of Roman power. Hadrian spent his mid-second century reign moving between cities. He put his hand in local governance but encouraged autonomy. He founded a wave of new settlements, the Empire's last. In addition to building in Rome, he encouraged provincial construction.[157] Boatwright estimates that 130 cities "were affected by the personal attention of Hadrian."[158] He was one of the five so-called good emperors despite startling eccentricity. Dio claims Hadrian killed his architect Apollodorus in a dispute over aesthetics. This may well speak to his fervor for city building. Inasmuch as we may call him "good," he understood that the Empire's continuity rested on intercity relations.

Statecraft on the Frontiers

Modern maps of the Roman Empire suggest the imposition of Roman military power over large swaths of territory. To reiterate, the Romans themselves may have been surprised at the underlying assumptions of such illustrations. Roman universalism meant that the Empire conquered people, cultures, and city-states rather than square kilometers. As far as the use of maps as a tool, the Antonine Itineraries detail Britannia's road systems on the basis of distance between cities and registered way stations. Frontiers themselves were a social construct.

Owen Lattimore's political histories of boundaries call the frontier "a zone rather than a line."[159] Frontiers delineated urban values from the "social crime" of nomadism.[160] The social criminals had distinct advantages over empires,

[156] Paul Erdkamp, "Seasonal Labour and Rural–Urban Migration in Roman Italy," in Luuk de Ligt and Laurens E. Tacoma (eds.), *Migration and Mobility in the Early Roman Empire* (Boston: Brill, 2016), 33–49, 38.

[157] Boatwright, *Hadrian and the Cities of the Roman Empire*, 37.

[158] Ibid., 5.

[159] Owen Lattimore, *Studies in Frontier History: Collected Papers 1928–1958* (Oxford: Oxford University Press, 1962), 469.

[160] Ibid., 417.

however. They did not depend on stationary, sackable cities to project power. Their smaller, nimbler forces raided cities and trading routes, even defeating less mobile organized armies. The total defeat of three legions by Germanic tribes in the Battle of Teutoburg Forest in 9 CE showed the limits of universalism. Empires in turn violated territorial agreements, embarking on punitive expeditions, forcibly relocating tribes, or simply seeking glory. All of this was the case with the Roman *limes*. This presents problems for Darwinian theories of state evolution. The "territorial empire" represented the social, political, and ideological doctrines of the city-state. It was not the city-state's alternative.

The borders were mostly peaceable. The army was inactive more often than it fought. It relied on local populations for its auxiliaries, and barbarians could embark on military careers. Sometimes this backfired as Arminius used his knowledge of Roman methods to defeat them at Teutoburg Forest. The bulk of the army was stationed on the frontiers, making it an important source of new settlements, cultural hybridization, and trade. Otherwise, the farther away from cities, the less the Romans actually governed, and the less Romanization took hold.[161] The cities were the heart of Roman administration and political activity. Those living outside them had to enter them to conduct trade and take part in elections. Rural dwellers had to enter cities for mandatory obligations such as census registration. In cultural terms, Christianity took generations to reach the countryside after Theodosius I made it the state religion in the Empire. Nor were "frontiers" synonymous with the outer *limes*. Tribal migration occurred well within the Empire. The physical geography of some provinces presented difficult governance challenges, requiring the time honored combination of diplomacy and force to control. Germania proved impossible to govern after 9 CE. Pannonia in the Balkans was nearly as problematic.[162] The frontier at the Danube River was in crisis in the late second century. The Empire was so dependent on barbarians to serve as buffers for Roman security that Marcus Aurelius monitored their movements and brutally restricted attempts to desert.[163]

Much has been made about "barbarian" migrations into the Empire, less of their attempts to flee. While modern neoliberal understandings associate globalism with nonviolence, experiences along the frontiers and marginalized hinterlands suggest that interdependence was hardly peaceful. For example, Julius Caesar's published commentaries are full of exploits that could qualify as genocide, had that term existed. Caesar's dispatches – still in print today – eerily recount episodes of extreme slaughter in cold, terse prose. On his war with the Nervii in the Gallic campaign in the 50s BCE, he asserted that the

161 Thomas S. Burns, *Rome and the Barbarians: 100 BC–AD 400* (Baltimore: The Johns Hopkins University Press, 2003), 149.
162 Ibid., 206. 163 Ibid., 240.

nation depopulated "from 60,000 people to scarcely 500."[164] In another instance, Caesar reports selling an entire town "in one auction lot." By his own figures, the numbers of enslaved reached 53,000, who were sold off to slave brokers.[165] These events were controversial even to Roman observers and historians. Pliny the Elder noted the likely stain on Caesar's conscience, and the loss to humanity from all the deaths in his wars. He believed that one-million people died in Caesar's campaign to plunder and pacify Gaul. Though the actual figures are unknown, the campaigns undoubtedly took a massive human toll, displacing scores of Gallic and Germanic tribes.[166]

Still less has been made of Roman soldiers and civilians deserting their Empire for life with the barbarians.[167] The walls of Hadrian and Antoninus Pius may well have kept exploited farmers from abandoning the pasturelands, much like China's Great Wall. Yet ancient urban-based nobilities always governed under the threat of *anachôrêsis* – collective desertion – the only recourse left to the poor.

North Africa and Southern Frontiers

The North African frontier zone likely served different purposes than the Northern European frontier. A series of forts flanked some of the empire's wealthiest provinces and largest cities. This was not a continuous line. The zone coalesced into a "double frontier" by the third century.[168] A string of forts protected a rough boundary expanded by the emperor Trajan (53–117 CE) and consolidated by his successor Hadrian (76–138 CE). Unlike the empire's northern frontiers, these forts seem not to have been staging grounds for the Roman army to launch mass incursions into foreign territory. There are few recorded examples of marches into the desert. Conversely the threat of invasion from the Sahara Desert was low, and the Roman military presence small.[169] One scholar suggests that the positioning of roads, forts, and ditches called the *fossatum* was meant to control the movements of pastoralists so that their products could be taxed and sold in cities along with agricultural goods

164 James J. O'Donnell's translation captures what he calls "the calm, matter-of-fact treatment of episodes beyond ghastly to imagine." His translation captures the economy with which Caesar wrote. Julius Caesar, *The War for Gaul* (Princeton: Princeton University Press, 2019), 57.

165 Ibid., 59.

166 Modern estimates of the dead in the Gallic wars were staggering. A 2015 discovery and study of a battle site by archeologists at the Vrije Universiteit estimated that 150,000 people died fleeing Caesar's legions. Ibid., 82.

167 Burns, *Rome and the Barbarians*, 243.

168 David Cherry, *Frontier and Society in Roman North Africa* (Oxford: Oxford University Press, 1998), 52.

169 Ibid., 53.

on market days.[170] In sum, the relationship between border settlements and transhumance was one of "exploitation," as one specialist described it.[171]

The goal was not to transform transhuman actors into sedentary societies, imposing culture from the outside as in many imperial ventures. It was to regulate rather than "Romanize" pastoral populations.[172] As a result, the social structures of the desert polities remained intact. To the north, African cities had been long established before Rome became the dominant power in 146 BCE with the destruction of Carthage. During this period of rapid expansion, late Republican administrators used land to settle colonists. Settlers included veteran troops, along the lines proposed early on by Gaius Gracchus.[173] A new syncretized urbanism gradually took form. Roman features of urban planning grafted on to the preexisting African network as port cities expanded.[174] Carthage had already embarked on key city foundings, especially Lepcis Magna, bequeathing a "Punic urbanism" that persisted into Roman times.[175]

Carthage reemerged to become a leading port city, which was the most "Romanized" of cities in the Roman-African synthesis of urban forms. This is because its near total destruction paved the way for rebuilding over the old city.[176] Buildings nevertheless retained North African construction techniques and materials, as local identity persisted.[177] Lepcis Magna also emerged as a leading Mediterranean port city by the reign of Augustus (who initiated Carthage as a Roman colony). It adopted the major components of Roman cities very early on, even as the Punic language persisted. Most likely the quick adoption of Roman-styled municipal structures were spurred by elites eager to promote their loyalty to the empire, rather than forced acculturation from without.[178] Still, the bathhouse, a center of social life in archetypal Roman cities, took centuries to fully catch on.[179]

It was under Septimius Severus (145–211 CE) that the "Romano-African" style reached its height. Septimius was from Lepcis Magna, the son of affluent Italian and Punic families who spoke Punic, Latin, and Greek. During his

170 Ibid., 58.

171 Ibid., 73; Gareth Sears, *The Cities of Roman Africa* (Gloucestershire: The History Press, 2011), 9.

172 Cherry, *Frontier and Society in Roman North Africa*, 73.

173 Sears, *Cities of Roman Africa*, 34.

174 J. Andrew Dufton and Elizabeth Fentress, "Roman North African Urbanism," in R. Bruce Hitchner (ed.), *A Companion to North Africa in Antiquity* (Hoboken: Wiley Blackwell, 2022), 173–201, 174.

175 Sears, *Cities of Roman Africa*, 22.

176 Ralph Bockmann, "African Rome: The City of Carthage from Its Roman Re-foundation to the End of the Byzantine Period," in R. Bruce Hitchner (ed.), *A Companion to North Africa in Antiquity* (Hoboken: Wiley Blackwell, 2022), 119–141, 120.

177 Ibid., 122.

178 Sears, *Cities of Roman Africa*, 38.

179 Ibid., 66.

reign, he awarded Lepcis Magna with Italian city status, exempting it from tributes commonly required of provincial cities. This happened alongside massive public works embraced by the local nobility. Travelers would enter through a grand colonnaded boulevard, leading to a massive bathhouse and a new fountain. Finally they would reach a forum complex forming the heart of the renewed city.[180] This was lined with shops. The centerpiece was a temple spanning 30 by 20 meters, most likely built by the Severan family.[181] In return, local elites erected an array of statues and inscriptions honoring the emperor. A major four-way arch chronicled his military victories and illustrated family piety by way of animal sacrifice – it was on ready display upon the emperor's visit.[182]

Conclusion: Varieties of Globalization

The Roman core–periphery system began its slow decline the same way it started its ascent, in concert with the fate of its imperial network. The army and the city in effect competed for resources. The more capital diverted to the army along the frontiers, the less the Empire lavished on the city. The frontiers had developed mid-sized towns while the city underwent a slowdown in new building projects. Constantinople replaced Rome in importance in the Late Empire. Its strategic position closer to the Empire's frontiers was the main reason it attracted capital.

Rome was no longer the Western capital when it was sacked in 410 CE. Upon hearing the news in Ravenna, the emperor Honorius famously breathed a sigh of relief when learning that it had been the sacking of the city rather than the death of his beloved chicken of the same name.

Roman studies regularly apply a world systems approach.[183] In concluding this chapter, it is worth stressing the relevance of Wallerstein's theory to the ancient city, of which Rome was the apotheosis. Rome's consumer economy implied that there were various far-off peripheries where "the trees will have been stripped bare" to supply the city. There was mutual dependence between the core and periphery, with the former in a position of power. Scholars of modern economic systems are shy about retroactively applying this material, including Wallerstein. For his part, Manuel Castells conceded that there may be "nothing new under the sun" in intercity relations (see Chapter 1). He stopped short of applying his own theories of power relations given important technological differences between then and now.[184] Scholars of

180 Ibid., 82. 181 Ibid., 83. 182 Ibid., 87.

183 For an overview of this application to the Roman Empire, see Greg Woolf, "World Systems Analysis and the Roman Empire," *Journal of Roman Archeology* 3 (1990), 44–58.

184 Castells, "Nothing New under the Sun?"158.

antiquity are less shy in retroactively applying such theories, particularly archeologists who continually analyze new physical evidence of far flung intercity networking. Cunliffe's study of Roman interactions outlines this relationship in the world systems mold:

> In the centre was the inner core, Rome and Italy, consuming raw materials, manpower and cash in enormous quantities, far above its own productive capacity, in order to maintain a high urban population and the full apparatus of the state. In simple terms, the inner core was a tax-importing zone. Around it lay an inner periphery of rich provinces – Spain, Gaul, Asia, Africa – producing far in excess of local needs. That is, they were tax-exporting, part of their product going to maintain the inner core and part to the third zone, the outer periphery of the frontier regions, where the fighting forces had to be supplied and paid. Outside all this lay the barbarian periphery, a zone from which, by process of exchange and trade, a further range of manpower and raw materials, some unobtainable elsewhere . . . were drawn into the empire.[185]

The Roman Empire involved not microsystems but something more expansive. Indeed vast enough to qualify as a political system that operated on a global scale with the aid of sea travel. In my view the city remained the primary unit of social organization in this undertaking. This happened even though one critical component of globalization, time–space compression, had not taken off.

That would change as navigation technology improved, which we will see in Chapters 9–11. After 410 CE, Rome, for its part, fell into terminal decline. It never recaptured economic or military hegemony. By the middle ages it was one of many great cities in a fractured Italy. No cities in Europe equaled ancient Rome's size until London and Paris in the 1800s.

The Italian peninsula revolved city-states in another era of state experimentation. As Italy grew less secure in the early 400s, refugees arrived on the Rialto, gambling correctly that the marshlands would protect them from barbarian incursions. Venice took form from this unwanted backwater on the Adriatic Sea, becoming the center of a city network and Europe's richest city. That polity – which will be explored in Chapter 9 – developed its own forms of power expression that are seminal in the history of world cities and in Italian political development.

Another city, however, was contemporary with Rome and an equivalent center of social gravity on earth at the turn of the first millennium: Chang'an. It is to imperial China, a superpower about which the Romans were at most dimly aware, that we now turn.

[185] Barry Cunliffe, *Greeks, Romans, and Barbarians: Spheres of Interaction* (London: Batsford, 1988), 3.

6 Tale of Two Chang'ans

Urban Power in Han and Tang China

When drums pounded across the walled city, all of its perhaps two million denizens knew where to go.[1] This daily routine started in the mid-600s CE, lasting more than two centuries. "Drums at dawn rumbling like thunder, hastening the sun," wrote the ninth century Tang poet Li He, "drums at dusk rumbling like thunder, calling out the moon."[2] The pounding lasted for hundreds of beats at dawn and dusk, giving people time to reach their registered wards before the gates closed. To be on main boulevards thereafter was to risk being shot by archers perched on watchtowers.[3] The internal network of gates reopened only in the morning as daily life began again.

The layout of Tang Chang'an and the daily routines it fostered were stunning expressions of state power at the heart of an urban network. The city was a microcosm of the vast empire it managed, down to the tightly controlled rural growing regions, with trading routes reaching far west. It was an empire rooted in spatial order, the city's modular layout designed to conform as closely as possible to the cosmos, the emperor at the heart of the city mandated to rule all under heaven.[4] In reality, emperors ruled nothing close to that, and they knew it. This was a period of heightened geographic awareness. Chang'an was the Silk Road's major terminus. Its tightly regulated markets demonstrated the burgeoning consumer demand for all things foreign.[5] This as teams of omnipresent regulators surveyed market activity from nearby watchtowers.

As in all the high periods of urbanization we have explored so far, city building required controlling personal movement and managing far-flung

1 Charles Benn, *Daily Life in Traditional China: The Tang Dynasty* (London: Greenwood Press 2002), 46.

2 Cited in Mark Edward Lewis, *China's Cosmopolitan Empire: The Tang Dynasty* (Cambridge, MA: Harvard University Press, 2009), 90.

3 Ibid.

4 Arthur Cotterell, *The Imperial Capitals of China: A Dynastic History of the Celestial Empire* (New York: Overlook Press, 2008), 113; Mark Edward Lewis, *The Construction of Space in Early China* (Albany: State University of New York Press, 2006), 151.

5 Cotterell, *Imperial Capitals of China*, 145.

resources. Forced population transfers were common in imperial China. Cities used modular design to create internal barriers, reinforcing strict hierarchies. This happened as China's dynastic empires constructed the Great Wall to delineate in-groups from out-groups, to hold insiders *in place* while keeping undesirable elements out. The city's internal walls served the same function.

For all these zealous efforts at social control, Chang'an was paradoxically the world's open city. Dependence on unfree labor created harsh conditions for most. For elites and the literati the city was intellectually liberating. Chang'an was where imported religions – Buddhism, Christianity, Islam, Zoroastrianism, and so on – existed alongside Chinese Taoist and Confucian thought, engaging intellectually curious palatial elites.[6] Those of us in thrall to modern global cities would understand the allure. It was a period of enlightenment well before any such thing existed in Europe, embodied in the rule of Emperor Taizong (598–649 CE), foreswearing superstition in running the state.[7] The chance to pass exams for admittance to the state bureaucracy attracted eager provincials, as did learning, writing, and fine arts.[8] Commercial and diplomatic opportunities drew what were probably the world's largest urban immigrant communities.[9]

This chapter explores Chinese innovations in urban networking that reached an apotheosis in Tang Chang'an. The central argument is that capital cities evolved in tandem with the expanding geographic reach of imperial China. Chinese antiquity featured its own unique version of the world city. Its governments cultivated elaborate knowledge sectors and built environments to meet the demands of managing vast resources and people. This occurred alongside increasingly complicated interstate relations across Eurasia.

Peter J. Taylor, a leading global cities scholar, contends that Chinese city-making has an understudied place in history as one of the "greatest creative arenas in the history of humanity."[10] He points toward the existence of urban networks in China at various points across time.[11] Historic globalization studies note that the rise of the Han in the second century BCE and the rise of the Tang in the seventh century CE each changed the center of gravity in world trade. They influenced economies as far as Europe, even when they did not have direct contact.[12]

[6] Benn, *Daily Life in Traditional China*, 59.

[7] He famously told aids that the health of the state depended on the quality of its administration rather than omens. Cotterell, *Imperial Capitals of China*, 118.

[8] Ibid., 115. [9] Ibid., 145; Lewis, *China's Cosmopolitan Empire*, 91.

[10] Taylor, *Extraordinary Cities*, 162. [11] Ibid., 163.

[12] Curtin, *Cross Cultural Trade in World History*, 105; Stearns, *Globalization in World History*, 19.

In fact, the Tang capital was not the first "Chang'an" (the name meaning "forever safe").[13] Its massive walled footprint stood near a previous city of the same name. The Tang capital referenced the ancient Han Dynasty, the first to unify China over an extended period. The old Chang'an was the capital of the Han Empire at its peak. Han Chang'an was indicative of urban power over laborers and peasants, in unceasing conflict with a menagerie of transhumant and pastoral polities. Flourishing at the same time as imperial Rome, Han Chang'an was the heart of an urban network that bookended a shrinking Eurasia. At this time, major civilizations established contact, dotted by emergent urban trading and administrative centers.[14] Han Chang'an, like Rome, was a prototypical world city, representing an ever-expanding geographic horizon. As one scholar put it, "the capital gradually evolved from simply the emperor's palace to the symbolic center of the entire realm, and thus a sublimely realized apex not only of the urban hierarchy but also of the court and all civilized people."[15]

There is a steep political ramification: China's world cities were enormously labor-intensive. Both iterations of Chang'an were planned largely from scratch. Their walls and palaces (the largest structures in first-tier Chinese cities) required exorbitant "unfree labor" to construct.[16] Designed to manage resources across the empire and beyond, the great metropolises needed infrastructure linking their spheres of influence via a remarkable system of roads and canals. This was especially urgent in China, where linkages were predominately inland rather than seaborne as in Mediterranean city networks. Entire populations were mobilized to make this urban system work. Cities drew from the hinterlands for conscript labor, drafting armies of men and (when desperate) women for construction projects in dire conditions.[17] Moreover, major cities were famine-prone, necessitating a network of state administrators to carefully monitor and regulate food production in the hinterlands.[18] For these reasons, peasant rebellions were frequent in antiquity and capable of destabilizing an entire empire.[19]

How did these dramatic expressions of centralized authority emerge?

13 Translation in Cotterell, *Imperial Capitals of China*, 41.
14 Stearns, *Globalization in World History*, 19.
15 Tang Xiaofeng, "The Evolution of Imperial Urban Form in Western Han Chang'an," in Michael Nylan and Griet Vankeerberghen (eds.), *Chang'an 26 BCE: An Augustan Age in China* (Seattle: University of Washington Press, 2015), 55–74, 55.
16 Cotterell, *Imperial Capitals of China*, 41.
17 Benn, *Daily Life in Traditional China*, 32; Cotterell, *Imperial Capitals of China*, 41.
18 Gang Deng, *The Premodern Chinese Economy: Structural Equilibrium and Capitalist Sterility* (New York: Routledge, 1999), 38.
19 Ibid., 221.

China's Urban Revolution

China was a site of pristine urbanization, beginning roughly in the 1600s BCE with the Shang dynasty. Like other pristine urban networks, ecological conditions shaped settlement patterns.[20] The combination of rich soil and regular rainfall in the ancient Chinese heartland was conducive to agrarianism, and the long cascade of political, cultural, and economic evolutions stemming from settled society.[21] As James C. Scott might put it, this was well within the grain line, and indeed grain was by far the most cultivated crop throughout China's pre-modern history.[22] Fluctuations in climate impacted migration patterns, with growing aridity along China's frontiers possibly influencing border pressures with transhumant polities to the east and north.[23]

The regions around which urban networks coalesced from the ancient to medieval periods presented massive environmental challenges, which would have political consequences. The Yellow River in the country's northern tier was China's most densely settled area from ancient times well into antiquity. This region housed 90 percent of the population in the Han Dynasty.[24] Between the Yellow River and the Yangtze River to the south is a series of tributaries useful for irrigation and trade, but not without immense physical modifications to meet the demands of emergent cities.[25] The constant ecological struggle is symbolized in the legend of Yu, sage emperor of the mythologized first dynasty, the Xia around 2100 BCE.[26] Yu purportedly constructed barriers that diverted floodwaters out to sea. In context, the Yellow River was capable of catastrophic floods, which occurred no less than 1,500 times in imperial China, destroying infrastructure and farmland, and displacing whole settlements.[27]

China's physical geography created a patchwork society that was relatively isolated. The agrarian heartland was flanked by the Pacific Ocean to the east. Recalling Plato from Chapter 2, this pond was by comparison far too large for even the most ambitious frogs to cross. Without natural harbors in northern China, coastal hopping as happened around the Mediterranean was cost-

20 David N. Keightley, "The Environment of Ancient China," in Michael Loewe and Edward L. Shaughnessy (eds.), *The Cambridge History of Ancient China: From the Origins of Civilization to 221 B.C.* (Cambridge: Cambridge University Press, 1999), 30–36, 32.

21 Ping-ti Ho, "The Loess and the Origin of Chinese Agriculture," *American Historical Review* 75, no. 1 (1969), 1–36, 2; Deng, *Premodern Chinese Economy*, 62.

22 Deng, *Premodern Chinese Economy*, 38.

23 Robert Orr Whyte, "The Evolution of the Chinese Environment," in David N. Keightley (ed.), *The Origins of Chinese Civilization* (Berkeley: University of California Press, 1983), 3–20, 8.

24 Mark Edward Lewis, *The Early Chinese Empires: Qin and Han* (Cambridge, MA: Harvard University Press, 2007), 7.

25 Keightley, "Environment of Ancient China," 33.

26 Ibid.

27 Lewis, *Early Chinese Empires*, 7.

prohibitive.[28] The two major rivers flowed eastward, hitting a dead end at this point. No navigable waterways connected them.[29] Arid climates dominated the north, with mountains and desert ensuring separation from the west. Natural barriers meant that humid southern regions were relative frontiers even during the expansive Han era.[30] The corresponding reliance on overland transport made bulk trade costly in early urban China. This also limited geographic awareness, leading Chinese civilization to see itself as the only settled cultured region on earth. Internally, jagged terrain created isolated spaces for dense settlements to grow, leaving scarcity in other zones. "The limited arable land was further compartmentalized into a series of core areas – alluvial plains, coastlands, and interior basins – separated by high mountain chains or elevated plateaus that divided the Chinese heartland into distinct regions," argued one expert.[31]

For these reasons, the early Shang (1600 to 1045 BCE) and Zhou (1045 to 771 BCE) dynasties were not contiguous territorial empires, but urban leagues comprised of cities "that controlled only their immediate hinterlands."[32] Kings did not rule directly. They had little to no bureaucratic state to govern far beyond their own cities, relying on ritual and diplomacy.[33] There was little territorial control from the urban leagues beyond the cities, so modern maps of early dynastic eras would be more accurately expressed as webs of towns threading together league members. Oracle bone inscriptions during the Shang dynasty record the names of 500 member towns.[34] These are the first known writings in China, dating from 1200 BCE.[35] These divinations represent an advance in public administration, as cities consulted them in policy decisions.[36] The late Shang capital of Anyang was a hotbed of innovation in writing, possibly even monopolizing the craft.[37] A likely abundance of unfree

[28] Ibid. [29] Ibid. [30] Ibid., 13. [31] Ibid., 6.

[32] Mark Edward Lewis, "The City-State in Spring and Autumn China," in Mogens Herman Hansen (ed.), *A Comparative Study of Thirty City-State Cultures* (Copenhagen: The Royal Danish Academy of Arts and Letters, 2000), 359–373, 359.

[33] Robin D. S. Yates, "The City-State in Ancient China," in Deborah L. Nichols and Thomas H. Charlton (eds.), *The Archeology of City-States: Cross Cultural Approaches* (Washington, DC: Smithsonian Institutions Press, 1997), 71–90, 72.

[34] William G. Boltz, "Language and Writing," in Michael Loewe and Edward L. Shaughnessy (eds.), *The Cambridge History of Ancient China: From the Origins of Civilization to 221 B.C.* (Cambridge: Cambridge University Press, 1999), 74–123, 75.

[35] David N. Keightley, "The Late Shang State: When, Where, and What?" in David N. Keightley (ed.), *The Origins of Chinese Civilization* (Berkeley: University of California Press, 1983), 523–564, 532.

[36] David N. Keightley, "The Shang: China's First Historical Dynasty," in Michael Loewe and Edward L. Shaughnessy (eds.), *The Cambridge History of Ancient China: From the Origins of Civilization to 221 B.C.* (Cambridge: Cambridge University Press, 1999), 232–291, 236.

[37] Robert Bagley, "Shang Archeology," in Michael Loewe and Edward L. Shaughnessy (eds.), *The Cambridge History of Ancient China: From the Origins of Civilization to 221 B.C.* (Cambridge: Cambridge University Press, 1999), 124–231, 183.

labor managed from the core was a sign of this advance in administrative power.[38] Major cities featured ritual centers, necropolises, and administrative facilities, all surrounded by large walls of rammed earth. They were designed to accommodate a mobile royal court and house armies consistent of nobles. By Zhou times the nobility and their retinues resided inside the walls while a feudal peasantry lived tied to the land outside.[39]

The Spring and Autumn era from the eighth to fifth centuries BCE was the high period for the city-state as the dominant form of social organization in the Yellow River Basin. Cities had spaces akin to the *agora* where nobles and citizens gathered to discuss politics.[40] Self-governing city-states formed various urban leagues. Their ability to project power was limited. The scale of conflict was small, with armies of noble charioteers and tradition-guided protocols of battle. Important changes occurred over time. Commercial functions grew, with increased roles for markets in cities, resulting in complex migration, production, and regulatory patterns.[41] Across the Yellow River region cities resembled one another, differing mainly in scale, modeled after capitals. A shared visual culture existed in all cities.[42] The largest cities had populations in the tens of thousands, allowing quasi-democratic face-to-face politics.[43]

Polities became fewer and larger over time, a trend that seems consistent throughout these phases.[44] The gigantism of the Warring States period (481 to 221 BCE) is analogous to the enormous polities in the Greek world that assumed supremacy over the *poleis* during the transition from Classical to Hellenistic times (see Chapter 4). By now seven polities dominated the known world.[45] (The *Tao Te Ching* was probably written in this period, indicative of the frequent folly of direct action as territorial empires engulfed cities). Here it is worth recalling our working definition for world cities. They are not necessarily autonomous city-states. City networks are not synonymous with "city-state cultures." World cities project power and influence over the broadest possible geographies. Things moved dramatically in this direction.

Cities lost autonomy but were the seats of expanding power bases. "The offices of the imperial government existed only in walled cities," noted Mark Edward Lewis, "so the cities alone were filled with the rich and mighty."[46]

[38] Keightley, "Shang," 282. [39] Lewis, "City-State in Spring and Autumn China," 361.
[40] Ibid., 359.
[41] Chen Shen, "Compromises and Conflicts: Production and Commerce in the Royal Cities of Eastern Zhou, China," in M. L. Smith (ed.), *The Social Construction of Ancient Cities* (Smithsonian Institution Press: Washington, DC, 1990), 290–310, 292.
[42] Lewis, *Construction of Space in Early China*, 143. [43] Ibid., 146.
[44] Lewis, "City-State in Spring and Autumn China," 362.
[45] These kingdoms were the Yan, Qi, Wei, Zhao, Han, Qin, and Chu.
[46] Lewis, *Construction of Space in Early China*, 150.

Rigid control from within the city walls over the hinterlands only grew, expanding the sphere of unfree labor.[47] Population was a source of power harnessed by mapping and cataloging. The peasantry, in Lewis' words, were "objects of registration, surveillance, and punishment" overseen by growing urban information sectors.[48] Major polities conscripted and commanded massive infantry-based armies, drawing on the peasantry. Cities grew markedly in population and architectural scale, dominated by elevated palaces that occupied vastly disproportionate shares of urban land.[49] The archetypal "double city" plan delineated the rigid class structure inside these walled cities. An internal barrier divided the governing nobility from every other class and function.[50] The administrative palatial nerve center was cordoned off from other residential and market activities. In the place of diplomatic agreements among relative equals, urban hierarchies emerged with imperial capitals at the top.[51]

Rise of the Han: Urban Power Projection

China was first unified under the Qin dynasty in 221 BCE, the culmination of a ferocious expansion in administrative command and control. This was a legacy of the Legalist philosopher Shang Yang, a fourth century Qin leader who espoused severe laws as the foundation of a strong state, and a system designed to marshal the peasantry for warfare, building, and increased agricultural output.[52] The Qin state abolished serfdom, assigning land directly to peasants Not to be confused with redistributive land reform, the move enabled the central state to regulate peasant activity directly, tethering them in place.[53] This established the formula for city building.

On unifying the empire, the famed First Emperor, Shi Huangdi (259–210 BCE), replaced local rule with commanderies, administrative districts answerable to the capital. To do what had never been done, rule over a unified China, "the flow of information between the central government and regional and

[47] Mark Edward Lewis, "Warring States in Political History," in Michael Loewe and Edward L. Shaughnessy (eds.), *The Cambridge History of Ancient China: From the Origins of Civilization to 221 B.C.* (Cambridge: Cambridge University Press, 1999), 587–650, 603.

[48] Ibid., 646.

[49] Wu Hung, "The Art and Architecture of the Warring States Period," in Michael Loewe and Edward L. Shaughnessy (eds.), *The Cambridge History of Ancient China: From the Origins of Civilization to 221 B.C.* (Cambridge: Cambridge University Press, 1999), 651–744, 651.

[50] Lewis, "City-State in Spring and Autumn China," 361.

[51] Lewis, *Construction of Space in Early China*, 151.

[52] Derk Bodde, "The State and Empire of Ch'in," in Denis Twitchett and John K. Fairbank (eds.), *The Cambridge History of China: Volume I, The Ch'in and Han Empires* (Cambridge: Cambridge University Press, 1986), 20–102, 36.

[53] Paul S. Ropp, *China in World History* (Oxford: Oxford University Press, 2010), 13.

local offices had to be swift and sure."[54] He forcibly relocated noble families – purportedly 120,000 in all – to his new capital, Xianyang, extracting a ready-made population for the city.[55] This was the highest profile of a series of population transfers, mostly for the sake of colonizing new territories.[56] From there, the First Emperor ordered a building program whose labor intensiveness can't be overstated.[57] A new road network radiated from the capital for thousands of miles. Xianyang sat astride a riverine network.[58] Such connectivity became necessary as alpha cities grew in scale, becoming more dependent on external resources. Conversely, alpha cities had to deploy equipment, soldiers, and labor to the empire's farthest reaches. Shi Huangdi dispatched a general, Meng Tien (c. 250–210 BCE), to the northern frontier to construct the Great Wall. The traditional figure of 300,000 laborers to build the wall is plausible, with one historian speculating that the "death toll too must have been enormous."[59]

The transformative Qin Dynasty fast combusted after Shi Huangdi's death, having paved institutional ground for the durable Han Dynasty. The brevity of Qin rule resulted in Xianyang going unfinished, despite drastic efforts to house the transplanted families.[60] A reputed 700,000 convicts went to work on the nearby Er Fang palace alone, which had a land cover comparable to the whole future capital of Chang'an.[61] Alas, the city was deserted for the new capital. This was a recurrent trend. Because of the cyclical portents of dynastic rule, founders tended to prefer constructing new capitals, abandoning old ones. "Planning the new and getting rid of the old is like a farmer looking forward to autumn," went the Sui edict in the construction of the later Chang'an.[62] These were not eternal cities. Primary building materials of wood and rammed earth allowed them to construct new cities quickly – against the ecological headwinds of deforestation – in comparison with Greco-Roman stone cities. Because these building materials perish easier, sadly far less survives, leaving nothing akin to the Roman Forum or Athenian Acropolis to walk today. The walls of Chang'an were constructed between 192 and 190 BCE in just two one-month spurts. Granted this occurred with two *corvée* labor forces of at

54 Robin S. Yates, "Body, Space, Time, and Bureaucracy: Boundary Creation and Control Mechanisms in Early China," in John Hay (ed.), *Boundaries in China* (Chicago: University of Chicago Press, 1997), 56–80, 69.

55 Bodde, "State and Empire of Ch'in," 55.

56 Ibid., 65.

57 Another case in point, historic figures report that it took 700,000 laborers to construct his burial site, although the number may be overstated. Discovered only in 1974, the mausoleum is replete with an army of terracotta warriors that are being slowly unearthed near present-day Xian and are a UNESCO heritage site.

58 Bodde, "The State and Empire of Ch'in," 61.

59 Ibid., 64.

60 Cotterell, *Imperial Capitals of China*, 42.

61 Ibid., 44.

62 Ibid., 113.

least 145,000 men and women working far from home with no state provisioned food or shelter.[63]

In the end, the millions of conscripts required to labor under severe conditions for this construction spree deserted and in some cases formed armies.[64] Riding this wave of resistance to power, the Han founder Gaozu (born Liu Bang, 256–195 BCE) went from humble beginnings to assume the throne in 202 BCE, but cycles of peasant abuse and revolt remained constant. Confucius' warnings from the 400s BCE in the *The Analects* were well founded in ancient Chinese politics: Workers must know their place in the hierarchy, but rulers must "worry about discontent."[65] Monarchs who abused their mandate risked revolt. This social contract essentially legitimated rebellion against rulers who overplayed their hands with the peasant classes. Farmers were exploited in the best of times and yet were lauded by the urban literary classes who viewed them as the nation's sole producers.

The abolition of feudalism theoretically freed peasants to own land. However, land inequality was a serious problem, leading one Han observer to lament that "the rich owned land piece after piece, while the poor did not own enough on which to stand an awl."[66] Many were engaged in tenant farming, surrendering half their harvest to landowners. A large number of farmers worked near cities, making up the lowest underclasses in urban areas, their makeshift hovels lined against city walls.[67] Peasant laborers were instrumental in overthrowing the Qin, with one initially leading the uprising.[68] Along with slaves, peasants deserted in defiance of the local registration system, becoming fugitives.[69] There was a thin line between refugee and bandit, as desperate wanderers made spaces between cities ungovernable. Organized peasantries even threatened cities, which, like nomadic invaders, saw cities as fixed targets of concentrated riches. Sometimes the state solved this problem with compulsory displacements ostensibly for the peasants' own good, wrenching as they were, relocating them to areas with more available land.[70] This omnipresent threat compelled the state to set up checkpoints at passes. Villagers were called on to report their neighbors' whereabouts. Regulated movements were so ingrained that Han peasants expected to register with an "underworld bureaucracy" in the afterlife.[71]

[63] Mu-Chou Poo, *Daily Life in Ancient China* (Cambridge: Cambridge University Press, 2018), 39.
[64] John Keay, *China: A History* (New York: Harper Collins, 2009), 112.
[65] Confucius, *The Analects* (Oxford: Oxford University Press, 2008), 65.
[66] Cited in T'ung-tsu Ch'ü, *Han Social Structure* (Seattle: University of Washington Press, 1972), 108.
[67] Ibid., 110. [68] Ibid., 108. [69] Ibid., 110.
[70] Cho-yun Hsu, *Han Agriculture: The Formation of the Early Chinese Agrarian Economy* (Seattle: University of Washington Press, 1980), 27.
[71] Poo, *Daily Life in Ancient China*, 68.

Han bureaucracy grew to 120,000 bureaucratic officials, tenfold that of imperial Rome. The core of which were located in Gaozu's new capital, Chang'an, located near Xianyang.[72] To tax, register, and conscript an empire of fifty-seven million, these officials needed access to villages and towns. An "outer" court ran the provinces while an "inner" court stayed in the capital.[73] Construction continued, eventually reaching 22,000 miles of roads designed to connect the two largest cities of Chang'an and Luoyang in one of the great dyadic relationships of ancient times. This is more than quadruple the number of roads completed by the Qin. Some roads were fifty feet wide and tree-lined. This road network emanated outward from these cities in an empire-wide hub and spoke system.[74] They were dotted with inns, rest houses, postal stations, as well as toll checkpoints.[75] This in no way implied freedom to traverse the country. Life for most meant staying in place. "Roads allowed movement throughout China," noted Mark Edward Lewis, "but it was a highly controlled movement to serve the purposes of the state."[76]

Han China reached an unprecedented size under emperor Wudi (141–87 BCE), taking the offensive against the weakened Xiongnu state in present-day Mongolia and pushing northwest into uncharted territory. The seminal odyssey of Zhang Qian (195–c. 114 BCE), an envoy dispatched from Chang'an during Wudi's reign, marked a new era in Chinese globalism. Wudi sent him ostensibly to recruit allies against the Xiongnu but also to learn about the west.[77] He returned after years abroad in 126 BCE with the first detailed information about Central Asia. He reported that Afghanistan had "cities, mansions, and houses as in China," confirming that China was not the only settled urbanized state and had been isolated for millennia.[78] "These oases resembled small city-states more than kingdoms," as Valerie Hansen put it, with some cities reaching the thousands in population.[79] Zhang Qian reached Bactria in what is now northern Afghanistan, once influenced by Hellenism from the conquests of Alexander the Great (see Chapter 4). More startling, he learned that Chinese merchants had already arrived in Bactria, their goods for sale in market stalls.[80] This was the heart of what early modern scholars dubbed the Silk Road.[81] The

[72] Dingxin Zhao, "The Han Bureaucracy: Its Origin, Nature, and Development," in Walter Scheidel (ed.), *State Power in Ancient China and Rome* (Oxford: Oxford University Press, 2015), 56–89, 56.

[73] The most detailed and referenced overview of the Han governing structure is still Hans Bielenstein, *The Bureaucracy of Han Times* (Cambridge: Cambridge University Press, 1980).

[74] S. A. M. Adshead, *China in World History* (New York: Palgrave, 1988), 15.

[75] Lewis, *Early Chinese Empires*, 55. [76] Ibid., 57.

[77] Adshead, *China in World History*, 25. [78] Cotterell, *Imperial Capitals of China*, 46.

[79] Valerie Hansen, *The Silk Road: A New History* (Oxford: Oxford University Press, 2012), 16.

[80] Ibid., 14.

[81] The Geographer Ferdinand von Richthofen coined the phrase "Silk Road" in 1877. It was not a misnomer. Silk was indeed a central commodity along these trails.

Silk Roads, plural, were not one single continental belt but an archipelago of cities connected by nearly invisible trails, requiring local guides. Like other land networks we have explored, the Silk Roads were strictly retail, transporting luxury items.[82] No known expeditions traversed the whole expanse at this time, but products did. Silk reached the Mediterranean. Roman textiles reached China.[83] Both sides knew little about the origins of the goods changing hands across Eurasia. Han expansion was critical to opening up these geographic horizons.[84]

Han influence grew through conquest and diplomacy, as the empire tried its best to exert authority westward. Seminal Han historian Sima Qian (c. 145–c. 86 BCE) records his contemporary emperor Wudi ordering large-scale resettlements westward to populate its new frontiers. His landmark history *Records of the Grand Historian* is the source of the traditional figure of 700,000 impoverished Chinese forcibly transplanted to distant colonies.[85] The state erected an elaborate system of towers with beacons to notify garrisons of unrest.[86] Wudi established new commanderies with earthworks built to lock in these foreign land grabs, a sign of the offensive nature of what appear architecturally to be defensive bulwarks against aggressive outsiders.[87]

For all of these expressions of state power, this terrain was impossible to govern permanently, overextending China's state capability. Chang'an engaged in a flurry of diplomacy in lieu of control, blurring the lines between tributary and ally. The imperial capital at Chang'an always preferred to project the image of universalism reminiscent of Rome's *orbis terrarum*, referring to the state as "the world" with the capital at the center. This was at best a partial truth. China did not directly control all of the dozens of kingdoms in Central Asia or its transhumant population, all of which were instrumental to this incipient globalization. Still, standardized rules smoothed the flow of trade, with goods circulating through Eurasia's major empires, including Parthia and India.[88] At its peak in size around the early first century BCE, the Han Empire approximately reached Uzbekistan. A kind of hegemonic stability prevailed, where the presence of a singular great power increased interstate interaction. Han China was now a known quantity, with emissaries across the Eurasian

82 Hansen, *Silk Road*, 9. 83 Adshead, *China in World History*, 38.

84 Peter Frankopan, *The Silk Roads: A New History of the World* (New York: Vintage, 2015), 10.

85 Sima Qian, *Records of the Grand Historian: Han Dynasty II* (New York: Columbia University Press, 1961), 68.

86 Hansen, *Silk Road*, 14.

87 Michael Loewe, "The Former Han Dynasty," in Denis Twitchett and John K. Fairbank (eds.), *The Cambridge History of China: Volume I, The Ch'in and Han Empires* (Cambridge: Cambridge University Press, 1986), 103–222, 165.

88 Ropp, *China in World History*, 28; Stearns, *Globalization in World History*, 26.

world arriving at Chang'an with tribute.[89] The new city was the greatest of all Silk Road landings.

Han Chang'an

Chang'an, at the height of the Early Han Dynasty in the first century BCE, was the largest city in the world, possibly three times the size of Republican Rome at the time.[90] It sat at the heart of a riverine network, served by eight rivers, possibly ten.[91] There were also valuable lakes and hot springs. It was not enough. The city grew far too large to be self-sufficient. A remarkable system of canals and wells offered clean water. It transported grain to the capital, and distributed food throughout the hinterlands. The system could even deliver supplies to the northern defenses, as Chang'an was perilously close to the transhumant frontier of present-day Mongolia.[92] The abundance of water made this an unusually lush "green city" with vast parklands.[93]

Beginning as the residence for emperor and court, the city and inner suburbs contained more than one million residents by the time of emperor Chengdi's reign from 33 to 7 BCE.[94] There were 30,000 bureaucrats in the city managing the empire. The first century BCE Han poet and historian Ban Gu's rhapsody captures this complexity:

> They erected a metal fortress a myriad spans long,
> Dredged the surrounding moat to form a gaping chasm,
> Cleared broad avenues three lanes wide,
> Placed twelve gates for passage in and out,
> Within, the city was pierced by roads and streets,
> With ward gates and portals nearly a thousand.
> In the nine markets they set up bazaars,
> Their wares separated by type, their shop rows distinctly divided.
> There was no room for people to turn their heads,
> Or for chariots to wheel about.
> People crammed into the city, spilled into the suburbs,
> Everywhere streaming into the hundred shops.
> Red dust gathered in all directions;
> Smoke blended with the clouds.

[89] Intriguingly, one such group claimed to be bearing gifts from the Roman Empire. They would have been sent by Marcus Aurelius, though there is no proof of their story. Hansen, *Silk Road*, 18.

[90] Michael Nylan, "Introduction," in Michael Nylan and Griet Vankeerberghen (eds.), *Chang'an 26 BCE: An Augustan Age in China* (Seattle: University of Washington Press, 2015), 3–54, 3.

[91] Ibid., 8.

[92] Michael Nylan, "Supplying the Capital with Water and Food," in Michael Nylan and Griet Vankeerberghen (eds.), *Chang'an 26 BCE: An Augustan Age in China* (Seattle: University of Washington Press, 2015), 99–130, 108.

[93] Nylan, "Introduction," 23. [94] Ibid., 18.

> Thus the people being both numerous and rich,
> There was gaiety and pleasure without end.
> The men and women of the capital
> Were the most distinctive of the five regions.
> Men of pleasure compared with dukes and marquises;
> Shop girls were dressed more lavishly than ladies Ji or Jiang.[95]

Ban Gu's rhapsody was intended as a bit of local boosterism. Still, it's hard not to feel its excitement leap off the page, and with reason. This was, as one recent study of daily life in Han times explains, the "most important place in the entire empire, the center of matters political, economic, educational, military, ritual, and cultural, or simply extravagant, and thus a model for every city to emulate."[96] More than one-quarter of the empire lived in or near sizeable cities. Distinctly Chinese aesthetics had matured throughout Chinese cities. So urban experiences wouldn't have been entirely new to every first-time visitor.[97] Chang'an stood at the top of a instituted urban hierarchy.[98] Just as sumptuary laws ensured no wealthy merchants or bureaucrats could mimic the styles of the emperor, no city was permitted to look quite like Chang'an.[99]

Travelers approaching the city would first pass through its outer sprawl, which was notably important for market and ceremonial functions. They would have been astonished at the massive wall surrounding the core city, probably the largest artificial structure they would have ever seen up to that point. At 12 meters high, this 25 kilometer perimeter of rammed yellow earth had three gates on each of four sides.[100] (For perspective, this dwarfed the Theodosian Walls that protected Constantinople from the fourth century CE) Chang'an wasn't contained in a perfect rectangle, which Chinese planners considered symmetrical to a universal order beneath the heavens. Modular planning within the walled city was disrupted by the rivers flowing along its northern and western sides. This may have been meant to resemble a constellation, Ursa Major or Minor, or maybe it was pragmatic conformity to the terrain.[101]

Once inside, palaces were the central architectural feature of capital cities in China, which were heavily planned in comparison with the cacophonous Roman street map. Palace complexes occupied two-thirds of the city within the walls, underscoring the drastic chasm between classes in this period of

95 Cited in Poo, *Daily Life in Ancient China*, 101. 96 Ibid., 102.
97 Nylan, "Introduction," 36.
98 Gilbert Rozman, *Urban Networks in Ch'ing China and Tokugawa Japan* (Princeton: Princeton University Press, 2015), 18.
99 Nylan, "Introduction," 18.
100 Nancy Shatzman Steinhardt, *Chinese Architecture: A History* (Princeton: Princeton University Press, 2019), 32.
101 Ibid.

concentrated authority.[102] By Chengdi's reign there were five palaces, each surrounded by massive ramparts with statement-making gates and towers. They were the residences of the emperor and other leading figures, especially the dowager empress and heir apparent. They were also important sites of religious ritual and administration.[103] The city's general emphasis on private space over public spectacle extended to gender roles, with women largely confined to domesticity within the nobility.[104] If poor, women worked in the court as singers and dancers.[105] Sports and gladiatorial games happened mainly in private spaces for select audiences. Shanglin Park in the palace district offered a bucolic setting for the ruling classes, its lush gardens even had hunting grounds.[106] This greenbelt contained artificial lakes and wooded areas containing wild exotic animals. Their importation spoke to the geographic reach of imperial might, but with limited public consumption.

Palace architecture was designed to conceal rather than reveal dynastic power, with a system of elevated corridors that hid emperors' movements. Horizontal architecture affirmed the distribution of power in the urban landscape. Large flat palaces avoided high-rise towers to which the public could affix its gaze on the court. They offer no dramatically elevated lookouts for casual viewing. That would have reminded observers of the limited size of the walled city whose spaces the state firmly controlled. By extension it would have laid bare the unfathomable and anarchic expanse leading to the horizon, which the state for all its power struggled to govern.[107] Palaces did stand on elevated platforms, ensuring that visiting dignitaries and ranking officials needed to climb wide staircases to reach heads of state, always looking up at them. Where the general public was concerned, towers represented surveillance rather than grandiosity, the places from which officials monitored the city's dense warrens. Beyond that, verticality was reserved for the gate towers along the walls and the imposing imperial tombs north of the city.[108]

Han China did not foster a slave society on the order of magnitude of the Roman Empire (see Chapter 5), but it relied heavily on various forms of unfree labor. Convicts and conscripts bore the brunt of city construction. War captives, convicts and their families, however, were often formally enslaved, as were debt-burdened rural peasants sold off by their families. They performed

[102] Ibid.
[103] Carlos F. Noreña, "Chang'an and Rome: Structural Parallels and Logics of Urban Form," in Walter Scheidel (ed.), *State Power in Ancient China and Rome* (Oxford: Oxford University Press, 2015), 75–98, 78.
[104] Ch'ü, *Han Social Structure*, 50. [105] Ibid., 53.
[106] Poo, *Daily Life in Ancient China*, 106.
[107] For a fascinating dialogue on this aesthetic, see Lewis, *Construction of Space in Early China*, 159.
[108] Noreña, "Chang'an and Rome," 88.

all manner of functions in the city, and were common sights, some of them with their faces tattooed for identification purposes.[109] At one point the Han government owned 100,000 slaves forced into work ranging from managing animals to working as messengers. They were also commonly owned among Chang'an's wealthy merchants, nobles, and officials, performing blue- and white-collar functions.[110] Analogous to modern world cities, Chang'an's remarkable concentration of wealth seldom trickled down, but instead created a large demand for a laboring underclass. In ancient alpha cities this burden always fell on unfree labor.

The Eastern and Western markets sat side by side in the north end of the city. These two markets occupied 500,000 and 250,000 square meters respectively, making them the largest of the nine markets documented around Chang'an, and referenced in Ban Gu's poem.[111] They were the most important public gathering places in the city. Like today's alpha cities, Chang'an's concentrated wealth made it a shopping haven. The Western Market was a site of industrial activity, producing pottery, sculpture, and coinage. The Eastern Market was arranged in rows of stalls selling "all kinds of consumer goods such as food, wine, cloth, utensils, tools, medicinal herbs, cattle, poultry, shoes, silk, swords, vegetables, funerary equipment, books, household items, and luxury items such as jewelry and cosmetics."[112] This was urban spectacle at its most raucous, where in Ban Gu's words there "was no room for people to turn their heads."

It was some *mise en scène*, a rare space where various walks of life converged, where thieves and the down and out watched ostentatiously dressed nobles enter in carriages, flouting sumptuary laws. You could edge past beggars, entertainers, and speech givers and into a tavern. But it was a scene that unnerved the state. These forums were walled and gated, overseen by five-story surveillance towers. The state tightly regulated prices. There was none of the bargaining we might imagine in such boisterous markets. Goods needed fixed price tags, and transactions had to be recorded.[113] Severed body parts on display in the markets warned against stepping too far out of line, as did the public executions occurring here. The displays of goods would have been familiar to modern eyes, but much probably disturbed onlookers even in their times. Urban air did not exactly make one free. This was literally so, as Han markets frequently featured enslaved women in embroidered clothes for sale in pens alongside livestock.[114] The city brought you closer to a

[109] Ch'ü, *Han Social Structure*, 136.
[110] Ibid., 142.
[111] Noreña, "Chang'an and Rome," 83.
[112] Poo, *Daily Life in Ancient China*, 111.
[113] Lewis, *Early Chinese Empires*, 85.
[114] Ch'ü, *Han Social Structure*, 141.

concentrated apparatus of state, which was dangerous in a society where public critics of the emperor were cut in two at the waist.[115]

More prosaically, the Chinese ruling elite were ambivalent about the merchant classes that prospered with increasing commercial complexity in cities. There was no independent bourgeoisie, and no threat of one, owing to a state-imposed glass ceiling. Commoners made fortunes in merchant trades, though many were impoverished peddlers. Laws curbed their wealth, influence, and purchasing power.[116] They were barred from official positions.[117] The city's literary classes of poets and scholars often frowned on merchant profiteering, even if city life couldn't quite exist without it. The atmospheres in the Eastern and Western markets reflected this culture of distrust. In all, commoners from every economic strata had reasons to avoid potent state regulation and escape scrutiny in the capital. By contrast, argues Lewis, "the outer cities remained alien to the government's ideal patterns of service and hierarchy," attracting rural deserters.[118] Lastly, high mortality in dense cities created miseries for rich and poor alike.[119]

Most of the rest of the city's 160 wards (*li*) were residential. Needless to say, living space was tight. The dearth of housing inside the city compelled the nonelite to build homes in the suburbs.[120] Broad, impressive boulevards with special lanes along class lines emphasized the planned nature of the capital, their width usefully serving as fire barriers in a wooden city. Once inside a typical ward in this sea of "walls within walls," spontaneity took over.[121] Behind each gate was a crowded self-contained community in tightly packed housing, doors opening out into narrow alleyways. These streets could only accommodate foot traffic. More affluent *li* had access to main streets, which handled horse and carriage traffic. As in later Tang Chang'an, the city gates locked each night. This was securitization in the extreme, the kind of measure in containing civil unrest that cities usually disguise today. At the same time, this could potentially have reduced the late night banditry common in other ancient cities. Lower level officials in service to the ruling family lived cramped lives in these wards. They shared space with pigs, disposing of human and animal waste in gutters along the street, which drained into the

115 Ibid., 69.
116 Attitudes toward merchants in China were strikingly similar to those of the Greeks and Romans. Ibid., 113.
117 Ibid., 119. 118 Lewis, *Early Chinese Empires*, 87.
119 Plagues, however, were less frequent and intense in ancient China than in Europe. Zhongwei Zhao, "Long-Term Mortality Patterns in Chinese History: Evidence from Mortality Patterns in Chinese History," *Population Studies* 51 (1997), 117–127, 121.
120 Poo, *Daily Life in Ancient China*, 107. 121 Noreña, "Chang'an and Rome," 81.

mote surrounding the city.[122] A Qin-constructed canal brought fresh water to them from a lake.

Remarkable as ancient Chang'an was, it was only the heart of a larger network.

A Radial Network

The number of cities in Han China grew from 800 in Gaozu's time to 1,500 by the turn of the millennium, concentrated in the Yellow River Basin.[123] Though Chang'an and Luoyang dominate the literary record, a number of large cities existed in a hub and spoke pattern radiating outward from this urban heartland.[124] Gaozu initiated an inner constellation of "tomb towns" near Chang'an for the purpose of maintaining the hulking Han mausoleums, artificial mountains to the north of the capital.[125] A canal enabled this string of cities to conquer otherwise inhospitable environments, which had populations upward of 300,000, so large they needed imported grain to survive. They were populated through a series of involuntary migrations of rich and poor alike, the largest of which uprooting nearly three-quarters of a million people.[126]

Over time these cities played diversified roles in Chang'an's artificial ecosystem. They provided human capital for city administration and a northern military bulwark.[127] Rooted in the ancestral values of the times, these relics and the state power that forced them into being are anathema to twenty-first century norms. Yet they anticipated something modern, a bona fide metropolitan region rather than a standalone city. This zone of two million people resembles the imbricated networks that are the building blocks of the world city system today.

Luoyang was the capital of the reconstituted Eastern Han (also called the Later Han) for most of the first and second centuries CE. Located 350 kilometers east of Chang'an, this was China's second city during Early Han times. Though he ruled from Chang'an, the "usurper" emperor Wang Mang (45 BCE–23 CE) called Luoyang "the centre of the earth."[128] He transferred resources to the city, creating a dual core in managing the empire. In short,

122 Poo, *Daily Life in Ancient China*, 110. 123 Nylan, "Introduction," 36.

124 Carlos F. Noreña, "Urban Systems in the Han and Roman Empires: State Power and Social Control," in Walter Scheidel (ed.), *State Power in Ancient China and Rome* (Oxford: Oxford University Press, 2015), 181–202, 185.

125 Lewis, *Construction of Space in Early China*, 178.

126 Michael Loewe, "The Tombs Built for Han Chengdi and Migrations of the Population," in Michael Nylan and Griet Vankeerberghen (eds.), *Chang'an 26 BCE: An Augustan Age in China* (Seattle: University of Washington Press, 2015), 201–217, 213.

127 Noreña, "Urban Systems in the Han and Roman Empires," 194.

128 Rafe de Crispigny, *Fire over Luoyang: A History of the Later Han Dynasty 23–220 AD* (Boston: Brill, 2016), 19.

China had not one Rome, but two. These cities sat definitively at the top of the urban hierarchy. A main highway connected them, running parallel to the river network.[129] The city was surrounded by a controlled water system that sped transport and communication.[130] This was vital in an age of rising Xiongnu threats (instigated by an antagonistic foreign policy route taken by Wang Mang).

The walled cities shared traditional Chinese imperial forms. As a near-perfect rectangle, Luoyang is a clearer overall example of the Chinese modular. Both were administrative centers. The two palace complexes dominated the urban footprint.[131] The city's topography was also designed to control and monitor movements, with underpasses allowing the state forces to reach trouble spots.[132] A drum tower in the heart of the city announced curfew, and traversing the city required passing checkpoints.[133] As the empire lost control of outlying territories, it lost its ability to prevent crime and civil unrest within the city, a sign of the connection between state power within and beyond the walls.[134] As in Chang'an, the markets were sites of boisterous city life and commercial prowess. The urban footprint was smaller than Chang'an's but more densely populated. Centrally planned broad boulevards gave way to crowded city life. The city was a center of intellectual frisson, with bookshops hosting scholarly debates.[135]

Tang Global

The Han Dynasty ended in 220 CE, initiating another extended period of division between powerful kingdoms. This was not a so-called dark age as we saw in Mesopotamia and Greece, where urbanization and writing receded, but a fluid and protracted period of conflict between rival dynasties. Systems of population control continued developing in the Early Medieval period, practices the Tang inherited.[136] The Sui Dynasty reunified China in 589 under emperor Wendi. Recalling the Qin, the breakneck Sui building spree helped fuel its overthrow, paving the ground for three centuries of Tang rule by 618. The Sui asserted administrative control over the hinterlands, doubling the number of taxable households.[137] This was comparable to the power structure

[129] Ibid., 24 [130] Ibid., 23. [131] Steinhardt, *Chinese Architecture*, 39.
[132] Cotterell, *Imperial Capitals of China*, 74. [133] Ibid., 73. [134] Ibid., 74.
[135] Poo, *Daily Life in Ancient China*, 119.
[136] See Yang Lu, "Managing Locality in Early Medieval China: Evidence from Changsha," in Wendy Swartz, Robert Ford Campany, Yang Lu, and Jessey J. C. Choo (eds.), *Early Medieval China: A Sourcebook* (New York: Columbia University Press, 2014), 95–107.
[137] Arthur F. Wright, "The Sui Dynasty: 581–617," in Denis Twitchett and John K. Fairbank (eds.), *The Cambridge History of China: Sui and Tang China, 589–906* (Cambridge: Cambridge University Press, 1979), 48–149, 67.

in previous eras, where "a network of cities extracted income from taxation on crops and cloth" from the hinterlands.[138] Architecture in Wendi's new capital Daxiangcheng ("Great Revival City") referenced Han glory.[139] Subsequent Tang rulers even renamed the city Chang'an, with the remains of the old eponymous city sitting neglected 10 kilometers away.

The emperor's successor Yangdi rebuilt Luoyang in "extraordinary splendor" according to observers.[140] Canal building dwarfed the Qin-Han epoch. Yangdi's Grand Canal – the name for a series of canals still in use today – laid the groundwork for the Sui-Tang city network. This was, as one historian put it, "without a doubt, the grandest navigation system ever undertaken by a single sovereign in pre-modern history."[141] It linked the port city of Hangzhou with Suzhou, Yangzhou, Kaifeng, Luoyang, and Tang Chang'an.[142] All of these cities would play important roles in Chinese history in the ensuing centuries. The canals enabled bulk trades, with supplies reaching cities that were once famine-prone. Barges carried diversified staples across China's remote, distinctive growing terrains in an interdependent food system.[143] However, the toll on the laborers who constructed the Grand Canal was so immense that, once the supply of men with pickaxes, shovels, and wheelbarrows (an invention still unique to China) ran thin, the state conscripted women.[144] Meanwhile, reconstructing and expanding the Great Wall to the north required one million *corvée* laborers. Only half returned home.[145] Famines ensued. Peasants deserted and eventually revolted. On top of it, the emperor drafted massive armies in an abortive attempt to conquer present-day Korea, all of this culminating in Yangdi's assassination.

The Tang looked back reverentially on the Han, drawing on traditional urban forms. But the new Chang'an departed from the Han capital in significant ways. The Tang dynasty assumed a leading position in a shrinking world, evident in the new Chang'an's urban landscape. Emperor Wendi had been a devout Buddhist, constructing skyscraper-scale pagodas that introduced a never before seen verticalism to the city.[146] These changed Chinese urban aesthetics. Giant Wild Goose Pagoda, constructed at the height of Tang rule and now a UNESCO heritage site in present-day Xian, attests to the cosmopolitanism of the times. Knowledge sectors also rendered Tang Chang'an distinct from its ancient predecessor. This is where the monk explorer Xuanzang (602–664 CE) translated a trove of Buddhist texts he returned with after a seventeen-year journey across South Asia in 645.[147] A goal of the new

138 Lewis, *China's Cosmopolitan Empire*, 26. 139 Keay, *China*, 224. 140 Ibid., 228.
141 Ibid., 230. 142 See the illustration in ibid., 228. 143 Ibid., 231. 144 Ibid., 232.
145 Ibid., 230. 146 Ibid., 224.
147 S. A. M. Adshead, *T'ang China: The Rise of the East in World History* (New York: Palgrave, 2004), 43.

Chang'an was to restore the education system. The Sui founders expanded it with new innovations. The examination system was redesigned to attract talent from outside powerful families. The university established the first organized faculty in calligraphy.[148]

Taizong, who was emperor during Xuanzang's time, at first took a lighter approach to the peasantry, mindful of how an abused public led to the downfall of the Sui. Taizong, known for his inquisitiveness, had a barrage of questions for the famed explorer. But there was more behind the inquiry: The empire was expanding mightily and needed reconnaissance.[149] On consolidating power, Taizong launched massive campaigns westward, expanding the empire to its greatest size since the Han. It was a period of intense diplomacy, with envoys traveling extensively.

Scholars struggle to situate the Tang Empire within these "outer realms." Adshead argues that Tang China's political, economic, and cultural power projection circa 700 made it hegemonic on par with the United States at its peak.[150] Wang Zhenping's extensive study of Tang Foreign policy complicates this picture, describing China as one player in a "multipolar" field. Statecraft was messy, as Tang China interacted with city-states, territorial empires, and nomadic polities.[151]

The rise of Islam saw the emergence of new great empires, the Umayyad and the Abbasid Caliphates, during the Tang era. The Indian Ocean was a hub of seaborne trade, fostering a high period of global interaction comparable to the Mediterranean *longue dureé* investigated by Fernand Braudel (which we will explore in Chapter 9), according to the magisterial studies of Indian Ocean trade by K. N. Chaudhuri.[152] Arab geographers, diplomats, and explorers accelerated this process. During the Tang period, sea travel increased in importance. The world came to China from the sea, convening in major port cities, with the Guangzhou and Yangzhou *entrepôts* home to Arab, Indian, Persian, and Southeast Asian merchants.[153] Chinese vessels themselves moved outward during the later Tang era, after the An Lushan rebellion of 755 disrupted Silk Road trade. In all, China was again the center of gravity in Eurasia with far ranging consequences. In Chaudhuri's words:

> The administrative unification and the economic achievements of Tang China ... led in the Far East to the emergence of a larger zone of Chinese cultural influence. In spite of periods of civil war, political disintegration, and foreign invasion, the Celestial empire

[148] Cotterell, *Imperial Capitals of China*, 115.
[149] Wang Zhenping, *Tang China in Multi-Polar Asia* (Honolulu: University of Hawaii Press, 2013), 191.
[150] Adshead, *T'ang China*, 1. [151] Zhenping, *Tang China in Multi-Polar Asia*, 231.
[152] K. N. Chaudhuri, *Trade and Civilisation in the Indian Ocean: An Economic History from the Rise of Islam to 1750* (Cambridge: Cambridge University Press, 1985), 21.
[153] Keay, *China*, 171.

> continued to act … as an area of economic high pressure, attracting itself overland caravans, tributary missions from foreign princes, and large oceangoing vessels engaged in a two-way traffic. The Sinicisation of a large part of Asia and its people was as much connected with the political and military expansion of China as a general economic and social acceptance of her cultural values and standards of life.[154]

Put simply, imperial China's reconstitution created booming business. Silk Road traffic grew, with trade flowing through this complicated menagerie of states. The adaptive – and frequently conquered – polity of Sogdiana unified by a shared Persian language illustrated this amorphousness. It changed forms over time to emerge as the richest country in Central Asia.[155] There were also Sogdian-speaking city-states. "Their customs are slippery and tricky, and they frequently cheat and deceive, greatly desiring wealth, and fathers and sons alike seek profit," asserted the traveler Xuanzang.[156] This stereotypical language speaks their critical mercantile role for a Chinese gentry skeptical of merchants yet in need of them. Sogdian cities flourished across Central Asia in Tang times, evidenced by shared urban forms. Sogdian communities were critical to the economies of Chang'an, Luoyang, and other major Chinese cities.[157]

Samarkand in present-day Uzbekistan was at its commercial peak. It was a critical node in a Eurasia-spanning city network between the Caliphate and China. The smaller city of Panjikent has left a trove of archeological records behind by its estimated 7,000 residents before the Arabs conquered the city in the eighth century. Today, archeologists are painstakingly uncovering the city's housing, streets, alleys, commercial bazaars, and temples showing religious syncretism. The city was an important stop for caravans between Samarkand and China. Differences in housing sizes show Panjikent's inherent inequalities, while the proximity of shops evince blurred boundaries between residential and commercial uses of space.[158]

The Silk Roads during the Tang era represent the most important expansion of geographic knowledge in medieval times. Map making developed in sophistication along with Silk Road travel.[159] In fact, the effort to map the Silk Roads never ended. A project initiated in 1988 by UNESCO, utilizing Geographic Information Systems (GIS) technology, reveals the dense system of primary and secondary cities managing what appear to be fairly compact routes.[160] *Silk Nodes* would be a less elegant but equally apt designation, as the routes required intensive management from cities. Urbanization happened in

[154] Chaudhuri, *Trade and Civilisation in the Indian Ocean*, 34. [155] Hansen, *Silk Road*, 12[illegible].
[156] Ibid., 116. [157] Ibid., 120. [158] Ibid., 124.
[159] Peter Whitfield, "Mapping the Silk Roads," in Susan Whitfield (ed.), *Silk Roads: People, Cultures, Landscapes* (Oakland: University of California Press, 2019), 20–39, 21.
[160] Ibid., 38.

conjunction with the flow of people and goods. This was the most geographically expansive world city network prior to the economic merger of the Americas with Africa and Eurasia (see Chapters 7 and 11). "By the thirteenth century," one specialist points out, "there were markets in the Mediterranean for Central Asian slaves, in Iran for Chinese rhubarb and tea, and in China for African and Indian ivory."[161] Textile imagery shows shared aesthetics from Tang China to the Middle East.[162]

Recent scholarship on the Silk Roads explores ties between Africa and Eurasia, looking at the routes in terms of cultural and religious exchange, which overlapped with economic production.[163] Buddhist monasteries were important conduits for trade between China and India.[164] The Buddhist complex at Dunhuang in China served as a repository for cross-cultural art and writing, housing materials, and artifacts spanning from 400 to 1000 CE.[165] In short, the Eurasia axis was the center of the world in Tang times. Byzantine, Sassanian, and later Islamic coinage flowed across these regions.[166] Between empires, Central Asian kingdoms minted silk currencies and coins. Islamic silver coins, the preferred currency in the trafficking of slaves, have been found as far afield as Scandinavia.[167] Cairo, Isfahan, and Baghdad each expanded markedly in tandem with Silk Roads trades.[168] These cities had remarkably cosmopolitan districts in their mercantile primes, home to multitudes of languages, religions, and foreign colonies.

*****

The Turkic and Uighur Khaganates, and the Tibetan Empire were ascendant powers at various points in the Tang era.[169] Steppe empires were pivotal in

161 Susan Whitfield, *Life Along the Silk Road* (Oakland: University of California Press, 2015), 201.

162 Mariachiara Gasparini, *Transcending Patterns: Silk Road Cultural and Artistic Interactions through Central Asian Textile Images* (Honolulu: University of Hawaii Press, 2020), 17.

163 See, especially, Susan Whitfield (ed.), *Silk Roads: People, Cultures, Landscapes* (Oakland: University of California Press, 2019). Whitfield's exploration of the Roads is expansive in both time and place.

164 Liu Xinru, "Buddhism and Trade: Moving Eastwards from Gandhāra to China," in Susan Whitfield (ed.), *Silk Roads: People, Cultures, Landscapes* (Oakland: University of California Press, 2019), 152–167, 155.

165 Gasparini, *Transcending Patterns*, 5.

166 Touraj Daryaee, "Great Empires of the Silk Roads," in Susan Whitfield (ed.), *Silk Roads: People, Cultures, Landscapes* (Oakland: University of California Press, 2019), 294–301.

167 Robert Bracey, "Money and Mints," in Susan Whitfield (ed.), *Silk Roads: People, Cultures, Landscapes* (Oakland: University of California Press, 2019), 303–309, 308.

168 Tim Williams, "Arteries of the Silk Roads," in Susan Whitfield (ed.), *Silk Roads: People, Cultures, Landscapes* (Oakland: University of California Press, 2019), 282–289.

169 Jonathan Karam Skaff, *Sui-Tang China and Its Turko-Mongol Neighbors: Culture, Power, and Connections, 580–800* (Oxford: Oxford University Press, 2012), 23.

what was the most remarkable zone of globalization in the Medieval world, with Turkic fashions all the rage in Chang'an. Christopher I. Beckwith's study of the Silk Roads reminds us that they stood at the center, not the periphery of Eurasia in the age of empires.[170] Transhumance was not urban civilization's polar opposite, contrary to Tang universalist discourses.[171] Standards of living were generally higher in nomadic societies, which relied less than China did on heavily exploited fixed agriculture.[172] These zones were militarily interdependent, with steppe battle tactics diffusing across Asia. Chinese emperors sought to augment their stables with steppe horses.[173] Tang China relied on Turkic armies to quell the catastrophic An Lushan rebellion.[174]

Chinese borderlands and migratory conditions recall the Roman *limes*, where the seminal twentieth century scholar of frontier histories Owen Lattimore saw important parallels.[175] A major difference, of course, is China's massive Great Wall, mythologized as a clean and neat boundary between tranquil civility and aggressive barbarism (Figure 6.1). The Great Wall's effectiveness in blocking maneuverable nomadic armies is doubtful. Sima Qian's *Records of the Grand Historian* reports nomadic marauders "crossing the border every year" during Han times, retreating back with ease.[176] The Chinese state engaged in marauding of its own, taking advantage of its swelling population to launch massive incursions beyond the wall. For this, the wall enabled imperial forces to assemble quickly over otherwise insurmountable terrain. "Thus military walls could be an integral part of an expansionist 'offensive' project," argues di Cosmo.[177] Even with fifty million people under Tang administration, the dynasty could never quite subdue much smaller pastoral nomadic populations, at least not for very long.[178] At the same time, the perilous proximity of China's great cities to the frontier – the bulk of the population was still concentrated in the northern Yellow River Basin at this time – led to constant fear of attack.[179]

As Lattimore implores us to understand, "the linear Frontier never existed except as a concept."[180] At most it was a rough line of best fit between differing, environmentally determined modes of living. Lattimore asserts that

[170] Christopher I. Beckwith, *Empires of the Silk Road: A History of Eurasia from the Bronze Age to the Present* (Princeton: Princeton University Press, 2009), xxiii.

[171] Shao-Yun Yang, *The Way of the Barbarians: Redrawing Ethnic Boundaries in Tang and Song China* (Seattle: University of Washington Press, 2019), 141.

[172] Beckwith, *Empires of the Silk Road*, xxiii.

[173] Liu Xinru, *The Silk Road in World History* (Oxford: Oxford University Press, 2010), 17.

[174] The rebel general was himself part Turkic. [175] Lattimore, *Studies in Frontier History*, 115.

[176] Qian, *Records of the Grand Historian*, 145.

[177] Nicola di Cosmo, *Ancient China and Its Enemies: The Rise of Nomadic Power in East Asian History* (Cambridge: Cambridge University Press, 2004), 139.

[178] Population figures cited in Skaff, *Sui-Tang China and Its Turko-Mongol Neighbors*, 26.

[179] Ibid., 30. [180] Lattimore, *Studies in Frontier History*, 115.

Figure 6.1 The Mutianyu section of the Great Wall, located 70 kilometers north of Beijing. Initiated by the Northern Qi dynasty in the 550s CE, this remarkable section of the wall purportedly required over a million laborers. It makes steep terrains traversable and its watchtowers allowed for frontier surveillance.
Photo by the author and Erin L. Leon.

there existed "a graduated series of social groups, from partly sinicized nomads and semibarbarized Chinese."[181] These groups largely coexisted, with the wall fostering interaction as well as it created division. Merchants arrived at its gates and frontier settlements with goods coming to or from the Silk Roads.[182]

The state did not always welcome the prevailing (unregulated) comity. Reflecting the cellular nature of the city, the wall was the outer shell of the empire, a point of official surveillance. It reflected a herculean effort at controlling an infinitely expansive terrain, something the state could only sporadically achieve. The city system required holding the lifeblood of premodern city networks, human populations, at their necessary posts. As cities were magnets for the literate classes, less labor-intensive pastoral lives appealed to a peasantry confined to a life of fixed toil. Conditions remained poor in the countryside as land concentrated into fewer hands with outsized

[181] Ibid. [182] Liu, *Silk Road in World History*, 12.

estates, underpinning an urban expansion.[183] The wall and an elaborate passport system prevented defections to freer societies. "The only way to avoid losing population, power, and wealth to Central Eurasia was to build walls, limit trading at frontier cities, and attack the steppe peoples as often as necessary to destroy them or keep them away," concludes Beckwith's extensive study.

The city in this geographical context drew the bulk of resources from Tang territory and beyond, including human resources. Taizong's frontier policy included the forcible resettlement of 100,000 Turks behind Chinese lines, with 10,000 living in Chang'an.[184] The city existed in this global context, becoming perhaps the world's most diverse metropolis.

Tang Chang'an: Medieval Apotheosis of Globalism

Tang Chang'an had 1.6 million residents, roughly the size of Philadelphia or Montreal today, with 2 million in the region.[185] Large numbers of unregistered denizens added to this count.[186] The largest Western European cities at 700 CE – the approximate heyday of Tang China – numbered only in the tens of thousands. Chang'an's scale strained the vocabulary of its literary scribes trying to describe it, as it had few parallels in its own time.

To reiterate, this new version of Chang'an aesthetically evoked its ancient namesake, but departed in key ways. Urban life reflected unprecedented geographic horizons and foreign religious influences. There were teahouses, a new concept. Tea drinks were imported by Buddhists from the humid south, where tea leaves grew, as the north and south of China became increasingly linked. There were restaurants and wine shops.[187] There were inns for travelers. The major markets – also called the Eastern and Western Markets – had warehouses where merchants stored goods, and proto-banks where they left money.[188] These markets spanned a half-square mile each, surrounded by walls. The Eastern Market specialized in domestic goods. On the opposite side of the city, the Western Market presided over the exotic. Camel caravans from the Silk Roads entered regularly to stock the dense stalls with foreign merchandise.[189] Much was unsettling, such as the sale of slaves alongside

[183] Denis Twitchett, *Land Tenure and the Social Order in T'ang and Sung China* (Oxford: Oxford University Press, 1962), 17.

[184] Howard J. Wechsler, "T'ai-tsung (Reign 626–49) the Consolidator," in Denis Twitchett and John K. Fairbank (eds.), *The Cambridge History of China: Sui and Tang China, 589–906* (Cambridge: Cambridge University Press, 1979), 188–241, 224.

[185] Victor Cunrui Xiong, *Sui-Tang Chang'an: A Study in the Urban History of Medieval China* (Ann Arbor: University of Michigan Press, 2000), 196.

[186] Ibid., 198. [187] Ibid., 190. [188] Hansen, *Silk Road*, 148. [189] Ibid.

animals.[190] Taizong forbade China's power elite from entering these markets, considering their cultures of consumption a corrupting influence.[191]

The walled, gated city was divided up by nine thoroughfares running north to south. These were bisected by twelve wide streets running east to west. The central north–south boulevard was 147 meters wide, while other avenues measured 69 meters in width.[192] This had cosmological significance. Chang'an was as symmetrical as a large city could be, a massive cellular rectangle, representing order to scale, from the universe down to the ward. Note the departure from the irregularly shaped Han city. These grand boulevards also encouraged a more earthly order, designed with a similar intention to Napoleon III's Parisian streets to enable crowd control. The central axis along Vermillion Bird Road reified divides along class lines, with the nobility located mainly in the more prosperous eastern half of the city. These streets ran through 110 distinct wards, which were larger than most modern city blocks and worlds unto themselves. These *li* comprised the vast majority of space in the core city. Inside some wards stood only a few mansions. While other wards were packed with thousands of residents in a maze of dense laneways. Improvisation within the central plan was a feature of the traditional Chinese layout. In the words of a widely quoted ninth century poem:

> Hundreds of houses, thousands of houses – like a chessboard.
> The twelve streets like a field planted with rows of cabbage.
> In the distance perceptible, dim, dim – the fire of a torchlight procession;
> And a single row of stellar lodges lying to the west of the Five Gates.[193]

Daming Palace ("Great Luminous Palace") sat just off the "chessboard" grid. The Xingqing palace sat at the city's eastern side. At the center of the northernmost tier presided Chang'an's palatial and administrative heart. The city had a larger footprint than Han Chang'an, approximately 9 by 10 kilometers. Height restrictions limited high-rise residences in the wooden city, but its uneven physical geography allowed for impressive vistas.[194] Still, emperors reserved the right to rule sight unseen, with "climbing up to a high place and looking down into the imperial palace" punishable by a year of labor servitude according to the *Tang Code*.[195]

The labor intensiveness of building at this scale unnerved the city's founding Sui emperor Wendi. This account recalls his observations on returning to a completed Daming Palace:

190 Ibid. 191 Ibid. 192 Cotterell, *Imperial Capitals of China*, 114.
193 Xiong, *Sui-Tang Chang'an*, 195.
194 Linda Rui Feng, *City of Marvel and Transformation* (Honolulu: University of Hawaii Press, 2015), 84.
195 Ibid.

> Finishing the palace, at a time of scarcity, entailed great sufferings on the part of the people. The superintendent of the work was a hard and unpitying master. When [Wendi] came to inspect the palace before he came to live in it, the superintendent had to hurriedly bury the bodies of workmen who had died of exhaustion. Their corpses were lying about everywhere. Seeing the enormous pile of buildings that had been erected for him, the emperor pointed his finger at the superintendent and said: "In this extravagance you have given reason to the people of the Empire to hate me with the bitterest hatred."[196]

The architect and engineer in charge of the project was Yuwen Kai, who recommended the location of the city, for its proximity to the Han past, but also as a place to start anew. He was in charge of major projects throughout the empire, including the Grand Canal. The emperor's concerns here speak to another less ethereal cycle, that of abuse and resistance by peasants.

Though Chang'an was unprecedented in its scale of planning and "open city" culture, conservative architectural traditions prevailed. Wood and rammed earth remained the favored building materials (the oldest surviving wooden buildings are from the Tang era). Sui emperor Wendi insisted the city follow traditional Chinese cosmology, deriding the Han for not consulting the ancestors in constructing their capital city. The modular form was standard in imperial buildings, later summarized in the twelfth century Song era building manual *Yingzao Fashi* ("State Building Standards").[197] There were prescribed forms of carpentry, décor, beams, and brackets. This system's emphasis on prefabricated, standardized components in timber frames prevented the emergence of any starchitects, but it was visionary nonetheless. The emphasis on "tree" and "orchid" bracketing anticipate the modernist organic.[198] There were no completed architectural plans for Tang buildings other than floor plans.[199] Using the *cai-fen* system, timbers whose cross-sections are at standardized scales, buildings could be constructed quickly at every size.[200] The result was a unique aesthetic across the Chinese sphere of influence that was replicable at proportions corresponding with cities' places in the urban hierarchy.[201] The major architectural features were understandable to travelers in any new city.

*****

196 Cited in Cotterell, *Imperial Capitals of China*, 113. Posthumous name inserted here.

197 Qinghua Guo, "Yingzao Fashi: Twelfth Century Chinese Building Manual," *Architectural History* 41, no. 1 (1998): 1–13, 1.

198 Jiren Feng, *Chinese Architecture and Metaphor: Song Culture in the* Yingzao Fashi *Building Manual* (Honolulu: University of Hawaii Press, 2012), 58.

199 Fu Xinian, *Traditional Chinese Architecture: Twelve Essays* (Princeton: Princeton University Press, 2017), 224.

200 Ibid., 209.

201 G. William Skinner, "Cities and the Hierarchy of Local Systems," G. William Skinner (ed.), *The City in Late Imperial China* (Palo Alto: Stanford University Press, 1977), 275–352, 287.

Tang Chang'an had large foreign communities, to the point where the city recognized foreign laws and customs provided offenses were committed within these groups. Central Asian fashions were all the rage. The most popular music and dance forms in Chang'an were from the steppe, Korea, and Southeast Asia.[202] Buddhist monasteries were economically powerful throughout the empire, with large caches of wealth and slaves.[203] Chang'an had Buddhist communities from India, Japan, Korea, and Tibet.[204] The city had Jewish and Christian settlers, and a large community of Zoroastrian Persians. Jewish, Arab, Turk, Sogdian, and Uighur merchants were constant presences in the city. This was a city whose diversity was unparalleled anywhere in the world, but the ward system served to sequester these communities.

This wasn't all. Chinese literati partook in this cultural flourishing. The road and canal networks smoothed the journey into the city for the annual exam period.[205] The examination system had been centralized, so examinees looking to forge careers in the bureaucracy had to find residence in Chang'an.[206] This group rhapsodized about the city, their London, their New York, their Paris. This, like all great cities, meant different things to different people. For this class it offered a sense of freedom, places to roam away from their small villages.[207] Class is a powerful force, but so is curiosity. Emperors could escape to the streets in disguise and play the *flâneur.*[208] Chang'an artists had a scene, albeit a male dominated one, with the literati descending on the city's famous Pleasure Quarter to consort with female courtesans. These were among the most educated women in the city but were largely forbidden from walking outside.

Conclusion: Finding the Modern

Scholars frequently refer to the Chinese system in the Han and Tang eras as modernist. In many ways this is overstated. The cellular structures of these two Chang'ans are archaic on the face of things. The scale of abuse in the labor system is hard to process in the context of modern norms. Like the Romanovs living in an antiquated paradigm well past its expiration date, dynastic China's rigid system today feels like a lost, barely understandable world.

Yet, from the stranger-than-fiction realities of the times, we see modern ideas prototyped. The Han bureaucracy was designed to express power across expansive geographies, much as governments and centralized corporations housed in global cities try to do today. Tang Chang'an was a "maximum city"

[202] Ropp, *China in World History*, 55. [203] Ibid., 62. [204] Ibid., 55.
[205] Feng, *City of Marvel and Transformation*, 46. [206] Ibid., 45. [207] Ibid., 50.
[208] Ibid., 71.

foreshadowing the modern megacity paradigm. The ward system belies the comparison, with its emphasis on sanitized top down planning that is more an attempt at Brasília than Mumbai. On the other hand it reinforces the notion of the megacity, as not a singular entity but an ecosystem of towns in one crushed space, operating simultaneously. Urban segregation is a central byproduct of the world city archetype. In Chang'an at the height of the Han and Tang empires, no subtlety was needed when it came to fostering divisions.

Tang Chang'an existed at the time when meaningful understandings of the world had expanded to their largest extent ever. Eurasia constituted a space of interaction that was unprecedented in world history at the peak of Tang times, with cities, trading links, and expansive empires rendering this expanse less mysterious. Chang'an was an artifact of this broadened conception of "the world," always a relative term in premodern times. There was no knowledge of what lay beyond the Pacific in Mesoamerica, a pristine civilization with its own urban circuitry.

7 City-State Civilizations

Mesoamerica's Urban Revolution

Mexico City has been continuously inhabited since the migratory Mexicas founded it in 1325 CE. As in Rome or Istanbul, its sedimentary history makes for fascinating strolls. The megacity sits atop centuries of history that pop out at passersby. The Zócalo, its crowded heart, is near where the administrative center was in the *altepetl*, or city-state, of Tenochtitlan. The pyramidal Templo Mayor – today a widely visited UNESCO Heritage site with ongoing excavations – towered over the island city once home to perhaps 200,000 people.[1] Mexico City's great sinking cathedral serves as a reminder of the environmental stresses Tenochtitlan faced during its pre-Columbian hegemony. Then, as now, the city was one of the world's great artificial constructs.

Mexico City today is an alpha world city according to the Globalization and World Cities index.[2] The essence of its functionality echoes the past: Tenochtitlan was a command center designed to manage resources around the known world. If such an index existed at the turn of the sixteenth century, Tenochtitlan would have had similar standing in the Mesoamerican universe.

No city in Mesoamerican history had a broader sphere of influence, stretching from coast to coast in what is now Central Mexico. The city layout maximized connectivity under the constraints of the time. Canals for canoe transportation with causeways for foot traffic allowed for human and material flows. Commercial relations blurred the line between trade and tribute, with a class of traders (*pochteca*) stocking its main market. A labor-intensive system of overland portage, carried out by a distinct laboring class, utilized intercity

[1] Michael E. Smith puts the population at 212,500, though scholarly estimates vary widely as with all pre-modern cities. Michael E. Smith, "Aztec Urbanism: Cities and Towns," in Deborah L. Nichols and Enrique Rodriguez-Alegría (eds.), *The Oxford Handbook of the Aztecs* (Oxford: Oxford University Press, 2017), 201–218, 208.

[2] Globalization and World Cities Research Network, "The World According to GaWC."

roads. (Draught animals were unknown and waterborne transportation options were minimal).[3] In short, Tenochtitlan was the apotheosis of pristine Mesoamerican urbanism, at its height when Europeans arrived in 1519. It did not directly hold territory, making the Spanish-derived term "Aztec Empire" somewhat misleading. It was an innovative force in intercity cooperation and coercion, but it was not by definition a territorial empire. Nor was it the first expansionist city in Mesoamerica, where urbanization had progressed and regressed for more than two millennia by that time.

This chapter is about the hegemonic city-states that emerged across time in Mesoamerica and the urban networks they sustained. From the 1940s, scholars have defined Mesoamerica not as a singular place, but as an "interaction sphere" encompassing many ethnicities, languages, migrations, and architectural styles shaped by widely varying environmental conditions.[4] This world stretched from Northern Mexico to Central America, with urban power centers clustering in different places at different times. Peter J. Taylor contends that its long history included some of the great "creative arenas" of city building and networking in the pre-modern world.[5] Olmec cities flourished along Mexico's Gulf Coast. There were Mayan urban clusters in present-day Guatemala, Belize, Honduras, and the Yucatan. Teotihuacan dominated Central Mexico. The Mexica mythologized its history, awed by the construction left over from the city's heyday around 250 CE. Like Eurasian spheres of interaction, these societies continually learned from one another, fostering "international styles" amidst local variation.[6] The evidence for this is built into urban topographies. For example, the distinctive *talud-tablero* platform architecture in the Teotihuacan style is present at Tikal, despite the vast distance separating these major cities.

Aesthetic influences flowed both ways between those major cities around the fourth century CE. As we will see, ideas about city building traversed Mesoamerica for centuries by then, a process of knowledge sharing that continued into the sixteenth century.

[3] Kenneth G. Hirth, *The Aztec Economic World: Merchants and Markets in Ancient Mesoamerica* (Cambridge: Cambridge University Press, 2016), 239.

[4] Paul Kirchhoff introduced the term in 1943. For discussion on this geographic construct, see George L. Cowgill, *Ancient Teotihuacan: Early Urbanism in Central Mexico* (Cambridge: Cambridge University Press, 2015), 27; Joshua D. Englehardt and Michael D. Carrasco, "New Perspectives on Interregional Interaction in Ancient Mesoamerica," in Joshua D. Englehardt (ed.), *New Perspectives on Interregional Interaction in Ancient Mesoamerica* (Louisville: University of Colorado Press, 2019), 3–33, 4.

[5] Taylor, *Extraordinary Cities*, 169.

[6] Englehardt and Carrasco, "New Perspectives on Interregional Interaction in Ancient Mesoamerica," 6.

New Political Horizons

Mesoamerica is one of only three world regions to have developed pristine cities, that is, without outside influence.[7] It was one of the same three regions to independently invent writing, a process that occurred in cities, though not until 600 BCE in the Monte Albán city-state in Oaxaca.[8] By V. Gordon Childe's criteria, true cities foster artistic culture, complex administration, writing, and long distance trade (see Chapter 2).[9] An urban revolution was underway by the start of the Early Formative period around 1250 BCE near Mexico's Gulf Coast. Olmec influence radiated from the major urban polities of San Lorenzo and La Venta.

Until then, Mesoamerica's settled agrarian villages were relatively egalitarian.[10] Maize was in cultivation for four millennia by that point.[11] As with the other urban revolutions, cities did more than expand on the largess of agricultural production. The first cities accommodated trade, with luxury items underpinning extraordinary increases in inequality. Ancient cities and inequality were practically coterminous. San Lorenzo "was the largest, most socially stratified, and hierarchically differentiated polity in Early Formative Mesoamerica," noted one specialist.[12] "Forging the first stratified society," argued another important work, "the elite of San Lorenzo were responsible for a political transformation that established the exploitive relations that defined all subsequent Mesoamerican societies."[13] Control over a riverine trading network was a critical source of the city's power.[14] Internally, luxury items – the more foreign the better – put social differentiation on display. Elites monopolized knowledge of trading routes. They also maintained exclusive protocols between intercity elites. Both kinds of knowledge were required at

7 The other regions are Mesopotamia's Fertile Crescent and China's Yellow River Basin (see Chapters 2 and 6, respectively).

8 Richard E. Blanton, Gary Feinman, Stephen A. Kowalski, and Linda M. Nicholas, *Ancient Oaxaca: The Monte Albán State* (Cambridge: Cambridge University Press, 1999), 23; Brian Dervin Dillon, "Aquí Nació El Mundo: Takalik Abaj and Early Mesoamerican Civilization," in Matthew A. Boxt, Brian B. Dillon, and David Carrasco (eds.), *Fanning the Sacred Flame: Mesoamerican Studies in Honor of H. B. Nicholson* (Louisville: University of Colorado Press, 2012), 93–136, 115.

9 Childe, "Urban Revolution," 9.

10 Christopher A. Pool, "The Formation of Complex Societies in Mesoamerica," in Deborah L. Nichols (ed.), *The Oxford Handbook of Mesoamerican Archeology* (Oxford: Oxford University Press, 2012), 169–187, 172.

11 Phillip J. Arnold III, "Not Carved in Stone: Building the Gulf Olmec from the Bottom Up," in Deborah L. Nichols (ed.), *The Oxford Handbook of Mesoamerican Archeology* (Oxford: Oxford University Press, 2012), 188–199, 193.

12 Pool, "Formation of Complex Societies in Mesoamerica," 173.

13 Robert M. Rosenswig, *The Beginnings of Mesoamerican Civilization* (Cambridge: Cambridge University Press, 2010), 304.

14 Pool, "Formation of Complex Societies in Mesoamerica," 174.

nodes along these networks, since no city had authority over all territories. This inequality was evident within Olmec cities and regional hinterlands, which show growing differentiation in housing and possessions. Large, elaborate decorated stone homes contrasted with rudimentary structures with dirt floors. The most elite housing showcased imported materials.[15]

Scholars use terms like "complexity" to describe this process of urbanization, which is apt given the elaborate social categorizations and economic output incubated in cities. However, this term should not be deployed moralistically. As in other precocious settlement regions, Mesoamerican urbanization ebbed and flowed. Periods of city building and the expansions of city networks were dispersed by what the literature calls "hiatuses" and "disruptions." These are akin to the periods of deurbanization we have explored in previous chapters, such as the "dark ages" in Mesopotamia and Greece. Social collapse would have been calamitous to those living through it. Commoners, whose labor was tied mainly to the land, might well have found life near a rising city equally unsettling. Major cities drew surpluses from smaller communities. Building cities and their material cultures added new demands on labor when subsistence was unpredictable enough.[16] The administrative capacities of these emergent cities meant new layers of authority, obligations, and restrictions. Their growing reach would have been hard to escape for those living in their orbits.

Specialists define the Olmec horizon by the geographic extent of its art and architecture, one of Mesoamerica's international styles, a period lasting from the mid-second millennium to roughly 400 BCE.[17] The Olmec horizon is most famous today for the extraordinary monumental head sculptures thought to represent city rulers in ball court regalia. The bulk of known pieces are from San Lorenzo. During this period several common features of Mesoamerican cities came into form. There were ball courts, pyramidal temples, and plazas with massive terraced earthworks in the major cities. Reflecting the social rank categorized in ancient cities, these built environments were immensely labor intensive.[18] This suggests an ability to project power over long distances, its sphere of influence enlarging the labor pool. Early city formations have been likened to Greek *synoikisms*, with villages compelled (or coerced) into larger

15 Ann Cyphers, "The Early Preclassic Olmec: An Overview," in Loa P. Traxler and Robert J. Sharer (eds.), *The Origins of Maya States* (Philadelphia: University of Pennsylvania Press, 2016), 83–120, 96.

16 Arthur A. Demarest, "The Collapse of the Classic Maya Kingdoms of the Southwestern Petén: Implications for the End of Classic Maya Civilization," in Charlotte Arnauld and Alain Breton (eds.), *Millenary Maya Societies: Past Crises and Resilience*, 22–48, 25. Electronic document. Available at www.mesoweb.com/publications/MMS/2_Demarest.pdf, last accessed February 21, 2024; Hirth, *Aztec Economic World*, 275.

17 Rosenswig, *Beginnings of Mesoamerican Civilization*, 49.

18 Dillon, "Aquí Nació El Mundo," 103.

polities.[19] Much remains unknown. The San Lorenzo aesthetic was evident across wide swaths of the Gulf region and beyond, prompting scholars to debate whether it was the "mother city," setting the Mesoamerican world on a seminal political, economic, and cultural path.[20] That debate is ongoing. What is clear is that human flows trafficked through cities, spreading material goods, power systems, and ideas to supplement local cultural variations. Unique styles in sculpture, building, and planning complemented and encouraged adaptation and hybridization.

Other power centers emerged as San Lorenzo declined around 900 BCE, including La Venta during the Middle Formative period. Takalik Abaj at Guatemala's Pacific Slope features both Olmec and Early Mayan remnants, having been occupied by what are essentially two distinctive cultures with unique style horizons.[21] What determined settlement patterns? The major urban regions of Mesoamerica across time lacked the advantages of other cradles of urban civilization. The river system is limited in comparison with the Fertile Crescent, Indus River, or Yellow River Basin. The coasts allow few robust natural harbors, lessoning the potential for port cities. As a result no city civilizations colonized the Gulf of Mexico such as those settling the Aegean like "frogs around a pond." Bulk trades appear to have been limited by the reliance on overland portage. Porters carried food products, but the caloric demands of portage itself reduced the amount of food that could arrive.[22] This made the food radius for basic staples relatively small. In all, the ability of cities to project power was limited when compared with Chang'an or Rome. Mesoamerica never had a period of unification along the lines of Han or Tang China, or imperial Rome. Correspondingly, no one enforced a single set of rules, weights, and measures in every trading node. Intercity relations required negotiation rather than top-down imposition. Secondary cities had relative autonomy even when intercity relations were hierarchal.

On the other hand ecological factors also fostered interdependence. The Mesoamerican environment is remarkably heterogeneous, with different regions producing different resources and crops.[23] Highly distinctive resource regions sit close to one another, an environment conducive to trade. One geospatial study concluded that the vast majority of households in pre-

19 Christina Elson, "Cultural Evolution in the Southern Highlands of Mexico: From the Emergence of Social Inequality and Urban Society to the Decline of Classic-Period States," in Deborah L. Nichols (ed.), *The Oxford Handbook of Mesoamerican Archeology* (Oxford: Oxford University Press, 2012), 231–244, 236.

20 Rosenswig, *Beginnings of Mesoamerican Civilization*, 300.

21 Dillon, "Aquí Nació El Mundo," 94.

22 Hirth, *Aztec Economic World*, 239.

23 Jeffrey R. Parsons, "The Development of a Prehistoric Complex Society: A Regional Perspective from the Valley of Mexico," *Journal of Field Archeology* 1, no. 1 (1974), 81–108, 87.

Columbian Central Mexico were within a reachable 30 kilometers of a different resource zone.[24] This led to distinctive specializations. Local scarcity led to trade, with cities arbitrating resource flows. "Environmental diversity was an important incentive for small-scale economic interaction to develop across the highlands," argued an extensive study of the Aztec economy. "The proximity of different resource zones made it possible for households in one ecological zone to procure resources from another."[25] Small size, high value luxury trades dominated long distance networks.

Mesoamerica scholarship, especially the influential work of Richard E. Blanton, have vigorously applied world systems theory to the region in a way reminiscent of Mesopotamia studies. Absent a unified territorial empire in the ancient Chinese mold, Blanton and his coauthors see a number of core and periphery regions shifting over time with the emergence and decline of power centers.[26] Blanton and colleagues see a core–periphery system evident beginning with the Olmec "heartland" in Veracruz and Tabasco.[27] These smaller cores emanated outward, in their estimation, from large cities to their rural hinterlands as far as 100 kilometers. The core city expanded its administrative capacity to these immediate hinterlands through a system of military and trading outposts.[28] This enabled core cities to administer what they call "displaceable labor," where "households were moved into/out of cores to realize goals of the state."[29] Populations were the most important of all resources. Households, for their part, felt this proto-globalization impacting their economic decisions and daily lives.[30] Core–periphery relations helped determine what to consume and bring to urban markets.

Mayan City Networks: The Case of Tikal

The forested ruins of Tikal located in Guatemala's Petén region are remarkable for their scale and expanse. The city was abandoned for good in the tenth century CE after seventeen centuries of habitation, leaving 13,000 structures hidden in the rainforest. Only 3,000 have been uncovered.[31] The encroaching forest finally overcame a city that kept it at bay for so many centuries. Once it had an orderly 65 square mile urban footprint that housed 60,000 inhabitants at

[24] Hirth, *Aztec Economic World*, 8. [25] Ibid., 274.
[26] Richard E. Blanton, Stephen A. Kowalewski, and Gary M. Feinman, "The Mesoamerican World System," *Review: Fernand Braudel Center* 15, no. 3 (1992), 419–426, 419.
[27] Ibid., 421. [28] Blanton et al., *Ancient Oaxaca*, 127.
[29] Blanton et al., "Mesoamerican World System," 423.
[30] Also see Richard E. Blanton, *Houses and Households: A Comparative Study* (New York: Springer, 1994), 152.
[31] Statistics cited in Peter D. Harrison, *The Lords of Tikal: Rulers of an Ancient Maya City* (New York: Thames, 1999), 9. For an excavation history, see Hattula Moholy-Nagy, *Historical Archeology at Tikal, Guatemala* (Philadelphia: University of Pennsylvania Press, 2012).

its peak around 700 CE, though population estimates vary considerably.[32] Today the tallest pyramids peer over the forest canopy at heights comparable to modern office towers.

Tikal was one of the ancient world's greatest cities in terms of its size, architectural scale, and geographic influence. That the Mayans forged large city-states in Petén's dense forests and similarly scarce regions is surprising, as few tropically forested societies constructed cities of this magnitude. A central theme running throughout this book has been that cities did not emerge entirely from local abundance. Instead they represent, at least in part, efforts to overcome local environmental scarcity through trade and extraction. They needed networks to acquire resources from other places, maintained by force if necessary.

The tropical lowlands of the Yucatan, Guatemala, and Belize supported the densest Mayan populations during the Classical period, although the highlands were more agriculturally productive.[33] Local production was a constant struggle around Tikal. Its agricultural ecology required intensive land management to overcome irregular rainfall and thin topsoil.[34] In Peter D. Harrison's estimation, Tikal "possessed no special or rare natural commodity to suggest settlement based on the presence of tradable source material."[35] The Mayan lowlands did produce cacao and cotton, which were important mediums of exchange. But this was a consumer city.[36] Harrison called Tikal a "toll site" for goods traversing the Mesoamerican world.[37] It was a defensible strategic post sitting at the heart of water channels linking it to the coasts and the rest of Mayan civilization.[38] Harrison speculated that the Mayans who eventually built Tikal may have simply been the first settlers brave enough to try establishing themselves in such an inhospitable environment.[39] Once they did, they could assert power over inland waterborne trade. Control over this lucrative crossroads invited a history of conflict, evidenced in Tikal's epic hegemonic struggles with the neighboring cities of Caracol and Calakmul.

32 David Webster, *The Population of Tikal: Implications for Maya Demography* (Oxford: Archeopress, 2018), 41. This monograph provides an overview of current debates in Mayan demography.

33 Lynn V. Foster, *Handbook to Life in the Ancient Maya World* (New York: Facts on File, 2002), 307.

34 Ibid.; Don S. Rice, "Late Classic Maya Population: Characteristics and Implications," in Glenn Storey, Rebecca Storey, Li Liu, Sarah M. Nelson, and Roger S. Bagnall (eds.), *Urbanism in the Preindustrial World* (Tuscaloosa: University of Alabama Press, 2006), 252–276, 255.

35 Harrison, *Lords of Tikal*, 15.

36 Foster, *Handbook to Life in the Ancient Maya World*, 307.

37 Harrison, *Lords of Tikal*, 14.

38 Ibid., 14, 46.

39 Granted, the question of where the Maya migrated from, including at Tikal, remains debated by archeologists, along with the origins of urban kingships. See Francisco Estrada-Belli, "Regional and Interregional Interactions and the Preclassic Maya," in Loa P. Traxler and Robert J. Sharer (eds.), *The Origins of Maya States* (Philadelphia: University of Pennsylvania Press, 2016), 225–269, 246; Harrison, *Lords of Tikal*, 14.

While liberal International Relations theory predicts reduced conflicts where complex trade relationships exist, the opposite was the case in Mayan regions. Control over trade routes was the catalyst for these all-or-nothing wars between Tikal and the two allied cities.[40] Tikal and Calakmul clashed over jade and obsidian trails which changed hands with Tikal's defeat.[41]

The city-state was the primary form of social organization in the Mayan regions, and that remained the case throughout the Classic period (250 CE to 900 CE).[42] This city-state culture had deep origins. La Blanca near the Pacific Coast – a region that saw early urbanization – emerged by 900 BCE.[43] The well-built, gridded city of El Ujuxte surpassed it by 400 BCE.[44] Around that time Kaminaljuyú emerged to eventually dominate the Valley of Guatemala.[45] Nakbe and the gargantuan city-state of El Mirador prefigured Tikal as major city-state powers in the lowlands.[46]

Grube likens this system to that of the Greek *poleis* explored earlier in this book, with "small, fiercely individualistic states engaged in a long and inconclusive struggle for dominance of their cultural realm."[47] These delicate balances were stitched together by diplomacy, with durable agreements between states. Cataclysmic wars occasionally reshaped the balance of power. From there, much remains unclear about this network of polities. No territorial empires subsumed city-states as happened during Greece's Hellenistic Age. This perhaps helps explain why there were no cities on the scale of Alexandria or Rome, consumer cities that grew in tandem with their spheres of extraction. The formal boundaries between these polities are generally unknown, aside from military outposts and earthworks. Second-tier cities assumed subordinate positions to the major city-states but retained local authority.[48] It is possible that a few cities held most of the Mayan regions in their spheres of influence, including dependent cities and rural areas. Although circumscribed by impassable swamps, Tikal's hinterland might have included 425,000 denizens under

40 Antonia E. Foias and Kitty F. Emery, "Politics and Economics: Theoretical Perspectives of the Motul de San José Project," in Antonia E. Foias and Kitty F. Emery (eds.), *Motul de San José: Politics, History, and Economy in a Classic Maya Polity* (Gainesville: University of Florida Press, 2012), 1–29, 14; Harrison, *Lords of Tikal*, 121.

41 Traci Ardren, Scott R. Hutson, David R. Hixson, and Justin Lowry, "Connections beyond Chunchucmil," in Scott Hutson (ed.), *Ancient Maya Commerce* (Louisville: University of Colorado Press, 2017), 273–297, 276.

42 Nikolai Grube, "The City-States of the Maya," in Mogens Herman Hansen (ed.), *A Comparative Study of Thirty City-State Cultures* (Copenhagen: The Royal Danish Academy of Arts and Letters, 2000), 547–565, 547, 553; Michael Love, "Early States in the Southern Maya Region," in Loa P. Traxler and Robert J. Sharer (eds.), *The Origins of Maya States* (Philadelphia: University of Pennsylvania Press, 2016), 271–327, 272.

43 Ibid., 277. 44 Ibid., 286. 45 Ibid., 321.

46 Arthur Demarest, *Ancient Maya: The Rise and Fall of a Rainforest Civilization* (Cambridge: Cambridge University Press, 2004), 83.

47 Grube, "City-States of the Maya," 550. 48 Ibid.

its kingship.[49] Long-distance trade occurred across these competing polities and was not confined by allegiances.[50] "Micro empires" like Tikal existed during periods of centralization, which rose and fell over time. Only a few powerful cities existed by the Late Classic period as authority became dispersed, with kingships mostly gone.[51]

*****

Most Mayan cities were near waterways.[52] Water systems were the primary physical linkages between cities and were essential for agriculture and water storage.[53] The largest cities, with populations upward of 100,000 people (which some have estimated for Tikal), likely required riverine networks for food supplies as immediate harvests could have been insufficient. The vast majority of Mayan cities were a small fraction of this size in terms of probable populations and built footprints.[54] These cities were more localized, with less power to acquire luxury goods, but were still tied to regional trading networks and intercity diplomacy. An unusually large share of the Mayan population lived in cities. The Mayan lowlands perhaps had a greater urbanization rate than much of medieval Europe in the eighth century. However, there was no clear delineation between urban and rural in Mesoamerica. Housing for commoners in the hinterlands looked much as it did in the city. These were rectangular units with thatched rooftops for extended families, sometimes constructed of wattle and daub.[55] Urban farming was common in Mesoamerican cities, further blurring these boundaries.[56] An estimated three-quarters of Mayans engaged in agriculture regardless of their proximity to core cities.[57] This provided large enough food surpluses to support urban specializations. Farming was not year round work, freeing the labor pool during off seasons for other tasks and professions. That said, Mayan cities incontrovertibly met Childe's definition, replete with a matured writing system monopolized by the elite.[58] City life was highly unequal compared with the hinterlands.

[49] Ibid., 556. [50] Ibid., 558. [51] Ibid., 561. [52] Demarest, *Ancient Maya*, 140.

[53] Ibid., 126.

[54] R. E. W. Adams and Richard C. Jones, "Spatial Patterns and Regional Growth among Classic Maya Cities," *American Antiquity* 46, no. 2 (1981), 301–322, 305.

[55] Elliot M. Abrams, *How the Maya Built Their World: Energetics and Ancient Architecture* (Austin: University of Texas Press, 1994), 22; Foster, *Handbook to Life in the Ancient Maya World*, 230.

[56] Rice, "Late Classic Maya Population," 267.

[57] Foster, *Handbook to Life in the Ancient Maya World*, 329.

[58] Karl A. Taube, "Tetitla and the Maya Presence at Teotihuacan," in Geoffrey E. Braswell (ed.), *The Maya and Teotihuacan: Reinterpreting Early Classic Interaction* (Austin: University of Texas Press, 2004), 273–314, 311.

Power and wealth was overwhelmingly in the hands of the nobility, which has been estimated at 10 percent of the urban population.[59]

Another part of Childe's criteria, monumental architecture, was on dramatic display in large city centers with shared architectural styles. Long after its defeat at the hands of Calakmul and Caracol and near abandonment – a 133-year hiatus – Tikal reasserted hegemony over those cities. It assumed control over important trading networks by 695 CE.[60] Most of the largest structures at Tikal were from this era despite the city's much longer history. The city's twenty-sixth ruler, Jasaw Chan K'awil ("Heavenly Standard Bearer") oversaw this resurgence. He correspondingly initiated a building spree in 692 that continued during this renewed period of dominance. His half-century reign from 682 to 734 CE initiated two of the city's iconic landmarks.[61] The 180-foot Temple I, completed in 732 CE, has nine levels, possibly representing the Mayan conception of the underworld. This was Jasaw's burial place. The smaller Temple II was dedicated to his wife. Both step pyramids feature the classic Mayan "roof comb," stone structures built at their summits serving as shrines. The dynasty continued constructing the city's palaces and temples. Jasaw's immediate successor Yik'in Chan K'awil (reigned 734–c. 755) built the 212-foot Temple IV.

Temples were built for funerary, religious, and ceremonial reasons.[62] Their appearances reflected carefully meted out cosmology rather than profit motive according to then-unknown capitalist logics. Yet these structures have an overlapping function with modern profit-driven skyscrapers: They communicate priorities and convey power structures. More than homes for the deceased, they presided over the plazas that conducted much of daily life. They served ceremonial functions and were central to the public spectacle of the city. This is distinct from large-scale tomb projects constructed outside core cities in other ancient societies. These were places urban dwellers witnessed up close (Figure 7.1). Larger and more grandiose than any artificial structures in the world known to the Mayans, they were proof to public eyes that the dynastic system as they knew it was very much anchored in place.[63] Toward this end, they resembled immutable natural formations in a society that took a long view of history.

Despite these well-orchestrated displays of authority, cities as a whole do not appear to have been built according to master plans. New structures were regularly constructed over old ones, with monumental buildings accruing in

[59] Mary Ellen Miller, *Maya Art and Architecture* (New York: Thames and Hudson, 1999), 26.
[60] Harrison, *Lords of Tikal*, 130. [61] Ibid., 140. [62] Miller, *Maya Art and Architecture*, 30.
[63] Elizabeth Drake Olton, "Spaces of Transformation at Temple 1, Tikal, Guatemala," in Maline D. Werness-Rude and Kaylee R. Spencer (eds.), *Maya Imagery, Architecture, and Activity* (Albuquerque: University of New Mexico Press, 2015), 271–307, 271.

Figure 7.1 Wandering into Tikal's central plaza in Guatemala, center of the Mayan world.
Photo by Erin L. Leon.

number over time.[64] The largest of these structures, by far, were the temples and palaces that make up the bulk of Mayan ruins today. By one estimate these buildings together comprise 90-percent of the built mass of classic Mayan cities.[65] They were covered in white stucco and at times red plaster with colorful sculptures.[66] Palaces were mixed use, housing the elite, who concentrated mainly at city centers. They were by extension administrative nerve centers with proto-bureaucracies. This is where important decision making occurred, judicial rulings for instance.[67] These masonry structures had distinctive international styles characterized by the ubiquitous corbeled vaults, which were load-bearing partial arches that allowed for impressive if narrow interiors.[68] This aesthetic pervaded temple chambers and palace quarters. Most rooms were characteristically narrow with high ceilings as a result of the Mayans' reliance on this form.

City centers were connected by a distinctly Mayan urban planning element, the *sacboeb* ("white roads"). These elevated causeways also connected important buildings. There were likely formal processions within cities via the *sacboeb*. Dating from the early Classic period, they also linked together city-states. The pattern of connecting *sacboeb* between city-states reflects either established alliances or tributary statuses in the region's complex intercity relations picture.[69] Vendors may have used them to smooth commerce within and between cities.[70] In any case the *sacboeb* were probably not casual pedestrian ways.

Walking through major Mayan cities involved moving from plaza to plaza rather than along surface streets. Unlike in other parts of Mesoamerica, these were largely "cities without streets."[71] Tikal had eighty-five plazas by one count, more than any other Mayan city.[72] It is uncertain if these plazas, which served ceremonial functions, were common spaces or if access was restrictive.[73] Temple platforms, tombs, and palaces would have been off limits to most. Major plazas concentrated public sculpture, official stelae, and royal burials in a mountain-cave motif reminiscent of Chinese tomb cities, which

[64] Demarest, *Ancient Maya*, 93.

[65] Adams and Jones, "Spatial Patterns and Regional Growth," 303.

[66] Demarest, *Ancient Maya*, 93. [67] Harrison, *Lords of Tikal*, 183.

[68] Demarest, *Ancient Maya*, 94. [69] Foster, *Handbook to Life in the Ancient Maya World*, 234.

[70] Marshall Joseph Becker, "Ancient Maya Markets: Architectural Grammar and Market Identifications," in Eleanor M. King (ed.), *The Ancient Maya Marketplace* (Tucson: University of Arizona Press, 2015), 90–110, 94.

[71] Miller, *Maya Art and Architecture*, 27.

[72] Adams and Jones, "Spatial Patterns and Regional Growth," 305.

[73] Flora Simmons Clancy, "Public Spaces in the Ancient Maya City," in Maline D. Werness-Rude and Kaylee R. Spencer (eds.), *Maya Imagery, Architecture, and Activity* (Albuquerque: University of New Mexico Press, 2015), 210–220, 210.

likewise conveyed immutability.[74] These plazas played host to lavish urban spectacles led by the nobility and priesthood, central components of Mayan political unity in what Demarest and other scholars call "theater states."[75]

*****

Tikal hosted considerable economic activity, with masonry platforms built for large fixed markets in the Late Classic period.[76] At its height it was an archetypal alpha city that fostered long distance as well as localized trade. Fixed markets seem to have had facilities for storage and may have featured built-in stalls.[77] Tikal's market infrastructure was unmatched during its height. However, other cities at this time had familiar "Tikal-style material cultures."[78] Some were "gateway cities" hosting long distance goods en route to other places, with facilities for storage.[79] A number of smaller cities played specialized roles in the Mesoamerican trading system, particularly if they resided in unique resource regions with access to materials such as rare stones or seafood.[80] Canoe transport was especially vital to linking this network, with cities deploying large trading vessels with upward of twenty-five rowers.[81] Merchant classes carried out long distance trade. Transport was especially arduous even when compared with the time-and-space challenges facing other societies. The lack of easy access to the coasts for most cities, and greatly varying terrain, heightened these problems.[82]

Inequality was formally embedded in the set of rules and norms governing the economic system. The Mesoamerican market had craft industries that were widely participatory, including for the off-season farmers pursuing other trades. In this sense, commoners were not entirely excluded from the broad spectrum of market activity. By contrast, salt, chocolate, obsidian, shells, and coral were essential to the Mayan class system. Their high values made it worth long arduous transport. Trades that connoted status were strictly controlled by the state and accessible only to the intercity nobility.[83] These fueled the "peer polity" system that bound the urban elite *as a class*, providing ready status symbols in an elaborate series of shared customs.[84]

By the 800s Mayan cities depopulated along with most of the lowland area. Construction largely stopped. This meant the gradual erasure of the class structure and of daily life as Mayans knew them. This process is the subject

[74] Ibid., 215. [75] Demarest, "Collapse of the Classic Maya Kingdoms," 23.
[76] Becker, "Ancient Maya Markets," 98. [77] Ibid., 102.
[78] Ardren et al., "Connections beyond Chunchucmil," 283, 288. [79] Ibid., 283, 286.
[80] Demarest, *Ancient Maya*, 166. [81] Ardren et al., "Connections Beyond Chunchucmil," 274.
[82] Traci Ardren and Justin Lowry, "The Travels of Maya Merchants in the Ninth and Tenth Centuries AD: Investigations at Xuenkal and the Greater Cupul Province, Yucatan, Mexico," *World Archeology* 43, no. 3 (2011), 428–443, 435.
[83] See Demarest, *Ancient Maya*, 160. [84] Ibid., 161.

of scholarly and popular fascination.[85] Jared Diamond's 2005 book *Collapse* famously emphasizes environmental causes made worse by deforestation. Resource limitations touched off conflicts that only worsened scarcity.[86] There is a theoretical implication here: Where Charles Tilly expects states to crystalize under conditions of regular warfare, the Mayan city-state slowly deteriorated. In the language of cities, the so-called collapse was in essence a period of deurbanization and dispersal comparable to Greece or Mesopotamia. With exceptions. Chichén Itzá in the northern Yucatan was an ascendant center of waterborne trade at the turn of the second millennium. Mayapán was a substantial urban center into the 1400s. Iximché, near modern Guatemala City, thrived in the late 1400s until its conquest by the Spanish in the 1520s. Tikal mostly ceased to function by the 900s. Interestingly, squatters lived in and around its magnificent buildings during hiatuses – until the forest engulfed it.

Arthur A. Demarest, a leading scholar of the Mayan collapse, contends that the causes were closely related to internal class and labor structures in cities. The greater a city-state expanded, the more energy-intensive it became. A term deployed by scholars; "energy" meant human exertion. As we have seen, the Mayans developed far-flung production, trade, and transport. They pulled off bolder building designs. City sizes rested on more elaborate irrigation systems for a method of terraced agriculture that was itself taxing on workers. The nobility grew in number. Professional classes did too. Agrarian classes – 90 percent of the population – faced growing pressure to create surpluses to support these urban functions.[87] As Demarest puts it:

All of this beauty, ceremony, splendid art, growing courts, and architecture had an escalating energetic cost in labor for all aspects of construction, crafting, and ritual, as well as for the intensification of agriculture to support multiplying elite classes and their retainers and full or part time specialists – whose own role in subsistence activities had been reduced or eliminated. These classes would have included royal and noble court members, artisans, priests, war leaders, architects and court staff from cooks to fan bearers to jesters. In some centers they would have also included rowers, porters and merchants.[88]

[85] Sometimes this fascination happens at the expense of forgetting that the culture is very much alive today. Millions of Mayans in Mexico and Central America speak thirty-one indigenous languages.

[86] Jared Diamond, *Collapse: How Societies Choose to Fail or Succeed* (New York: Penguin, 2011), 176.

[87] David Webster, "The Classic Maya Collapse," in Deborah L. Nichols and Enrique Rodríguez-Alegría (eds.), *The Oxford Handbook of the Aztecs* (Oxford: Oxford University Press, 2017), 325–334, 326.

[88] Demarest, "Collapse of the Classic Maya Kingdoms," 25.

Social imbalances augmented environmental scarcity. Urban construction disproportionately strained labor, much more than DIY periphery housing.[89] Given the demand for protracted backbreaking work, *corvée* labor was common.[90] For Demarest, labor demands for cities outstripped what these networks could sustain and the army of laborers they could conscript.

Teotihuacan: Power and Interdependence

It was the most powerful city in Mesoamerica around 500 CE, the sacred place the Mexica later mythologized. "It is not surprising that the web of connections reflected its size and grandeur," argued one scholar in a widely cited volume on the city.[91] This far-ranging series of interactions reached Mayan cities. Ample archeological evidence shows that visitors from Teotihuacan had long ties with Tikal and other important Maya centers. Just as Teotihuacan's *talud-tablero* style is found in Tikal's ruins, there are Mayan artistic forms evident in Teotihuacan.[92] Specialists contest the exact nature of this relationship. What was "Teotihuakal" like?

Teotihuacan was a path-breaking example of state development. Like San Lorenzo it is sometimes called a "mother city" for its influence on Mesoamerican culture. The population peaked at between 100,000 and 150,000 people, making it one of the world's largest cities.[93] It was probably the largest city in Mesoamerica until Tenochtitlan reached its apogee eight centuries later.[94] The region was highly urbanized, with three-quarters of the residents in the area living in the core city.[95] Located near Mexico City, Teotihuacan's urban layout differs markedly from Mayan cities. The city

[89] Abrams, *How the Maya Built Their World*, 83. [90] Ibid., 91.

[91] Geoffrey E. Braswell, "Introduction: Reinterpreting Early Classic Interaction," in Geoffrey E. Braswell (ed.), *The Maya and Teotihuacan: Reinterpreting Early Classic Interaction* (Austin: University of Texas Press, 2004), 1–43, 40.

[92] Juan Pedro Laporte, "Architectural Aspects of Interaction between Tikal and Teotihuacan during the Early Classic Period," in Geoffrey E. Braswell (ed.), *The Maya and Teotihuacan: Reinterpreting Early Classic Interaction* (Austin: University of Texas Press, 2004), 199–216, 200; Joyce Marcus, "The Maya and Teotihuacan," in Geoffrey E. Braswell (ed.), *The Maya and Teotihuacan: Reinterpreting Early Classic Interaction* (Austin: University of Texas Press, 2004), 337–355, 338.

[93] Saburo Sugiyama, "Ideology, Polity, and Social History of the Teotihuacan State," in Deborah L. Nichols (ed.), *The Oxford Handbook of Mesoamerican Archeology* (Oxford: Oxford University Press, 2012), 215–229, 215.

[94] George L. Cowgill, "State and Society at Teotihuacan, Mexico," *Annual Review of Anthropology* 26 (1997), 129–61, 130.

[95] Rebecca Storey, "Mortality through Time in an Impoverished Residence of the Precolumbian City of Teotihuacan," in Glenn Storey, Rebecca Storey, Li Liu, Sarah M. Nelson, and Roger S. Bagnall (eds.), *Urbanism in the Preindustrial World* (Tuscaloosa: University of Alabama Press, 2006), 277–294, 278.

Figure 7.2 Teotihuacan in Central Mexico, which shared architectural features and dense political, social, and economic ties with Tikal – a quintessential dyadic relationship.
Photo by the author.

was clearly centrally planned, including streets and alleys.[96] Its grand axis was one of the most imposing in the ancient world (Figure 7.2). Creating such unusual order would have been a wrenching process, one imagines.[97] As Cowgill wryly puts it, such immense planning and construction "is unlikely to have been the work of committees."[98] Some propose that Haussmann-esque rulers may have been in charge during periods of remarkable construction while at other times a more decentralized "corporate system" prevailed.[99] Either way, the enormous Sun and Moon Pyramids bring a scaled symmetry to the skyline, to this day an impressive scene to walk across. This ruin is unique in another respect: No ball court has been found.[100] Nearly all Mesoamerican cities had them. Far from trivial, the poorly understood game likely involved intercity relations, with foreigners attending matches and competing in them.

96 Sugiyama, "Ideology, Polity, and Social History," 217.
97 Because Teotihuacan did not leave a written record, little is known about its historic experiences.
98 Cowgill, *Ancient Teotihuacan*, 133. 99 Ibid. 100 Ibid., 151.

Teotihuacan was the military and commercial center of Mesoamerica, strategically located along an important trade route.[101] It was "the central node of a network gradually expanded to establish links with other systems," argued Chávez and Spence on the weight of archeological evidence.[102] "Over several centuries," they continued, "it maintained absolute hegemony over all of the Basin of Mexico, dominating numerous communities that provisioned the city with the resources needed" by such a large population.[103] This was an internal web spun in a series of webs, a forerunner to the modern world city network. How did this core interact with cities outside its radius in the Mexican Basin? This remains uncertain. Clearly Teotihuacan had a ubiquitous presence in the Mayan regions. The dyadic "Teotihuakal" was only part of this complex of interactions. Teotihuacan influences in art, architecture, and social systems are evident in many Mayan cities from circa 400 CE. Few believe that Teotihuacan had direct imperial control over all of these distant cities.[104] "Very likely [Teotihuacan's] administrative control extended somewhat beyond the Basin of Mexico, but perhaps not much beyond," argued Cowgill, a leading specialist.[105] There are Tikal rulers with Teotihuacan names, but these could be marital alliances.[106] We see similar relationships with a dynasty founded at Copán.[107] Some scholars leave open the possibility of a conquest of Kaminaljuyú, though there is no clear proof of a takeover.[108] It is more likely that Mesoamerica's world city relied on vigorous diplomacy, dependency, and indirect coercion instead of sovereign territorial authority. Like great cities then and now, its cultural influence and geopolitical prestige radiated farther than its armies.

Such extensive regional interactions were evident in the city's built environment and lived experiences. There were more than 2,000 apartment compounds housing denizens "from distant areas like Oaxaca, Veracruz, and northwestern Mexico."[109] A Mayan population lived in Teotihuacan.[110] (For this population the city must have felt like the far side of the planet). Living spaces were standardized, differentiated mainly by size according to social

[101] Cowgill, "State and Society at Teotihuacan, Mexico," 145.

[102] Sergio Gómez Chávez and Michael W. Spence, "Interaction among the Complex Societies of Pre Classic Period Mesoamerica," in Deborah L. Nichols and Enrique Rodriguez-Alegría (eds.), *The Oxford Handbook of the Aztecs* (Oxford: Oxford University Press, 2017), 283–297, 285.

[103] Ibid. [104] Webster, "Classic Maya Collapse," 326.

[105] Cowgill, "State and Society at Teotihuacan, Mexico," 134.

[106] Marcus, "Maya and Teotihuacan," 348.

[107] Robert J. Sharer, "Founding Events and Teotihuacan Connections at Copán Honduras," in Geoffrey E. Braswell (ed.), *The Maya and Teotihuacan: Reinterpreting Early Classic Interaction* (Austin: University of Texas Press, 2004), 143–165, 144.

[108] Elson, "Cultural Evolution in the Southern Highlands in Mexico," 239.

[109] Sugiyama, "Ideology, Polity, and Social History," 218.

[110] Taube, "Tetitla and the Maya Presence at Teotihuacan," 273.

status.[111] The neighborhoods were the building blocks of the city.[112] They had their own plazas and communal shrines. The relative sameness housed a remarkable cacophony of languages, ethnicities, and customs. Some neighborhoods were segregated along ethnic lines. Others were organized around commercial function, or perhaps both. One neighborhood, Tlajinga, specialized in ceramic production.[113] There were apparent merchant neighborhoods.[114] One apartment complex housed Mayans living just steps from the major Street of the Dead.[115] Though Teotihuacan lacked a writing system, these apartments had Mayan writing. Their literacy indicates that these Mayans were wealthy and, hence, mobile. Leaving behind a trove of Mayan art, they were traders, diplomats, or both, much the way foreign dignitaries inhabit capital cities today.[116]

Proto-world cities had their hazards. Life may have been less severe in Mesoamerican cities than in Eurasian ones. Many lethal European diseases did not exist in Pre Columbian times. Plagues were fewer. Still, bringing large populations in close proximity created population sinks, with life expectancies comparable to pre-modern Europe.[117] Pathogens know no boundaries, but the consuming nobility was at least spared the routine toil of the producer classes. Elite neighborhoods, unlike commoner housing, lacked attached manufacturing sites.[118]

Tenochtitlan in the Age of *Altepetl*

Hernán Cortés's second letter to the Hapsburg King Charles V ignited Europe's geographic imagination. Cortés (1485–1547) compared Tenochtitlan's watery setting to Venice. "The causeway is as wide as two lances, and well built, so that eight horsemen can ride abreast," Cortés said of

111 Cowgill, "State and Society at Teotihuacan, Mexico," 137.

112 Linda R. Manzanilla, "Neighborhoods and Elite 'Houses' at Teotihuacan, Central Mexico," in M. Charlotte Arnauld, Linda R. Manzanilla, and Michael E. Smith (eds.), *The Neighborhood as a Social and Spatial Unit in Mesoamerican Cities* (Tucson: University of Arizona Press, 2012), 55–66, 66.

113 Randolph J. Widmer and Rebecca Storey, "The 'Tlajinga Barrio': A Distinctive Cluster of Neighborhoods in Teotihuacan," in M. Charlotte Arnauld, Linda R. Manzanilla, and Michael E. Smith (eds.), *The Neighborhood as a Social and Spatial Unit in Mesoamerican Cities* (Tucson: University of Arizona Press, 2012), 102–129, 111.

114 Ibid., 102; Cowgill, *Ancient Teotihuacan*, 163.

115 Taube, "Tetitla and the Maya Presence at Teotihuacan," 280.

116 Ibid., 311.

117 See Rebecca Storey, Lourdes Márquez-Morfín, and Luis F. Núñez, "Teotihuacan Neighborhoods and the Health of the Residents: The Risks of Preindustrial Urban Living" in M. Charlotte Arnauld, Linda R. Manzanilla, and Michael E. Smith (eds.), *The Neighborhood as a Social and Spatial Unit in Mesoamerican Cities* (Tucson: University of Arizona Press, 2012), 117–129, 119; and Storey, "Mortality through Time," 179.

118 Manzanilla, "Neighborhoods and Elite 'Houses'," 88.

his approach in 1519.[119] From there, he describes a grand avenue "which is very wide and beautiful and so straight that you can see from one end to the other."[120] This central axis was flanked by "very good big houses, both dwelling and temples" according to Cortés' descriptions.[121]

He wasn't alone. In soldier Bernal Díaz del Castillo's words:

> When we saw so many cities and villages built in the water and other great towns on dry land and that straight and level causeway going towards Mexico, we were amazed and said that it was like the enchantments they tell of in the legend of Amadis, on account of the great towers and pyramids rising from the water, and all built of masonry. And some of our soldiers even asked whether the things that we saw were not a dream.[122]

Cortés described the Templo Mayor, the city's presiding building "whose great size and magnificence no human tongue could describe."[123] It was the centerpiece of a vast walled religious district. Under the Templo Mayor's omniscient watch, canoes busily paddled the canals selling water.[124] Urban agriculture was a remarkable site in the city, with so-called floating gardens, some of which can still be seen in Mexico City's Xochimilco lake district. The only quarter of Mexico City not drained after the conquest; it offers a glimpse of the city's past. Some of Cortés's most vivid descriptions are of the commercial life across the city:

> The city has many squares where trading is done and markets are held continuously. There is also one square twice as big as that of Salamanca, with arcades all around, where more than sixty thousand people come each day to buy and sell, and where every kind of merchandise produced in these lands is found; provisions as well as ornaments of gold and silver, lead, brass, copper, tin, stones, shells, bones, and feathers.[125]

His figures for the major market of Tlatelolco, located in a neighboring city, are exaggerated. But the daily crowds were staggering. He described the assortment of food products and businesses ranging from cloth sales to barber shops. There was an elaborate portage system within the city.

It is important to note the biases in these accounts, coming as they did from the eventual founders of "New Spain." Cortés is justifiably notorious for highly destructive, even genocidal campaigns. He was anxious to justify an unsanctioned war on the Mexica. Still, there are good reasons to believe this stream of superlatives by Spanish chroniclers was genuine. For starters, Tenochtitlan was bigger than any city most of them had seen, triple the size of Seville, the largest Spanish city at the time. As we see from these two

[119] Hernán Cortés, *Letters from Mexico* (New York: Grossman Publishers, 1971), 83.
[120] Ibid., 84. [121] Ibid.
[122] Bernal Díaz del Castillo, *The History of the Conquest of New Spain* (Albuquerque: University of New Mexico Press, 2008), 156.
[123] Cortés, *Letters from Mexico*, 105. [124] Ibid., 108. [125] Ibid., 103.

accounts, it was not the only city that awed the Spanish. They were leapfrogging a network of 400 city-states and smaller towns.[126] Tenochtitlan housed 212,500 people. The second largest Late Post Classic (1200 to 1520) city had a population of 30,000. But there were many cities in this size range that had large imposing city centers.[127] The median city size of over 10,000 was large by any standard of the time.[128]

What these outsiders witnessed was a new era of cities after a long period of deurbanization in Central Mexico following the fall of Teotihuacan, reversing centuries of dispersed living patterns.[129] It was an ascendant urban age in the region, what Smith describes as a city-state culture, albeit one dominated by the primate city of Tenochtitlan.[130] The *altepetl* was the primary form of political organization, with an estimated fifty polities in the Valley of Mexico.[131] They followed similar plans, with public plazas at the heart of each city-state, which was technically a capital. (Tenochtitlan's closed walled plaza is an outlier). Each city had the requisite administrative and religious elements needed for governing: Palaces, temples, and ball courts in city centers. This entailed top-down planning on gridded streetscapes.[132] Further out, housing became more dispersed. Land tracts were larger. The urban–rural boundary was still nonexistent.[133] Nobles had estates outside of cities, in addition to clustering in exclusive urban neighborhoods. They were mobile, traveling frequently between *altepetl* in diplomatic roles.[134]

*****

The Mexica were one of many tribes for whom the binding language was Nahuatl. The Mexica origin story starts at the presumably mythical island of Aztlan, from which the umbrella term Aztec derives. In 1168, the Mexica embarked on an extended great migration to the Valley of Mexico, probably from what is now Mexico's northern tier.[135] This mythical wandering, with the guidance of the god Huitzilopochtli, doesn't end until Year 2 House (1325 CE) on an island in the middle of Lake Texcoco with mountains rising out of the

[126] Figures from this paragraph cited in David Carrasco, *The Aztecs: A Very Short Introduction* (Oxford: Oxford University Press, 2012), 2.

[127] Michael E. Smith, "City Size in Late Postclassic Mesoamerica," *Journal of Urban History* 31, no. 4 (2005), 403–434, 411.

[128] Ibid., 412.

[129] Michael E. Smith, "Aztec City-States," in Mogens Herman Hansen (ed.), *A Comparative Study of Thirty City-State Cultures* (Copenhagen: The Royal Danish Academy of Arts and Letters, 2000), 581–595, 581.

[130] Ibid., 582. [131] Ibid., 585. [132] Ibid., 586. [133] Ibid. [134] Ibid., 587.

[135] José Luis de Rojas, *Tenochtitlan: Capital of the Aztec Empire* (Gainesville: University of Florida, 2012), 14.

water on all sides. A prickly cactus marked the site for their future city, the story goes, just as a vision had predicted.

The Mexica also found serious environmental obstacles to city building that still challenge planners and engineers today. The Valley of Mexico had a water system that consisted of five distinct lakes. The shallow Lake Texcoco had brackish water unsuited to farming, so in the 1400s it was split in two by a dike.[136] This created the desalinated Lake Mexico to its West, enabling *chinampas*, the floating gardens that were actually rooted in the shallow lakebeds. The Mexica extracted algae from the lakes to make spirulina, a source of protein.[137] A wide variety of plant crops could be transferred to *chinampas* nearer the city. The result was a relatively balanced diet in comparison with pre-modern cities whose lower classes survived mainly on grain, which might explain Europeans' wonderment at how healthy the Aztecs appeared.[138]

In its early years, Tenochtitlan was one of many important cities in the valley and was a tributary to the Tepanec city of Azcapotzalco.[139] The nobility began electing rulers (*tlahtoani*) in 1372. This was a growing city of 18,000 whose built environment remained austere.[140] A dramatic turn occurred in the early 1400s, when Tenochtitlan ruler Itzcoatl (1380–1440 CE) forged a series of alliances that successfully toppled Azcapotzalco hegemony. His legendary diplomat and nephew, Tlacaelel (c. 1397–1487), engineered a pact with the commoners to foment rebellion in Tepanec city-states. He shrewdly agreed to strip the nobility of their titles, consigning the Tenochtitlan elite to lives of servitude if the gambit failed.[141] One can only imagine the painstaking negotiations behind what Tlacaelel masterminded next: An alliance between Tenochtitlan, Texcoco, and Tlacopan cemented by 1430.[142] The Triple Alliance formed the basis for what became the Aztec Empire. A landmark in the annals of intercity relations, it institutionalized a set of norms and resource sharing.[143] As with the Athenian-dominated Delian League (see Chapter 3), the Triple Alliance prefigured a period of expansionism. The empire reached its maximum extent under Ahuitzotl (reigned 1486–1502), who spoke of world conquest.[144]

Tenochtitlan swelled in tandem with the expansion of its vassal cities. Tribute and goods poured in as imperial relations reached further out. Cities

[136] Ibid., 7. [137] Ibid., 9. [138] Ibid. [139] Ibid., 23. [140] Ibid., 24. [141] Ibid., 27.

[142] Lane F. Fargher, Richard E. Blanton, and Verenice Heredia Espinoza, "Aztec State-Making, Politics, and Empires: The Triple Alliance," in Deborah L. Nichols and Enrique Rodriguez-Alegría (eds.), *The Oxford Handbook of the Aztecs* (Oxford: Oxford University Press, 2017), 143–160, 151.

[143] Ibid., 152.

[144] Frances Berdan, "Late Postclassic Mesoamerican Trade Networks and Imperial Expansion," *Journal of Globalization Studies* 8, no. 1 (2017), 14–29, 23.

in the region also grew in size, along with the overall population in Central Mexico. "The city lived for itself and its mission: the seat of government of a great empire," argued one study. "The growth of the city was tied to the empire."[145] And the empire grew almost unimpeded. By the end of the reign of Motecuhzoma I (1440 to 1469), it established hegemony over most of Central Mexico from coast to coast.[146] There was substantial migration into the city, giving the city a multilingual cosmopolitan feel as the empire grew.[147] The built environment became denser as new rulers constructed their own palaces. The city's footprint expanded on reclaimed land.[148] The enclosed central district had at least seventy buildings used by the nobility.[149] From there, Tenochtitlan became a city of cities, divided into four zones bisected by main streets. Zones were divided further into *calpulli*, settlement groups held together by kinship and occupations.[150] These apparently closely knit neighborhoods had their own leadership structures, schools, temples, and plazas. School attendees were conscripted for construction labor.[151]

Spanish accounts of tens of thousands of sacrificial victims at the time were highly exaggerated and are unsupported by the forensic record.[152] They justified forced conversions to Christianity, and ginned European audiences for a protracted dirty war involving enslavement and extreme resource extraction. But human sacrifices did occur, likely more often in Aztec societies than in Classic Mayan cities. Why? First, the urban scene reminded domestic factions that wars of expansion were can't lose propositions: "In our city, we win all battles."[153] The most extensive such ritual turned the city into a mock battlefield where soldiers slaughtered defenseless captives from other cities. Some captives were force fed *pulque*, an alcoholic drink, and flayed alive by priests in bearskin brandishing obsidian blades.[154] These were harrowing scenes, and they were meant to be. Like the Roman gladiatorial games, they were spectacles of order rather than anarchy. Second, architecture was foreign policy. The city center was a controlled ceremonial space. The *tlahtoani* and priesthood chose their audiences. These pointedly included foreign dignitaries. They passed racks of skulls from enemy soldiers. The built environment where this took place was comparable only to natural formations in scale, anchored by the Templo Mayor (on whose alter priests cut out the beating hearts of

[145] José Luis de Rojas, "Tenochtitlan," in Deborah L. Nichols and Enrique Rodriguez-Alegría (eds.), *The Oxford Handbook of the Aztecs* (Oxford: Oxford University Press, 2017), 219–228, 226.

[146] Rojas, *Tenochtitlan*, 31. [147] Rojas, "Tenochtitlan," 219.

[148] Barbara Mundy, *The Death of Aztec Tenochtitlan, The Life of Mexico City* (Austin: University of Texas Press, 2015), 27.

[149] Rojas, *Tenochtitlan*, 41. [150] Ibid., 42. [151] Ibid.

[152] Excavations of mass burials uncovered hundreds, not thousands, of executed bodies. See an overview in Carrasco, *Aztecs*, 62.

[153] Ibid., 77. [154] Ibid.

victims). This mega structure and its plaza present Tenochtitlan as the center of a reasoned universe. If onlookers were from cities on the frontiers, they might remember scraps of female flesh posted as taunts to male warriors.[155] This was realist diplomacy, not warfare, a reminder that diplomacy and peace are not synonyms.[156]

*****

The island city was nowhere near self-sufficient. It did not have the resources to grow as it did without substantial importation. It is unlikely the city could feed its peak population, causing it to lean heavily on its growing tributary system.[157] Nor did it have enough building materials.[158] For these reasons, city building was geared toward ingress and egress for human and material flows. This includes three long causeways linking the city to the mainland. The task of moving things from one place to another was a logistical undertaking requiring the mobilization of a large share of the urban population.[159] Like Venice, canoes lapping against the water would have been a common sight at all times, particularly near the markets. Land portage entailed laborers foisting loads in special frame containers on their backs for extended periods.[160] The physical stress could well have caused severe pains and disfiguration for this distinct underclass called *tlamemehque* who answered to city leaders. This did not just happen within cities. Long distance trade was more substantial than at any time in Mesoamerican history.[161] An elaborate road system linked major urban centers. Roads were more likely to be in disrepair the further away the *tlamemehque* went from city centers. Only an incredible stamina by this class of workers could have compensated for the physical constraints on overland travel.[162]

The spaces between cities and their hinterlands went largely ungoverned. Modern notions of sovereignty did not exist. "Instead of having borders that were marked and defended, membership in the *altepetl* was defined by personal relationships," explains one study of this system. "All people who were

155 Ibid., 78.

156 There were also ritual forms of warfare. "Flower wars" were battles for the purpose of enabling warriors and nobles to prove themselves in combat, rather than for plunder or conquest.

157 Manuel Aguilar-Moreno, *Handbook to Life in the Aztec World* (New York: Facts of File, 2006), 60; Rojas, *Tenochtitlan*, 90.

158 Aguilar-Moreno, *Handbook to Life in the Aztec World*, 60.

159 Rojas, "Tenochtitlan," 223.

160 Aguilar-Moreno, *Handbook to Life in the Aztec World*, 341.

161 Smith, "City Size in Late Postclassic Mesoamerica," 420.

162 For an analysis of overland mobility and its caloric costs, see Robert D. Drennan, "Long Distance Transport Costs in Pre-Hispanic Mesoamerica," *American Anthropologist* 86, no. 1 (1984), 105–112.

subject to a [*tlahtoani*] were members of his *altepetl*."[163] Maps characterized by shaded territorial boundaries do not capture this easily. The Aztec Empire, really a series of allegiant cities, has open spaces within it. Nearby cities may be independent while remote *altepetl* were politically integrated. Tlaxcala managed to hold out against the Mexica onslaught despite being surrounded by Mexica allies. Tenochtitlan left local elites in charge of most cities. They provided the empire with labor, goods, and military support. At times the empire dispatched settlers to colonize the frontiers and construct fortifications.[164] The Aztecs regularly deployed locals to traverse its distant provinces as traders, couriers, or spies. Locals knew regional languages and unmarked road systems and were less subject to harassment.[165]

*****

The Aztec economy, its land, and commodities markets were rooted in a rigid social hierarchy. The nobility (*pipiltin*) had hereditary title and monopolies on important resources. *Mecehualtin* were commoners in the *calpulli* units. They provided much of the farm and construction labor for *calpulli* leaders. *Mayeque* labored directly for noble households. Slaves (*tlacohtin*) were deployed in mostly urban settings rather than for farm labor.[166] Slavery came in the form of indentured servitude or was a criminal punishment. It was not hereditary or as pervasive as in the Greco-Roman world. Nor was there a true equivalent to European serfdom. Commoners who deserted, and many did, could not legally be captured and returned. Most commoners in the city were actually farmers working urban plots or venturing out to land in the nearby hinterlands.[167]

Commoners partook in city markets, which they used to provision their households. This inclusivity only went so far. Sumptuary laws limited wardrobe and house sizes, should a family become prosperous.[168] Most commoners were doubtless stuck in place in any case, save for the merchant *pochteca* who walled their homes to keep their wealth out of sight.[169] Commoners could not

[163] Smith, "Aztec Urbanism," 211. Italics mine. Spelling of *tlahtoani* slightly altered for consistency.

[164] Michael Ohnersorgen and Marcie L. Venter, "Aztec Boundary Interactions," in Deborah L. Nichols and Enrique Rodriguez-Alegría (eds.), *The Oxford Handbook of the Aztecs* (Oxford: Oxford University Press, 2017), 525–536, 528.

[165] Ibid.

[166] See the detailed overview of this class structure in Hirth, *Aztec Economic World*, 25; and Hugo G. Nutini and Barry L. Isaac, *Social Stratification in Central Mexico, 1500–2000* (Austin: University of Texas Press, 2009), 22.

[167] Michael E. Smith and Frederic Hicks, "Inequality and Social Class in Aztec Society," in Deborah L. Nichols and Enrique Rodriguez-Alegría (eds.), *The Oxford Handbook of the Aztecs* (Oxford: Oxford University Press, 2017), 423–437, 427.

[168] Ibid., 425. [169] Ibid., 428.

own land. So while they had greater mobility than other ancient societies, peasants depended on landlords wherever they moved. They owed taxes to the city-state and rent to the noble estate whose lands they worked.[170] This formed the basis for inescapable exploitation.

The fact that this was a warrior society complicates the hierarchy further. Cities were patriarchal, rooted in strictly delineated gender roles. Multi-room housing seems to have had "women's rooms" where women performed a variety of household tasks in isolation.[171] However, women were not solely relegated to the private sphere. Women headed city-states in rare circumstances. Gender division in society put them in parallel leadership positions in the priesthood and schools.[172] They had influence at market as producers of food and textiles.[173] At the same time, life in the *calpulli* would have been a repressive human experience. The unit made critical life decisions for young teenagers. Girls married in their early teens. Husbands prepared for war. Population demands dictated they have children young. The harsh conditions of childbirth likely took their toll on female bodies at an early age, shortening life expectancy.[174]

In the end, the tributary system orchestrated by Tlacaelel was buckling when Cortés arrived. The conquistador forged alliances with subordinated cities in the urban hierarchy, much as Itzcoatl had.[175] Cortés also found an ally in embittered Tlaxcala. The Spanish conquest was a rebellion.

Conclusion: Birth of the Globe

Ahuitzotl "had such faith in the Aztecs that in time they would conquer the entire world."[176] The world known to the Aztecs stretched northward to the desert, and south to roughly Peru. The feared leader, whose name meant "water beast," understood the limitations of his empire's sphere of influence. Just as Augustus did, and Taizong did. The vast unknowns beyond their empires enabled them to nevertheless claim world dominance, to each their own *orbis terrarum*.

[170] Ibid., 432.
[171] Susan Kellogg, "The Woman's Room: Some Aspects of Gender Relations in Tenochtitlan in the Late Pre-Hispanic Period," *Ethnohistory* 42, no. 4 (1995), 563–576, 563.
[172] Ibid., 566.
[173] Caroline Dodds Pennock, "Gender and Aztec Life Cycles," in Deborah L. Nichols and Enrique Rodriguez-Alegría (eds.), *The Oxford Handbook of the Aztecs* (Oxford: Oxford University Press, 2017), 387–398, 393.
[174] Ibid., 390.
[175] For an illustration of this hierarchy, see Mary G. Hodge, *Aztec City-States* (Ann Arbor: University of Michigan Press, 1984), 147.
[176] Berdan, "Late Postclassic Mesoamerican Trade Networks," 23.

No more. The conquests meant no continent would be fully unknown to any other. Tenochtitlan was in a sense the first world city whose image projected worldwide. "The Great City of Mexico" captured Europe's imagination. An illustration by Cortés became famous in Europe. Reproduced illustrated codices of Mexica history circulated around Europe. The German renaissance painter and sketch artist Albrecht Dürer was fascinated by an exhibition in Brussels of Aztec artifacts in 1520. For Europeans, the canals of Tenochtitlan drew comparisons with Venice (which we will explore in Chapter 9). Meanwhile resources plundered from the Americas were traded with Asia. "The world" finally encompassed the globe.

8 Baghdad

Crossroads of the Universe

The caliph Al Mansur (c. 714–775 CE) forged the city in fire. A renowned Persian-Jewish astrologer considered the time in 762 CE fortuitous for breaking ground on a new capital.[1] On the caliph's order, workers outlined the city's layout in lines of cotton soaked in naphtha, a flammable liquid, setting it ablaze for the sake of gaining perspective on the grounds.[2] The circular radius was part homage to the Greek mathematician Euclid, who Al Mansur read enthusiastically.

The charred ground must have been a remarkable sight for the tens of thousands of laborers arriving to do the crushing job of assembly. In four years they fastened its roughly half-million sunbaked bricks, which weighed upward of 200 pounds.[3] Their combined encampments were more populous than any city in Christian Europe – with settlers hailing from further and wider – a proverbial Babylon existing only in lines drawn on the ground. White-collar workers were much better paid, but wages for everyone were reportedly good. One specialist renders the scene as a mix of "humble laborers, carpenters, blacksmiths, diggers, architects, engineers, surveyors, and legal experts," all "sweating in the sun" together.[4]

Sadly no traces exist of Al Mansur's citadel on the Tigris River. It was purportedly 2 miles in diameter or more. A series of heavily fortified concentric rings segregated functions and people, compartmentalizing the caliph's vast support staff along class lines. The transient population existed outside this carefully regulated royal quarter. Al Mansur abruptly ended their presence

[1] This was the year 145 AH in the Islamic lunar calendar, which dates from Muhammad's *hegira* from Mecca to Medina in 622 CE. This chapter uses the solar Gregorian calendar for the sake of consistency. The day was June 30th. See Christopher I. Beckwith, "The Plan of the City of Peace: Central Asian Factors in Early Abbasid Design," *Acta Orientalia Academiae Scientiarum Hungaricae* (1984) 38, no. 1, 143–164, 147.

[2] Benson Bobrick, *The Caliphs' Splendor: Islam and the West in the Golden Age of Baghdad* (New York: Simon and Schuster, 2012), 15.

[3] Justin Marozzi, *Baghdad: City of Peace, City of Blood* (Boston: Da Capo, 2014), 12.

[4] Justin Marozzi, *Islamic Empires: The Cities That Shaped Civilizations from Mecca to Dubai* (New York: Pegasus, 2019), 53.

in the teeming market at the suggestion of a Byzantine diplomat. He moved the bazaars outside the hulking 60-foot outer walls for security reasons.

The two most monolithic pieces of architecture stood at the center of the original plan. Al Mansur's Golden Gate Palace was 360,000 square feet. It had a 120-foot high green dome, possibly straddled by a figure of a lancer on horseback.[5] All of this was apparently visible for some distance past the city walls. Next to it stood the massive Great Mosque where the caliph gave religious orations. From there, class distinctions in the complex ran outward via four streets. This was a members-only city within a city. On the outer ring there was housing for junior nobility, barracks for royal guardsmen, bakers, servants, and a litany of government staffers working in the citadel's administrative offices.[6] Dense arcades linked them.

With his hands-on approach to urban planning, historians count Al Mansur as one of history's most forceful city builders, a Haussmann, a Moses, a Kubitschek, and then some. The painstaking planning and vast costs are clear signs that he meant the city to carry out an unparalleled litany of functions. This was no temporary home for a mobile court but the seat of an empire that was settled and urban. If nomadism was a source of power projection in the century-and-a-half of Arab conquests then much had changed. This was a rationalized nerve center intended to project political might, assimilation, and economic connectivity.[7] Its space of flows had broad bandwidth, channeling all of these forms of power across long distances.

The Round City was an architectural symbol of order in a vast combustible empire. It resembled a compass. Four cardinal boulevards led past heavily guarded gates to movable pontoon bridges straddling a moat. The equidistant gates required whole companies of attendants to open and close. They were signposts aimed roughly toward key regions in the empire. The Basra and Kufa gates opened to the south in the direction of two established Iraqi cities. The Sham gate faced the former imperial heartland of Syria. The Khurasan gate faced the new power base to the east that helped the Abbasids topple their Umayyad predecessors by 750. Recalling Augustus' hyperbolic architectural language from Chapter 5, the Round City put a universalizing stamp on the caliphate. The caliph territorially and metaphysically ruled the world's four corners, even if this wasn't literally true. He was, for city dwellers, commander and religious authority of a still mostly geographically unified *Dar al Islam* ("abode of Islam").[8]

5 Figures cited in ibid., 15. Other medieval historians dispute accounts of the horseman, which derive from Khatib al Baghdadi's incredibly detailed descriptions.

6 Ibid., 53.

7 Charles Wendell, "Baghdad: Imago Mundi, and Other Foundation Lore," *International Journal of Middle East Studies* 2, no. 2 (1971), 99–128, 106.

8 Ibid., 119.

As with other world cities whose fortunes were tied to territorial empires, the scale of the city coincided with the expanse of the Abbasid Caliphate. Its rule extended from Central Asia where the Abbasids clashed with Tang Chinese armies, to the Eastern Mediterranean, Egypt, and North Africa. The ninth-century historian Yaqubi claimed there were 100,000 laborers working on Al Mansur's citadel, forming a large base population. Like Brasília in the twentieth century, the central city was meticulously top-down. The peripheries were do-it-yourself. Further migrations followed from across Eurasia, reported in detail by the prolific medieval historian Al-Tabari (839–923 CE). Soon the population grew to levels unknown outside Tang China. Its self-contained narrow streets, dense cul-de-sacs, local mosques, and markets fired literary imaginations. (This was the Baghdad glamorized in *The One Thousand and One Nights*). It attracted generations of scientists, philosophers, planners, and literati, especially from Central Asia, who contributed mightily to the city's cultural aesthetic. Migratory flows included a durable revolving network linking Baghdad to Merv and other key centers of learning and trade along the Silk Roads.[9]

Baghdad was by design the heart of a vast city network at a time of pronounced urbanization, an urban golden age by standard reckonings. At the height of Abbasid power its population was an estimated 840,000. Cairo, founded in 969 CE, had as many as 450,000 denizens. Numerous other centers had populations in the tens of thousands.[10] The likes of Fez, Kufa, Basra, and Isfahan flourished simultaneously, sharing planning and architectural motifs. This was also the case with the many ancient Silk Road cities of Asia under the caliphate that had not been founded by Muslims, especially Merv and Samarkand. The Islamic common market harmonized trade, finance, and incentivized migration across the network. These places were resultantly locked in intensive intellectual dialogue for centuries.

To put the reach of Abbasid interactions in perspective, large tranches of its coins have been found as far afield as Scandinavia.[11] For our purposes, Baghdad marks a major turn in the history of world cities. As we will see, the new capital tapped into an emergent city network that was altered greatly by the Islamic expansion that was splintering by that time.

[9] S. Fredrick Starr, *Lost Enlightenment: Central Asia's Golden Age from the Arab Conquests to Tamerlane* (Princeton: Princeton University Press, 2013), 158.

[10] Figures for this paragraph cited in Jonathan Bloom and Sheila A. Blair, *Islam: A Thousand Years of Faith and Power* (New Haven: Yale University Press, 2002), 112.

[11] Also, the eighth century Anglo-Saxon king Offa in the present-day United Kingdom made his own coins modeled on those of the Abbasids.

The Islamic Conquests: A New Urban Network

Muhammad was born around 570 CE, claiming visions around the age of forty. He embarked on the *hegira* from his home city of Mecca to Medina in 622, touching off a remarkable campaign of conflict and diplomacy that upended centuries-old political orders.[12] The master statesman unified the Arabian Peninsula by the time he died a decade later, but that was just the start. The Islamic conquests reconfigured statecraft and settlement patterns on an unprecedented scale.

The Arabia of the sixth century was an eclectic menagerie of state types claiming different forms of spatial authority. Three territorial empires competed for influence there: The Byzantines (the enduring Eastern Roman Empire), Sasanian Persians, and the Christian Axumite Empire in Ethiopia across the Red Sea, which was fully capable of invading the peninsula.[13] The densest settlements – replete with high-rise housing – were port cities in present-day Yemen handling maritime trade. Landlocked Mecca's power must have been considerable, having wrested control of interstate trading routes to compensate for extreme environmental scarcity.[14] It was also a shade of its future self, a religious center catering to then polytheist pilgrims.

Trade between empires had sustained cities for millennia in the deserts of the Mideast. According to Richard W. Bulliet's classic research, domesticated camels enabled high volumes of overland trade. This allowed multifaceted exchange across isolated regions to continue in the absence of the paved roads that existed in the Roman Empire. Camel caravans fully replaced wheeled carts, which slowly disappeared with Rome's decline.[15] The caliphates that emerged built extensive caravanserai lodging networks to bridge their vast expanses, but never needed an equivalent to the Roman road system that once flourished in the second century CE.[16] As camel caravans averaged about 25 miles per day, caravanserais in the Islamic city network tended to be about that far apart, contingent on water availability.[17]

In context, the cities in the region were on the periphery but hardly backwaters. The exact characters of Mecca and Medina at this time are nevertheless unclear. There is halting evidence that a "city-state culture" existed in Arabia at

[12] From 622 on the dates from Muhammad's life become more certain.

[13] Tim Mackintosh-Smith, *Arabs: A 3,000-Year History of People, Tribes and Empires* (New Haven: Yale University Press, 2019), 89.

[14] Patricia Crone, *Meccan Trade and the Rise of Islam* (Princeton: Princeton University Press, 1987), 4; Jørgen Baek Simonsen, "Mecca and Medina: Arab City-States or Arab Caravan Cities?" in Mogens Herman Hansen (ed.), *A Comparative Study of Thirty City-State Cultures* (Copenhagen: The Royal Danish Academy of Arts and Letters, 2000), 242–249, 243.

[15] Richard W. Bulliet, *The Camel and the Wheel* (New York: Columbia University Press, 1990), 17.

[16] Ibid., 14, 19.

[17] Bloom and Blair, *Islam*, 112.

this time.[18] At the very least these cities were independent polities capable of asserting control over trade routes. Their populations were unknown but thought to number in the thousands, perhaps 20,000 for Mecca.[19] During the famous conflicts between Mecca and Medina, both cities conducted diplomacy and raised armies. Mecca was a world center with long distance caravans arriving and departing seasonally. Itinerant traders and bandits (or both) told stories of India and the Eastern Mediterranean and beyond.[20] The local polytheist elite needed broad geographic awareness to maintain its fragile commercial power, impacted as it was by events in far off empires.[21] The Quraysh tribe that came to blows with Muhammad – its once minor member – monopolized key trade routes for goods such as leather, clothing, and domestic animals.[22] Rising inequality was a defining feature Muhammad rebelled against, helping explain the pro-poor tenor of early Islam.[23] The legendary statesman Umar (c.582–c.644 CE), the second of the caliphs who succeeded Muhammad, erected a substantial redistributive program predicated on taxing the rich for public goods, including child support.[24]

Despite the relative urbanity, the predominate mode of living was nomadic, with mobile societies carrying out trade between imperial markets. Arabia's physical geography was conducive to transhumance, owing to barren growing regions in comparison with the historically sedentary Fertile Crescent. There was relatively little impassable terrain to obstruct access to the large economies to the east and west.[25] Most settlements were little more than way stations.

Here we see an important contrast with previous cases of unifying diplomacy explored in this book. Rome and Athens expanded on the basis of intercity agreements (Chapters 3 and 5). Muhammad united tribal factions which were not tied to fixed settlements or at most partially so.[26] These highly mobile forces on camelback were the source of Arab power during the early conquests. Arab armies wrested Egypt and North Africa from the Byzantines and entirely destroyed the Sasanian Empire by the mid-seventh century despite

18 See the discussion in Simonsen, "Mecca and Medina," 247.

19 Ibid. Population figure in Mackintosh-Smith, *Arabs*, 122.

20 Mackintosh-Smith, *Arabs*, 121.

21 Fred M. Donner, "Muhammad and the Caliphate: Political History of the Islamic Empire up to the Mongol Conquest," in John L. Esposito (ed.), *The Oxford History of Islam* (Oxford: Oxford University Press, 1999), 1–61, 4.

22 Patricia Crone, a leading authority on Meccan trade, disputes the traditional accounts of Mecca as a leading dealer in frankincense and spices. Crone, *Meccan Trade and the Rise of Islam*, 87.

23 Mackintosh-Smith, *Arabs*, 122. 24 Ibid., 211.

25 Ibid., 20, 57; Vernon O. Egger, *A History of the Muslim World to 1750* (New York: Routledge, 2018), 38.

26 For the nuance here, see Mackintosh-Smith, *Arabs*, 27, 127.

being outnumbered by both powers.[27] Bedouins turned the economic advantage of the camel to military advantage.[28] There was an immediate tension as the Arabs enlisted the very "social group that posed a threat to the personal, political, and economic security of the town dwellers."[29] Plunder at the expense of the old regimes underscored a shift in wealth in favor of the new empire.[30] As the Arab-led armies moved out of Arabia they rolled back old civilizations but erected a new one. This is not without parallel. Transhumant societies that overpower city networks build new ones in their stead.[31]

During the era of the austere "rightly guided" caliphs who ruled from Medina (632–661), *Dar al Islam* expanded drastically following the apostasy in the wake of Muhammad's death. Islamic territories reached their maximum expanse in the early eighth century. The conquest of Spain over the Visigoths put them at the doorstep of present-day France. The Umayyad Caliphate (661–750) governed five million square miles from Damascus in former Byzantine Syria. The caliphate made decisions for – and collected taxes from – lands near the Atlantic coast to Central Asia. *Dar al Islam* was a novel territorial concept. The religion and the empire were coterminous. Yet these were not wars of conversion. Arab Muslim tribes comprised the top of the class structure in cities. This tiny minority ruled over a vast population. In fact they did not always welcome converts. The system eliminated taxes for Muslims. New Muslims sought equal status in conquered territories. This as Arab rulers sought to physically cordon off their military officers in growing garrison towns, ideally ruling in an insular style.[32]

Indeed, early on there was much that did not change. Conversions happened slowly.[33] "There was no attempt at converting the peoples of imperial territories who practically all adhered to some form of confessional religion already," argued Hodgson in his classic study *The Venture of Islam*. "Islam was felt to be primarily, if not exclusively, meant for Arabs."[34] As with Christianity in antiquity, Islamic movements happened in the cities serving as conduits for new ideas (or incentives for social climbers). Islam was one of many

27 Chase F. Robinson, "The Rise of Islam, 600–705," in Chase F. Robinson (ed.), *The New Cambridge History of Islam: The Formation of the Islamic World, Sixth to Eleventh Centuries* (Cambridge: Cambridge University Press, 2010), 173–224, 197.

28 Egger, *History of the Muslim World to 1750*, 18.

29 Ibid., 38.

30 Robinson, "Rise of Islam, 600–705," 199.

31 For example, Mongol conquerors such as Kublai Khan and Timur would found or rebuild major cities in Asia in later centuries, notably Kublai's Beijing and Timur's reimagined Samarkand.

32 Paul M. Cobb, "The Empire in Syria, 705–763," in Chase F. Robinson (ed.), *The New Cambridge History of Islam: The Formation of the Islamic World, Sixth to Eleventh Centuries* (Cambridge: Cambridge University Press, 2010), 226–267, 252.

33 Jonathan P. Berkey, *The Formation of Islam: Religion and Society in the Near East, 600–1800* (Cambridge: Cambridge University Press, 2003), 77.

34 Marshall G. S. Hodgson, *The Venture of Islam I: Conscience and History in a World Civilization, The Classical Age of Islam* (Chicago: University of Chicago Press, 1974), 199.

transmissions in the slipstream of the space of flows, to borrow from Castells. For all the plunder of objects concomitant with conquests, one confiscated asset was immovable: Land.[35] Consolidating control over expansive territories required modifying the network of cities rather than ripping it up wholesale.

For existing cities "the conquest effects were far from catastrophic" in the words of one historian.[36] Early caliphs left much of the Byzantine and Sasanian bureaucracies intact for the sake of managing rich growing regions. The shifting world order meant little to the non-Muslim peasant laborers who constituted the majority of the population. The caliph Umar, a state builder in the foundational decade between 634 and 644, taxed these laboring classes conservatively.[37] The key difference was that they no longer paid out to the Christian nobility or landed clergy. The largess now accrued to a new over-class of Arab soldiery and governors.[38] Conditions may have improved for farmers who strained under the heavier-handed Sasanian land system. The young superpower could afford relative benevolence as new wealth poured in from expansions.

*****

During these formative decades a new city network emerged in two ways. The caliphates took control of existing cities from conquered lands. They also founded garrison towns that were modest at first but evolved into permanent cities by Abbasid times. The Umayyad Caliphate's power base was in greater Syria, including the present-day Levant. The Umayyads ruled from Damascus, having acquired other Byzantine cities of major significance, especially Jerusalem.

It was the Umayyads who initiated massive building sprees, leaving their imprimatur on the inherited cities to this day. Surviving buildings from this time are not so much masterpieces by way of newness. Like Mozart's compositions, they are famous for reimaging existing forms from Uzbekistan to Italy. The empire's eclectic composition enabled architectural knowledge to coalesce.[39] The Dome of the Rock in Jerusalem is the first major public work commissioned by an Islamic ruler, completed in 691. It sits atop the elevated clearing where Solomon's temple stood.[40] The octagonal structure, replete with mosaics, evokes Byzantine aesthetics. The caliph Al Walid's Great Mosque of Damascus, complete in 715, also shares form with Byzantine

35 Robinson, "Rise of Islam, 600–705," 200. 36 Ibid., 199. 37 Ibid., 208.
38 Ibid., 200, 208.
39 Richard Ettinghausen, Oleg Grabar, and Marilyn Jenkins-Madina, *Islamic Art and Architecture: 650–1250* (New York: Penguin, 2001), 19.
40 The Romans destroyed the temple under then military commander (and future emperor) Titus in 70 CE. This is also the spot where Muhammad purportedly ascended to heaven.

churches featuring seminal shades of Islamic decorative art.[41] An architectural language developed.[42]

Architecture gave form to shifting geopolitical situations, as is common in city networks in their metamorphic stages. Both landmark buildings reflect the waves of regional interactions brought about by rapid conquests. Large-scale construction projects hastened such interactions, including country palaces commissioned by the new nobility. The *corveé* system in greater Syria drew labor from across the empire. Liturgical financiers also imported skilled artisans from outside Islamic boundaries. This labor, free or unfree, had leeway to implement their skill sets. This gave early Islamic architecture a cosmopolitan feel. Classical Greek and Italian arches and columns mingled with Byzantine mosaics and domes. There were Persian molds and Coptic sculptures.[43] These varied styles were disciplined by a need to conform to the traditional uses of space from Mecca and Medina. Muhammad's home was essentially the first mosque, remaining the prototype thereafter. His bustling home foreshadowed a distinctly Islamic urban life. It was a congregational space for social interaction, a place of worship and a network of redistributive economic support.[44] Distinctive styles emerged from these seminal designs over time, crystalizing over centuries until minarets became a common marker of urbanity.

In short, the kinds of city building emerging in inherited cities were hardly a shock of the new. Onlookers would recognize their various forms from previous eras. Urban topography changed gradually from the Hippodamian grid to narrower winding streets. It is unclear when this shift happened. These changes associated with Islamic cities likely began under Christian rule as the camel replaced the cart, lessening the need for wide thoroughfares to transport goods.[45] Large plazas, which allowed space for bulky cart transport, were also superfluous to the times.[46]

In daily life Greek remained widely spoken in former Byzantine cities, remaining the language of administration until its eventual replacement with Arabic. The caliphate and its governors were administratively ensconced in cities. It often employed holdovers from the Byzantine bureaucratic apparatus to extract revenues from the agricultural hinterlands in early years.[47] Thus, the in-person targets for local loathing were usually Christians, not Muslims.[48]

41 Robert Hillenbrand, *Islamic Art and Architecture* (New York: Thames and Hudson, 1999), 25.
42 Stefano Bianca, *Urban Form in the Arab World: Past and Present* (New York: Thames and Hudson, 2000), 24.
43 Hillenbrand, *Islamic Art and Architecture*, 14.
44 Bianca, *Urban Form in the Arab World*, 102. 45 Bulliet, *Camel and the Wheel*, 14
46 Robinson, "Rise of Islam, 600–705," 198; Bloom and Blair, *Islam*, 112.
47 Cobb, "Empire in Syria, 705–763," 243. 48 Ibid., 244.

While many chose to stay, scores of Greeks and Persians saw it in their best interests to desert the inherited cities. A number of cities depopulated alarmingly for the new rulers.[49] We have already learned that freedom of movement was far from an acknowledged right in fledgling empires. Variants on the *synoikism* were key to any imperial strategy. Ergo the caliphates checked the outflow through a series of harsh policies. They settled Persians, Greeks, and Jews across the depopulating towns and newly acquired provinces, shoring up their tactical map.[50]

The best known new towns offer more of a tabula rasa from which we can glean the essence of an emerging urban experience. These too grew in fits and starts. They featured mosques at their center, surrounded by shaded markets (*suqs*). The symbiosis of market and mosque was to become a hallmark of medieval social life later obscured by modern clearances.[51] Baths returned as a central feature of urban life, harkening back to Roman cities.[52] These would eventually become the main features of all cities under the caliphates, growing more elaborate as an empire conquered by transhumant armies converted to settled life.[53] Caravanserais developed along with them, replicating many of the common urban trappings. Merchants stabled their animals and stored their goods at these specialized inns featuring cloistered courtyards. A weary traveler would enjoy a steam bath. This was a welcome comfort as well as a means of cleanliness that reduced disease transmission upon entering crowded cities.[54]

The first large settlements were Basra and Kufa in Iraq, Qayrawān in Tunisia, and Fustat in Egypt. All four evolved into critical nodes in the emerging city network. Their original intent was to consolidate power over newly conquered territories. Cities were, put simply, places where "surplus could be brought to market, and their income and rents spent."[55] These were

[49] E. Ashtor, *A Social and Economic History of the Near East in the Middle Ages* (Berkeley: University of California Press, 1976), 13.

[50] Ibid., 14. [51] Bloom and Blair, *Islam*, 110.

[52] Donald Whitcomb, "An Urban Structure for the Early Islamic City," in Amira K. Bennison and Alison L. Gascoigne (eds.), *Cities in the Pre-Modern Islamic World: The Urban Impact of Religion, State and Society* (New York: Routledge, 2007), 15–26, 16.

[53] The term Islamic city is subject to much deliberation if not abandonment. This is because not all urban forms are religiously motivated, despite the importance of Islamic norms. Later scholarship on cities in the Islamic world sought to counter orientalist perspectives blinded by Western-centric understandings of Islam. Though beyond the scope of this discussion, a leading orientalist perspective can be found in G. E. von Grunebaum, *Classical Islam: A History 600–1258* (New York: Barnes and Noble, 1996). For representative works that counter this perspective, see Janet L. Abu-Lughod, "The Islamic City: Historic Myth, Islamic Essence, and Contemporary Relevance," *International Journal of Middle East Studies* 19, no. 2 (1987), 155–176; and André Raymond, "Islamic City, Arab City: Orientalist Myths and Recent Views," *British Journal of Middle Eastern Studies* 21, no. 1 (1994), 3–18.

[54] Bloom and Blair, *Islam*, 113. [55] Cobb, "Empire in Syria, 705–763," 248.

forward positions stationing troops in newly subdued territories. Arab soldiery concentrated in these new towns as part of a controlled migration designed to colonize potentially hostile zones.[56] Mass migrations were largely involuntary, part of a centrally planned resettlement to the *amsar* as the garrison towns were called. Immigration was a sanctified part of state ideology, evoking Muhammad's *hegira*.[57] The strategy had the "smack of Stalin" as one recent history colorfully put it.[58] Settlers lived under the constant specter of relocation. In one instance in 671, fifty thousand settlers living in Basra were dispatched to Merv 2,000 kilometers away.[59] That is half a world in medieval time and space, entailing a sure sense of disorientation, exhaustion, and loss. The new towns consisted of modest buildings that could themselves be uprooted on short notice, despite having large populations.[60]

Political power tilted in favor of cities in the contest between *badw* (transhumant) and *hadar* (settled). "Desert dwellers were not fully developed human beings," as Patricia Crone explained.[61] Religious authorities dubiously claimed that Muhammad had cursed any deserter who turned to their Bedouin roots.[62] The emergent post and road system monitored human flows, intended to keep today's settlers from becoming tomorrow's transhumant raiders.[63]

Age of Revolutions

Populations in cities mixed more organically over time. Early on the Arabian tribal system held. Colonists retained clan identities along with their requisite rights to new lands and confiscated treasure. These identities weakened or were at the very least subject to complications brought about by the waves of cultural interaction. New converts gave allegiance to the ruling tribes but were denied their attendant status. The deceleration of the conquests by the eighth century strained resources, raising uncomfortable questions of who got what, when, and how.

Increased productivity happened on the backs of the peasantry. If new lands could not be acquired or irrigated into use, then the burden of rising productivity fell hard on their backs. Conditions worsened for peasants in

[56] Hugh Kennedy, *Caliphate: The History of an Idea* (New York: Basic Books, 2016), 11.
[57] Mackintosh-Smith, *Arabs*, 204. [58] Ibid., 205. [59] Ibid.
[60] Sylvie Denoix, "Founded Cities of the Arab World from the Seventh to the Eleventh Centuries," in Salma K. Jayyusi (ed.), *The City in the Islamic World* (Boston: Brill, 2008), 115–139, 118.
[61] Patricia Crone, *God's Rule: Government and Islam* (New York: Columbia University Press, 2004), 343.
[62] Mackintosh-Smith, *Arabs*, 204 [63] Ibid.

the decades before the Abbasid revolution.[64] Their taxes increased, ending the relatively benign period initiated by Umar.[65] City leaders mutually resented the peasants whose surpluses they extracted. They resorted to branding farmers with marks indicating their rural districts. An elaborate system developed to catch fugitive farmers, promising rewards for informers. Severe punishments for escapees included whippings and impossibly large fines.[66] Growing administrative power enabled the caliph and governors to initiate a passport system regulating movements and a service that specialized in captures.[67]

Back in town the soldiery adjusted to sedentary life, mingling with non-Arab populations, adopting civilian professions.[68] Cities became less Arab and more cosmopolitan. Even the elite had qualms with a system requiring them to send large sums to the capital.[69] These trends were particularly pronounced in and around the centers of learned urbanity in Central Asia, catapulting the entire polity into an unstoppable entropy. The third *fitna* – civil war – simmered for decades until it exploded, leaving the Abbasids in power when the dust settled in 750.

The Abbasid powerbase was in Khurasan, a territory spanning northern Iran and neighboring eastward regions. It was from here that the revolutionary tidal wave swept over the Umayyads by an eclectic mix of opportunistic and dispossessed factions. This was, not coincidentally, where the remarkably successful Arab conquest met by far its stiffest resistance.[70] Present-day Uzbekistan, Turkmenistan, and Afghanistan featured a jagged mix of urban, rural, and transhumant authority. There was a venerable network of cities, established nodes in the Silk Roads, including Nishapur, Merv, Bukhara, and Samarkand. They held sway over a seething *corvée* labor force. These peasants from various hinterlands harvested, built, and fought for the nobility in towns and villages.[71] The caliphate was determined to maintain its own stake in this production. The conquests were not complete there until 654, and then only tentatively as cities frequently declared independence or revolted outright. The 50,000 transplants from Basra mentioned in the previous section were an act of desperation by the Ummayad caliph Mu'awiya (reign 661–680) against chronic unrest.[72]

[64] Ashtor, *Social and Economic History*, 67. [65] Ibid., 38. [66] Ibid., 67. [67] Ibid., 68.
[68] Ira M. Lapidus, *A History of Islamic Societies* (Cambridge: Cambridge University Press, 1988), 198.
[69] Hodgson, *Venture of Islam I*, 213. [70] Egger, *History of the Muslim World to 1750*, 41.
[71] Elton L. Daniel, *The Political and Social History of Khurasan under Abbasid Rule* (Chicago: Bibliotheca Islamica, 1979), 17.
[72] Egger, *History of the Muslim World to 1750*, 45.

Revolts from below were common throughout the late Umayyad Caliphate. Nearly all of them were reflexive responses to immediate conditions.[73] Central Asia had the combustible mix of full-blown revolution: Heavy recruitment, religious fervor, and shrewd organizing. The fertile valleys that enable settled life are interspersed with ungovernable mountain terrains. Intellectual malcontents in well-linked urban centers added fuel to the sparks. Merv, in present-day Turkmenistan, was awash with revolutionary ideas. For centuries tourists visited the city to see the house where the underground Abbasid movement was organized, and where the Abbasids' startling black outfits were dyed.[74] Outcasts from the nobility frequently offered to arm and lead the repressed populations in the hinterlands. In the poetry of the Umayyad Khurasani governor:

> Fire's kindled with two fire sticks,
> war with words,
> And if no men of sense extinguish it,
> its fuel will be of corpses and of heads.[75]

So it went. The revolutionary commander Abu Muslim brought the Abbasids to power by harnessing broad swaths of rural discontent.[76] He made promises to disparate factions including discontented Shiites, a form of Islam with populist leanings.[77] "An important factor in the success of the Abbasid movement was the support it received from the peasant and lower class population of Khurasan," one social history pointed out.[78] The Abbasid movement promised spiritual and material salvation.[79] Adorned in their trademark black, its leadership spoke to these classes, but only for a time. The Abbasids later assassinated Abu Muslim, settling on a new status quo that was itself the target of revolts by so-called *ghulāt* (extremists). The idiosyncratic *ghulāt* revolts together "represented the efforts of the peasant communities to resist subjugation by the new 'Muslim,' Arabo-Iranian urban elite in Khurasan" taking place in "isolated, usually very mountainous rural areas."[80] Politicized banditry outside cities remained perpetual problems for the urban aristocracies. Peasant revolts persisted as a standard feature of the caliphate.

In the end, the Abbasid Revolution was not all that revolutionary. An elite Arab family assumed rule, happy to exploit farmed regions. These social conditions were nevertheless clear in the brick-layered DNA of Al Mansur's new city, where new arrivals flowed en-masse.

73 Ashtor, *Social and Economic History*, 30, 68. 74 Kennedy, *Caliphate*, 70.
75 Mackintosh-Smith, *Arabs*, 264.
76 Moshe Sharon, *Revolt: The Social and Military Aspects of the Abbasid Revolution* (Jerusalem: Hebrew University, 1990), 47, 121.
77 Ibid., 135. 78 Daniel, *Political and Social History of Khurasan*, 125. 79 Ibid.
80 Ibid., 126.

Baghdad, Order, and Empire

It is hard to overstate Al Mansur's ambitions for Baghdad. According to the ninth-century geographer Yaqubi, Mansur predicted Baghdad would become "the crossroads of the universe," and beating heart of a Eurasian network. Yaqubi writes in his *Book of Countries*:

> Ships on the Tigris, coming from Wasit, Basra, Obolla, Ahwaz, Fars, Oman, Yamama, Bahrain and neighboring countries will land and drop anchor there. It is there that merchandise will arrive by way of the Tigris from Mosul, Azerbaijan and Armenia; that too will be the destination of products transported by ship on the Euphrates from Rakkah, Syria, the borderlands of Asia Minor, Egypt, and the Maghreb. This city will also be on the route of peoples of Jebel, Isfahan and the provinces of [Khurasan]. By God I will build this capital and live in it all my life. It will be the residence of my descendants. It will certainly be the most prosperous city in the world.[81]

Up to this point rulers were mostly mobile. The Umayyads showed limited interest in residing full time in Damascus. Here Mansur envisions a settled court in the new city for generations. The plan represented a herculean effort to control an impossibly over-scaled *Dar al Islam*, minus much of North Africa and the Umayyad remnant in Spain.[82] This was a protected inland city that had riverine access to world markets. Geographer Muqaddasi (945–991) explained this dynamic, channeling one of Mansur's advisors who recommended a site near water. Should nearby lands turn fallow, foodstuffs could be imported from longer distances. In his words:

> [S]upplies can come to you by the vessels plying the Euphrates; the caravans from Egypt and Syria will come across the desert, goods of all different kinds from China will reach you by sea, and from the Byzantines and al Mosul by the Tigris. Again, you are in a place between rivers so that the enemy cannot reach you except by ship, or by bridge, by way of the Tigris and Euphrates.[83]

Political factors were at work. The caliph needed to manufacture a population that omitted anyone faithful to the old regime, so greater Syria was a non-starter. The empire was hardly consolidated. Large swaths of territory remained unsafe. Power shifted east, limiting the Arab character of the city. A controlled flow of artisans entered from Central Asia, leaving an indelible

81 Cited in Marozzi, *Islamic Empires*, 52. Spelling of Khurasan altered for consistency.

82 In one of history's most dramatic escapes, Abd al-Rachman, son of the last Umayyad caliph, narrowly avoided murder by the Abbasids, the fate of most of his family. He evaded the merciless pursuit, in one instance swimming across the Euphrates. Dodging dangers all the way to Spain, he was proclaimed ruler and initiated a lasting dynasty in Cordoba, soon to be Western Europe's most cosmopolitan city.

83 Muqaddasi, *The Best Divisions for Knowledge of the Regions* (Reading, UK: Centre for Muslim Contributions to Civilization, 1994), 108.

stamp on its art and architecture. Christopher I. Beckwith argues strenuously that an elite from Merv named Khalid ibn Barmak (708–782) played the most hands-on role in planning the Round City, not Mansur himself.[84] A recent convert to Islam from Buddhism, he was an experienced architect versed in the circular designs that were unique in that region, including at Merv.[85] Its enormous citadel of Erk Kala may have influenced the caliph during a visit to the revolutionary city.[86] Erk Kala was similar in scale and function to the Round City. A Buddhist monastery from Barmak's birth city of Balkh was also an influence.[87] The use of the circular – costlier to build than rectangular footprints – stemmed from its history as a symbol of power in Persian cities.

The symbiosis between Baghdad and Merv comprised one of the densest dyadic relationships in the early middle ages, evident in ways large and small. The Round City had a major avenue named for Merv, the only street commemorating another city. In a few years the Barmak family became the empire's most powerful clan after that of the caliphs. The hard labor to build the city came from Syria and Iraq, but the artisans came mainly from Merv.[88] "Much the way that Greek culture eventually conquered a triumphant Rome," asserted a specialist, "Central Asian culture was now positioned to conquer the Abbasids and their new capital, Baghdad."

*****

The lands near Baghdad suffered gradually worsening scarcity. Its site by the Fertile Crescent enabled ample cultivation, shoved along by new hydraulic innovations.[89] There was a network of cities along the rivers, indicative of the enduring food surplus that supported Sumerian cities for millennia. At the peak of Abbasid power the amount of revenue Baghdad extracted from its hinterlands was notably less than previous periods. It was substantially lower than in Persian epochs.[90] Yet full-blown ecological crisis was way off in the eighth century golden age.

Baghdad grew well beyond these limitations. What made the Abbasid period singularly golden in the annals of political economy was the caliphate's success in creating a single market with an alpha city at its center. Neither Mecca nor Medina had forged such extensive economic ties despite their

84 Beckwith, "Plan of the City of Peace," 146. 85 Ibid., 150.
86 Starr, *Lost Enlightenment*, 130. 87 Beckwith, "Plan of the City of Peace," 147.
88 Starr, *Lost Enlightenment*, 128.
89 Edmund Burke III, "Islam at the Center: Technological Complexes and the Roots of Modernity," *Journal of World History* 20, no. 2 (2009), 165–185, 174.
90 Robert McCormick Adams, *Land behind Baghdad: A History of Settlement on the Diyala Plains* (Chicago: University of Chicago Press, 1965), 74.

ruling over the whole of *Dar al Islam*. Basran intellectual Amr ibn Bahr's ninth century *Investigations of Commerce* lists the goods in Baghdad's emporiums arriving from Europe, East Asia, the Indian subcontinent, and Africa.[91] The conquests brought the Persian Gulf and Red Seas into the orbit of Islam.[92] Innovations in shipbuilding and navigational techniques followed.[93] By extension, Philip Curtin contends that Baghdad's rise to prominence permanently altered patterns of Indian Ocean trade.[94] Curtin points out that traders, not armies, spread Islamic culture across Asia where Abbasid merchants were active. His classic study *Cross Cultural Trade in World History* describes seaborne Silk Roads "where the Tang were strong at one terminus and the Abbasids at the other."[95] There were Abbasid outposts in India, Indonesia, and China (see Chapter 6), places with some of the largest Muslim populations in the world today.[96] Chinese junks were a common sight in the city's wharf, docking alongside ships from Africa.[97]

Curtin argues that Baghdad's tilt eastward prefigured these interactions.[98] The shift away from the Umayyad's western outlook meant a high period for overland networks as well. The spaces of flows along the Silk Roads expanded apace. As Central Asian architectural forms "conquered" Baghdad, Islam spread along trading circuits to Central Asia.[99] Baghdad's place as a centrifuge for itinerant scholars helped this process along, as did new forms of mass communication.[100] Abu Muslim's victory over the Tang at the battle of Talas in 751 resulted in the capture of Chinese paper artisans. The first paper mill in the Islamic world was in Baghdad.[101] Baghdad eventually became a center of printing, using paper to strengthen administrative capacity.[102] Not even war

[91] Robert S. Lopez and Irving W. Raymond, *Medieval Trade in the Mediterranean World: Illustrative Documents Translated with Introductions and Notes* (New York: Columbia University Press, 1967), 28.

[92] Chaudhuri, *Trade and Civilization in the Indian Ocean*, 15; For the archeological record see Lynne S. Newton and Juris Zarins, *Dhofar through the Ages: An Ecological, Archeological and Historical Landscape* (Oxford: Archeopress, 2019), 42.

[93] Stearns, *Globalization and World History*, 39.

[94] Curtin, *Cross Cultural Trade in World History*, 106. [95] Ibid., 108. [96] Ibid., 107.

[97] Philip Hitti, *Capital Cities of Arab Islam* (Minneapolis: University of Minnesota Press, 1973), 92.

[98] Curtin, *Cross Cultural Trade in World History*, 107.

[99] Peter Webb, "Islam: A New Faith along the Silk Roads," in Susan Whitfield (ed.), *Silk Roads: People, Cultures, Landscapes* (Oakland: University of California Press, 2019), 256–268, 263.

[100] Jonathan Bloom, "Paper and Printing," in Susan Whitfield (ed.), *Silk Roads: People, Cultures, Landscapes* (Oakland: University of California Press, 2019), 331–338, 336.

[101] James M. Lindsay, *Daily Life in the Medieval Islamic World* (Indianapolis: Hackett, 2008), 102.

[102] Bloom, "Paper and Printing," 332.

terminated the brisk market in luxury pottery between China and Iraq, where artistic forms began a long process of mutual imitation.[103]

Peter J. Taylor's use of population rank sizes hints at the scale of the network around 900 CE, which he calls "the most impressive world network to have been developed outside East Asia before modern industrialization."[104] His statistics suggest a population of 1.2 million for Baghdad, a clear primate city though this estimate is admittedly on the high end. From there Cordoba weighs in at 450,000 inhabitants. Egyptian Fustat and Alexandria had 200,000 and 175,000 denizens, respectively. Samarkand, Nishapur, Bukhara, Isfahan, and several other cities along the Silk Roads sustained populations of between 100,000 and 200,000 each.[105] These economies could not be self-sustaining, relying instead on intercity trade. Cities developed narrow specializations. Basra exported luxury foods and textiles. Kufa made silk turbans. Baghdad processed paper, apparel, and textiles. Draperies came from Wasit. The Jazira shipped horses, soap, and grains. Mosul exported dried meats, and so on, in an emergent world system.[106]

Baghdad was a consumer city, a site of importation and reassembly. Raw materials from the hinterland reached urban power centers for processing into higher value goods, which were often sold back to rural hinterlands at profit.[107] This trapped the peripheries in a state of dependency.

Dense interactions required complex diplomacy. There were Abbasid delegations in Tang courts, for example. Baghdad's outlook was not exclusively to Asia. The caliph Harun al-Rashid (reigned 786–809) sent diplomats to Charlemagne's court at Aachen. Harun reportedly gifted Charlemagne a live elephant, which the emperor traveled with for years. This was part of an effort to isolate the Byzantines, who also sent important delegations to Baghdad at times.[108] The eleventh century chronicler Khatib al-Baghdadi's seminal *History of Baghdad* contended that Al Mansur took Byzantine diplomats' critical advice seriously on planning and architecture matters. A fickle diplomat from Constantinople said the city was too far from water sources, that the palace lacked green space, and that the commoners at market

[103] Rosalind Wade Haddon, "Ceramics from Mesopotamia to China," in Susan Whitfield (ed.), *Silk Roads: People, Cultures, Landscapes* (Oakland: University of California Press, 2019), 338–346, 342.

[104] Taylor, *Extraordinary Cities*, 210.

[105] Figures compiled in ibid., 212.

[106] For further detail here, see Lindsay, *Daily Life in the Medieval Islamic World*, 102.

[107] André Raymond, "The Economy of the Traditional City," in Salma K. Jayyusi (ed.), *The City in the Islamic World* (Boston: Brill, 2008), 731–751, 734.

[108] Alexandre M. Roberts, "Al Mansur and the Critical Ambassador," *Bulletin d'Études Orientales* 60, no. 1 (2012), 145–160, 146.

in the Round City posed a security risk. The caliph ordered his lieutenants to "dig two canals, landscape [the palace], and transfer the populous to Karkh."[109]

This so-called golden age did not just entail trade in pottery. Slave labor was exploited mainly in wealthy urban households rather than for agriculture. The famed Indian Ocean winds carried slave ships bound for these networked cities.[110] Slaves were also sold and transferred along the Silk Roads.[111] They were a routine sight in urban markets. In Baghdad aristocratic buyers subjected them to humiliating inspections in the public slave emporium located by the Karkh Gate.[112] After long painful journeys, the women at Karkh could only look on as men bid on them for use as household concubines. Long distance slave transfers from Europe, Asia, and Africa showed the reach of urban power over individuals, reminders that the migrations behind Taylor's figures were often involuntary. Moreover the slave trade contributed to the cosmopolitan character of the elite. Nobles born to captive foreign women retained their status in society, caliphs included, who had diverse geographic and ethnic backgrounds.

Death and Life in a City of Cities

Harun al-Rashid was the wise caliph fictionalized in *The One Thousand and One Nights*. Harun and his vizier (a Barmak) dress as commoners to wander the streets undetected, to understand life outside their citadel. Whether this happened or not, the element of truth is in the city's segregated layout. Few residents of Baghdad saw the city in its totality. It was an imbricated network within a network, a constellation of classes, clans, ethnicities, and professions.[113]

As the greatest of all founded cities in the Islamic network to that point, everyone was originally from somewhere else. The initial population was organized according to "their city or region of origin: Kufa, Yamama, Fars, Kirman, Khurasan, Khwarizm, Bukhara, [Merv], Balkh, Sughd, Isbijab,

[109] Jacob Lassner, *The Topography of Baghdad in the Early Middle Ages: Texts and Studies* (Detroit: Wayne University Press, 1970), 58.

[110] Elizabeth Lambourne, "Slavery and Servitude in the Indian Ocean," in Susan Whitfield (ed.), *Silk Roads: People, Cultures, Landscapes* (Oakland: University of California Press, 2019), 408–413.

[111] Angela Schottenhammer, "Pirates and Slaves on the South China Sea," in Susan Whitfield (ed.), *Silk Roads: People, Cultures, Landscapes* (Oakland: University of California Press, 2019), 415–419, 416.

[112] Marozzi, *Baghdad*, 47.

[113] André Raymond, "The Spatial Organization of the City," in Salma K. Jayyusi (ed.), *The City in the Islamic World* (Boston: Brill, 2008), 48–70, 59.

Khuttal, Jurjan, Fergana" lists one detailed study.[114] Though less prone to plagues and famines during its apogee, the city was most likely a population sink where deaths outweighed natural births.[115] Such a large population required steady influxes of migration.

What is striking here is that the first settlers came mainly from far away. Unlike Alexandria, Baghdad's population was not pieced together through *synoikisms* involving nearby settlements. One can imagine the trauma facing the craftsmen recruited by the caliphate to design and build the city. These involuntary migrants faced perilous crossings to a city that did not yet exist. From there, the city's appeal voluntarily attracted opportunity seeking merchants and mobile elites.[116] Few planned cities were so successful at self-generation, the later capital of Samarra included. This was by necessity an open city tolerant of Christian, Jewish, Zoroastrian, and other faiths.[117] Arabs, Persians, and Turks were the largest overarching identities. Medieval historians record 40,000 Jews in Baghdad. If correct this would give Baghdad one of the largest Jewish populations of the middle ages. This community centered on a lavish colonnaded synagogue and ten Jewish academies.[118] There were twenty Christian churches. Nestorian patriarchs had high standing in Baghdad and Christian festivals were a common public image.[119] There was a "street of the Zoroastrians."[120] Language gave coherence to these disparate populations. Just as English gives viscosity to globalization today, Arabic became the unifying language spoken in public, although Persian remained important.[121] Where European cities created ghettos for religious minorities, these populations mixed freely with Muslims. They were restricted from fewer professions and there were greater chances for social rank.[122]

Baghdad's knowledge sectors are singularly important to intellectual history, reaching new heights during the caliph Al Mamun's reign (813 to 833). The translation movement already existed when he assumed rule in a calamitous civil war. Innovations in organized education continued thereafter. But the intellectually curious caliph had a profound impact on the city's culture. Three scientists commissioned by Mamun, the Banu Musas, came close to estimating the exact circumference of the earth. The modern world owes a debt to the translation efforts accelerated by Mamun, including recovering, translating,

[114] François Micheau, "Baghdad in the Abbasid Era: A Cosmopolitan and Multi-confessional Capital," in Salma K. Jayyusi (ed.), *The City in the Islamic World* (Boston: Brill, 2008), 221–245, 235. Spelling of Merv changed for consistency.

[115] Ibid., 235. [116] Ibid., 236. [117] Ibid., 237.

[118] Martin Jacobs, *Reorienting the East: Jewish Travelers to the Medieval Muslim World* (Philadelphia: University of Pennsylvania Press, 2014), 131.

[119] Micheau, "Baghdad in the Abbasid Era," 237. [120] Ibid., 238. [121] Ibid., 236.

[122] Amira K. Bennison, *The Great Caliphs: The Golden Age of the Abbasid Empire* (New Haven: Yale University Press, 2009), 125.

and preserving Indian and Greek texts. Going beyond translation, Abbasid scholars built on these texts, using them as starting points for lively debates in the natural sciences, medicine, philosophy, history, law, and literature.[123] The terms Greco-Arab, Greco-Persian, and Greco-Asian or Greco-Jewish are no less apt than Greco-Roman. Intellectuals assembling in Baghdad from all of these backgrounds saw themselves as inheritors of the Greek classicism actively revived in Baghdad.

Concomitant with the world city archetype, power and the metaphysical agglomeration of knowledge intertwine. Early medieval Europe was no "dark age," as it has often been called. Charlemagne's court at Aachen was actively collecting manuscripts, as were Constantinople and Cordoba. Baghdad's purchasing power, patronage potential, and imperial reach enabled it to do so on a much greater scale.[124] It's position as a major link to the communities in Merv, Samarkand, Balkh, and other knowledge capitals enabled a flow of white-collar migration that no other city in Europe or the Middle East could match. Notably a large share of Baghdad's intellectual elite hailed from these centers, as well as from Constantinople, Kufa, Syria, and other points to the west. Mamun could call on scholars from around the known world. His House of Wisdom was the ultimate expression of these assemblages, a study center, library, and translation office, called by one historian the most important learning institution since the founding of Alexandria's library.[125] Cartographers made advances in mapmaking in order to better make sense of imperial networks. A caliphate that subscribed to universalist ideology necessitated expanded geographic imaginaries.[126] The city's location and form conveyed cosmological and therefore social ordering. This required reifying investigation as Mamun initiated one of the world's first astronomical observatories.[127]

*****

The topography of Baghdad displayed yawning gaps between rich and poor, worsening over time.[128] At the very top, caliphs lived cloistered lives, eventually deserting the Round City for suburban palaces. Power over city land

123 Hitti, *Capital Cities of Arab Islam*, 95.

124 Jens Schneider and Damien Janos, "Baghdad: Political Metropolis and Intellectual Center," in Jens Schneider and Damien Janos (eds.), *The Place to Go: Contexts of Learning in Baghdad, 750–1000 CE* (Berlin: Gerlach Press, 2014), 1–45, 30.

125 While attributed to Mamun, some historians believe the House of Wisdom may have been initiated earlier. Bobrick, *Caliphs' Splendor*, 207.

126 Marozzi, *Baghdad*, 69.

127 Samer Akkach, *Cosmology and Architecture in Premodern Islam* (Albany: State University of New York Press, 2005), 156; Marozzi, *Baghdad*, 69.

128 Micheau, "Baghdad in the Abbasid Era," 242.

flowed downward. Fortunes in real estate were made or broken by the central administration, which granted land parcels to civilian and military loyalists. These local leaders and their clients made relatively unregulated micro decisions that gave form to most districts.[129] Rank and file neighborhoods were isolated, such as those in the teeming suburb of Karkh. The mosque and market motif repeated itself ad infinitum in scaled down form. Smaller less extravagant markets serviced locals, whose needs were met in the neighborhood. There were a vast number of gender-segregated bathhouses to serve locals. The system of clientelism meant the poor clustered around the affluent, giving neighborhoods a cross class feel.[130] Dense warrens of narrow winding dead end streets, gates separating neighborhoods, and the deployment of local toughs for security lent an inward essence to these neighborhoods.

There would have been little incentive for most commoners to leave, even if allowed. The whereabouts of women, in particular, were tightly monitored. Public space was considered a threat to the chaste female whose primary role was procreation.[131] Women were confined largely to the private sphere in a culture of surveillance. A well-organized morals squad called the *muhtasib* policed markets and neighborhoods for unacceptable gender mixing.[132]

Indoors, strict rules prevented men from entering gender-delineated rooms. In her landmark work in this area, Janet L. Abu Lughod pointed out that "Islamic law regulated the placement of windows, the heights of adjacent buildings and the mutual responsibilities of neighbors toward one another so as to guide visual privacy."[133] Women's rooms were kept invisible from courtyards or any other public spaces adjoining houses in the packed city. Lughod and other scholars have challenged just how Islamic these forms are. Cultural hybridization was essential to Abbasid identity, including adopting gender norms from conquered areas.[134] Recall that the otherwise democratic Athens had housing designed for the sake of female confinement.

In Islamic cities, women exited the house for proscribed reasons such as funeral rights and other social rituals.[135] In daily life women performed prayers at home.[136] Reminiscent of the Greek *symposium*, housing for the affluent featured guest rooms or private courtyards that played host to men only gatherings. Sadly, the intellectually boisterous affairs in one of the world's

[129] Hugh Kennedy, "Elite Incomes in the Early Islamic State," in John Haldon and Lawrence I. Conrad (eds.), *The Byzantine and Early Islamic Near East* (Berlin: Gerlach Press, 2021), 13–28, 15.
[130] Bianca, *Urban Form in the Arab World*, 77. [131] Bennison, *Great Caliphs*, 112.
[132] Ibid., 119. [133] Abu-Lughod, "Islamic City," 167.
[134] Nadia Maria El Cheikh, *Women, Islam, and Abbasid Identity* (Cambridge, MA: Harvard University Press, 2015), 6.
[135] Lucienne Thys-Şenocak, "The Gendered City," in Salma K. Jayyusi (ed.), *The City in the Islamic World* (Boston: Brill, 2008), 877–893, 886.
[136] Lindsay, *Daily Life in the Medieval Islamic World*, 125.

preeminent knowledge capitals relegated women to the background.[137] If any attended, they were educated concubines. Wealthy women entertained separately.[138] Lower class women in families that could not afford multi-room sequestration were compared with prostitutes.[139] This section of humanity survived in makeshift hovels, trying their best to retain social respectability.[140]

Conflict, Class, and Collapse

As with Rome, Baghdad's fortunes were closely tied to the empire. "If the dynasty is of short duration, life in the town will stop at the end of the dynasty," theorized the fourteenth century historian Ibn Khaldun with Baghdad's vicissitudes in mind.[141] The caliphate's ability to control its vast territories diminished by the mid-ninth century. The empire's problems blew back into the city in myriad ways. The caliphate's reliance on Turkish mercenary armies courted chaos. Soldiers threatened city dwellers, galloping on horseback over citizens on narrow streets. Pitched battle broke out between the army and the city's denizens.[142] This is why Al Mutasim moved the capital to nearby Samarra in 835, where it stayed until returning to Baghdad in 892.

The inability to assert control over the hinterlands came ricocheting hard back to the city. Neighborhood segregation was no mere voluntary social phenomenon. The city's stunning layout reflected its microcosmic geopolitical instability, with physical barriers everywhere. Waterways lacing the city, bringing material connectivity to neighborhoods, were straddled by moveable pontoon bridges that could isolate unrest on short notice. The city's supply networks diminished with the empire's decline. A city known for the worldliness of its spice markets and bookstores suffered routine famines in the tenth century.[143] The city's chroniclers made increasing note of the *ayyarun*, a transient underclass struggling to survive on the streets. Nobles could arm this apparently growing population in defense of the city. Or the poor could rise against them.[144] Revolts were commonplace in this era. The poor resorted to force against the rich, with riots over food prices or against extractive public officials, often with religious inspiration.[145]

Increasingly cash-strapped caliphs paid the restive soldiery in land, using *iqta* grants.[146] This feudal agricultural system allowed the titleholder to

[137] Ibid. [138] Bennison, *Great Caliphs*, 104.
[139] Lindsay, *Daily Life in the Medieval Islamic World*, 125. [140] Ibid., 182.
[141] Ibn Khaldun, *The Muqaddimah: An Introduction to History* (Princeton: Princeton University Press, 2015), 263.
[142] Marozzi, *Baghdad*, 88. [143] Micheau, "Baghdad in the Abbasid Era," 241.
[144] Ibid., 242. [145] Ibid.
[146] Michael Campopiano, "State, Land Tax and Agriculture in Iraq from the Arab Conquest to the Crisis on the Abbasid Caliphate," *Studia Islamica* 3 (2012), 5–50, 33.

capitalize on crop yields. *Itqa* land was not hereditary, freeing up land for later grants but perversely reducing incentives to maintain the hydraulic systems that made the hinterlands viable.[147] Revenues plunged further. The need to drive up short-term productivity put whole new burdens on the peasantry. We are now a long way from the relatively benign agricultural system left in place by Umar. Land masters resided in the city, rarely laying eyes on deteriorating environmental and labor conditions.[148] They did little to stop raiders from attacking the exposed villages and fields. Peasants could either desert or revolt. They did both. Some joined transhumant societies, becoming raiders themselves.[149] Others migrated into the cities, swelling the ranks of Baghdad's *ayyarun* subaltern strata.[150]

The Abbasids took drastic measures to stem ecological decline in Baghdad's shrinking sphere of influence. In the mid-800s the empire forced Zanj slaves to reclaim the marshlands of southern Iraq by stripping its topsoil. This is the only example of large-scale agricultural slavery in the early Islamic world. Inhuman conditions propelled the Zanj to revolt in 869, one of the most dramatic slave rebellions in history. The landholding nobility fled to Basra, pleading to Samarra for help. But the harsh marshlands were ungovernable spaces. The Zanj army seized Basra, Wasit, and other major cities, forging a new government beyond Abbasid control. Their charismatic leader promised the Zanj their own gold and slaves. The new state made good on the promise by enslaving their plantation-owning masters, confiscating their wealth and holding them in peonage. The Zanj were not defeated until 893. By this time much of the empire devolved to local control.[151] Iraq, once the empire's richest region, was in terminal decline. Viable growing lands shrank. Whole cities and scores of smaller townships were deserted.[152]

Conclusion: Renaissances

In 945, Buyid invaders assumed de facto control over Baghdad, essentially keeping caliphs in gilded captivity. Seljuk invaders assumed hegemony in the eleventh century. In 1258, Mongols under the command of Hulegu devastated the city. Timur invaded the city again in the fifteenth century.[153] Other alpha

[147] Bennison, *Great Caliphs*, 98. [148] Ibid.
[149] Marshall G. S. Hodgson, *The Venture of Islam II: The Expansion of Islam in the Middle Periods* (Chicago: University of Chicago Press, 1974), 103.
[150] Bennison, *Great Caliphs*, 98.
[151] For two excellent accounts of the Zanj rebellion in detail, see Michael Bonner, "The Waning of Empire, 861–945," in Chase F. Robinson (ed.), *The New Cambridge History of Islam: The Formation of the Islamic World, Sixth to Eleventh Centuries* (Cambridge: Cambridge University Press, 2010), 305–359, 323; and Ashtor, *Social and Economic History*, 115.
[152] Campopiano, "State, Land Tax and Agriculture in Iraq," 32.
[153] Known as Tamerlane ("Timur the Lame") in the West.

cities supplanted Baghdad, especially Cairo, established in 969 near Fustat, reaching apogees under Fatimid and Mamluk rule.[154]

These cities in the Islamic network continued a protracted renaissance that prefigured Europe's. Baghdad was seminal to this development. It continued developing intellectual capital as long as it could, retaining a proud intellectual heritage down to the present. In this way it persisted well beyond the imperial decline, as once-great cities often do.[155] In the 1200s the diminished city was experimenting in institutional education.

The medieval histories of Baghdad were written well after the city's height. There are no known histories available from Harun al Rashid's time. This gave these writings a nostalgic feel, contributing to the trope of Baghdad as the last center of a unified Islam.[156] (Even if this label applies more aptly to the less historically well-regarded Ummayads.) Al Tabari's voluminous writings from the tenth and eleventh centuries referenced poetry to convey the loss:

> By destruction and fire her people have been annihilated;
> a punishment has encompassed whoever sought refuge.
> How good time's changes will be, if Baghdad,
> for lack of people, does not again become Baghdad![157]

Dar al Islam remained fragmented. Even the most powerful caliphs had to settle for an Islamic world that resembled Christendom, bisected by competing sovereignties and shifting territorial claims. The Islamic city network continued as a conduit for physical and metaphysical connections. Form followed flows. Baghdad's early architecture is lost to history but found in Cairo and other later power centers. Islamic architectural forms are evident farther afield in sites of later urban renaissances, especially in Italian communes and Venice, where we now turn.

[154] For studies on this complicated evolution after Abbasid hegemony, see Janet L. Abu-Lughod, *Cairo: 1001 Years of the City Victorious* (Princeton: Princeton University Press, 1971); and Ira Marvin Lapidus, *Muslim Cities in the Later Middle Ages* (Cambridge: Cambridge University Press, 1967).

[155] Caliphs on occasion briefly regained real power, though their influence was moral and spiritual in the later Abbasid period. See D. G. Tor, "The Political Revival of the Abbasid Caliphate: Al Muqtafi and the Seljuks," *Journal of the American Oriental Society* 137, no. 2 (2017), 301–314.

[156] See Mona Hassan, *Longing for the Lost Caliphate* (Princeton: Princeton University Press, 2016).

[157] Al Tabari is lamenting Mamun's siege, the beginning of protracted Abbasid decline. Cited in Al Tabari, *The History of Al Tabari XXXI: War between Brothers* (Albany: State University of New York Press, 1992), 138.

9 Italian Communes and the Rise of Venice

Cities express power unpredictably. In 1204 the blind nonagenarian doge went it alone in the face of Constantinople's impossibly scaled walls. In a series of bizarre twists, the Fourth Crusade had arrived outside Christendom's richest, most populous city. Many Venetian sailors were familiar with Constantinople's skyline. Frankish soldiers and sundry volunteer knights from provincial Europe were not. "They looked on Constantinople for a long time because they could scarcely believe there could be such an enormous city in all the world," wrote Frankish leader Geoffroi de Villehardouin (1140–1213). "There was no one so brave that his flesh did not tremble" upon seeing the scale of the city's walls, towers, churches, and vast residential tracts.[1] It was a natural response to a city larger than the ten largest European cities combined. The moment was made even more surreal by throngs of Greek civilians staring back at the spectacle of a Venetian fleet. Doge Enrico Dandolo (c. 1107–1205) famously charged ahead in his state flagship under the banner of St. Mark, daring the apprehensive, undersized crusader force to match his courage. The assault worked.

It could not have worked without Venetian maritime power. In his ambassadorial role in the bid to raise a crusader force against Muslim occupied Jerusalem, Villehardouin reminded the Venetians "there is no nation so powerful at sea as you." The crusaders were to "throw ourselves at your feet and not get up until you have agreed to take pity on the Holy Land overseas."[2] The doge conscripted virtually the whole city to build the largest European naval fleet since Roman times.[3] The result was not the conquest of Jerusalem, but the dismantling of the Byzantine Empire, the Roman Empire's eastern

[1] Cited in Roger Crowley, *City of Fortune: How Venice Ruled the Seas* (New York: Random House, 2011), 63. For the full text of Villehardouin's important accounts, albeit in an older translation, see Geoffroi de Villehardouin, "Memoirs or Chronicle of the Fourth Crusade and the Conquest of Constantinople," Project Gutenberg, available at www.gutenberg.org/files/6032/6032-h/6032-h.htm, last accessed May 23, 2019.

[2] Cited in Crowley, *City of Fortune*, 28.

[3] Thomas F. Madden, *Venice: A New History* (New York: Penguin, 2013), 121.

remnant. The gamble paid off for Venice, if not the faith. Venice acquired a series of littoral territories across the eastern Mediterranean, shrewdly opting for ports over vast land domains. The Venetian maritime empire, the *Stato da Mar*, crystalized into a complex network of harbors intended as way stations for Mediterranean trade. As of 1204 this extended to the Black Sea, a market once cornered by Constantinople. Venice already dominated the Adriatic, the so-called Venetian Sea, which the crusade's meandering journey reinforced. Venetian doges meticulously referred to themselves as lords of "a quarter and half a quarter" of Byzantium. Expansionist doctrines ensued. Life in Venice – never much larger than 100,000 residents – changed permanently. Ascension Day became an annual ceremonial claim to de facto ownership of the seas. Trading vessels left the city regularly to ceaseless fanfare. As we will see, Venetian city building took on global themes. Venice conveyed a strange foreignness to Italians.

A city-state comparable in size to a modern suburb, Venice's geopolitical influence punched well above the city's weight even in the face of hostile territorial empires. The *Stato da Mar* contained strongholds all along the eastern Adriatic coast. It controlled strategic points at the mouth of the Adriatic, from the island of Corfu in the Ionian Sea to Crete in the Greek Isles. It also had vital holdings throughout the Aegean Sea. Venice governed important islands in the eastern Mediterranean, notably Cyprus, south of Turkey. It had port cities as far afield as Tana in present-day Russia. This helped it capture the spice trade that was invigorated under Mongol rule across Eurasia in the thirteenth century.[4] Beyond asserting direct authority over trading networks, Venetian shipping linked eastern wealth with continental Europe, particularly Germany. Venetian traders reached rising Atlantic *entrepôt* cities in England and the Netherlands. As a result, Venice forged increasingly complex financial relations. The rise of new territorial empires in the fifteenth and sixteenth centuries meant a surprisingly gradual erosion of Venetian power. The *Stato da Mar* was perilously situated next to an ambitious Ottoman Empire. By this time Venice acquired a land-based empire of its own in Italy, the *terraferma* stretching close to Milan.

Jacob Burckhardt's classic nineteenth century history *The Civilization of the Renaissance in Italy* assigns Venice a pivotal role in the establishment of Western modernity. Whatever its cultural deficiencies in Burckhardt's mind, Venice's complex economic system made it "the birthplace of statistical science."[5] On the basic question of the city's importance to matters far beyond

[4] The holdings in the *Stato da Mar* were ever shifting. For a detailed inventory of acquisitions and losses, see Benjamin Arbel, "Venice's Maritime Empire in the Early Modern Period," in Eric R. Dursteler (ed.), *A Companion to Venetian History* (Boston: Brill, 2013), 125–254, 132.

[5] Jacob Burckhardt, *The Civilization of the Renaissance in Italy* (New York: Penguin, 1990), 63.

its lagoon, the most admired big histories of modern scholarship agree. Major works by Henri Pirenne, Fernand Braudel, Robert S. Lopez, Janet L. Abu-Lughod, and Michael McCormick assign crucial roles for Venetian statecraft during European economic revivals, remarkably, from the ninth to the sixteenth centuries. William H. McNeill described Venice as the "hinge of Europe," and the Venetians as "principle mediators and links between the Adriatic, Aegean, and Black Sea regions."[6] Characteristic of world cities at the heart of city networks, the Venetian Republic developed the organizational prowess to manage expansive diplomatic, financial, and economic relations abroad. When it came to hard power projection, the city's arsenal complex could assemble a complete war galley in less than an hour's time using a system of prefabrication.[7]

Unique in its globalism, Venice was not alone in its ascendancy. The commune system predominated in politically fragmented northern Italy by the twelfth century. Communes were legally recognized autonomous city-states. Neither papal nor imperial authorities were sufficient to control them, not for lack of trying. Venice's impenetrable offshore location made it immune to imperial invasions. Northern Italian city republics had the strength to bandwagon against the relatively weak Holy Roman Empire. The emergence of communes in Italy was evolutionary, but evident with the first formally declared communes at Cremona in 1078 and Pisa in 1081.[8] Though technically part of Byzantium, Venice had been effectively autonomous since the early Middle Ages. Genoa's declaration as a commune in 1098 was consequential.[9] Its mortal rivalries with Pisa and Venice serve as reminders that the Italian city network entailed conflict as well as cooperation.

This was a time of decentralization, but not dispersal. No city managed control over Italy as ancient Rome had. Yet there were the familiar power dynamics that we have seen throughout this book. Cities grew in population. They were centers of governance, usurping land-based feudal authority. The peasantry, whose position improved after the collapse of Rome's empire of cities, found themselves increasingly subject to exploitation by city-based elites.[10] This urban age coincided with growing trade. Italian cities were at the forefront of these changes in Europe, reorienting their built environments to accommodate unprecedented commercial activity. In Marxian terms we see

6 William H. McNeill, *Venice: The Hinge of Europe 1081–1797* (Chicago: The University of Chicago Press, 1974), xvii; Robert C. Davis, *Shipbuilders of the Venetian Arsenal: Workers and Workplace in the Pre-Industrial City* (Baltimore: Johns Hopkins University Press, 2007), 80.

7 Ibid., 6.

8 Stephan R. Epstein, "The Rise and Fall of Italian City-States," in Mogens Herman Hansen (ed.), *A Comparative Study of Thirty City-State Cultures* (Copenhagen: The Royal Danish Academy of Arts and Letters, 2000), 277–293, 279.

9 Ibid., 279.

10 Chris Wickham, *Land and Power: Studies in Italian and European Social History* (London: British School at Rome, 1994), 34.

a revolution of sorts: The rise of an independent mercantile bourgeoisie. Venice emblematized this revolution from day one. With no land, it had no landed aristocracy.

This was a resurgent period for intercity relations. How did it emerge?

The Italian City-State System in the Middle Ages

Writing in the fourteenth century high period for cities, Petrarch (1304–1374) used the term "dark age" to periodize the centuries after the Roman Empire's fading. He described a world of "darkness and dense gloom."[11] In Petrarch's dichotomy, the forthcoming renaissance was a revival of the classical light. What the so-called dark ages were, in reality, were centuries of deurbanization alien to Italian intellectuals in Petrarch's time. Command functions moved to the countryside. Much of the European population followed. Economies localized, though never entirely.

Metaphors of "collapse" misleadingly describe the gradual transition from the Roman urban age to an epoch of dispersal. Significant continuities remained after the last western emperor's overthrow in 476 CE. The Senate continued to meet throughout the sixth century, before the papacy apparently absorbed it.[12] Chris Wickham's research on this period suggests that ancient city-managed modes of production coincided with medieval manorial systems from 300 to 700 CE.[13] The former system was rooted in heavy taxation "mediated through cities" with the latter scheme "going to a more immediate, though often absentee, landlord."[14] The *limes* became ever harder to maintain, border armies less and less effective. Roman patricians, he argues, gambled on the Germanic land-based system of power as taxes became more costly while yielding fewer returns. They lost. The rich got poorer, a fact reflected in built environments.[15] Noble estates in the sixth century were smaller, more remote, and less differentiated from other strata.[16] Village settlements grew less complex. The *latifundia* were deserted or repurposed. Housing for all castes was less durable.[17] Gathering points in Tuscany resembled the pre-*polis* days, constructed on defensible hilltops with walls for protection.[18]

[11] Cited in Theodore E. Mommsen, "Petrarch's Conception of the Dark Ages," *Speculum* 17, no. 2 (1942), 226–242, 227.

[12] Stefano Gaspari, "The Aristocracy," in Christina La Rocca (ed.), *Italy in the Early Middle Ages 476–1000* (Oxford: Oxford University Press, 2002), 59–84, 63.

[13] Wickham, *Land and Power*, 26. [14] Ibid.

[15] Chris Wickham, *Framing the Early Middle Ages: Europe and the Mediterranean, 400–800* (Oxford: Oxford University Press, 2005), 649.

[16] Riccardo Francovich, "Changing Structures of Settlements," in Christina La Rocca (ed.), *Italy in the Early Middle Ages 476–1000* (Oxford: Oxford University Press, 2002), 144–167, 146.

[17] Ibid., 148. [18] Ibid., 150.

The collapse of the western empire blurred the urban–rural divide that is characteristic of city networks. Wickham finds that the age may have been less dark for the peasantry – 90 percent of the population – who in some cases fled to the newly formed barbarian kingdoms to escape exploitative taxation.[19] In his estimation, the peasantry "profited more than anyone else" from the Empire's collapse, freed once and for all from its land taxes.[20] Early medieval Italy was poorer and smaller scaled than the Roman Empire in virtually every way. But, as Wickham put it, "the richer the [pre-industrial] civilization, the greater the exploitation of the producer."[21] During these centuries, the peasantry produced food at subsistence but "kept more of it themselves."[22] The contractual relationship between the peasantry and nearby rural aristocrats was more equitable. This was bolstered by peasant participation in military service, which gave the lower classes leverage as badly needed soldiers. It was not until the emergence of the Carolingian dynasty in the ninth century that European aristocrats asserted themselves by way of "subjection and expropriation" of the peasantry, hardening in to strict feudal hierarchies.[23] The Merovingian aristocracy, which ruled the Frankish kingdom from the 400s to the 700s, resided mainly outside cities.[24] Itinerant Carolingian rulers did not have a fixed capital city. Charlemagne (747–814) fashioned himself a Roman emperor, but he ruled a rural empire.

The lived experience in Italy was correspondingly different than in ancient times. Land once used for large farms reverted to forests. Long distance trade declined in tandem with many formerly great commercial centers, though coastal cities declined at different rates.[25] Evidence based on the decreased number of shipwrecks from late antiquity to the early Middle Ages provides convincing evidence of the overall drop.[26] Diplomatic communiqués between cities appear to have decreased, according to the compiled data.[27] Just as built environments reoriented themselves to commercial activity, they adjusted to a lack thereof. City walls sprang up across Italy. Urban footprints from ancient times exceeded potential uses, leaving stacks of ruins ripe for pilfering. This aesthetic change was especially stark in Rome, whose population shrank from 800,000 to 60,000 between 300 CE and 530 CE.[28] Some town centers became waste sites.[29] Population contractions led nearly a hundred Italian cities to lose diocesan status in the church.[30] Urban forms changed over time. Dense

19 Wickham, *Land and Power*, 21. 20 Ibid., 113. 21 Ibid., 115. 22 Ibid., 34.

23 Ibid. 24 Wickham, *Framing the Early Middle Ages*, 606.

25 Philip Jones, *The Italian City-State: From Commune to Signoria* (Oxford: Oxford University Press, 1997), 58.

26 Michael McCormick, *Origins of the European Economy: Communications and Commerce, A.D. 300–900* (Cambridge: Cambridge University Press, 2001), 66.

27 Ibid., 80. 28 Ibid., 66. 29 Jones, *Italian City-State*, 58. 30 Ibid.

insulae – ancient apartment buildings – gave way to open fields within cities.[31] Perishable wooden materials used for housing construction replaced the favored Roman bricks.[32] Increasingly autarkic economies with less geographic range required less skilled administration, prompting formerly prosperous white-collar urbanites to sell their holdings, mainly to church authorities. Squatting was common as this population of *insulae* dwellers shrank.[33] Despite constant crisis, daily life had a bucolic feel that was different from the dense, noisy, built-in cities of the ancient world. Even members of the nobility typically lived in small two story wooden houses.[34]

The major architectural elements of the ancient city lost their uses, or those uses shifted. Bathhouses disappeared. Forums became fields, albeit with some market activity. Yet nearly all the Italian cities founded by the Roman Empire remained inhabited, their street layouts intact. Church dioceses were organized around cities, another important continuity. As imperial magistracy withered away, bishops assumed municipal power. As Tom Scott points out, most of the future city-states had once been Roman municipalities, around which the church leadership structure had organized.[35] Cathedrals located next to old forums were now the largest building projects. The stage was set, pitting ecclesiastical authority against imperial statecraft. Italian cities were far from passive in these struggles.

*****

A complex series of economic revivals occurred throughout Europe in the Middle Ages. These expansions and their causes are widely contested, their details subject to regular revision by historians. We will explore this broader economic context further in the following section, but it is clear that Italian cities were critical to these growth periods. First, to reiterate, they were well positioned for a return to growth as residual authorities kept them alive through the upheavals of late antiquity. Second, Italy was well placed to reach major world markets via the Mediterranean.

Seaborne trade increased markedly in the eleventh century as communes formed. Venice, Pisa, and Genoa, with extensive knowledge of seafaring, were ready to accommodate changed conditions. Landlocked Milan returned to prominence. Europe's territorial empires to the north proved slower to adjust to the times, still ensconced in landed manorial economies. Instead of

[31] Wickham, *Framing the Early Middle Ages*, 646.

[32] Sauro Gelichi, "The Cities," in Christina La Rocca (ed.), *Italy in the Early Middle Ages 476–1000* (Oxford: Oxford University Press, 2002), 168–188, 183.

[33] Ibid., 184. [34] Wickham, *Framing the Early Middle Ages*, 651.

[35] Tom Scott, *The City-State in Europe, 1000–1600: Hinterland, Territory, Region* (Oxford: Oxford University Press, 2012), 10.

overwhelming the less populous cities in their quest to control Tuscany and Lombardy, these polities were decreasingly effective against city-states. Why? Stephan R. Epstein contends trade in the Middle Ages thrived on social trust that was only plausible in small concentrated communities.[36] Long distance trading was a risky undertaking requiring transparency, legal recourse, and property rights, which cities were best placed to institutionalize. Intercity relations were increasingly dense in northern Italy, where cities forged financial and monetary agreements for the sake of trade.[37] Banking activities grew more complex, especially in Florence and Genoa. Cities developed specializations, even establishing trading districts in other cities. The Mediterranean became a single market in search of lowered transaction costs. "Constant interaction," Epstein adds, "also made it easier to learn about neighboring cities' experiences and to share institutional and commercial improvements."[38]

Cities grew steadily, along with the doubling of Italy's population as a whole between the tenth and fourteenth centuries, accompanied by "a wholesale movement townwards from the countryside."[39] There were 300 city-states in Italy in the 1300s.[40] Twenty-three of them had populations in excess of 20,000.[41] Venice was Europe's third largest city.[42] Lombardy and Tuscany had the West's most advanced economies. "By the year 1000 Italian towns were overtaking all but the greatest Byzantine and Islamic cities," according to Philip Jones.[43] In the twelfth century, Bishop Otto I of Freising wrote in awe of the city-state system from an imperial perspective:

> The entire land is divided among cities; each of them requires its bishop to live in cities, and scarcely any noble or great man can be found in all the surrounding territory who does not acknowledge the authority of a city ... Also that they may not lack the means of subduing their neighbors, they do not disdain to give the girdle of knighthood or the grades of distinction to young men of inferior status and even to some workers of the vile mechanical arts whom other people bar like the plague from the more respected and honorable pursuits. From this it has resulted that *they far surpass all other states of the world in riches and power.*[44]

This oft-cited passage from *The Deeds of Fredrick Barbarossa* shows awareness of the leading positions Italian cities assumed in the high Middle Ages. Otto of Freising astutely noticed the revolution at hand. Professional and mercantile classes gained formal recognition by the nobility. This he saw as

[36] Epstein, "Rise and Fall of Italian City-States," 281. [37] Ibid. [38] Ibid., 283.
[39] Daniel Waley, *The Italian City-Republics* (New York: Longman, 1988), 4.
[40] Epstein, "Rise and Fall of Italian City-States," 284. [41] Waley, *Italian City-Republics*, 22.
[42] Luciano Pezzolo, "The Venetian Economy," in Eric R. Dursteler (ed.), *A Companion to Venetian History* (Boston: Brill, 2013), 255–318, 257.
[43] Jones, *Italian City-State*, 96.
[44] Emphasis mine. Otto of Freising, *The Deeds of Fredrick Barbarossa* (New York: Columbia University Press, 2004), 127.

a source of city-state power, however distasteful from a manorial perspective. "In northern phraseology Italy acquired a 'bourgeoisie'," explained Philip Jones.[45]

Historic estimates support Otto of Freising's perspective of Italy as a wealthier, more urbanized region with emergent artisanal sectors. Its population reached an estimated 12.5 million before the plague of the fourteenth century.[46] North-central Italy, with the most autonomous city-states, also had Europe's highest population density by a wide margin.[47] More telling, 20 percent of this population lived in cities in 1300. By that year, the four "super cities" of north-central Italy – Florence, Milan, Genoa, and Venice – had populations of at least 100,000.[48] The urbanization rate was almost quadruple Europe's as a whole, and at least double what it was in 1000.[49] In all, nearly 1.7 million north-central Italians lived in cities, and the number of large cities grew.[50] Per capita GDP during this time is believed to be well above England, Spain, and Holland, the clear leader and most urbanized region by the 1600s.[51] Non-agricultural sectors accounted for half of this output in 1300.[52] Living standards appear to have been among Europe's highest.[53] The statistics also show extreme property inequality.[54]

The neighbor that Italian cities subdued, to borrow Freising's words, was the Holy Roman Empire itself. In conflict with continental Europe's largest territorial empire, communes won the day. Legally speaking, Italian cities were nominally part of the Empire. They had de facto autonomy as the Empire's most advanced polities. Fredrick I Barbarossa sought to reassert control and revenue from these zones. The campaign succeeded, it seemed, with the destruction of rebellious Milan in 1162. The victory convinced rival communes that forming an alliance was necessary for survival. Two years later the Lombard League formed. By 1167 it aligned most of the major communes of Lombardy, a formidable front that included Venice.[55] The emperor signed a conciliatory treaty with the cities in 1183 after trying for three decades to subdue them.

[45] Jones, *Italian City-State*, 205.
[46] Paolo Malanima, "Italy in the Renaissance: A Leading Economy in the European Context, 1350–1550," *The Economic History Review* 71, no. 1 (2018), 3–30, 6.
[47] Ibid., 6.
[48] Edward Coleman, "Cities and Communes," in David Abulafia (ed.), *Italy in the Central Middle Ages 1000–1300* (Oxford: Oxford University Press, 2004), 27–57, 50.
[49] Malanima, "Italy in the Renaissance," 8. [50] Ibid., 9. [51] Ibid., 16.
[52] Paolo Malanima, "The Italian Renaissance Economy (1250–1600)," International Conference at Villa La Pietra, Florence (May 2008), 18.
[53] Malanima, "Italy in the Renaissance," 14. [54] Ibid., 17.
[55] Gianluca Raccagni, *The Lombard League, 1167–1225* (Oxford: Oxford University Press, 2010), 36.

As city-states grew in capability, they increasingly exploited their hinterlands. Once again, most elite Italian landowners lived in cities.[56] Italy as a whole had a relatively even rank-size distribution in terms of city populations. However the leading cities were definitive primate cities within their spheres of control. This created permanent imbalances of power that enabled them to take extractive measures with impunity.[57] The countryside became the *contado*, the sphere of direct control. The rural laborer became the *contadino*, the "boorish peasant" subject to ridicule in satirical fourteenth century literature.[58] Cities leaned on *contados* for everything imaginable, going well beyond food production. *Contadini* provided labor for earthworks such as fortifications, canals, and improved roads helping link Europe.[59] They provided the military manpower that enabled cities to defeat larger polities. In hard times, rural migrants to the city could be denounced as "unproductive" by the commune and expelled wholesale. Conversely there were compulsory population transfers to the most vulnerable, least desirable settlements (*borghi nuovo*) strategically located around the *contado*.[60] *Contadini* would have to swear oaths not to desert these posts. Far from benign neglect, cities had the administrative capacity to micromanage their *contados*. City managers were omnipresent, and likely loathed by the producing peasantry during periods of excessive taxation. "The primary goal," in the words of one scholar, 'was concentrating the population to consolidate jurisdiction and control."[61] Remote, mountainous spaces in the *contado* were far more difficult to govern. Either way, overly repressed peasantries sometimes trickled away or deserted altogether.[62]

There was remarkable discord *within* cities. The urban nobility was notoriously clannish, making cities tinderboxes for conflict. Neighborhoods in some cities were cordoned off by noble families, effective ganglands for hapless passersby subject to attacks for little reason. Noble clans constructed fortified towers atop their homes for the purpose of hurling projectiles at victims.[63] These otherwise picturesque architectural features were among the tallest

[56] Chris Wickham, *Sleepwalking into a New World: The Emergence of Italian City Communes in the Twelfth Century* (Princeton: Princeton University Press, 2015), 8; Giorgio Chittolini, "Cities, 'City-States,' and Regional States in North-Central Italy," *Theory and Society* 18, no. 5 (1989), 689–706, 693.

[57] S. R. Epstein, "Town and Country: Economy and Institutions in Late Medieval Italy," *Economic History Review*, 46, no. 3 (1993), 453–477, 458.

[58] Epstein, "Rise and Fall of Italian City-States," 285.

[59] Coleman, "Cities and Communes," 44. [60] Waley, *Italian City-Republics*, 22.

[61] Duane Osheim, "Rural Italy," in David Abulafia (ed.), *Italy in the Central Middle Ages 1000–1300* (Oxford: Oxford University Press, 2004), 161–182, 162.

[62] Waley, *Italian City-Republics*, 22.

[63] Lauro Martines, *Power and Imagination: City-States in Renaissance Italy* (New York: Knopf, 1979), 34.

buildings in Italy – upward of 80 meters – though cities imposed height restrictions on them for the sake of public order.[64] They were numerous in Florence, Verona, Siena, and Pisa, in particular, but not Venice. Noble families staked out territories by running chains around streets, posting knights to harass workers, with catapults and bowmen on the rooftops.[65] The new world clashed with the old. Out of control noble clans (*consorterie*) helped galvanize the *popolo* ("the people," or non-nobles of all wealth levels) to organize safer, business friendly neighborhoods.[66] Guilds expanded out of this crucible. Artisanal associations armed themselves against noble gangs and sought inclusion in the halls of power. These segments of the *popolo* were not poor. This was a direct challenge to the titled nobility by a rising mercantile middle class. For their part, the *consorterie* organized to maintain their prestige, positions, and wealth. Tower societies were their way of extracting resources, loyalty, and opportunity through kinship.[67] The towers also served as defensive refuges in such conflicts, not to mention showpiece architecture.[68]

Increased verticality also owed itself in part to the rising costs of urban real estate after around the year 1000.[69] First off, it made more sense to build taller on smaller parcels. Some cities had to address overcrowding. Mass housing emerged to accommodate these conditions. Standardized apartment buildings were conjoined. They added upper floors and used overhangs to create space.[70] Multiple families at times occupied these units in cramped conditions. Housing for the very poor was so shoddy that there is little trace of it. These are thought to be wooden, single story homes with miniscule floor spaces that could be transplanted to new sites once tenants' leases ran out.[71] In these ways urban growth led to squalid conditions for most residents in cities. Safety and sanitary regulations came into play about two centuries into Italy's urban age. Disputes between families emerged over waste disposal, which happened in streets, alleys, and very public dumping sites.[72] It was a recipe for disease. Untreated illnesses were rampant. Infant mortality was high. The average person died at between thirty and forty years of age.[73] Making matters far worse, Italy's precocious interdependence with the rest of the world meant that it was among the earliest and hardest hit by plagues. Venetian traders may have ushered in the crushing mid-fourteenth century epidemic that wiped out approximately half of Venice's population and Europe's. This led to Venice's famous quarantine for arriving traders.

[64] Coleman, "Cities and Communes," 51. [65] Martines, *Power and Imagination*, 40.
[66] Ibid. [67] Ibid., 36. [68] Waley, *Italian City-Republics*, 127.
[69] Jones, *Italian City-State*, 93. [70] Ibid., 154.
[71] Patricia Skinner, "Material Life," in David Abulafia (ed.), *Italy in the Central Middle Ages 1000–1300* (Oxford: Oxford University Press, 2004), 147–160, 148.
[72] Ibid., 149. [73] Ibid., 150.

Italian globalization also meant a beautification of the urban experience, informed by foreign styles of architecture and intended to impress foreign visitors. According to the council at Siena, "among those matters to which men who undertake the city's government should turn their attention . . . beauty is the most important."[74] The Sienese council also noted that "it is a matter of honor for each city that its rulers and officials should occupy beautiful and honorable buildings, both for the sake of the commune itself and because strangers often go visit them on business."[75] Palaces were the largest secular buildings. These were not simply residences for the rich. They carried out assembly and judicial functions. In Venice, only the doge's palace could formally be called a "palace," despite the ostentation of the rest of the nobility. Construction on other public works grew more elaborate. City walls were a point of civic pride as well as defense, requiring compulsory labor for construction and maintenance.[76] Wealthy communes competed to construct the most elaborate churches and cathedrals. The Florentine Duomo was built large enough to hold mass for the city's entire post-plague adult population.[77] These undertakings subsidized artisanal labor, a creative class of architects, engineers, craftsman, and artists working on a range of projects. This reinforced the importance of craft guilds in society.[78]

European Revivals

By the 1200s Venice controlled the Adriatic Sea, with free trade in Constantinople after the Fourth Crusade. Venetian and Genoese ships were familiar sights across the Mediterranean world. Italian merchants congregated in important nodes such as Alexandria and Acre. These cities were sites of key innovations in ship design, mapping, and navigation. Powerful rudders enabled better steering. Previously this required enormous effort on the part of oarsmen. Because of the stronger steering capability, Italian shipping in the Middle Ages could leave sight of shore, using magnetic compasses instead of eyeing the coastline for navigation.[79] The shipping season became year round for the first time. Vessels grew in size, enabling higher volumes of lower margin nonluxury commodities. For a time, only the Venetians and Genoese had merchant ships that displaced more than 1,000 tons, the largest vessels on earth.[80]

[74] Waley, *Italian City-Republics*, 107. [75] Ibid. [76] Ibid., 110. [77] Ibid., 111.

[78] Ibid., 115; Peter Burke, *The Italian Renaissance: Culture and Society in Italy* (Princeton: Princeton University Press, 2014), 70.

[79] McNeill, *Venice*, 48.

[80] Marco Tangheroni, "Trade and Navigation," in David Abulafia (ed.), *Italy in the Central Middle Ages 1000–1300* (Oxford: Oxford University Press, 2004), 127–146, 141.

The world market was Venice's chessboard. What did this big picture look like?

To start with, Venice rode the waves of commerce but also stoked them. Scholars agree that an epochal shift in economic activity took place in the 1100s. Henri Pirenne's influential *Medieval Cities* contended that Venice deserved "a singular place in the economic history of Europe."[81] Observing processes of urbanization and trade, he sees Venice as *in* but not *of* Europe, a city isolated within a bleak lagoon keeping trade alive as Christendom was under "a state of blockade."[82] Venetian ties with Constantinople mattered more than with its neighbors – VENCON as today's world city scholars might say. The rollback of Islamic domination of the Mediterranean opened the door for greater European involvement in trade, led by this dyadic relationship with Constantinople. More trade meant invigorated and repurposed cities, which in turn challenged feudal and religious norms, making this a consequential century in statecraft. Robert S. Lopez calls the period spanning the tenth to the fourteenth centuries a "commercial revolution" comparable to modern industrialization.[83] Here too the relationship between Italian cities and the Byzantine Empire was paramount. As in Pirenne's telling, Venice was the more commercially dynamic partner in its relationship with the ageing giant. Constantinople's defeat in the Fourth Crusade broke the lock, as he put it, throwing open long distance markets in Asian trade once monopolized by the Empire. This explains the timing of European expansion.[84]

Janet L. Abu-Lughod's *Before European Hegemony* defines this as a high period for global interaction. The 1200s were extraordinary for cultural flourishing not just in the West but, remarkably, in Europe, Asia, and the Middle East at once. This was a multipolar world that existed with no notion of Western hegemony and, I would add, no singular codified form of statecraft.[85] The nation-state system was four centuries from solidifying. A world market existed, without a singular core, consisting of "subsystems."[86] As we have seen, Italy was firmly in a city-state system by this time. It is worth scanning the political horizon: "Christendom" constituted an important overlapping authority. For example, the city republics of Venice and Genoa crusaded more than any other states. Territorial empires expanded. The Mongol Empire, in

81 Henri Pirenne, *Medieval Cities: Their Origins and the Revival of Trade* (Princeton: Princeton University Press, 1939), 82.
82 Ibid., 111, quotation from p. 91.
83 Robert S. Lopez, *The Commercial Revolution of the Middle Ages 950 to 1350* (Cambridge: Cambridge University Press, 1976), 85.
84 Ibid., 109.
85 Janet L. Abu-Lughod, *Before Western Hegemony: The World System A.D. 1250–1350* (Oxford: Oxford University Press, 1989), 4
86 Ibid., 33.

nomadic form, was instrumental in stabilizing the silk road trade on which the Venetian city-state thrived. It was a world in which a menagerie of state types intermingled. In a multipolar setting, statecraft suited the purposes of its craftsmen rather than emerging from precedent or imposition from without. Governance itself occurred in shades of grey. Piracy happened in cooperation with states. It occurred so regularly that Venetian ships in the Middle Ages were dual use. Merchant ships were prepared for battle while naval convoys had goods ready to sell. In this tumultuous milieu, Italy transitioned from a peripheral zone to one of the cores of the world economy as Arab dominance receded.[87]

For Abu-Lughod, Venetian behavior was seminal in Europe's centuries-long shift toward state-capitalism, though the feudal scaffolding of society remained.[88] The state led a popular investment culture in which casual Venetian "dandies" were shareholders.[89] Even the lower ranks in society had goods for sale in Venetian galleys. Just as importantly, she sees Italian seafaring as the most direct cause of Europe's return to core status. Its role was that of "middleman or jobber, transferring goods from where they are produced and plentiful to where markets for them exist."[90] In this way Venice offers another foreshadowing, a managerial city more interested in capturing value from resources produced elsewhere than in producing goods itself.

In this heterogeneous age of state experimentation, Venice and Genoa voraciously competed to establish ties with Mamluk and Mongol powers, also forging links in the European world cities of Antwerp, Lübeck, and Bruges. Interdependence fostered war rather than the peace through trade that international relations theory might predict. Open warfare ensued for centuries between the two seaborne powers. Not even the decimation of both of their populations by the plague halted fighting over the shipping lanes. Both sides fought ferociously with depleted crews. This lasted until Venice gained the upper hand after the decisive Battle of Chioggia in 1380. "It was not until Venice established a virtual monopoly over the Mediterranean routes that trade once again became more secure," concluded Abu-Lughod.[91] Whatever the broader economic fortunes from then on, Europe won a core place in the world system that it has never fully relinquished.

Michael McCormick's *Origins of the European Economy* challenges the oft-cited tenth century timing of the recovery, dating Europe's commercial emergence from the 800s.[92] He cites a plethora of factors for this, making the case that Venetian merchants spearheaded the shift. Much of the Venetian activities Abu-Lughod described also occurred in the 700s, he argues, calling it the "Venetian breakthrough" in long distance sea traffic.[93] Shipping studies

[87] Ibid., 105. [88] Ibid., 115. [89] Ibid., 114. [90] Ibid., 113. [91] Ibid., 130.
[92] McCormick, *Origins of the European Economy*, 791. [93] Ibid., 523.

from these years based on merchant records show Venice to be the "epicenter of change" accounting for enormous shares of Mediterranean travel.[94] Its outsized role echoed in a thicket of diplomatic agreements with various imperial powers across the Mediterranean and continental Europe. The doge's wealth may have rivaled or exceeded that of the papacy by then.[95] He pinpoints the Venetian emergence as a maritime power from the early 700s, gradually surpassing its nominal Byzantine overlords in naval capability.[96] This made the Empire more reliant on Venice, incentivizing Venetian support through favorable access to Constantinople's gargantuan market. This is when the Adriatic gradually became the "Venetian Sea," where emperors frequently called on Venice to defend their holdings. Back home, the city was awash in foreign currencies and new building projects, especially ever more numerous churches.[97] The Venice we know today gradually took form, with village dwellers coalescing on the Rialto. Venice played a central role in a network tying it to Muslim Egypt and Syria as well as Byzantium. Increasing Venetian assertiveness in the Adriatic managed to turn back northbound Arab fleets. At the same time it capitalized on trade relations with Islamic powers, which were integral to its newfound wealth. In his exhaustive exploration of shipping records in the early Middle Ages, McCormick asserts that no other European power had Venice's long distance capability, "extraordinary" for the time. His words best describe the city's geographic range and relations at this stage:

> Early on, the Venetian ships ranged astonishingly widely: From Rome to somewhere in the Caliphate, between Africa – perhaps indeed Morocco rather than Tunisia – and Sicily, to the Holy Land, to Egypt. All across the Mediterranean, the Venetian vessels were active. But predominantly, they sailed to the Islamic world, in contrast to the Byzantine harbors that would become their favored destinations a little later.[98]

The slave trade was a financial force behind Europe's revival. Despite bans, slavery continued in Europe. Slave markets existed throughout the network, including in Italy. Venice capitalized on the trade, supplying Islamic markets.[99] War captives were sold as chattel. Pirates raided coasts, abducting people to sell at market. Denizens of port cities feared approaching Venetian ships where they could be "taken away just like slaves to a land we do not know."[100] The slave trade in the Middle Ages involved a variety of backgrounds, including Italians, Slavs (from which the term derives), Byzantines, Africans, Jews, and Arabs. McCormick's analysis came to the tentative conclusion that most slave trafficking ran from Europe to points south by seaborne

[94] Genoa had yet to emerge as a rival. Ibid., 632. [95] Ibid., 633. [96] Ibid., 526.
[97] Ibid., 530. [98] Ibid., 546. [99] Ibid., 545. [100] Ibid., 244.

"middlemen" merchants carrying people in much the same way as commodities.[101]

As has been shown, Europe's core position has been in place since at least the late Middle Ages, with the benefit of hindsight. This reflection would have been news to patricians horrified at Ottoman advances into Europe by land and sea – borrowing Venetian ship design – centuries into the period of Western hegemony. The renaissance was an age of economic stagnation in Europe, despite the cultural flourishing led by Italy. Severe plagues in the 1300s halted economic expansion. Italy declined economically relative to the rest of Europe. Intercity travel, the engine of growth, remained a massive struggle throughout the Middle Ages. Disorganization after the Roman Empire's collapse slowed travel and communications. The postal system declined. Inns fell into disuse. The roads crumbled. Only in the later Middle Ages did revitalized infrastructure and renewed innovation improve connections incrementally.[102] Travel remained exhausting. Mountainous regions in Italy were isolated from urban-based authority, the church included.[103]

Fernand Braudel's classic study *The Mediterranean: And the Mediterranean World in the Age of Phillip II* centers around a peculiar time period. Phillip II of Hapsburg's sixteenth century reign occurred after a prolonged economic slowdown, and a decline in the relative strength of Italian cities. The navigational advancements that enabled blue water seafaring hastened Venetian decline. Vasco da Gama's (1460s–1524) route to India around the horn of Africa at the turn of the sixteenth century was a commercial threat that stirred trepidation when the news reached Venice. Portuguese shipping could potentially reach the spice trade without the old Mediterranean routes monopolized by Venice, though the process was gradual.[104] Fully aware of Venice's loss of influence, Braudel still calls it "unquestionably the vigorous heart of the Mediterranean."[105] A loss in geopolitical weight, for Braudel, did not equal an economic decline. Despite his subtitle's reference to Hapsburg dominance at this time, the dual volume work places significant emphasis on Venice's role in the Mediterranean. He defined the region as a "self-contained universe," with an urban "quadrilateral" of Genoa, Milan, Venice, and Florence at its heart.[106] Still arguably the most powerful

[101] Ibid., 248. [102] Ibid., 475.

[103] C. J. Wickham, *The Mountains and the City: The Tuscan Appennines in the Early Middle Ages* (Oxford: Oxford University Press, 1988), 353.

[104] An important Venetian diarist lamented that the Portuguese breakthrough was "more important to the Venetian state than the war with the Turks," with the potential to "rip out the heart of the city of Venice." See Robert Finlay, "Crisis and Crusade in the Mediterranean: Venice, Portugal, and the Cape Route to India, (1498–1509)," *Studi Veniziani* 28 (1994), 45–90.

[105] Fernand Braudel, *The Mediterranean: And the Mediterranean World in the Age of Phillip II Volume I* (Berkeley: University of California Press, 1995), 387.

[106] Ibid.

city in Italy, Venice relied increasingly on economic interdependence with these cities. Prefiguring world city studies, Braudel points out that cities had specialized noneconomic forms of power. He credits Rome for being a centrifuge of culture throughout the region. This despite the fact that it was not part of the quadrilateral. All told, "the hegemony of the four 'great powers' remained uninterrupted" until France's invasion of Italy under Charles VIII in 1494, which destabilized intercity relations.[107] The city-state itself was an entity in decline, though Braudel's seminal thinking on the role of cities focuses on their resilience. More European cities had risen to prominence. Far from declining, intercity relations were vital to the burgeoning European empires. Braudel summarizes the situation:

> In short the cities were not to be so easily eliminated from the land of the living and powerful. Their position remained good at least until 1530. In the new constellation, in which Seville and Lisbon were in the ascendant, a chain of cities from Antwerp to Venice ruled the world, with Venice still maintaining her supremacy in the eastern Mediterranean, though not without difficulty, for there was only to be lasting peace with the Turks after 1574.[108]

Not only that, by the sixteenth century these cities, led by Venice, found themselves "in a position to exploit the whole world."[109] Braudel's choices of time and place mark a region in conspicuous, observable transition. Continental Europe was establishing "European" (not simply Christian) political identity where for millennia the sea-linked Mediterranean was a more powerful social engine. The Atlantic was in the early stages of becoming the new Mediterranean, a circuit board of transoceanic commerce and communication (although we should not forget that the Europeans forged the Atlantic network with genocidal colonial rapacity). The second volume of *The Mediterranean* culminates with the allied Venetian and Hapsburg victory over the Turks at the Battle of Lepanto in 1571. This marked a psychological end to perceived Ottoman invincibility. As a whole, *The Mediterranean* evinces a fascination with things evolving away. This includes the independent city-state system of the Middle Ages, yet another transition.[110]

The rest of this chapter explores Venice's place in its city network and its local impacts.

Venice: Prototypical Alpha City

Venice was a city of refugees fleeing the Germanic invasions of the Roman Empire in the 400s CE. Its historic trajectory was a product of its natural environment. Put bluntly, it occupied a territory in Italy that no one else

[107] Ibid., 388. [108] Ibid., 390. [109] Ibid., 342. [110] Ibid., 326.

wanted. Abandoning *terraferma*, they carted with them what valuables they could. When land was the most valuable commodity, Venice had little more than a stretch of islands and sea barriers (the *lidi*) separated by a shallow lagoon unreachable by any army. For much of its history, Venetians had to reclaim needed land. Later they fought silting, flooding, and coastal erosion.[111] The Venetian lagoon could yield few crops, especially as the city used more space for construction, forcing it to look outward for sustenance. Cassiodorus' letter to Venetian nobles in 523 CE describes a series of villages (Venice was not yet a cohesive metropolis) physically isolated from its neighbors yet integrated through exchange:

> For you live like sea birds, with your homes dispersed, like the Cyclades, across the surface of the water. The solidity of the earth on which they rest is secured only by osier and wattle; yet you do not hesitate to oppose so frail a bulwark to the wildness of the sea. Your people have one great wealth – the fish which suffices for them all. Among you there is no difference between rich and poor; your food is the same, your houses are all alike. Envy, which rules the rest of the world, is unknown to you. All your energies are spent on your salt fields; in them lies your prosperity, and your power to purchase those things which you have not.[112]

Note the simple building materials of osier (a plant used for weaving) and wattle reportedly used for housing. Yet Venice was a formidable shipbuilder early on. Empires stomping through the northern tier of Italy – the Ostrogoths, Lombards, and Byzantines – never truly controlled the lagoon. The latter required the support of Venice's fleet. This sheltered geographic position engendered tough talk. The Venetians apparently informed the Byzantine exarch, its technical sovereign, that "we fear no invasion or seizure by any of the kings or princes of this world, or even by the Emperor himself."[113] Despite this scarcity, the retreat to the lagoon turned out to have immense environmental advantages. Although Venice could never be self-sufficient in basic necessities, it was strategically well positioned at the north end of the Adriatic Sea. This zone, with a narrowed, controllable southern entry point, was the heart of the *Stato da Mar* for centuries. Just as crucially, Venice had riverine access to continental Europe. It was a crossroads between land and sea from its founding.

The city's commercial peak was so long-lasting that the timing of its true heyday is hotly debated. Onlookers awed at the mature city's abundance. In contrast to Cassiodorus, an observer visiting Venetian warehouses centuries later noted that "it seems as if the world flocks there, and that human beings

111 Elisabeth Crouzet-Pavan, "Venice and Its Surroundings," in Eric R. Dursteler (ed.), *A Companion to Venetian History* (Boston: Brill, 2013), 25–84, 37.

112 Cited in John Julius Norwich, *A History of Venice* (New York: Vintage: 1989), 6.

113 Cited in ibid., 9.

have concentrated there all their force for trading."[114] In another superlative description:

> There is such a variety of things here, pertaining both to man's well-being and to his pleasure, that, just as Italy is a compendium of all Europe, because all the things that are scattered through other parts are happily concentrated in her, even so Venice may be called a summary of the universe, because there is nothing originating in any far-off country but it is found in abundance in this city.[115]

These descriptions actually came as Venice lost influence, as old trading lanes diminished.[116] The city remained an *entrepôt* whose overseas networks and *Stato da Mar* shaped its culture.

Venice's *Stato da Mar* far predates its land acquisitions in Italy. For centuries, this was the source of its power. As we will see in the passages that follow, the *Stato da Mar* enabled far-reaching contacts that greatly affected city planning, architecture, and the lived experience for Venetians. Venice was the hive of a prototypical maritime empire later emulated by the Portuguese, British, and Dutch. From at least the Fourth Crusade until well into the 1400s, Venice was a first-tier power in Europe and the Mediterranean. Fredric C. Lane argued that Venice's transformation from a local player to a maritime power was apparent by 1000 CE.[117] In the formative years, Venice ran profitable trade along the rivers leading into Northern Italy according to the rules of territorial empires. Venice asserted control of river outlets in its vicinity, at the expense of local rivals, foreshadowing expansionist aims.[118] As the city neutralized competitors in its vicinity, it looked outward to the Adriatic. Venice's great power status was undoubted in the 1200s and 1300s.

Along with basic commodities like salt and lumber, the slave trade tragically drove the city's financial growth. McNeill contends that slavery played a "far greater role than scholars recognized" in the city's emergence as a great power.[119] The Latin church tried curbing the enslavement of Catholics but allowed the trafficking of captured, so-called infidel Muslims and "heretical" Orthodox Christians. Neither religious nuance nor human empathy mattered to traders capitalizing on what to them was brisk business. They sold at Italian and Islamic slave markets alike.[120] Although it was not as prevalent as in Roman times, slave traders shipped thousands of people from European markets to the Middle East annually.[121] Here the ecological source of

[114] Cited in David Chambers and Brian Pullan (eds.), *Venice: A Documentary History, 1450–1630* (Toronto: University of Toronto Press, 2001), 167.
[115] Cited in ibid., 168.
[116] Braudel illustrates this decline in graphics, noting that private convoys helped make up for the loss. See Braudel, *Mediterranean Volume I*, 392.
[117] Fredric C. Lane, *Venice: A Maritime Republic* (Baltimore: Johns Hopkins University Press, 1973), 1.
[118] Ibid., 6. [119] McNeill, *Venice*, 54. [120] Lane, *Venice*, 7. [121] McNeill, *Venice*, 54.

Venetian power was apparent. From its isolated position it evaded any empire seeking to impose rules on trade. The rules had to be negotiated, leaving latitude even with the likes of church and empire. Distant colonies away from creeping anti-slavery mores on the European continent further enabled slave trading. For example, the outpost at Tana was a way station for Russian and Tatar slaves. Venice had a slave market on the Rialto until 1366, only to reemerge in its colony at Crete after its banishment.[122] Larger shipping enabled more slave trafficking. Chillingly, Venice increased the ratio of slaves to crewmembers as the slave trade fell harder on children and women sold as concubines. They were perceived to be less likely to revolt.[123]

*****

The arguable founder of the *Stato da Mar* was Pietro Orseolo II (961–1009), who initiated an eastward expansion on assuming the dogeship in 991. In a nominal effort to combat piracy, his navy acquired tributaries up and down the Dalmatian coast. It installed warehouses and ports in these places, ensuring control of Adriatic seaborne traffic. Another reward was access to Dalmatian farming regions to ensure Venice's growing population a food surplus.[124] The most important strategic nodes acquired from the Fourth Crusade were the port cities of Modon and Coron, the "eyes of the Republic."[125] They were located near one another on the Peloponnese and usually mentioned in the same breath by historians. Fixed midway between the Adriatic and Middle East, these ports provided the safe harbor needed for Venetian fleets to restock and repair. These junctions in the Ionian Sea extended the projection of naval power. They ensured that Venice could marshal formidable force beyond the Adriatic and would be a match for rival Genoa at points east.[126] Formerly Byzantine Crete was one of the largest colonies in the *Stato da Mar*, inclusive of 10,000 Venetian settlers (Figure 9.1). Venetian rule, often allowing for a modicum of self-governance, was particularly severe there. The Venetian colonists "mulcted Crete with particular ferocity, worked its peasantry hard to extract grain and wine for the mother city, and repressed the Orthodox church," as one historian put it.[127] This resulted in nearly thirty peasant-led revolts.

The urban–rural divide was as pronounced in the *Stato da Mar* as in any city network. Venice relied heavily on its maritime state for its food supply. Conditions worsened in places with high levels of agricultural output and peasant workforces. There was immense pressure on these select regions,

[122] Ibid., 133. [123] Ibid. [124] Norwich, *History of Venice*, 54.
[125] Crowley, *City of Fortune*, 120.
[126] Thomas F. Madden, *Enrico Dandolo and the Rise of Venice* (Baltimore: Johns Hopkins University Press, 2003), 199.
[127] Crowley, *City of Fortune*, 123.

Figure 9.1 Venetian fortification in Candia (present-day Heraklion, Crete), a critical node in the *Stato da Mar.* Completed in the sixteenth century, this fortress was under Venetian control until Venice capitulated to the Ottomans in 1669. One can imagine Venetian sentinels scanning these seas for the Turkish navy.
Photo by the author.

because there was little fertile land under Venetian control. Making matters worse, as a city-state of limited size Venice always had too few workers and pressed provincials into military service, resource extraction, and farm labor under poor conditions. Debt, famines, and disease wracked the countryside in the fertile holdings around Crete, Corfu, and Negroponte.[128] Desertions magnified manpower problems. "In particular it is necessary to give confidence to fleeing debtors so that they return to work their land," went a fourteenth-century missive from the Signoria to the Cretan administration. "The landlords lack men."[129] Escaped slaves from these hinterlands further threatened production. Whatever the *Stato da Mar* did produce had to flow through the city of Venice, a core–periphery model under tight administrative control from the center. This economic scheme prefigured the state mercantilism of later empires. The Venetian monopoly on the "white gold" salt trade in the colonies was a prime example.[130]

[128] Ibid., 248. [129] Ibid., 249. [130] Arbel, "Venice's Maritime Empire," 220.

Despite top-down oversight when it came to resource extraction, the *Stato da Mar* was enormously difficult to guard against external threats in remote ungovernable spaces. The Venetian navy's primary responsibility was to shield these territories from piracy or the threat of takeover from rival powers. Land-based travelers around its holdings were frequently robbed. Coastal property was constantly at risk. Pirates commonly raided the coasts to abduct inhabitants for sale at slave markets. The practice was common enough for the Venetians to maintain a fund for recovering its colonial populations from slavery.[131] Venetian naval hegemony in the Mediterranean differed from ancient Rome's. In a multipolar world there was no Pompey the Great to effectively eliminate piracy in a matter of months. Keeping the shipping lanes open required constant warfare, first principally with Genoa, then with the Ottoman Empire. Venice fought eleven wars against the Ottomans, mainly over Mediterranean possessions.[132] The expansion of the *Stato da Mar* paradoxically created more points on the map to battle over. For this reason, Venetians were expansionist and minimalist at the same time, foregoing control over large land tracts or other great cities that would be difficult to protect and unprofitable.[133] The state resultantly spent the bulk of its budget on overseas security in typical years.

In all, the *Stato da Mar* reached its maximum geographic extent in the 1400s. Population size peaked in the 1500s.[134] No city in the *Stato da Mar* approached Venice in size. It was the primate city in the network under Venice's control, to put things in perspective. Venice was still small enough to foster the personal relationships that were central to its governance and business culture. The *Stato da Mar* provided ample potential for travel. Large portions of the community were overseas for extended periods. Most Venetian families had someone or knew someone serving in administration, trading, or fighting abroad. The cities in the *Stato da Mar* were themselves small communities in an "intimate empire" ripe for close-knit social relations.[135] Venice's population was remarkably well adapted to long running Cold Wars with rival powers. On the home front, the arsenal comprised a large workforce by necessity. They were essential to Venetian power, prone to strike under poor conditions, and therefore had a degree of power themselves. These *arsenalotti* could double or quadruple the size of the navy in wartime, helping explain Venice's significant technological edge in the Middle Ages.[136] From an economic vantage point, Venice's complex trading networks ultimately required more traders to stay home to arrange business ventures. The state

[131] Ibid., 128. [132] Ibid., 199. [133] Ibid., 137. [134] Ibid., 142.

[135] See Erin Maglaque, *Venice's Intimate Empire: Family Life and Scholarship in the Renaissance Mediterranean* (Ithaca: Cornell University Press, 2018).

[136] Arbel, "Venice's Maritime Empire," 210.

organized trading convoys (*muda*) that emerged in the 1300s required innovations such as double entry bookkeeping. A knowledge economy emerged to handle finances and contracts, helped in part from lessons learned by Venetian traders abroad.[137] In this area too, the Venetians had an organizational competitive advantage over rivals. This financial capability made long distance trade viable.[138] Profits on *muda* reached as high as 40 percent and helped Venice maintain a near monopoly on the spice trade.[139] The *muda* gave the state control over merchandise traffic in a way that benefitted the nobility.[140]

The rivalry with the Genoese was instructive of city networks in history, where control of commercial routes between cities was grounds for conflict. Genoa emerged from a seemingly restrictive ecology at the north end of an important waterway, the Tyrrhenian Sea. As with Venice, ancient settlers largely avoided the region due to its remoteness and scarcity. Genoa, sandwiched between coast and mountains, was far from self-sufficient.[141] These were "two flourishing cities or, to put it briefly, two bright lights of Italy, which it seems to me Mother Nature has so strategically located on the opposite sides of [Italy]," wrote Petrarch in the mid-1300s.[142] Genoa rose to prominence in the east through the First Crusade in 1095, advancing its commercial interests through crusader ports. These ports accounted for nearly three-quarters of overall trade by the 1200s.[143] At its peak in the later Middle Ages, Genoa occupied most of Corsica and Sardinia. It temporarily controlled Crete, with colonies in the Aegean. The most advanced long distance navigators, Genoa dominated Black Sea trade with numerous colonies. This is a remarkable projection of power for a city with a population estimate of only 40,000 in 1348.[144] Its immediate *contado* had an additional 95,000 people, also relatively small.[145]

The Genoese maintained even more extensive trading routes. Genoa's location on the western shores of Italy made it well positioned to reach the

[137] Pezzolo, "Venetian Economy," 259.

[138] Diego Puga and Daniel Trefler, "International Trade and Institutional Change: Medieval Venice's Response to Globalization," National Bureau of Economic Research, Working Paper 18288 (August 2012), 2.

[139] Pezzolo, "Venetian Economy," 259.

[140] Stefania Montemezzo, "Galley Routes and Merchant Networks between Venice and the North Sea in the Fifteenth Century," in Andrea Caracausi and Christof Jeggle (eds.), *Commercial Networks and European Cities, 1400–1800* (London: Pickering and Chatto, 2014), 153–169, 155.

[141] Steven A. Epstein, *Genoa and the Genoese, 958–1528* (Chapel Hill: University of North Carolina Press, 1996), 10.

[142] George L. Gorse, "Architecture and Urban Topography," in Carrie L. Beneš (ed.), *A Companion to Medieval Genoa* (Boston: Brill, 2018), 218–292, 219.

[143] Jeffrey Miner and Stefan Stantchev, "The Genoese Economy," in Carrie L. Beneš (ed.), *A Companion to Medieval Genoa* (Boston: Brill, 2018), 397–426, 401.

[144] Scott, *City-State in Europe*, 72.

[145] Ibid.

western Mediterranean and the northern center of Bruges.[146] Genoa circulated high value, high margin luxury goods from spices to silk.[147] It competed ferociously with Venice for advantageous trade relations with Byzantium, losing access after 1204, but gaining the upper hand after Constantinople returned to Byzantine rule in 1261 with Genoese help. The Genoese retained a colony in nearby Galata, from which the Galata Tower constructed by the Genoese in the 1300s is a popular architectural artifact in present-day Istanbul.

A changing balance of power endangered Venice's position by the turn of the sixteenth century. The fall of Constantinople in 1453 under expansionist Ottoman ruler Mehmet II threatened to cut off Venetian access to eastern trade, jeopardizing most of its maritime empire. Another conqueror, Charles XIII of France, launched an advance through Italy in 1494 that revealed weaknesses in small, divided city-states against territorial empires. The city-state system as a whole was an endangered species. Communal structures eroded, becoming more dictatorial. Italy's relative economic and technological edges ebbed. The northern trading cities, as we will see in Chapters 10 and 11, grew stronger. Venice's glorious victory at Lepanto, for example, required imported northern shipping construction and knowhow. Europe plundered the Americas, prying open the West African slave trade. Venice sat apart in the old heart of the transcontinental economy, the Mediterranean. The Republic was a second-class power in a changed playing field. It stemmed these losses by land, expanding its *contado* in Italy.

The Venetian *terraferma* empire does not emerge until the fifteenth century, well after the *Stato da Mar*. Its annexations eventually encompass most of the northeastern section of Italy, including the important cities of Brescia, Padua, and Verona in addition to crucial waterways.[148] Brescia was the largest city in the *terraferma*, with 50,000 people, followed by Verona with 40,000 inhabitants – very large cities by the standards of the time. As with the *Stato da Mar*, the *terraferma* empire was intended to provide a security buffer for Venetian interests, especially trade. By accepted estimates, the *terraferma* was about 30,000 square kilometers encompassing 1.4 million people by the mid-sixteenth century.[149] Nearly a quarter of the population in the greater region lived in cities.[150] As a result of these conquests, Spanish ambassador Don Alonso de la Cueva could report in 1618 that, "[i]n the unanimous opinion of all men, the Venetian Republic is deemed to be the first and greatest in dignity,

[146] For a detailed mapping of Genoese colonies and trade routes, see Carrie L. Beneš, "Introduction," in Carrie L. Beneš (ed.), *A Companion to Medieval Genoa* (Boston: Brill, 2018), 1–24, 15.

[147] Miner and Stantchev, "Genoese Economy," 403.

[148] Michael Knapton, "The *Terraferma* State," in Eric R. Dursteler (ed.), *A Companion to Venetian History* (Boston: Brill, 2013), 85–124, 87.

[149] Ibid., 86. [150] Ibid., 108.

power and authority in Italy today."[151] Venetian rule in the *terraferma* brought new tensions. Rival cities, particularly Rome, bridled at this expansionism, forming the League of Cambrai. Most of the power of Europe backed the League, dealing Venice a crushing defeat in the battle of Agnadello in 1509. As often happens when force is used, the result of the war itself was inconclusive.[152] Still, it reinforced the hard fact that empires ruled the age and showed weakness in the city's ability to hold on to its *contado*. Internally, the urban-minded Venetians continually grated against the peasant *contadini* in a frenzy of land acquisitions by urban elites in which rural living standards "worsened substantially."[153]

All told, Venice's golden age lasted a remarkably long time.

City of the World

"This city, amidst the billowing waves of the sea, stands on the crest of the main, almost like a queen restraining its force," wrote the Venetian chronicler Marin Sanudo in praise of his city in 1493.[154] Then as now the city evokes a remarkable image of compact districts reachable by foot or boat. Venice's famed canals expanded with the city's commercial reach, intended primarily to move goods efficiently (and later to filter out waste).[155] From there, Sanudo describes the bountiful markets and the well-connected specialized districts later praised by the twentieth century architecture critic and urban visionary Lewis Mumford. The homes of the wealthy doubled as warehouses with access to Venice's waterways.

The Rialto market was the heart of the city, where merchants coalesced. The Grand Canal was the main thoroughfare, accommodating ships of up to 200 tons.[156] Functions were separated out over time, away from the central area to reduce traffic congestion. Shipbuilding was the most important industry, enabling the *Stato da Mar*, with shipyards eventually housed at the east end of the city. The arsenal was started in 1104 and was reconstructed many times over. It had "a particular identity" with each craft group in the *arsenalotti* assigned "special privileges and responsibilities," according to Sanudo.[157] The Venetian government grew more proactive in urban planning, reclaiming land for construction and shoring up the canals to reduce silting.

151 Cited in Chambers and Pullen, *Venice*, 31.
152 Norwich, *History of Venice*, 398.
153 Knapton, "*Terraferma* State," 104.
154 Cited in Chambers and Pullen, *Venice*, 4.
155 Crouzet-Pavan, "Venice and Its Surroundings," 44.
156 Venetian ships tended to be smaller than their Genoese counterparts due to the shallowness of the lagoon. Lane, *Venice*, 14.
157 Cited in Patricia H. Labalme and Laura Sanguineti White (eds.), *Venice, Cítà Excelentissima: Selections from the Renaissance Diaries of Marin Sanudo* (Baltimore: Johns Hopkins University Press, 2008), 245.

Venice required constant migration from the Italian mainland and beyond, prompting a French envoy to remark that "most of their people are foreigners."[158] First, Venice was a classic population sink with death rates exceeding birthrates. Migration was particularly important after plagues, but public health conditions were always harsh.[159] In the Grand Council's own words, "cities are rich and powerful when they are copiously populated."[160] The city simply could not have existed without an inflow of new residents. The *terraferma* also served this role, providing a flow of human resources in addition to commodities. Second, its complicated international economy required skilled labor from all over Europe and the Middle East. Greeks, Germans, Turks, Armenians, Dalmatians, and Jews from abroad all contributed to a polyglot city that could not work without them. In cases of badly needed professions, the government offered naturalization or permanent residency to foreigners.

The architecture of Venice strongly reflects its role as a world city in the Middle Ages, with Islamic and Byzantine forms melded into "Venetian Gothic." Quoting Goethe, one of the foremost experts of Venetian architectural history, Deborah Howard, points out that Venice "can only be compared to itself."[161] For Howard, Venetian architecture has its foundations in the Byzantine period.[162] This was hardly limited to the theft of relics such as the four bronze horses from Constantinople that Venice absconded with in the Fourth Crusade (or for that matter the bones of St. Mark, heisted from Alexandria by Venetian traders in 828). Byzantium, fading as it may have been, was still the cultural center of Christendom. Venice's medieval windows, domes, and building materials, Howard observes, closely reflect those of Constantinople.[163] St. Marks Cathedral heavily reflects foreign influences. As Howard meticulously shows, it was remarkably bold in its incorporation of Islamic and Greek Orthodox (e.g. "heretic") aesthetics in a place of worship.[164] As Howard's research shows, this was brought about through Venice's extensive intercity trading network. The further away figuratively or geographically, it appears, the more interested the Venetians were in incorporating the style. The Venetians imported building-types from eastern cities, particularly

158 Cited in Chambers and Pullen, *Venice*, 325.
159 Venice may have been somewhat more sanitary than most large cities in Europe, as the canals doubled as sewers for human and animal waste. See Lane, *Venice*, 20.
160 Dennis Romano, *Patricians and Popolani: The Social Foundations of the Venetian Renaissance State* (Baltimore: Johns Hopkins University Press, 1987), 26.
161 Deborah Howard, *The Architectural History of Venice* (New Haven: Yale University Press, 2002), 1.
162 Ibid., 6. 163 Ibid., 24.
164 Deborah Howard, *Venice & the East: The Impact of the Islamic World on Venetian Architecture 1100–1500* (New Haven: Yale University Press, 2000), 100.

the *fondaco* designed to facilitate travel and trade, going to the heart of the city's commercial functionality.[165]

According to the longstanding "myth of Venice," the city enjoyed internal stability that enabled it to concentrate resources on its empire. Conservative governance was evident in the *serrata* in 1297, which closed access to important leadership positions. This left offices almost exclusively to the titled nobility. Strong urban patriotism papered over class difference, but for a few bumps in the road. Modern scholars challenge this view.[166] As we have seen elsewhere in Italy, the Venetian elite commonly engaged in uncivil, even violent behavior. Nobles were particularly indignant toward public officials alleging corruption, which was in fact rampant.[167] There was a great deal of poverty, even among those with noble title. Still, the nobility formed a closed circle, pulling the levers of state to provide sinecure positions.[168] In total, only about 1 percent of the population was eligible for government councils after 1297.[169] Those standing outside this power elite, namely the *popolo*, rioted in the wake of the *serrata*.[170] Although the *popolo* could become wealthy through merchant activity, the majority of the wealthiest citizens were noble.[171]

As much as observers over the centuries have lauded Venice's urban form, inequality, tribalism, and competition seem to have been imbued in its built environment. The Rialto Bridge was the only crossing at the Grand Canal, apparently serving to separate rival factions.[172] The Spanish ambassador cited previously, Don Alonso de la Cueva, also took the time to contrast "extreme" riches with an "unspeakable poverty" that "beggars belief."[173] He recounts the children of the so-called shamefaced poor, fallen nobles living in "hovels" lying on mats "covered with filthy rags."[174] Famines fell hardest on the rural poor, who entered the city in search of food. According to one Venetian observer:

> Such was this terrible famine in 1569 and 1570 that great numbers of peasants who were dying of hunger came to Venice from the villages, and at home one could do nothing but answer the door to these peasants who hammered on doors in the town for two months on end . . . such poverty and wretchedness were truly pitiful sights.[175]

165 Ibid., 126.
166 See John Martin and Dennis Romano, *Venice Reconsidered: The History and Civilization of an Italian City-State 1297–1797* (Baltimore: Johns Hopkins University Press, 2000); and Donald E. Queller, *The Venetian Patriciate: Reality Versus Myth* (Chicago: University of Illinois Press, 1986).
167 Ibid., 234. 168 Ibid., 29. 169 Romano, *Patricians and Popolani*, 29. 170 Ibid., 4.
171 See estimates in ibid., 34. 172 Ibid., 20.
173 Cited in Chambers and Pullen, *Venice*, 258. 174 Cited in ibid. 175 Cited in ibid., 111.

In contrast to the myth, inequality made for volatile situations. According to the aforementioned account of a famine, a group of *arsenalotti* "attacked and robbed a number of persons who were selling bread in the city."[176] During work shortages, the *arsenalotti* spearheaded labor unrest. In one case, on hearing from the Doge that there was no work "they all made for the storehouses at St. Mark's and began to rob it of flour with great force and fury."[177]

The private sphere was fraught with inequality. Indeed, for the nonwealthy there was technically no private sphere at all. Here is one middle class resident's account of crowded, squalid lodgings from his journal entry in the mid-sixteenth century:

> I have the most wretched room (if you can call it that) in the whole town, and the worst company, and I suffer the worst discomfort in the world. For the consolation of sleep, I have a solid mattress, a good, soundly made hard bed, an empty pillow, coarse sheets and a blue counterpane of the type used in hospitals; at night, in the manner of a cruel doctor, an army of huge bedbugs . . . and a mob of fat fleas, test my pulse and bleed me; above my head, in an old loft, I think there is a consistory of cobwebs; below, there is a street where all night long wretches who waste the daytime pass up and down singing strombotti [lewd songs] noisily.[178]

The city's welfare system, run via religious organizations, shifted over time along with attitudes toward poverty.[179] There was no true social housing system. For women laborers, conditions in crowded rental housing were potentially terrifying. So were the city streets, rife as they were with an aggressive male dominated culture (where fist fights were a form of recreation!).[180]

Privacy in housing construction was only possible for the wealthy, and for half of the wealthy it was a gilded cage. Women were confined to cloistered spaces inside palaces. There were few spaces in the city available for them to roam freely outside the home, other than the local parish.[181] Strict segregation between men and women in urban spaces was unusual even for the time, a point of note for the foreign dignitaries who so often chronicled city life in Venice.[182] Even *within* single unit residences, there were rooms for men only. This was also true of parish architecture.[183] The bottom floor of the typical private *palazzo* was for men only. This was where they conducted business, the mercantile spaces that made the Venetian Republic tick.

It was a prototypical world city, but only for some.

176 Cited in ibid., 110. 177 Cited in ibid., 289. 178 Cited in ibid., 181.

179 For a magisterial account of this dynamic, see Brian Pullan, *Rich and Poor in Renaissance Venice: The Social Institutions of a Catholic State, to 1620* (Oxford: Oxford University Press, 1971).

180 Anne Jacobson Schutte, "Society and the Sexes in the Venetian Republic," in Eric R. Dursteler (ed.), *A Companion to Venetian History* (Boston: Brill, 2013), 354–377, 362.

181 Romano, *Patricians and Popolani*, 131. 182 Schutte, "Society and the Sexes," 355.

183 Ibid., 359.

Conclusion: Afterlives

Venice lost independence to Napoleon in 1797. This made it the longest lasting continually independent city-state in history. Long after it was a leading power on par with any territorial empire in world influence, it was finding new ways to retain relevance. In a certain sense the late Venetian Republic resembled a modern world city in a new way. In the later stages of its life, Venice trafficked not in direct military coercion, or even physical trade, but in knowledge and information. At the turn of the fifteenth century it was Europe's most important center of book publishing (despite this having been a northern invention) and correspondingly it was a global center for communications.[184] As Jane Jacobs might say, Venice excelled in finding new work. No longer a world "middle-man," Venice produced more manufacturing of its own.[185] Cultural production continued to flourish in the baroque period – think Tiepolo and Vivaldi – as Venice became a "grand tour" stop for tourists from the increasingly wealthy Atlantic polities.

In terms of geopolitical influence, Venice's peak was in the Middle Ages when it was central to the Italian city network, and part of a transcontinental city network inclusive of Asia, Africa, and the Middle East. The *Stato da Mar* could be thought of as a part of this broader world network, albeit under direct Venetian control, or rather a hybridized entity that positioned it geographically close to these places. In cities such as Constantinople, the network existed in a state of overlapping authority, with Venetians operating semi-autonomously in their own special zones. As much as territorial authority existed in full, unadulterated sovereignty had yet to take form, allowing a fomentation of trial, error, and convenience in state making.

In Chapter 10, we turn to one of the most important experiments in global urban governance happening around the northern seas: The Hanseatic League.

184 Mario Infelise, "Book Publishing and the Circulation of Information," in Eric R. Dursteler (ed.), *A Companion to Venetian History* (Boston: Brill, 2013), 652–674, 652.

185 Recalling the "middleman" characterization of Venice used by Abu-Lughod and McCormick.

10 Profit and Power

The Hanseatic Network

In 1284, the Hanseatic network, led by the northern German city of Lübeck, was a rising power capable of coercing territorial states. The German speaking Hanse had a virtual monopoly on the lucrative Norwegian trade in dried stockfish, a transportable commodity suitable for long-distance delivery that personified the integrated urban consumer markets of the high Middle Ages.[1] Bergen at this time was Norway's largest city, containing half the country's urban population.[2] It had trading contacts all over Europe.[3] Hardly any of the traders forging these ties were Norwegian.

As they controlled the tonnage of stockfish leaving Bergen's harbor, Hanse traders also controlled the grain shipments coming in. Norway was, to some degree, dependent on the Hanse to feed itself.[4] At the very least, Hanseatic grain made large swaths of Norwegian territory habitable.[5] The Hanse network found sufficient support among its membership to blockade the country, placing ships along the Danish straits to prevent food imports. "Then," noted the fourteenth-century medieval chronicler Detmar from Lübeck, "there broke out a famine so great that they were forced to make atonement."[6] The Hanse retained control of Norway's entire foreign trade with few exceptions.[7]

What, then, was the Hanse? Or *who* were *they*?

What is certain is that Hanseatic cities projected immense power, at times waging all out naval wars against territorial governments to protect preferential trading rights. Merchants from Hanse member cities dominated commerce

[1] Phillipe Dollinger, *The German Hanse* (New York: Routledge, 1999), 49.
[2] Geir Atle Ersland, "Bergen 1300–1600: A Trading Hub between the North and the Baltic Sea," in Wim Blockmans, Mikhail Krom, and Justyna Wubs-Mrozewicz (eds.), *The Routledge Handbook of Maritime Trade around Europe 1300–1600* (New York: Routledge, 2017), 428–445, 431.
[3] See the illustrations in ibid., 436.
[4] The ability of the Hanse to start an all-out famine in Norway has been questioned. For a skeptical view, see Arnved Nedkvitne, *The German Hanse and Bergen 1100–1600* (Köln: Böhlau Verlag, 2014), 566.
[5] Ibid., 540. [6] Cited in Dollinger, *German Hanse*, 49.
[7] Nedkvitne, *German Hanse and Bergen 1100–1600*, 277.

across the Baltic and North Seas in the fourteenth and fifteenth centuries before their primacy tapered off. The Hanseatic Diet, based primarily in Lübeck, convened over network-wide matters, seeking consensus where possible. When pressed to define itself to the English government in 1469, an official statement from the Hanse couched itself in modest terms:

> [The Hanse are] a firm *confederatio* of many cities, towns and communities for the purpose of ensuring that business enterprise by land and sea should have a desired and favorable outcome and that there should be effective protection against piracies and highwaymen, so that their ambushes should not rob merchants of their goods and valuables.[8]

This was its way of escaping responsibility if its members resorted to norm breaking, such as piracy, against trading partners. This could make the group as a whole vulnerable to indemnities. As a matter of course, the Hanse revealed little about itself. It usually declined to maintain a list recording the names of the 200 member cities whose merchants traded under its rules over the course of the organization's life.[9] Contrary to this artful dodge, the Hanse zealously pursued much more than mercantile security, creating what was in effect a system of exclusion among merchants in key trading zones consistent of clearly delineated in-groups and out-groups.[10] Maintaining trading rights at the expense of its competition was a life and death matter. In the 1200s, around the time of the Norwegian embargo, the Hanse transitioned from a social network of merchants to an increasingly formal organization whose membership consisted of cities. "In all of its activities," according to Phillipe Dollinger's study *The German Hanse*, "the Hanse was urban."[11] It was a product of increasingly complex medieval urbanization under which cities reemerged as the core sites of global interaction. Traditionally referred to as a "league" – the common designation this chapter uses for reference purposes – the Hanse did not have its own navy, official seal, or treasury. For some, this is too monolithic of a characterization of the Hanse, which suffered chronic collective action problems. One scholar calls it instead "a loose-jointed confederation with a complex structure and numerous protagonists, each with their

[8] Cited in T. H. Lloyd, *England and the German Hanse, 1157–1611* (Cambridge: Cambridge University Press, 1991), 7.

[9] Peter Johanek, "Imperial and Free Towns of the Holy Roman Empire: City-States in Pre-Modern Germany?" in Mogens Herman Hansen (ed.), *A Comparative Study of Thirty City-State Cultures* (Copenhagen: The Royal Danish Academy of Arts and Letters, 2000), 295–319, 311.

[10] Justyna Wubs-Mrozewicz, *Traders, Ties and Tensions: The Interactions of Lübeckers, Overijsslers and Hollanders in Late Medieval Bergen* (Hilversum: Uitgeverij Verloren, 2008), 12.

[11] Dollinger, *German Hanse*, 12.

own interests."[12] No treaty marked its creation, as historians continue to contest its start date. What the League had was superior shipbuilding capabilities and organizational skill.

During the institution's lifespan – roughly the 1100s to the 1600s – the term "hanse" meant something along the lines of "group," or "company," or "crowd." It came to imply entities with specific legal rights in towns. Over time the word became singular, in reference to the organization.[13] It was not until the year 1266, at least a century after the Hanse merchants began collaborating, that the term "Hanse" starts to formally describe it.[14] Eventually the League was identified in the phrase "towns of the German Hanse."[15] Complicating matters further, its major members were not true city-states, existing under the porous sovereignty of the Holy Roman Empire with varying degrees of autonomy. Despite the League's deliberate ambiguities, it was very real to the countries it marshaled force against, including Denmark, England, Holland, and Norway. It was very real to merchants from these countries who challenged Hanse monopolies for centuries. In daily life the Hanse presence was tangible in cities across northern Europe, encouraging the spread of artistic aesthetics, city planning, and architecture. Hanse towns were instantly recognizable in a peripatetic world unencumbered by national boundaries, starting with the buildings used to administer commercial ties. These, most ubiquitously, were the large "step gabled" row houses and mixed use town halls in the distinctive northern brick Gothic style that emphasized commercial over ecclesiastical strength.[16]

More than that, the Hanseatic League was at the heart of something larger than itself, a city network spanning the Atlantic shores, to England, across the northern seas to present-day Russia. For our purposes, the League was essentially a city network within a network. Recent historians have analyzed it in the context of network analysis, hence this chapter's references to the Hanse as a "network."[17] Hanse cities were way stations to places outside of the League. Many (though not all) of these cities were not the point of origin for traded

[12] Carsten Jahnke, "The City of Lübeck and the Internationality of Early Hanseatic Trade," in Justyna Wubs-Mrozewicz and Stuart Jenks (eds.), *The Hanse in Medieval and Early Modern Europe* (Boston: Brill, 2013), 37–58, 38.

[13] Justyna Wubs-Mrozewicz, "The Hanse in Medieval and Early Modern Europe: An Introduction," in Justyna Wubs-Mrozewicz and Stuart Jenks (eds.), *The Hanse in Medieval and Early Modern Europe* (Boston: Brill, 2013), 1–25, 6.

[14] Dollinger, *German Hanse*, 41.

[15] Jürgen Sarnowsky, "The 'Golden Age' of the Hanseatic League," in Donald J. Harreld (ed.), *A Companion to the Hanseatic League* (Boston: Brill, 2015), 64–100, 68.

[16] David Gaimster, "A Parallel History: The Archeology of Hanseatic Urban Culture in the Baltic c. 1200–1600," *World Archeology* 37, no. 3 (2005), 408–423, 412; Dollinger, *German Hanse*, 268.

[17] Mike Burkhardt, "Networks as Social Structures in Late Medieval and Early Modern Towns: A Theoretical Approach to Historical Network Analysis," in Andrea Caracausi and Christof

goods. Nor were they their destinations. Hanse cities were brokers and shippers controlling distribution. The League maintained dozens of outposts. The most important were the *kontors* – headquarters – cloistered in Bruges, Bergen, London, and Novgorod, the most important medieval commercial center in what is now Russia. The *kontors* housed merchants from the Hanse cities, playing by rules set by the Hanse Diet but also operating under the laws of the host governments. These four cities were not members, and crises dot their relations. For example, Hanse blockades also created famines in the alpha city of Bruges.[18] But they were crucial to its role in circulating commodities in the north, as important to the Hanse's existence as the member cities themselves.

New Worlds

The northern seas were *terra incognita* for much of the rest of Europe in antiquity. These zones were well beyond the Roman *limes*, for starters, and to the Romans the "barbarian seas" were the stuff of mythology. These lands were the last parts of Europe to convert to Christianity. Scandinavia, for its part, "was scarcely part of Europe in the Roman-Catholic, Western sense of the word."[19] Like the Mediterranean, the Baltic Sea and North Sea, separated by the Jutland peninsula, fostered their own unique maritime cultures.[20] These were pagan frontiers to the crusaders in the Middle Ages who attempted conversions.[21] Also analogous to the south, their populations had extensive navigational expertise and a long history of trading. Frisian society ran along the coastline of the Netherlands and northern Germany. Frisian traders landed from beach to beach to conduct exchanges in a proto-mercantile economy removed from the land-based power of the seventh century where the feudal Frankish Empire dominated.[22] Vikings from the North Sea sought trade relations as far as Constantinople.[23] These were not urban societies. Large-scale urbanization did not emerge until Christian missionaries arrived en-masse.

Scarcity created a need for northern civilizations to look outward. These were desolate climates, the land barely capable of sustaining human life. For centuries cities were few and far between because deep forested, agriculturally

Jeggle (eds.), *Commercial Networks and European Cities, 1400–1800* (London: Pickering and Chatto, 2014), 13–44, 14; Ewert and Selzer, *Institutions of Hanseatic Trade*, 33.

18 Jürgen Sarnowsky, "'Golden Age' of the Hanseatic League," 92.

19 Nils Blomkvist, *The Discovery of the Baltic: The Reception of Catholic World-System in the European North* (Boston: Brill, 2005), 2.

20 Andres Kasekamp, *A History of the Baltic States* (London: Palgrave, 2018), 1; Michael North, *The Baltic: A History* (Cambridge, MA: Harvard University Press, 2015), 2.

21 Blomkvist, *Discovery of the Baltic*, 3.

22 Michael Pye, *The Edge of the World: A Cultural History of the North Sea and the Transformation of Europe* (New York, Pegasus, 2015), 28.

23 Ibid., 107; Blomkvist, *Discovery of the Baltic*, 36.

poor land lacked the surpluses to sustain them. The further north you went, the less likely animal agriculture could work because cattle froze to death.[24] Grain harvests were so bare that remote Scandinavian communities mixed tree bark with flour to make bread.[25] This desperation fueled harsh labor conditions for peasants for centuries.

Environmental disadvantage merged with geographic advantage. The North and Baltic Seas made possible east to west trade, which would later become the principle function of the Hanse network. Trade networks running along an east to west axis existed well before the Hanse, and cultural interaction was significant. Proximity was aided further by the fact that the great northern seas are together a fraction of the size of the Mediterranean, one-seventh by one estimate.[26] All this was evident in the cosmopolitan qualities inherent in the Scandinavian sagas. Many of their adventure stories were passed down orally for centuries before they were put into writing in the later Middle Ages. Islamic influence was considerable, evidenced by the large caches of Arabic coinage found across the Baltic region from the ninth century, and in interactions with Islamic traders in Russia.[27] Northern trading networks sent fur, wax, and amber westward from the early Middle Ages onward, while cloth and manufactured goods sailed eastward. In the early Middle Ages a brisk market in slaves existed along these routes.[28]

The church declared its first crusade against pagans in the littoral regions of the Baltics in the twelfth century, catalyzing German eastward migrations into these lands that were motivated by opportunity as well as piety. The polyglot Swedish island of Gotland in the Baltic Sea emerged as a crucial space open to migration and trade.[29] In what may be marked as a genesis for the later Hanse, German merchants coalesced there, establishing the commercial city of Visby in the 1160s.[30] Visby became their early base for long distance trade. The Christian missionaries – beyond their history of forced conversions – changed the built environment greatly. They created a new Baltic aesthetic, constructing castles, churches, and abbeys.[31] The German eastward migration into pagan lands led to the founding of new towns, or the overrunning of existing ones. These settlements gave Christian forces a power base from which to reduce "the native Slavic peasantry to serfdom," as one historian put it.[32] These cities would become major names in the Hanse trading circuit: Lübeck, Gdańsk, Wismar, Riga, and Rostock, among others. Denmark, a

24 David Kirby, *Northern Europe in the Early Modern Period: The Baltic World 1492–1772* (New York: Longman, 1990), 15.
25 Ibid. 26 Ibid., 3. 27 Blomkvist, *Discovery of the Baltic*, 40.
28 Jahnke, "City of Lübeck," 39. 29 Blomkvist, *Discovery of the Baltic*, 397.
30 Kasekamp, *History of the Baltic States*, 10. 31 North, *Baltic*, 28.
32 David Nicholas, *The Northern Lands: Germanic Europe, c. 1270–c. 1500* (Oxford: Wiley-Blackwell, 2009), 63.

regional power, founded the city of Tallinn (then known as Reval) in Estonia. The Teutonic Order, a group of crusading knights that veered from Palestine to the Baltics to seize territory there, founded nearly 100 towns by itself. The Teutonic Order established or renewed infrastructure linking these cities after its defeat of pagan Prussia, later becoming a member of the Hanseatic League.[33] This nascent network of cities asserted colonial power over the local rural population, gathering raw materials for western markets.[34] This created a giant periphery in what Blomkvist calls a "Catholic world system."[35]

Businessmen maintained social networks linked by sea, from Visby to the other new towns across the Baltic. Low German was the shared dialect spoken by the Hanse merchants, forming the basis for linguistic connection. As settlers with common backgrounds, the Hanse traders depended on social trust to maintain the predictable business relationships on which risky seafaring ventures depended. German settlers comprised majorities in many of these towns, especially in the leading merchant and noble strata. As a merchant from Reval wrote to an associate in Lübeck in 1274, "the two towns belong together like the arms of Christ crucified."[36]

Europe's medieval expansions in population size and economic complexity (see Chapter 9) heavily impacted the north. "Europeanization" reached these formerly isolated territories. Colonization movements stretched as far west as Greenland. They even forged a brief beachhead in North America by around the year 1000 with the Viking settlement of Vinland in what is now Canada's Newfoundland.[37] Europe's population grew from less than forty million people that year to over seventy-five million on the eve of the plague of the mid-1300s.[38] Blomkvist identifies a vast economic core region stretching from Italy to southern England in 1200.[39] This comprised the highly developed urban areas of Bruges and London on its northern tier, with Venice and Genoa at its southern tier. The Champagne Fairs were located conveniently inland between these economic poles. These were the markets where northern and southern trade intersected seasonally.[40] This was the most international of the

[33] Christian Oertel, "Road Networks, Communications, and the Teutonic Order," in Alison L. Gascoigne, Leonie V. Hicks, and Marianne O'Doherty (eds.), *Journeying along Medieval Routes in Europe and the Middle East* (Turnhout: Brepols, 2016) 205–230, 206.

[34] Nicholas, *Northern Lands*, 63.

[35] Blomkvist, *Discovery of the Baltic*, 53; For the changing dynamic in urban–rural power relations, see Fritz Rörig, *The Medieval Town* (Berkeley: University of California Press, 1967), 32.

[36] Cited in Rörig, *Medieval Town*, 36. [37] Pye, *Edge of the World*, 114.

[38] Michael North, *The Expansion of Europe, 1250–1500* (Manchester: Manchester University Press, 2007), 362.

[39] Blomkvist, *Discovery of the Baltic*, 74.

[40] Edwin S. Hunt and James M. Murray, *A History of Business in Medieval Europe, 1200–1550* (Cambridge: Cambridge University Press, 1999), 28.

many annual fairs that sprouted up across Europe in the 1200s, attracting scores of merchant pilgrims.

By this time the Baltic region remained on the periphery, a rough frontier still undergoing a harsh process of Christianization. The north struggled to find enough valuable merchandise to trade for the luxury goods arriving at the Champagne Fairs from the core Mediterranean cities, having to cede silver coinage to make up the difference. Capital moved north to south.[41] Rural hinterlands sent raw goods to urban centers for processing, which were sent still further to *entrepôt* cities for purchase.[42] Change nevertheless happened quickly. In all, 38 cities were founded in the 1100s, with more than 200 new towns chartered in the 1200s.[43] Lübeck was founded in a devastating series of fits and starts.[44] German settlers were in conflict with Slavic oft-unconverted populations in the Wendish areas (in what is now northern Germany). After a round of conflicts, the German duke Henry the Lion (1129–1195) refounded a new city of Lübeck in 1159, combining the populations of nearby cities.[45] Located at a defensible position near the mouth of the Trave River by the German coast, the city was founded for the express purpose of commerce. Not long after the city's founding, Henry the Lion forged trade agreements with Russian and Scandinavian merchants.[46] Lübeck soon challenged Visby for regional trade supremacy. The first cogs, special ships used in Hanse convoys, were under construction in its shipyards. "The market at Lübeck also developed by the day," the chronicler Helmold of Bosau wrote of the city in the 1100s, "and the ships of its merchants multiplied."[47]

The foundations for the Hanseatic League were in place.

Northern City Network

Voltaire said that the Holy Roman Empire was "neither holy, nor Roman, nor an empire."[48] Inasmuch as this was true, the super-state centered on what is now Germany was highly decentralized in the Middle Ages despite expansive territorial claims. The sheer size of the Empire conspired to make it less centrally governable. In a polity where traversing two points could take at

41 Ibid., 29.

42 Carsten Jahnke, "The Baltic Trade," in Donald J. Harreld (ed.), *A Companion to the Hanseatic League* (Boston: Brill, 2015), 194–240, 196.

43 Ibid., 197.

44 For a full overview, see Dollinger, *German Hanse*, 21.

45 See Carsten Jahnke, "City of Lübeck."

46 Dollinger, *German Hanse*, 22.

47 Helmold of Bosau, *Chronica Slavorum*, Book I (Ann Arbor: University of Michigan Press, 1935).

48 Cited in Jason Lavery, *Germany's Northern Challenge: The Holy Roman Empire and the Scandinavian Struggle for the Baltic, 1563–1576* (Boston: Brill, 2002), 1.

least one month, important decisions simply had to be made locally.[49] Geography also worked against it. Where feudal lords could toll and blockade riverine trade, fragmented empires did not have the naval power to govern the northern seas.[50] The deterioration of the roads from Roman times took centuries to recover, and were dangerous, encouraging cities to take security matters into their own hands. Politically, emperors tended to be figureheads whose direct authority in reality extended only to their personal fiefdoms. Elections by the Empire's power elite decided emperors, not heredity. Therefore, they were no strangers to the imperatives of bargaining. Collective action required negotiation as though the cities under ostensible imperial sovereignty were foreign powers.[51] At times this weakened the state further, as conquerors seeking to mobilize empire-wide resources promised power to local nobles and town councils in exchange for favors.[52] In sum, cities had broad leeway to conduct their own foreign affairs, although imperial princes routinely contested the authority of the councils. Guarding local powers from imperial encroachments was an important function of the Hanseatic League.

The Empire granted some cities special legal status. "Imperial towns" formally accepted the emperor as "our only lawful, and legitimate Lord" in a relationship one historian describes as a partnership with the throne.[53] "Free towns" had theoretically greater autonomy and fewer responsibilities to the Empire or bishops. Some of the most important Hanse cities had one of these two designations. Lübeck was an imperial city, as was the formidable Hanseatic power of Cologne. Hamburg was the only free town in the League.[54] The vast majority of Hanse cities in the Holy Roman Empire had no special status at all. This reflects the broader makeup of the Empire, in which only about 100 of its 4,000 cities were imperial or free towns.[55] In all, the Empire's population was highly dispersed. Ninety-five percent of cities had 2,000 residents or fewer. Cologne was Germany's largest city, with 40,000 inhabitants. Lübeck's power was far greater than its population, which only numbered 28,000. Bear in mind that only sixteen cities passed the 10,000

49 Peter Moraw, "Cities and Citizenry as Factors of State Formation in the Roman German Empire of the Late Middle Ages," in Charles Tilly and Wim P. Blockmans (eds.), *Cities and the Rise of States in Europe, A.D. 1000 to 1800* (Boulder: Westview Press, 1994), 100–127, 110.

50 Job Westrate, "The Organization of Trade and Transport on the Lower Rhine and Waal Rivers around 1550," in Hanno Brand (ed.), *Trade, Diplomacy and Cultural Exchange: Continuity and Change in the North Sea Area and the Baltic c. 1350–1750* (Hilversum: Uitgeverij Verloren, 2005), 95–112, 100.

51 Nicholas, *Northern Lands*, 68.
52 Ibid., 69.

53 Johanek, "Imperial and Free Towns of the Holy Roman Empire," 296.
54 Ibid., 297.

55 Ibid., 296.

threshold, and a scant nine reached 20,000.[56] There was no "primate city" that existed on a scale inordinately larger than other leading centers. The legal statuses of these cities, which grew blurrier over time, may have been less important factors for urban autonomy than their locations. Imperial power was weak in the north.[57]

In Europe the broader trend was to see the power of the feudal lords over the towns diminished.[58] In Cologne, for example, emperors shared power with city officials. The crown could issue judgments on the most serious matters in the city, but this required consultation with local elites who wrote many of their own laws. The city conducted diplomacy with other towns under its own seal and issued tolls.[59] Certain cities were very close to functioning as city-states. This was by no means limited to the exceptionally fragmented Holy Roman Empire. Novgorod's elite managed to expel their prince to the countryside, expanding their power in his absence.[60] The Polish king who assumed control over the Hanse city of Danzig (now Gdańsk) after conflict with the Teutonic Order granted the city autonomy over maritime and trade policies.[61] Its city charter was harmonized with Lübeck's, further integrating it into the Hanse network.[62] Tallinn also adhered to Lübeck Law despite being under the ostensible authority of a multitude of empires in the Middle Ages. The city's German-speaking upper classes dutifully maintained its position in the city network, particularly as it was an important gateway to Russia.[63]

This milieu was conducive to renewed experiments in intercity relations.[64] The Swabian League of cities in southern Germany led by Ulm challenged imperial power. This helped instigate the Golden Bull of 1356 which

56 Figures cited in ibid., 297; and Gisela Naegle, "Revolts and Wars, Corporations, and Leagues," in Justine Firnhaber-Baker and Dirk Schoenaers (eds.), *Routledge History Handbook of Medieval Revolt* (New York: Routledge, 2017), 236–264, 236.

57 Rolf Hammel-Kiesow, "The Early Hanses," in Donald J. Harreld (ed.), *A Companion to the Hanseatic League* (Boston: Brill, 2015), 15–63, 52.

58 Dollinger, *German Hanse*, 13.

59 David Nicholas, *The Growth of the Medieval City: From Late Antiquity to the Early Fourteenth Century* (New York: Longman, 1997), 145.

60 Ibid.

61 Beata Mozejko, "Late Medieval Gdańsk as a Bridge between Regions," in Balázs Nagy, Felicitas Schmieder, and András Vadas (eds.), *The Medieval Networks in East Central Europe: Commerce, Contacts, Communication* (New York: Routledge, 2019), 227–235, 227.

62 Justyna Wubs-Mrozewicz, "Danzig (Gdańsk): Seeking Stability and Autonomy," in Wim Blockmans, Mikhail Krom, and Justyna Wubs-Mrozewicz (eds.), *The Routledge Handbook of Maritime Trade around Europe 1300–1600* (New York: Routledge, 2017), 248–272, 252.

63 Ivar Leimus and Anu Mänd, "Reval (Tallinn): A City Emerging from Maritime Trade," in Wim Blockmans, Mikhail Krom, and Justyna Wubs-Mrozewicz (eds.), *The Routledge Handbook of Maritime Trade around Europe 1300–1600* (New York: Routledge, 2017), 273–291, 273.

64 There are some ironies here. Recall from Chapter 9 that the Lombard League effectively resisted the Empire's attempt to assert authority in Northern Italy where it was technically sovereign. The emperor's absence in those wars against cities opened up space for more city autonomy in Germany.

ineffectually tried to ban autonomous city leagues.[65] In the north, bilateral agreements occurred frequently to protect trade, including an agreement between Lübeck and Hamburg in 1241. Westphalian cities forged an alliance in 1246, the same year cities in Lower Saxony began forging similar agreements. Lübeck and Visby signed a treaty in 1280, joined later by Riga to protect trade going to and from Novgorod.[66]

*****

Where did the northern city network begin and end? An inventory from the London *kontor* in 1554 offers answers. To the east, Hanse member cities were located as far as the critical trading nodes of Riga, Reval, and Dorpat. To the west, Hanse membership at this time concentrated densely along the Rhine River, reaching the Overijssel region of the Netherlands.[67] There were Hanse outposts dotting Britain's eastern coast as far north as Scotland. Lynn (now King's Lynn) and Boston were sites of dense Hanse trading activity. There were Hanse traders in Lisbon, which was then at its geopolitical pinnacle. The Low Country cities of Bruges, Amsterdam, Antwerp, and Ghent were crucial to the Hanse at various points in history. Hanse outposts existed as far east as Smolensk at the Dnieper River. To the north, Visby was no longer a member in 1554, but Bergen remained a Hanse stronghold. The Hanse reached inland to central Europe, capitalizing on overland and, especially, riverine trade. The Rhine carried traders as far south as Köln.[68]

The level of city engagement with the League varied considerably among members. However beneath this bird's eye view of the northern network were extensive political, social, economic, and military ties. Records are far from complete, but documented arrivals and departures show dense dyadic relationships between cities. Danzig saw Lübeck ships arrive two to three times per week on average.[69] Bergen was the Hanse's most entrenched and longest lasting stronghold. Extensive data in Arnved Nedkvitne's *The German Hanse and Bergen, 1100–1600* shows that its trade was particularly tied to Lübeck, though the *kontor* housed merchants from several cities.[70] From Bergen the Hanse distributed Norwegian goods across Europe.[71] Migration altered the social landscape in the northern network. Social and familial ties

65 Moraw, "Cities and Citizenry," 111.
66 For more detail on the specifics of these agreements, see Hammel-Kiesow, "Early Hanses," 56.
67 As mapped in Wubs-Mrozewicz, "Hanse in Medieval and Early Modern Europe," 28–29.
68 Ibid.
69 Dutch shipping overtook the Hanse in the 1500s. Based on the chart published in North, *Baltic*, 98.
70 Nedkvitne, *German Hanse and Bergen 1100–1600*, 50.
71 Ibid., 111.

deeply impacted intercity relations.[72] Social trust, aided by the smaller, person-to-person scale of the network's alpha cities, obviated the need for the complex bookkeeping used in Italian contracting. Cogs enabled high volume commodities shipping at lower profit margins. This in addition to high margin luxury goods. The old, early medieval shipping lanes intensified with new activity, with large markets in amber, herring, cereals, honey, furs, beer, copper, and timber.[73]

Bruges was the most important city in Northern Europe during the heyday of the Hanse. The Venice of the north, if you will. To reiterate, it was not a member city with a place in the Hanse Diet, but was the site of one of the four main *kontors*. Its geographic position along inland waterways emptying into the North Sea underscored its commercial potential. But keeping its waterways accessible required immense feats of engineering. This included an elaborate canal system within the city to facilitate the flow of goods. But first, merchandise passed through multiple satellite towns, including a Hanse trading post.[74] The system was prone to silting, a cause of its eventual decline. Characteristic of any alpha city in the history of city networks, inequality soared in Bruges in tandem with its success. Commercially driven migration into the city drove up demand for housing, pushing poor and lower class immigrants to the periphery.[75] The city center at Bruges – now a cherished UNESCO heritage site – exemplifies commercial power and its darker side. The last stop for shipments was the visionary "Waterhalle," a large commercial structure built in 1294 near the canal and central markets.[76] The fantastical element nearby was a massive crane designed to hoist heavy cargo out of the water. It was powered by so-called crane children walking endlessly on a treadmill.[77] The cloistered yet open city was, like Venice, a machine built for commerce. In the words of James M. Murray:

> In short, a merchant community drawn from all corners of Europe, permanently resident in the same city, supported by trading and financial institutions, resulted in far greater trading possibilities, just as a hundred networked computers are far more powerful than a hundred isolated ones. Yet like a computer network, Bruges as a network city derived its power in proportion to its use by individual merchants and merchant communities In other words, Bruges's European importance owed much to the sum of the networks it incorporated.[78]

[72] Ulf Christian Ewert and Stephen Selzer, "Social Networks," in Donald J. Harreld (ed.), *A Companion to the Hanseatic League* (Boston: Brill, 2015), 162–193, 167.

[73] Derived from Jahnke, "Baltic Trade," 207; and Dollinger, *German Hanse*, 431.

[74] James M. Murray, *Bruges, Cradle of Capitalism, 1280-1390* (Cambridge: Cambridge University Press, 2015), 33.

[75] Ibid., 51. [76] Ibid., 65. [77] Ibid., 72. [78] Ibid., 218.

The Hanse was the most powerful of these merchant communities, having gained special trading privileges in 1252.[79] They were also the most populous and well-integrated into the desirable cosmopolitan city life of Bruges, whose population hovered around 40,000 people, ranking it among northern Europe's largest metropolises.[80] This was a choice post. By 1360, Bruges effectively underwrote Hanse business deals among traders in the city, covering Hanse loses at its own expense – a strong indicator of how important Hanse trade must have been.[81] The Hanse purchased luxury goods found in Bruges, brought into the city from the east. It sent spices and fine fabrics back to the Hanse cities.[82] Unlike the other three *kontors*, however, Bruges did not grant the Hanse land to construct its own semi-sovereign trading center until 1450.[83] The urban experience among Hanse merchants during those years was markedly different than in London, Novgorod, or even relatively open Bergen. They lived among the other residents in the city and understood the dominant Flemish dialect. On the other hand, relations between the Hanse and the city were contentious.[84] In 1358, the Hanse made good on a threat to desert Bruges temporarily for Dordrecht, leading to the aforementioned concession two years later.[85] The Flemish navy, for its part, stood idly by as Hanse ships fell victim to piracy.[86]

Life for the Hanse merchants in the *kontors* was isolated from the host cities in a variety of ways, starting with architecturally imposed separation. In all four cases, the urban experience for the merchants was different from the host cities at large. *Kontor* complexes were designed to be self-contained in most daily functions, even separated from the town centers by wooden palisades.[87] They contained housing, warehouses, common recreation spaces, and places of assembly designed to promote in-group cohesion, but also to clearly delineate who was not in the group.[88] The Peterhof at Novgorod, the most cloistered *kontor*, had its own church and priest.[89] Apprentices in their teens lived offsite

[79] Ibid., 220.

[80] James M. Murray, "That Well-Grounded Error: Bruges as *Hansestadt*," in Justyna Wubs-Mrozewicz and Stuart Jenks (eds.), *The Hanse in Medieval and Early Modern Europe* (Boston: Brill, 2013), 181–190, 185.

[81] Murray, *Bruges, Cradle of Capitalism, 1280–1390*, 221.

[82] Mike Burkhardt, "*Kontors* and Outposts," in Donald J. Harreld (ed.), *A Companion to the Hanseatic League* (Boston: Brill, 2015), 127–161, 143.

[83] Murray, *Bruges, Cradle of Capitalism, 1280–1390*, 221.

[84] For all their contentious relations, the city of Bruges celebrates its Hanse history. The city's Hanse heritage was at the forefront of its European Cultural Capital initiatives in 2002. During that year the Hanse starred in a major popular exhibition, Hanze@Medici. Moreover, the former *kontor* cities are vital to Hanse research.

[85] Murray, *Bruges, Cradle of Capitalism, 1280–1390*, 220.

[86] Murray, "That Well-Grounded Error," 188.

[87] Burkhardt, "*Kontors* and Outposts," 132.

[88] Wubs-Mrozewicz, *Traders, Ties and Tensions*, 28.

[89] Burkhardt, "*Kontors* and Outposts," 132.

in the countryside with Russian families for language training. At the same time, the *kontor* restricted Russian visits.[90] Cold climates in Novgorod and Bergen made life harsh for the merchants, who endured a confining daily ennui with often only each other for company in buildings with limited heating.[91] In Bergen only the common room was heated in tenement buildings, in part for fire safety, and partly to bring the merchants together each evening. Residents in the *kontors* all came from the Hanse cities, which must have felt worlds away if not for shared architectural and planning styles across the northern archipelago of cities. Residents in the *kontors* were almost all men, who were forbidden to bring spouses or to start relationships with women in the town. Sex workers clustered near *kontors*, to the point where Norwegians blamed the Hanse for Bergen's supposed moral degeneration. Hanse politics cast shadows on daily life. Host cities were potentially hostile rivals whose merchants resentfully competed with the Hanse. In Novgorod, the Hanse powerhouses of Lübeck, Visby, Riga, and Tallinn negotiated such extensive trading rights that the authorities began pushing back against their control of fur exports.[92] In one dispute, the Hansards were hauled in front of the prince, "imprisoned and forged into irons."[93]

The *kontor* at Bergen was in the historic harbor of Bryggen. Founded in 1366, it is now an exceptionally well-preserved UNESCO heritage site.[94] This was the largest of the four *kontors* by population, housing at least 1,000 Hansards year-round and 2,000 annually during the high trading season in the summers.[95] In perspective, the latter figure constituted as many as one-third of the city's inhabitants.[96] Located on valuable land in the commercial heart of the medieval city, the architecture at Bryggen exemplifies Hanse separation (Figure 10.1). The fact that this was the most desirable neighborhood in Bergen probably did little to assuage local hostility. Row housing opened into a shared alley that was sheltered away from public street life. The wooden structures face inward toward common yards, symbolic of this highly secretive merchant guild. These buildings were decidedly mixed use, and therefore self-contained. Tenements housed the *stave*, special units that combined offices,

90 Erik Tiberg, *Moscow, Livonia and the Hanseatic League 1487–1550* (Stockholm: Almqvist & Wiksell International, 1995), 24.
91 Burkhardt, "*Kontors* and Outposts," 133.
92 Henrik Birnbaum, "Kiev, Novgorod, Moscow: Three Varieties of Urban Society in East Slavic Territory," in Bariša Krekić (ed.), *Urban Society of Eastern Europe in Premodern Times* (Berkeley: University of California Press, 1987), 1–62, 44; Tiberg, *Moscow, Livonia and the Hanseatic League 1487–1550*, 16.
93 Tiberg, *Moscow, Livonia and the Hanseatic League 1487–1550*, 49.
94 This despite several rebuilding efforts over the centuries because of fires in the wooden structures.
95 Nedkvitne, *German Hanse and Bergen 1100–1600*, 12.
96 Wubs-Mrozewicz, *Traders, Ties and Tensions*, 112.

Figure 10.1 The Hanseatic outpost at Bryggen, along the harbor in Bergen, Norway.
Photo by the author.

warehouses, and sleeping quarters for employees.[97] *Stave* quarters, each run by a merchant, served to subdivide the Bryggen *kontor* into administrative units. Separation between the Hanse and the city was evident in rules: Hanse members were forbidden to sell real estate at Bryggen to non-Hansards.[98] The *bergenfahrer* – German merchants trading in Bergen – were required to dine together in the evenings.[99] The *schutstave*, cooking rooms, called the companies together.[100]

This masked internal divisions. By decree, "nobody is allowed to trade at the Kontor unless he is a citizen, or has paid his fee for citizenship, and has his household in a Hanse town."[101] Bluntly put, the rules restricted who benefited from Hanse privileges on the basis of class and geography. At the same time, the notorious initiations at the Bergen *kontor* (which seem not to have occurred in other Hanse strongholds) were designed in part as an equalizer between the

97 Ersland, "Bergen 1300–1600," 438.
98 Wubs-Mrozewicz, *Traders, Ties and Tensions*, 109.
99 Justyna Wubs-Mrozewicz, "Rules of Inclusion, Rules of Exclusion: The Hanseatic *Kontor* in Bergen in the Late Middle Ages and Its Normative Boundaries," *German History* 29, no. 1, (2011), 1–22, 13.
100 Ersland, "Bergen 1300–1600," 438.
101 Nedkvitne, *German Hanse and Bergen 1100–1600*, 338.

upper and lower strata in the Hanse ranks. They were perhaps even meant to dissuade the wealthiest noble families' children from becoming overseas merchants.[102] *Spelen* ("ordeals") plied new members with alcohol and forced them under the keel of a ship, dangled them over burning garbage, and ritually beat them up.[103] In general, Hanse rules and customs were, in whatever way, shape, or apparently bizarre form, meant to keep hard-fought trading privileges from becoming diluted. They also limited competition. For example, a craftsmen leaving the Bergen *kontor* to operate independently in the city risked having their shop destroyed and fingers broken.[104] The prospect of expulsion also served to limit transgressions.

The Hanse secured special trading privileges in England by 1317.[105] London's Steelyard was the most important British Hanse site, although Boston and Lynn exported massive amounts of English cloth.[106] At peak, the German merchants achieved a larger share in this market than their English competition, and relations were predictably fraught with contention. Like Bryggen, to which it is most often compared, the London *kontor* was fenced in with rules limiting how much its merchants could integrate into city life. Its occupants tended not to stay as long.[107]

The four *kontors* comprised the outer geographic extremes of the northern city network for the Hanse, the most important limits of their world. As the *kontors* evolved, they challenged local sovereignties without so much as title or seal, or even sword in most cases. Their power was prototypically urban. Invisible and yet omnipresent.

Hanseatic Power in the State Menagerie

In 1361, Danish King Waldemar IV, in a move to reassert Denmark as a regional power, invaded Gotland and overran Visby. He continued Hanse trading rights, but Wendish cities in the League felt threatened. In 1362, the mayor of Lübeck led a naval assault against Denmark, failed, and was likely executed when returning home with what was left of the city's fleet.[108]

Waldemar followed up on his military success with diplomacy, curtailing free trade agreements across Scandinavia, compelling Norway to switch sides. In 1367, Hanse cities spearheaded the Confederation of Cologne. The Confederation did not comprise the whole of the Hanse but constituted a broader front than the previous, mainly Wendish, actions against Denmark.

102 Wubs-Mrozewicz, *Traders, Ties and Tensions*, 133. 103 Ibid., fn 40. 104 Ibid., 138.
105 Lloyd, *England and the German Hanse, 1157–1611*, 50. 106 Ibid., 76.
107 Wubs-Mrozewicz, *Traders, Ties and Tensions*, 112.
108 Sarnowsky, "'Golden Age' of the Hanseatic League," 71.

This was a key juncture in the evolution toward "the Hanse of the towns."[109] By the end of 1369 the Hanseatic fleet captured all of the Danish forts along the strategically vital Øresund, razed Copenhagen, and achieved hegemony over the Danish straits. The Peace of Stralsund, concluded the next year, abolished the recent trade restrictions against the Hanse. The agreement remarkably also granted the cities a say in Denmark's imperial succession. The year 1370 is widely cited as the pinnacle of Hanse power and a peculiar era in statecraft to modern eyes. In the words of leading Hanse historian Phillipe Dollinger:

> The Peace of Stralsund marks the emergence in Northern Europe of a new power, which here replaced the lapsed imperial authority. It was not a sovereign power, since the towns which composed it remained legally subject to many different territorial rulers. Its only basis lay in the will to defend its commercial interests, if need be by force of arms. It was a strange phenomenon, unique in the Europe of those days.[110]

Lübeck's importance was evident in other ways. It was not the most prominent destination for goods or a hive of foreign merchants. Therefore the urban experience there was markedly different from the alpha city of Bruges, an international emporium with some of virtually everything. Lübeck was the midpoint between Baltic and North Sea trade, growing rich from goods coming to and leaving from its astonishingly busy port. Even as conflict in all probability depressed business in 1368, its medieval port saw 680 ships make a total of 1,775 arrivals.[111] At least thirty-five cities harmonized their laws with Lübeck. "Lübeck Law" meant that the newly formed cities in the north were automatically integrated into the Lübeck-led trading system.[112]

In practice, the following lament by flummoxed Holland merchants trying to operate in Bergen is indicative of the futility of competing with the Hanse in Norway:

> Most of the Hanse merchants are from the Wendish towns or are their factors or servants. Everybody knows what the result will be if we bid the King to protect our rights according to our privileges. The King rarely visits the country, and the merchants from the Hanse towns there are so strong that they respect the King little.[113]

In short, approximately four millennia after their emergence as a form of statecraft, cities were ascendant throughout northern Europe. Other forms of state organization and authority receded to enable this. Like the periods of urban ascendance we have explored in this book, this was an age of

[109] Ibid., 73; Dollinger, *German Hanse*, 45. [110] Dollinger, *German Hanse*, 71.
[111] Carsten Jahnke, "Lübeck and the Hanse: A Queen without Its Body," in Wim Blockmans, Mikhail Krom, and Justyna Wubs-Mrozewicz (eds.), *The Routledge Handbook of Maritime Trade around Europe 1300–1600* (New York: Routledge, 2017), 231–247, 234.
[112] Ibid., 238. [113] Cited in Nedkvitne, *German Hanse and Bergen 1100–1600*, 470.

experimentation in many forms of statecraft. The church influenced urban politics through bishops. The Teutonic Order had no deeply ingrained ties to any one stretch of land, acquiring territory through a combination of conquest, deal making, and outright purchase. Max Weber, Henri Pirenne, Fernand Braudel, and Lewis Mumford head a list of many intellectuals who saw the medieval city as a crucial byway en route to the modern state system.[114] An important volume edited by Charles Tilly and Wim P. Blockmans, *Cities and the Rise of States in Europe*, points to the advantages cities had as islands in the land-based, feudal power structure still dominant at the start of Europe's medieval revival. "Cities shape the destinies of states chiefly by serving as containers and distribution points for capital," argued Tilly in the introduction.[115] The relationship between the city and overarching state, if there was one, was crucial to state development, according to Tilly.[116] This gave cities "access to capital, credit, and control over the hinterlands that, if seized or co-opted, can serve the ends of monarchs as well."[117] However, territorial monarchs could stifle urban production, and thus inhibit state development. Or, in the case of the northern network, economically complex urban centers could resist central power *for centuries*, leaving layers of authority incomplete, and open spaces largely ungoverned. For those living and operating organizationally under such durable if ambiguous conditions, the age of powerful cities must've felt like the endgame rather than the route to something else. In any case, for the Hanseatic League all that mattered was expedience.

Piracy remained a fact of life in the stateless, ungovernable waters and littoral spaces of medieval Europe. The term itself meant many different things, as privateers formed guilds, collaborated with states, and occasionally bargained with leaders on equal terms. The Victual Brothers (*vitalienbrüder*) were a force to be reckoned with by the late 1300s, at one point taking over Gotland. They were enemies of Lübeck, the great centrifuge of civilization. In fact the Victual Brothers emerged from a band of nobles seeking to secure their interests, but over time tapped into the class politics of the age. They gained the name *likedeeler* (which alludes to the words "in like parts"), because they reputedly distributed spoils fairly among members. Their membership increasingly drew on the peasantry and the dispossessed, which they illustrated in their standards.[118] "These activities must be evaluated as a social

114 For an overview of this dialogue, see S. R. Epstein, "Introduction: Town and Country in Europe, 1300–1800," in S. R. Epstein (ed.), *Town and Country in Europe, 1300–1800* (Cambridge: Cambridge University Press, 2001), 1–29, 5.

115 Charles Tilly, "Entanglements of European Cities and States," in Charles Tilly and Wim P. Blockmans (eds.), *Cities and the Rise of States in Europe, A.D. 1000 to 1800* (Boulder: Westview Press, 1994), 1–27, 8.

116 Ibid., 3. 117 Ibid., 8.

118 Johannes Schildhauer, *The Hansa: History and Culture* (Leipzig: Edition Leipzig, 1985), 51.

protest against the rich trading bourgeoisie by the oppressed, the outcasts of contemporary society," argues one scholar.[119]

As elsewhere in premodern times, the seas were paramount to forging ties across northern Europe. In medieval time and space, sea travel bridged distances much faster than diminished land routes. The growing trend of bulk cargoes in the 1300s made the waterways even more critical.[120] Land-based empires could seldom compete with cities in traversing the seas or controlling them. The northern seas were, in the words of specialists, "very much a weak frontier" for territorial empires.[121] They were effectively anarchic despite the existence of maritime laws. Under these conditions merchant groups bargained over the rules of seafaring in the Middle Ages.[122] Feudal power structures were poorly adapted to assert real power over these waters. Lords relied on cities and their merchants to provide naval forces when needed. Cities monopolized power over shipping technology. The most sophisticated craft construction was concentrated in metropolitan areas. Lords could not simply command urban ship owners to supply fleets with impunity. That is, not without resistance. Naval activity and troop transports required for conquests diverted plaintive entrepreneurs from profitable mercantile missions. This made royal fleets extremely hard to maintain, reinforcing monarchal reliance on merchants.[123] Hanse convoys were by contrast in service constantly for approximately 500 shipping seasons. Based on rough estimates, Lübeck alone housed around 250 registered ships.[124] True, territorial empires could boast populations in the millions, potentially staffing land armies in droves. But smaller polities were more than capable of ruling the all-important seas.

A leading scholar of shipping history argues that there were marked improvements in sailing and navigation technologies in the 1300s in the north as well as the south.[125] Capturing these technological advantages was a critical component of Hanse dominance. To reiterate from Chapter 9, magnetic compasses, rudder systems, speed measurements, and innovations in charting dramatically expanded shipping range and travel seasons. But boat designs

[119] Ibid.

[120] Wim Blockmans, Mikhail Krom, and Justyna Wubs-Mrozewicz, "Maritime Trade around Europe 1300–1600: Commercial Networks and Urban Autonomy," in Wim Blockmans, Mikhail Krom, and Justyna Wubs-Mrozewicz (eds.), *The Routledge Handbook of Maritime Trade Around Europe 1300–1600* (New York: Routledge, 2017), 1–35, 2.

[121] David Kirby and Merja-Liisa Hinkkanen, *The Baltic and the North Seas* (New York: Routledge, 2000), 117.

[122] Blockmans et al., "Maritime Trade around Europe 1300–1600," 2.

[123] Kirby and Hinkkanen, *Baltic and the North Seas*, 118.

[124] Jahnke, "Lübeck and the Hanse," 234.

[125] Richard W. Unger, "Ships and Sailing Routes in Maritime Trade around 1300–1600," in Wim Blockmans, Mikhail Krom, and Justyna Wubs-Mrozewicz (eds.), *The Routledge Handbook of Maritime Trade around Europe 1300–1600* (New York: Routledge, 2017), 17–35, 17.

in the north differed from the south, where large Italian galleys utilized oarsmen.[126] Cogs carried the bulk of Hanseatic trade in the north. They were dual use, fighting the League's battles as well carrying its goods. In service from the eleventh century, albeit with continually improved designs, cogs traversed the Baltic and North Seas en-masse by the end of the 1200s.[127] Cogs had space efficient square bottoms for cargo, the shape of which also helped the crafts pilot Northern Europe's shallow harbors.[128] Powered by wind, the lack of oarsmen opened up space below deck, also enabling relatively small crews to pilot them.[129]

Simply put, having superior shipping technology meant the practical competitive advantage of being able to freight goods more cheaply. Historians also hypothesize that the League had superior organizational advantages over the states under whose jurisdictions they functioned. They made sure their merchants were literate for the purposes of recording transactions. This was not always the case among the competition. A literacy gap between Hanse and Norwegian merchants may help explain the Hanse's unusually persistent, apparently self-reinforcing dominant relationship there.[130] Nedkvitne's thorough exploration of Hanse advantages in Bergen concluded that the Hanse could call on a permanent long-range network around Europe while the Norwegians had no equivalent.[131] It had links to a vast intercity market of stockfish buyers. The *bergenfahrer* in turn had more capital to purchase fish than local merchants.[132] For Nedkvitne, access to the network was a key variable explaining centuries-long dominance in Norway. English competitors, he notes, were every bit as professionally organized but had no equivalent to the Low German speaking mercantile network maintained by the League. In England, however, the Hanse's considerable power was weaker and less enduring.[133]

Of course the Hanse were not above base coercion, which no doubt extended the life of its power and allowed it to bully its way through collective action problems. One of the institution's functions was to smooth over competing interests within its ranks. When diplomacy failed, the Hanse expelled cities from the League as a last resort. Cologne was ousted in 1471 for five years after it declined to support multilateral actions against England.[134] In the end, Cologne accepted Hanse terms. It paid out a large sum in order to return to the fold. As we have seen, the Hanse ferociously wielded boycotts and at times military force against nonmembers. The Hanseatic Diet (the *Hansetag*) first

126 Ibid., 22. 127 Ibid., 23. 128 Kirby and Hinkkanen, *Baltic and the North Seas*, 94.
129 Unger, "Ships and Sailing Routes," 24.
130 Nedkvitne, *German Hanse and Bergen 1100–1600*, 278. 131 Ibid., 295.
132 Ibid., 294. 133 Ibid., 331.
134 Johanek, "Imperial and Free Towns of the Holy Roman Empire," 305.

met in 1358, another bellwether date, to deal with a conflict against Bruges. The assembly rarely met and had spotty attendance unless such weighty matters of power politics were involved. By then the Hanse was a self-aware great power in northern Europe. The *Hansetag* enabled negotiations over how best to throw its weight around.

Life and Death in the Hanse Cities

Europe's population plummeted after the devastating plague of the 1340s, shrinking cities along with it. Interestingly, the Hanse heyday came after that catastrophe. The medieval urban age in northern Europe fundamentally continued.[135] City sizes rebounded steadily after the plague losses. By far the fastest growing European cities in the following centuries were port cities.[136] "The large increases in the number of residents suggests that cities served as nodes of networks," asserted one scholar.[137] These transitory networks carried far more than merchandise.

Brick Gothic architecture made cities recognizable to the mobile classes in the northern network. Brick often had to be used because stone – used in Gothic variants elsewhere – was hard to come by in the Baltic and North Sea regions.[138] St. Mary's church in Lübeck, originally completed in 1350, inspired church designs in dozens of littoral cities. The brick Gothic cathedral of the same name in the Hanseatic city of Gdańsk initiated in the later 1300s is considered an apotheosis of the form. Church construction and mercantile growth were intertwined as an emergent wealthy bourgeois class financed the new buildings. Moreover, steeples were the most visible objects for ships hugging the shore in search of port destinations. They were frequently constructed in Hanseatic commercial districts, as is the case with St. Mary's in Lübeck. Lübeck was a font of design influence, exporting large alter pieces across northern Europe, most famously the ornately carved masterworks of Bernt Notke.[139] The major German portrait artist Hans Holbein gained commissions through the Hanse network, serving in Henry VIII's court and painting Hanse merchants in the London *kontor*.

Secular buildings including merchant association headquarters and town halls were built in the brick Gothic style as well. The latter rivaled churches in prominence. Frequently topped by imposing bell towers, they joined the

[135] This is not to gloss over the social changes that occurred in the wake of the plague. See, for example, Hunt and Murray, *History of Business in Medieval Europe*, 132.
[136] Unger, "Ships and Sailing Routes," 27. [137] Ibid., 28. [138] North, *Baltic*, 79.
[139] Sadly, the original Lübeck cathedral was mostly destroyed along with Notke's massive *Dance of Death* alter in World War II. A fragment of a Notke *Dance of Death* is on display in St. Nicholas church in Tallinn.

church steeples in the skyline. Lübeck's town hall was widely imitated.[140] Town halls were much more than just the seats of the town councils. The rectangular structures served a variety of purposes to accommodate the commercial revolution of medieval society at the time, incorporating warehouses and marketplaces.[141] Merchant guildhalls were also sites of concentrated power and global interaction, where mainly Low German was spoken. They played host to visiting dignitaries, wealthy businessmen, and visiting ship captains among other travelers.[142] These multi-purpose meeting places created in-groups and out-groups in the trading economy. They were where the guilds staged town festivities. Festivals were both public and private affairs. Exclusive games, banquets and music happened inside guildhalls, but parades, decorations and other forms of public posturing spilled out into the city.[143]

Fortifications comprised the third massive building-type characteristic of cities in the Hanse network. Their walls, watchtowers, and turrets are still on display in former Hanse strongholds such as Visby and Tallinn (Figure 10.2). Visby still has thirty-eight towers and a wall running more than a mile.[144] These reach up to 8 meters, with gates featuring trenches, ramparts, and drawbridges.[145] New walls were built to expand development within the towns, as was the case with Bruges. Many were constructed around cities across the network in the 1400s as territorial states sought to assert their sovereignty.[146] In a sense they symbolized city-state independence as conditions grew increasingly uncertain in the early renaissance. This as they became quickly obsolete as development sprawled on outside them. Walls regulated the flow of people, enabling many an open city to close itself off to migration when conditions warranted exclusion in the minds of the upper classes. Most city-dwellers were always on the brink of poverty.[147] The "shamefaced poor" with noble title had access to support, while masses of displaced peasants searched for what help they could find, if any. Their migration into cities ebbed and flowed with conditions in the countryside, which were dictated by urban-based landowners.[148]

Anyone entering a city would find "a cosmopolitan Hanseatic signature, which was articulated physically through a shared vocabulary of town plan," in the words of one archeologist.[149] The wide avenues flanked by narrow streets connected the waterfront and the central market, the two centers of activity.[150] Wide avenues always led to the central square, which was the hive of business

140 Schildhauer, *Hansa*, 69. 141 Dollinger, *German Hanse*, 268.
142 Anu Mänd, *Urban Carnival: Festive Culture in the Hanseatic Cities of the Eastern Baltic* (Brepols: Turnhout, 2005), 98.
143 Ibid., 256. 144 Schildhauer, *Hansa*, 70. 145 Ibid.
146 Dollinger, *German Hanse*, 269.
147 Murray, *Bruges, Cradle of Capitalism, 1280–1390*, 90. 148 Ibid., 91.
149 Gaimster, "Parallel History," 412. 150 Ibid.

Figure 10.2 Tallinn's (then known as Reval, in Estonia) medieval city center, replete with its walls dating from the 1200s and the Baltic Sea in the background. It was a stronghold for German merchants.
Photo by Erin L. Leon.

activity. Hanse towns had merchant districts surrounding the central market. Merchants owned homes facing the square.[151] The gabled burgher houses were warehouses as much as homes, with room to cart goods into the main halls.[152] These grew more ornate and luxurious over time. Everyone else – that is, the poor and middle strata – lived in far less durable huts or crammed into cellars along the unpaved side streets.[153] Specialized districts were evident in abundance, with neighborhoods inhabited by organized professions, with corresponding street names. For example *Böttcherstrasse* ("Cooper Street") referred to the coopers working in the city while *Gerberstrasse* ("Tanner Street") was where the tanners could be found.[154] Reflecting growing social stratification, dirty and degrading work was relegated to the town periphery.[155] Lest this still sound too neat and tidy, remember that the unlit streets were lined with refuse in this time period. Livestock roamed the streets, which housing

[151] Schildhauer, *Hansa*, 65. [152] Ibid., 73. [153] Ibid., 66. [154] Ibid. [155] Ibid.

encroachments made narrower.[156] Diseases, famines, and casual violence checked populations even in the most dazzling cities.[157] Three percent of the population died each year in a typical city.[158] This necessitated migration to keep cities in existence.

Inns in the Middle Ages were more multipurpose than today's hotels. They were integral to the economic system, playing host to itinerant "stranger" merchants. Hostels sprang up all over Europe as commercial activity intensified.[159] City authorities viewed them in terms of necessity and suspicion. As such they encouraged their construction but tightly regulated them, sometimes confining their guests to specialized districts. In alpha cities such as Bruges, innkeepers doubled as financial brokers and were members of brokers' guilds.[160] Because the stranger merchants brought goods with them, hostels charged warehousing fees in addition to standard lodging.[161] For all the efforts at containment, inns were sites of worldly mingling. By one account, Bruges had stranger merchants from all over Europe, the Middle East, and Central Asia.[162] Yet the clergy reviled the "evil inn" because of the vice economies clustered around them, from taverns to bathhouses which doubled as brothels.[163] Women avoided walking near them because of the risk of assault by male travelers.[164] Globalization was, after all, a patriarchy.

Renaissance illustrations of Hanse cities omit lower-class housing, replacing it with sturdy step gabled affluent homes associated with the Hanse aesthetic – creating the image of a classless society.[165] In fact, the clay *bude* housing lining the city streets away from the market were not gabled at all.[166] These small huts constituted the majority of urban housing, according to registry records. In Wismar, there were nearly 1,500 huts or inhabited basements, compared with less than 600 houses. In Rostock, more than 2,500 huts, basements, and sundry makeshift shelters outnumbered the 149 gabled houses.[167] This situation comports with tax records compiled by historians on the class structure in Hanse cities. In Tallinn, the upper classes constituted 16 percent of the population and were all German merchants. The artisanal middle class comprised another 19 percent of the city and were mostly German, with a mix of Estonian and Scandinavian craftsmen. The remaining 65 percent of the population were three-quarters Estonian, a precarious mix of

[156] Ibid. [157] Murray, *Bruges, Cradle of Capitalism, 1280–1390*, 97. [158] Ibid.
[159] Ibid., 196. [160] Ibid. [161] Ibid., 200.
[162] Donatella Calabi and Derek Keene, "Merchants' Lodgings and Cultural Exchange," in Donatella Calabi and Stephen Turk Christensen (eds.), *Cultural Exchange in Early Modern Europe, Volume II: Cities and Cultural Exchange in Europe 1400–1700* (Cambridge: Cambridge University Press, 2007), 315–348, 328.
[163] Murray, *Bruges, Cradle of Capitalism, 1280–1390*, 205. [164] Ibid.
[165] Schildhauer, *Hansa*, 66. [166] Ibid., 74. [167] Statistics derived from ibid.

poorly paid craftsmen and day laborers.[168] The ethnic record reflected the persistent colonial legacy of the German migrations and Christianization.

Crop failures could send formerly self-sufficient peasants migrating into cities, where there was modest potential for upward mobility. Cities sometimes protected serfs from the weakening feudal power structure, making it difficult for lords to reclaim them. This gave rise to the German saying *stadtluft macht frei*, "urban air makes you free." The breakup of the manorial system in much of the Baltic region enabled greater independence.[169] But the urban age meant increased control over the countryside, directed from the center. Lübeck alone had 240 villages in its sphere of influence.[170] The core cities slowly built up their *contados*, acquiring labor and raw goods to integrate into world production. Towns assembled the materials imported from the countryside in a core–periphery model.[171] Upper class merchants sought out cheaper rural labor as an end run around guild regulations.[172] Cologne, for example, left the early stages of wool and metalworking to the satellite villages of its hinterlands. The city's artisans completed the assembly of finished goods at higher value.[173] As we have seen, cities remained population sinks, to which the hinterlands provided a "demographic reservoir."[174] Moreover, the Hanse cities were especially concerned with protecting trade routes. Their *contados* were distinctive from southern German towns for this reason, comprising transportation arteries.[175] The urban age coincided with increased peasant revolts. This was even the case in the smaller Hanse hinterlands.[176]

Rural migrants made up the largest share of the poor in restive cities.[177] Though the exploited poor in the core–periphery network were cognizant of their conditions and rebelled, the bourgeoisie class posed the greatest threat to the nobility, at times mobilizing the dispossessed. The commercial revolution touched off unrest as growth exacerbated class tension.[178] The poor, noncitizens, and non-property holders were left out of city councils.[179] Between 100 and 150 German towns endured revolts in the late Middle Ages.[180] Rebels followed a similar pattern: Namely, forcing their way into town halls

168 Mänd, *Urban Carnival*, 28. 169 North, *Expansion of Europe, 1250–1500*, 182.

170 Scott, *City-State in Europe*, 140. For a map of its hinterlands, see Ulrich Müller, "Network of Towns, Networks of Periphery?" in Sunhild Kleingärtner and Gabriel Zeilinger (eds.), *Raumbildung Durch Netzwerke?* (Bonn: Habelt, 2012), 55–77, 67.

171 Tom Scott, "Town and Country in Germany, 1350–1600," in S. R. Epstein (ed.), *Town and Country in Europe, 1300–1800* (Cambridge: Cambridge University Press, 2001), 202–228, 215.

172 Ibid., 222. 173 Scott, *The City-State in Europe*, 147.

174 Scott, "Town and Country in Germany," 219. 175 Ibid., 215.

176 North, *Expansion of Europe, 1250–1500*, 184.

177 Murray, *Bruges, Cradle of Capitalism, 1280–1390*, 91.

178 Michel Mollat and Phillippe Wolff, *The Popular Revolutions of the Late Middle Ages* (London: George Allen & Unwin, 1973), 18.

179 Naegle, "Revolts and Wars, Corporations, and Leagues," 245. 180 Ibid., 243.

and confiscating the keys to the city and treasury.[181] The butcher's guilds were especially prone to revolting. Weavers rebelled in Cologne in 1369.[182] Hanse politics tended toward the reactionary, as entrenched elites kept city councils closed to newcomers. When craft guilds or new money merchants staged revolutions, the Hanse cities retaliated.[183] In Brunswick, a tax increase triggered a guild revolt that overran the government in 1374. Despite Brunswick's pleas to maintain business as usual with the rest of the League, the Hanse expelled the city.[184] Even mighty Lübeck was pushed out of the League temporarily after a cross-class revolution in 1408 that put parvenu craftsmen and merchants in power. Once the dust settled, the *Hansetag* declared that agitators in cities would face death. They declared further that any city altering its councils would be met with immediate loss of membership.[185]

Conclusion: Last of the Hanse

The last *kontor* administrator left Bergen in 1761. The last Hanse merchant on the planet became a citizen of Bergen in 1766. The Hanse was defunct. You wonder if this person thought of the historic context of no longer calling himself a Hansard, of being singularly the final person standing in a medieval institution that was a force in the Baltic for centuries. The Hanseatic League died the way it was born: Ambiguously. The merchant simply joined the rest of society.

The last *Hansetag* met a century before in 1669. By then it was reduced to a bit player in European politics transformed by the Thirty Years War, a continent painfully in the process of building nations. Eliminating the conditions that allowed virtual city-states to form a powerful network in the first place, the Reformation divided cities that were already prone to discord. The *kontors* in Bruges and Novgorod shuttered in 1494. The London Steelyard ran its course in 1598.

I gloss over all of this on purpose. What's most notable about the Hanseatic League is how *long* it lasted. Its longevity as the preeminent economic force in the north upends realist notions of power. With small populations and no land armies, the Hanse and its power center at Lübeck shrewdly maintained independence and facilitated other cities in doing the same. Small, concentrated populations proved superior to large territorial empires when it came to control of the all-important seas. The Hanse was not in its own category. Venice, as we have seen, had astonishing durability as a sea power. Another small polity

181 Ibid. 182 Ibid., 244. 183 Ibid., 242.

184 Mollat and Wolff, *Popular Revolutions*, 208.

185 Rhiman A. Rotz, "The Lübeck Uprising of 1408 and the Decline of the Hanseatic League," *Proceedings of the American Philosophical Society* 121, no. 1 (1977), 1–45, 15.

contributed greatly to the Hanse decline – the Dutch. Gradually, but surely, the Dutch assumed hegemony in Baltic trade. Even as it was dominated by a territorial empire in the 1500s. In 1581, the fragmented Low Countries forged an empire in their own right, changing economic, social, and class relations in the process.

11 Urban Power in the Dutch Empire

They called it the door of no return. Today it frames the vast Atlantic Ocean. In the 1600s the prisoners forcibly herded through the slaveholding castle's claustrophobic confines would have focused on the merchant ship awaiting them offshore. The agitated, sickly soldiers leading them through these dark, reeking passageways, echoing with sobs and screams, were not the main beneficiaries of the slave economy. Drawn from throughout Europe, these soldiers and sailors had the ill paying jobs no one wanted. A little more than one-third of the impoverished, indebted, and frequently defrauded laborers who left the Netherlands on the merchant fleet ever returned.[1] Like the slaves they brutalized, they dreamed of desertion and often fled their commanders. In this new economy, the top rung exploiters seldom met the exploited. The wooden vessels in view of the captives ducking through that infamous door could very well have been joint ventures of investors in Amsterdam.[2] Though the investment structure often changed, these ships could be owned by far off shareholders in Europe's increasingly complex financial system.[3]

The steamy coastal town of Elmina, in present-day Ghana, was a crucible of proto-capitalism. For centuries the Amsterdam-based Dutch West India Company (WIC), arguably one of the world's first global corporations, maintained strongholds like Elmina Castle along this crucial stretch of West African coastline.[4] That is, it was crucial to the forcible abduction of thousands of West Africans to the Americas, and to the wholesale extraction of gold by Europe's

[1] David Onnekink and Gijs Rommelse, *The Dutch in the Early Modern World: A History of a Global Power* (Cambridge: Cambridge University Press, 2019), 130.

[2] Jaap R. Bruijin, "Productivity, Profitability, and Costs of Private and Corporate Dutch Ship Owning in the Seventeenth and Eighteenth Centuries," in James D. Tracy (ed.), *The Rise of Merchant Empires: Long Distance Trade in the Early Modern World, 1350–1750* (Cambridge: Cambridge University Press, 1990), 174–194, 184; and Willie F. Page, *The Dutch Triangle: The Netherlands and the Atlantic Slave Trade, 1621–1664* (New York: Garland, 1997), 20.

[3] Page, *Dutch Triangle*, 119.

[4] Henk den Heijer, "A Public and Private Dutch West India Interest," in Gert Oostindie and Jessica V. Roitman (eds.), *Dutch Atlantic Connections, 1680–1800: Linking Empires, Bridging Borders* (Leiden: Brill, 2014), 159–182, 170.

burgeoning empires that helped shift the geography of wealth northward. Early urban-based capitalism was rooted in power, not entrepreneurship. The WIC was in effect a military outfit, comprising the western half of the Dutch military–industrial complex that was intended to outmuscle Spanish, Portuguese, British, French, and Swedish market share in the Atlantic. Naval warfare was constant at the height of Dutch power in the mid-seventeenth century, with West Africa's Gold Coast among its most lasting possessions. Eventually the struggling WIC settled on slavery as its primary business as long as transatlantic human trafficking persisted.[5] The slave plantations in the Americas controlled mostly by other empires had yawning labor demands, providing the market. The WIC was a state-backed mercantilist enterprise. Its corporate structure reflected a remarkably decentralized Dutch polity dominated by cities, especially Amsterdam. The city housed its headquarters – the elegant West India House situated between the city's waterways – and held its largest stake. Win, lose, or draw, the fortunes of far off overseas ventures directly impacted Amsterdam's culture, planning, architecture, and economic development.

The East India House from this era is also located in the heart of the city. The Dutch East India Company (*Verenigde Oostindische Compagnie*, or VOC) was WIC's more stably solvent counterpart operating from Southern Africa to points east. It had strongholds in present-day Indonesia, India, and South Africa, establishing trade relations as far afield as Japan. The WIC at times controlled territory in the Caribbean, South America, and North America's eastern seaboard. For a time, the Dutch wrested a large share of Brazil from the Portuguese. Together these companies founded what would later become the megacities of New York, Cape Town, and Jakarta. Smaller settlements in Curaçao, Suriname, Luanda, and Elmina were nodes in the slave trade, also transporting lucrative raw materials such as sugar for processing in Amsterdam refineries. This made Amsterdam central in the advent of the first truly planetary core–periphery network, a cardinal moment in the forging of the world political economy as we know it.[6]

The urban experience in Amsterdam changed dramatically at this time, as the city grew both in terms of sheer population size and architectural scale. The architect Jacob van Campen's (1596–1657) town hall reflected the governing ideology of globalism. Construction on the building started in 1648 and was

5 Pieter C. Emmer, "The Rise and Decline of the Dutch Atlantic," in Gert Oostindie and Jessica V. Roitman (eds.), *Dutch Atlantic Connections, 1680–1800: Linking Empires, Bridging Borders* (Leiden: Brill, 2014), 339–356, 342.

6 Karel Davids and Jan Lucassen, "Introduction," in Karel Davids and Jan Lucassen (eds.), *A Miracle Mirrored: The Dutch Republic in European Perspective* (Cambridge: Cambridge University Press, 1995), 1–25, 13; and Jan de Vries, *European Urbanization 1500–1800* (Cambridge, MA: Harvard University Press, 1984), 166.

not completed until 1665, a time when Dutch trading hegemony reached its apogee. This architectural masterpiece "propagated the idea of Amsterdam as the absolute center of world trade."[7] To start with, it was dramatically larger than older town halls, which had been relatively austere displays in the previous centuries in the Low Countries. This reflects the power of Holland within the Dutch Republic, and the power of Amsterdam within Holland. The clear message was that managing relations across hitherto unimaginable distances required expanded administrative authority. The Hague was the ostensible capital, but the de facto power was concentrated in Amsterdam, probably the world's wealthiest city. A marble Maid of Amsterdam faced Dam Square flanked by mythical sea creatures, symbolizing the oceans paying homage to the city. Stereotyped representatives of Europe, Asia, North America, and Africa approach her bearing bounty. This, in the words of two historians, displays "the self evident moral virtuousness of this seaborne empire" to visiting dignitaries and passersby who may never see these imperial domains and nodal networks.[8] The metropolis grew increasingly unequal after a period of strong wage growth in the earlier part of the seventeenth century. A merchant bourgeois class dominated urban planning initiatives in ways that cemented class hierarchies, most significantly the famed canal system. A few false steps and any middle class male laborer could find himself on the dreaded merchant fleet, itself a product of administrative efficiency that gave Dutch carriers astonishing cost advantages.

The likes of Charles Tilly, Wim Blockmans, and above all Immanuel Wallerstein assign a high degree of importance to the so-called Dutch Golden Age of the seventeenth century, the focus of this chapter.[9] Indeed, this period is historically important for a variety of reasons. First, it is a milestone in the advent of state capitalism, ushering in the age of mercantilism. Wallerstein's classic *The Modern World System II* places considerable emphasis on Dutch hegemony, brief as it was, as marking the beginnings of a globally scaled economy. It was, he argues, a rare moment of hegemony in world history, owing to Dutch preponderance in maritime trade as Britain, France, and Germany endured decades of divisive warfare, and as Spain and Portugal declined.[10] This period also marks advancements, not yet wholly apparent, toward the North–South geopolitical power imbalance impacting today's international relations.

[7] Onnekink and Rommelse, *Dutch in the Early Modern World*, 119. [8] Ibid., 120.

[9] The term "golden age" has gained controversy of late, owing to revised understandings of the significance of slavery and colonial repression during this period.

[10] Immanuel Wallerstein, *The Modern World System II: Mercantilism and the Consolidation of the European World Economy* (Berkeley: University of California Press, 2011), xxiii.

Dutch hegemony was also the beginning of the end of an era marked by seaborne power, dominated by port cities, punching well above their weight in geopolitics. The Netherlands dominated trade in an era of emerging giants, with just a fraction of the populations of its closest rivals, Britain and France. The following section makes the case that the source of Dutch power was not due to its position as an emerging modern nation state, like its rivals, but as a network of autonomous cities. The city-state culture is embedded in the structure of the highly decentralized republican state, and in the WIC and VOC. It is embedded, as well, in the composition of the Dutch navy. The emergence of the Dutch Republic as a world power was prefigured by a storied struggle against environmental scarcity, pushing against seawaters to reclaim lands. Canals linked Dutch cities, enabling internal trade, as well as trade with continental Europe. The city network in the Low Countries underwent drastic upheavals but proved effective against the much larger territorial empire of Hapsburg Spain. The core of the European economy shifted northward by the sixteenth century, led by Holland and Britain.[11] This left Amsterdam and neighboring cities in the unlikely position of forging a new state that was Europe's most urbanized, projecting power even further afield.

City Network Formation in the Low Countries

The Low Countries correspond roughly to the present-day Netherlands in the north and Belgium in the south. They were subject to dramatic shifts in authority from the Middle Ages onward. Cities were powerful, particularly in the south, with Ghent, Ypres, and Bruges dominating their hinterlands.[12] This was followed by the emergence of Antwerp as the undisputed alpha city in the region well into the sixteenth century.[13] The cities bridled against inherited Burgundian and later Hapsburg Spanish rule spanning the late 1300s until the Dutch revolts in 1568.[14] The state menagerie was alive and well, a hodgepodge of bishopric, municipal, and ducal authority. The vicissitudes of the revolts, not fully resolved until 1648, entailed the sharp decline of Antwerp as economic power headed north – along with a large migration of

[11] Ibid., 37.

[12] W. P. Blockmans, "The Formation of a Political Union, 1300–1588," in J. C. H. Blom and E. Lamberts (eds.), *History of the Low Countries* (New York: Berghan Books, 2015), 54–140, 70; Oscar Gelderblom, *Cities of Commerce: The Institutional Foundations of the Low Countries, 1250–1650* (Princeton: Princeton University Press, 2013), 15.

[13] Blockmans, "Formation of a Political Union," 121.

[14] See Marc Boone and Maarten Prak, "Rulers, Patricians and Burghers: The Great and Little Traditions of Urban Revolt in the Low Countries," in Karel Davids and Jan Lucassen (eds.), *A Miracle Mirrored: The Dutch Republic in European Perspective* (Cambridge: Cambridge University Press, 1995), 99–134.

refugee urbanites with business knowhow. This war left Amsterdam as the undisputed commercial power in the region.

Early on, Holland was isolated from the rest of Europe, occupying what Jonathan Israel called "a waterlogged, marshy land, dangerous, thinly populated, and marginal to the life of the Low Countries as a whole."[15] A harsh environment relegated the Low Countries to the periphery for most of their long history. As we have seen in Chapter 10, Frisian traders took advantage of their coastal access, but they were itinerant and did not construct large cities. Most economic activity took place inland on higher, drier ground.[16] The Low Countries seemed an unlikely site for the precocious urban network that emerged there. Much of Holland is below sea level, subject to flooding.[17] Land reclamation dates from ancient times, though the large-scale polder projects that created fertile land in Flanders began only in the Middle Ages.[18] This was by no means a linear process. Arable land was frequently lost. Water channels required vigilant management. The extraction of peat as a fuel source caused land to sink.[19] Local authorities managed the water system tightly, exercising considerable autonomous power, gaining expertise later exported throughout Europe. In sum, massive amounts of land were reclaimed after 1200, enough to transform the region and give the coastal areas access to the rest of the continent.[20]

By the early sixteenth century, more than half of Holland's population lived in cities.[21] There was a fairly even rank-size distribution, as Amsterdam was still smaller than Leiden and Gouda, and just larger than Haarlem, Dordrecht, and Delft.[22] The Netherlands was the most urbanized region in Europe, well surpassing Italy. In 1650, the Netherlands was 31.7 percent urbanized according to de Vries' extensive data. England was 8.8 percent urbanized. For Scandinavia, this figure was 2.4 percent. For France, 7.2 percent. For Germany, 4.4 percent. Spain, from which the Dutch had wrested independence, was 9.5 percent urbanized.[23]

Dutch cities gradually became rivals to the dominant centers in the south.[24] Urban elites steadily acquired rural land, forming their own *contados* and

[15] Jonathan Israel, *The Dutch Republic: Its Rise, Greatness, and Fall 1477–1806* (Oxford: Oxford University Press, 1995), 9.
[16] Ibid., 9.
[17] Paul Arblaster, *A History of the Low Countries* (London: Red Globe Press, 2019), 4.
[18] Ibid., 5. [19] Blockmans, "Formation of a Political Union," 74.
[20] Israel, *Dutch Republic*, 11.
[21] Marjolein 't Hart, "Intercity Rivalries and the Making of the Dutch State," in Charles Tilly and Wim P. Blockmans (eds.), *Cities and the Rise of States in Europe, A.D. 1000 to 1800* (Boulder: Westview Press, 1994), 196–217, 197.
[22] Ibid., 198.
[23] Urbanization figures cited in de Vries, *European Urbanization 1500–1800*, 39.
[24] Israel, *Dutch Republic*, 113.

assuming control over reclamations. Canalization occurred in tandem with the construction of ports, enabling trade for vital goods for a region that was far from self-sufficient. Moreover, the canals furthered the cause of city-state autonomy, enabling cities to construct competing waterways and issue tolls.[25] Major periods of construction occurred as central authorities weakened. The canal system enabled the mobility of crop staples, extending control over agricultural hinterlands. By the high period of Dutch trade hegemony, the independent republic had an internal network linked by canals wide enough to allow freight vessels.[26] The canal network was famous across Europe for enabling fast intercity public transportation, impacting the distribution of knowledge as well as physical goods. The route between Haarlem and Leiden carried 136,000 passengers annually by the 1660s, with the system as a whole capable of notching nearly 400,000 passenger kilometers daily.[27] With enhanced connectivity, cities played increasingly specialized roles in a dense system of exchange. Leiden was a center of education. The Hague housed government bureaucracy. Delft produced dairy and beer. Utrecht became a religious center. Middleburg linked the region to French goods. Dordrecht and Amsterdam were the most important long distance trading ports in the Netherlands, while Antwerp remained the leading *entrepôt* in the Low Countries.[28] The Low Countries had prototyped the modern megalopolis, an interdependent city network with multiple cores. However, not completely. Locks and gates regulated human flows as the cities' merchant elites saw fit. Expulsions were common. The highly unstable political context of Europe in the first half of the seventeenth century complicated matters even further. The Low Countries were the richest parts of the war weary, cash strapped Habsburg Spanish Empire. The cities were sites of rebellious Protestantism living under fervently Catholic rule. Rebellion gathered momentum toward full-blown separation.

Put simply, the "towns provided a fertile breeding ground for the Reformation, while values of urban autonomy and independence made the

[25] Claire Billen and Chloé Deligne, "Urban Space: Infrastructure, Technology and Power," in Bruno Blondé, Marc Boone, and Anne-Laure Van Bruaene (eds.), *City and Society in the Low Countries, 1100–1600* (Cambridge: Cambridge University Press, 2018), 162–191, 166.

[26] This is diagramed in Marjolein 't Hart, "The Dutch Republic: The Urban Impact upon Politics," in Karel Davids and Jan Lucassen (eds.), *A Miracle Mirrored: The Dutch Republic in European Perspective* (Cambridge: Cambridge University Press, 1995), 57–98, 64.

[27] Maarten Prak, "The Dutch Republic's City-State Culture," in Mogens Herman Hansen (ed.), *A Comparative Study of Thirty City-State Cultures* (Copenhagen: The Royal Danish Academy of Arts and Letters, 2000), 343–358, 350.

[28] This overview of specialized roles as outlined in ibid., 349; Peter C. M. Hoppenbrouwers, "Town and Country in Holland, 1300–1550," in S. R. Epstein (ed.), *Town and Country in Europe, 1300–1800* (Cambridge: Cambridge University Press, 2001), 54-79, 62; and 't Hart, "Intercity Rivalries," 198.

population allergic to autocratic rule."[29] Historians have deemed the Dutch Republic in its formative years as both "a country of cities" and "a state of fifty-eight cities."[30] The heavily fortified cities in the Netherlands that eventually comprised the Dutch Republic proved costly for the Spanish to besiege. In Charles Tilly's interpretation of events, "a contingent federation of city-states" proved too much to handle for Christian Europe's most powerful territorial empire.[31] For Tilly, alpha trading cities were difficult if not impossible for land-based empires to control. The imperatives of constant warfare pressed them to further refine systems of banking and finance, a considerable advantage during protracted conflicts. These were centers of advanced capital accumulation in a Europe that remained agrarian on balance. Amsterdam was by far the leading financial power in the nascent republic. "Without its financial strength it's hard to see how the Dutch could have become a world power in the seventeenth century," argued Tom Scott.[32] This crucial source of power enabled Dutch cities to retain autonomy in an age of centralizing states, so long as they maintained dominance in market hierarchies (Spain routinely flirted with insolvency).[33] It enabled them to finance a first tier navy, the world's most powerful merchant fleet, and a mercenary army that partially offset the Dutch disadvantage in population size. Tilly elaborates:

> As a consequence, major trading cities and city-states mounted more effective resistance to the penetration of consolidated states than did cities in mainly agrarian regions. Most often, consolidated states only gained genuine control over major trading cities when the cities had begun to lose their predominate positions in international markets.[34]

The city retained advantages even in this time period when the city-state as an independent entity was at an ebb. Its ability to accumulate capital was crucial to state development. In the extraordinary case of the Dutch Republic, a city network was competitive with its centralizing rivals for approximately a century, due to its exceptional ability to manage resources.[35]

The Dutch Republic had a loosely knit government that demonstrated the strengths and weaknesses of a highly decentralized state. Spain was ultimately able to hang on to the southern part of the Low Countries. That left seven formally sovereign provinces that struggled to maintain coherent policies

[29] Henk van Nierop, "Similar Problems, Different Outcomes: The Revolt of the Netherlands and the Wars of Religion in France," in Karel Davids and Jan Lucassen (eds.), *A Miracle Mirrored: The Dutch Republic in European Perspective* (Cambridge: Cambridge University Press, 1995), 26–56, 36.

[30] For example, respectively, ibid., 35; and 't Hart, "Intercity Rivalries," 199.

[31] Tilly, "Entanglements of European Cities and States," 21.

[32] Scott, *City-State in Europe*, 205.

[33] Tilly, "Entanglements of European Cities and States," 22.

[34] Ibid., 22.

[35] Gelderblom, *Cities of Commerce*, 10.

frequently finding themselves at odds with one another on the major questions of the day.[36] They were not bound by any special coherence beyond the fact that they were the territories that resisted Spanish rule by the war's end. Dutch national identity had yet to meaningfully form.[37] Life centered on the city and hinterland as the primary forms of social organization, with cities regulating human flows. Cities conferred or denied citizenship status. A person belonged to a metropolitan region rather than a country or even a province.[38] Holland was the center of power owing to its overwhelming share of the national tax base. It contributed 60 percent of the fledgling country's budget, with Amsterdam comprising the bulk of that figure. Maarten Prak's contribution to the edited volume *A Comparative Study of Thirty City-State Cultures* identifies the Dutch Republic as in effect "a confederation of city-state type of polities."[39] The urban hierarchy in the Low Countries shifted. Refugees from Antwerp after its recapture in 1585 reinforced power shifts northward. Amsterdam benefitted from Antwerp's commercial network. A Dutch naval blockade against Antwerp sealed the fate of the city's decline. A total of 100,000 people left Flanders and Brabant during these years, largely to the Netherlands. One-third of Amsterdam's population was of Flemish origin by the turn of the seventeenth century. The stream of refugees included Antwerp merchants specializing in high-value trades. Amsterdam's population tripled during these years, reaching 105,000 by 1622.[40]

The governmental structure of the Republic was designed in the crucible of the Eighty Year's War against Spain, with the Union of Utrecht binding the provinces in 1579. It reflected the dispersal of urban authorities and the power of the narrow bourgeois elite in the burgher classes who permanently retained power regardless of the changes in form. Though hardly progressive, the Dutch Republic doubtless offended the absolutist sensibilities of Europe's monarchal, increasingly consolidated states. William Temple (1628–1699), British Ambassador to The Hague and an important chronicler of the Dutch Republic, described the system as reducible to "many little states or cities, which have several marks of sovereign power within themselves, and are not

[36] These were Friesland, Groningen, Guelders, Holland, Overijssel, Utrecht, and Zeeland, in addition to territories governed directly by the States General.

[37] Marjolein C. 't Hart, *The Making of the Bourgeois State: War, Politics and Finance during the Dutch Revolt* (Manchester: Manchester University Press, 1993), 5.

[38] See Maarten Prak, "Burghers into Citizens: Urban and National Citizenship in the Netherlands during the Revolutionary Era," *Theory and Society* 26, no. 4 (1997), 403–420.

[39] Prak, "Dutch Republic's City-State Culture," 343.

[40] Figures cited in James C. Kennedy, *A Concise History of the Netherlands* (Cambridge: Cambridge University Press, 2017), 144.

subject to the sovereignty of their province."[41] Contemporary scholarship estimates that about fifty cities had influence at The Hague.[42] As Temple explained to audiences back home, town halls were critical centers of power. For its part, the States General focused primarily on foreign affairs, and the management of the empire. Each of the provinces sent delegations there, and each had one vote. Stadtholders served as heads of state – this was the office held by William "the Silent" of Orange (1533–1584) who became the leader of the revolt – but this was a controversial office, at times abolished. Provinces had their own Stadtholders who shared local power with the Stadtholder at The Hague. Towns and cities tended to dominate the provincial assemblies, extending power over the countryside. Amsterdam's power was limited on paper, but the city held inordinate sway both in Holland and the Republic as the center of economic strength.

More to the point, Amsterdam was the center of *military* strength, the main function of the Republic which absorbed 90 percent of its funds.[43] The city's advanced markets were the conduits for borrowing in the wartime "fiscal military state," shouldering most of the national debt.[44] The influence of Amsterdam and other cities in the Dutch city network went well beyond finance, as cities constructed the ships that plied the globe. The Dutch Navy was city-managed. It was peculiarly divided into five admiralties, based in Amsterdam, Rotterdam, Hoorn, Middleburg, and Harlingen.[45] Haarlem constructed upward of 250 ships each year. Holland managed more shipping than the entire Hanseatic League by 1500.[46] Though the navy was a match for much larger powers, it was the merchant fleet that enabled Amsterdam to dominate European trade. Holland surpassed the Hanse to become the preeminent low cost shipping carrier of Europe. The *fluyt*, developed in full by the late 1500s, could take on maximal loads with minimal crews. Dutch shipping yards produced them rapidly and cheaply, and shipbuilding was absolutely critical to the urban economies. Holland had a merchant fleet of 1,800 vessels, 500 of which were based in Amsterdam. No other country or city approached these figures.[47] At peak, the Dutch owned half of the world's stock of seagoing vessels.[48] The understaffed *fluyts* were easy enemy targets, but no matter. Cities easily replaced them. Seaborne herring and whaling fleets were also

[41] William Temple, "Observations upon the United Provinces of the Netherlands," University of Michigan, available at https://quod.lib.umich.edu/e/eebo/A64324.0001.001/1:6?rgn=div1;view=fulltext (last accessed October 6, 2019).

[42] Kennedy, *Concise History of the Netherlands*, 150.

[43] 't Hart, *Making of the Bourgeois State*, 218.

[44] Onnekink and Rommelse, *Dutch in the Early Modern World*, 67.

[45] 't Hart, *Making of the Bourgeois State*, 39.

[46] Kennedy, *Concise History of the Netherlands*, 107.

[47] Israel, *Dutch Republic*, 117.

[48] Jonathan I. Israel, *Dutch Primacy in World Trade* (Oxford: Oxford University Press, 1989), 12.

crucial to the Dutch economy. Shipbuilding was one of the largest sources of employment in the Netherlands, employing an estimated 10,000 workers.[49]

At this stage it is important to note that the urban military–industrial complex was entirely intertwined with trading activities. Trade was the *raison d'être* for the Dutch military state, which was in constant warfare over its sacred shipping lanes. Far from a state of "complex interdependence" in which mutual reliance between states reduces warfare, in this case globalization in the 1600s created the conditions for conflict.[50] Dutch trading hegemony formed the background to the jurist Hugo Grotius' arguments for *Mare Liberum*, or open seas. They make the case for Dutch intervention in markets deemed off-limits by other empires.

By the seventeenth century, about 1,000 Dutch ships passed the Danish Sound, four-fifths of them from Amsterdam, which dominated Baltic Sea trade.[51] This tripled the number of Northern German ships in the region by this time, and was well ahead of England.[52] The Dutch assumed hegemony over the Baltic city trading network well before independence. Amsterdam was the center of bulk trades, especially grain and timber.[53] In 1583, Dutch captains carried about three-quarters of trade going in and out of Danzig, once a Hanse stronghold.[54] Even the mighty Spanish Empire could not sustain its embargo against the rebellious provinces, owing to their dependence on Dutch carriers in the Baltics. Amsterdam had extensive trade with Danzig, Riga, and Reval, and overtook the English as leading traders in Russia.[55]

This trading network was so integral that the Dutch called it "the mother trade," and for good reason. Trade from the Baltics had transformative impacts on both urban and rural life in the Netherlands. The Dutch depended on this market for more than mere profit. In fact, these tended to be high volume, low margin trades. The economic efficiency of the merchant fleet made this bulk

[49] Jan de Vries and Ad van der Woude, *The First Modern Economy: Success, Failure, and Perseverance of the Dutch Economy, 1500–1815* (Cambridge: Cambridge University Press, 1997), 297.

[50] See Robert O. Keohane and Joseph S. Nye, *Power and Interdependence* (New York: Longman, 2011).

[51] Israel, *Dutch Republic*, 117.

[52] See the data collected in Michael North and Frits Snapper, "The Baltic Trade and the Decline of the Dutch Economy in the 18th Century," in Michael North (ed.), *From the North Sea to the Baltic: Essays in Commercial, Monetary and Agrarian History* (Brookfield: Ashgate, 1996), 263–286.

[53] Aksel E. Christensen, *Dutch Trade to the Baltic about 1600* (Copenhagen: Munksgaard, 1941), 39.

[54] Maria Bogucka, "Dutch Merchants' Activities in Gdansk in the First Half of the 17th Century," in Maria Bogucka (ed.), *Baltic Commerce and Urban Society, 1500–1700* (Brookfield: Ashgate, 2003), 19–32; Kennedy, *Concise History of the Netherlands*, 143.

[55] See Maria Bogucka, "Amsterdam and the Baltic in the First Half of the Seventeenth Century," in Maria Bogucka (ed.), *Baltic Commerce and Urban Society, 1500–1700* (Brookfield: Ashgate, 2003), 433–447.

carrying viable. The leading Dutch cities and their *contados* could import grain in vast quantities, overcoming their own environmental deficiencies. Holland's population rose considerably as grain supplies poured in. Amsterdam became Europe's grain depot, as middleman, not producer. This created an international market for grain, corresponding to its price at major ports.[56] Urban land masters who controlled large shares of their hinterlands could commit the reclaimed land to dairy production, for which it was better suited. The hinterlands were consolidated into ever larger farms for commercial rather than subsistence production.[57] In the words of one historian, "farmers increasingly needed to buy in services that they formerly provided for themselves."[58] The displaced peasantry underwent proletarianization, producing for export, migrating to cities, and staffing the bitterly harsh ranks of the fleets.[59]

The Dutch city network nevertheless saw wages rise in the early years of its trade hegemony as the new economy had a yawning demand for labor to staff its prototypical industries. Dutch cities had Europe's highest living standards, which encouraged more than enough migratory inflows to overcome their persistent high death rates. However, in what David Harvey and other critical scholars might call a "spatial fix," peasant exploitation continued on via dense trade networks in the Baltics. It did not go away, it simply moved. "The urban growth and rural specialization of the northern Netherlands depended upon an ability to command the surplus of literally hundreds of thousands of serfs and millions of hectares of land" in Poland, noted de Vries.[60] More than half of Holland and other provinces lived on Baltic grain entering through Amsterdam's port.[61] This freed up labor for other things, namely shipping[62]

The city network was poised to go global.

Dutch Global Network

Walking the pained corridors of Elmina Castle, and exploring its bleak courtyard, I observed the differing architectural styles grafted on to the building across its 500 year history (see Figure 11.1). First built by the Portuguese, the Dutch successfully overran the fort in 1637, occupying most of the Gold Coast

[56] de Vries and van der Woude, *First Modern Economy*, 199.

[57] Danielle van den Heuvel, "A Market Economy," in Helmer J. Helmers and Geert H. Janssen (eds.), *The Cambridge Companion to the Dutch Golden Age* (Cambridge: Cambridge University Press, 2018), 149–165, 151.

[58] J. L. Price, "Water and Land," in Helmer J. Helmers and Geert H. Janssen (eds.), *The Cambridge Companion to the Dutch Golden Age* (Cambridge: Cambridge University Press, 2018), 32–48, 40.

[59] van den Heuvel, "Market Economy," 154.

[60] Jan de Vries, *The Dutch Rural Economy in the Golden Age, 1500–1700* (New Haven: Yale University Press, 1974), 170.

[61] Ibid., 172. [62] Ibid., 173.

Figure 11.1 Elmina Castle, in present-day Ghana, the site of many of the horrors of the West African slave trade that helped capitalize Amsterdam's expansion during its "golden age." This was the site of the "door of no return" for abducted slaves headed to the Americas to satiate European labor demands.
Photo by the author.

by 1642. This made the West India Company a key player in the transatlantic slave trade, forcing abducted laborers into its fields in the Americas and Caribbean. Half of the European West India Company workforce in Africa was stationed here, the most important of a dozen fortified towns controlled by the company.[63] The fort feels like the holocaust memorials in Europe, reminders of historic eras of severe, mechanical anti-humanism and the extreme suspension of empathy. By the time the captives arrived here, they would have been branded by hot irons to denote ownership. There would have been humiliating fitness inspections.[64]

The fort is now a UNESCO heritage site. Its oppressively hot dungeons are stacked with flowers in remembrance of the people once fastened there in chains by the thousands at a time. WIC soldiers fed them the minimum to keep them in profitable fitness. They were forced to sit in their own feces and urine

[63] Johannes Menne Postma, *The Dutch in the Atlantic Slave Trade 1600–1815* (Cambridge: Cambridge University Press, 2008), 63.
[64] Ibid., 236.

as they were restrained in the darkness for weeks and sometimes months on end before being marched aboard the *fluyt* awaiting them. Women were frequently pulled from their gender-separated dungeon and raped by the WIC officials occupying the staterooms and quarters above (this was also the colonial administrative center). If they became pregnant, their transfer to the Americas was delayed until childbirth. They resided in maternal quarters outside the fort until their enslavement resumed, or until they were detained as mistresses for the officers. Dutch governors lived in the top floor apartment, duly insulated from the sounds below. Outside in the courtyard there is a church reflecting austere protestant aesthetics. Near that is a room with a skull and crossbones grafted above the door. This is the chamber where soldiers trapped insubordinate slaves in perfect darkness without a hint of outside light. The punished slaves never walked out, dying either from starvation, disease, or heat, when their bodies were carried out as examples to others.

This was one of the longest surviving colonies in the Dutch Atlantic, lasting until the British finally took control of the Gold Coast in the late nineteenth century. Incredibly, governors worked just steps away from the atrocities below. Since there was no organized resistance to chattel slavery in the Dutch Republic, there was no need for deniability. Elmina Castle and its nearby cousin, Cape Coast Castle, are nonetheless studies in compartmentalization. From the staterooms, the apartments, or even the cloistered, closed-off courtyard, one need not be forced to cope or justify the teeming human misery behind closed doors and below ground. This was a prototypical design in the annals of European overseas empires. It prefigures modern concentration camp and industrial slaughterhouse archetypes, separating the functions of forced labor and mass killing in the modern era. It was emblematic of the organizational architecture of the Dutch global network. This was an advanced system of nodal specialization. This system was the cheaper alternative to the territorial management of other empires with larger populations, including the vast Spanish Main, the preponderant empire at the time of Dutch emergence.

Segmented functions make the imperial nodes in the network seem worlds apart. The elegant Mauritshuis at The Hague in the Netherlands is now a museum housing Dutch paintings by the likes of Rembrandt, Steen, and Hals among other master oil painters. Vermeer's "Girl with a Pearl Earring" can be viewed there in elegant quietude. The Jacob van Campen and Pieter Post (1608–1669) designed project was built for Johan Maurits, Prince of Nassau. As governor of Brazil, Maurits launched the attacks on West Africa that finally took Elmina from Portugal in 1637. The principle aim of this war against Portugal was to connect West Africa's slave market with Brazil, leaving the WIC a lucrative share in the overall transatlantic slave trade. As Mauritshuis was under construction, Maurits "engaged in unparalleled building between

1636 and 1644" in the colony.[65] Bosman notes the close similarities between the Mauritshuis floor plan (for which construction was underway when Maurits departed for Brazil) and the Pieter Post-influenced plans for Recife (dubbed "Mauritiopolis") and its palace.[66] This aggressive attempt to lay infrastructure for a transoceanic slave labor network underpinned the Dutch Empire's most concerted if brief city building effort in the Atlantic.

*****

The East and West India companies were similar in corporate structure, and both were global extensions of the decentralized Dutch city network. In myriad ways, they connected Dutch cities – including public and private actors – to the emergent extractive colonial empire. They were also critical junctures in North–South relations theorized by Wallerstein and others. The Amsterdam-based East India Company was the first joint stock company, founded by the States General in 1602.[67] It was led by a board of directors called the Heeren XVII (or gentlemen seventeen). The directors came from city chambers, reflecting the power of the head offices in the economically dominant maritime cities. Eight were from Amsterdam alone.[68] The cities divided revenues accordingly. They also shared expenses, providing the shipping and recruiting investors from potentially all walks of life within the towns.[69] Each region had its own board comprised of investors.[70] The West India Company, created in 1621, mirrored the VOC. Like its counterpart, the WIC had a board of directors that reflected the urban hierarchy. In this case, eight of the nineteen directors (Heeren XIX) were from the Amsterdam chamber.[71] The States General supported the companies militarily, and both were in essence naval powers. They employed thousands of soldiers.[72]

The WIC was typically less profitable than the East India Company, owing in part to the loss of New Netherland and its fur trade to Britain in 1664, and the loss of its prized Brazilian colony after Portuguese settlers revolted there

[65] Lex Bosman, "Government Buildings in the Dutch Colonies (Seventeenth and Eighteenth Centuries)," in Konrad Ottenheym, Krista de Jonge and Monique Chatenet (eds.), *Public Buildings in Early Modern Europe* (Turnhout: Brepols, 2010), 119–130, 122.

[66] Ibid., 124.

[67] Michiel van Groesen, "Global Trade," in Helmer J. Helmers and Geert H. Janssen (eds.), *The Cambridge Companion to the Dutch Golden Age* (Cambridge: Cambridge University Press, 2018), 168–185, 169.

[68] Another four came from the Zeeland chamber. Rotterdam, Delft, Hoorn, and Enkhuizen each sent one director, in addition to a member from a lesser city.

[69] van Groesen, "Global Trade," 169. [70] Ibid.

[71] The differences are as follows: Zeeland also had four directors; Dordrecht, Enkhuizen, Hoorn, and Rotterdam each had one; Groningen had two; and another seat was reserved for a representative of the States General.

[72] van Groesen, "Global Trade," 172.

ten years earlier. Important scholarship deems it less critical to the Dutch economy in comparison with the Asian and Baltic trades.[73] This may understate the historic importance of the core–peripheral world system that was reshaping Dutch cities. Even after the loss of key colonies, the WIC doubled down on the slave trade and Amsterdam merchants sought to keep unfinished goods flowing, especially sugar and tobacco. As one study illustrates low margin crops were converted to high value goods in cities:

> In addition to profit for merchants, sugar, tobacco and other products also provided employment. After all, almost all Atlantic products had to be processed, which created many jobs. Amsterdam and Rotterdam had dozens of sugar refineries and tobacco mills within their walls. For the survival of these companies, not to mention to ensure their continued success, the supply of raw materials from the Atlantic was essential.[74]

Hence we see the start of the North–South value chain that persists in modern form today, with Amsterdam as its principle broker in the 1600s. Enslaved labor and raw materials extracted an ocean away led to higher value employment and processing in Europe's leading cities.

As the Dutch position weakened in the Atlantic relative to Britain, it gained strength in Asia after the VOC's all-out multipronged assault on Portuguese positions. The East India Company had broad ranging authority to wage war and conduct treaties and used it aggressively. The company wrested key parts of the Indonesian archipelago that formed the heart of its Asian network. This includes territories formerly held by local kingdoms that had been competitors in the spice trade, in addition to ports taken from the flagging Iberian empires.[75] There were crucial garrisoned strongholds in Ceylon, Java, Malacca, and points throughout present-day Indonesia.[76] The VOC established trade with Japan for vital silver as an alternative source to that plundered from the Americas by Spain. It was a match for China at sea, possessing a fort in Taiwan.[77] The company wrested the Chinese silk trade from the Spanish and Portuguese by force, even though the Chinese themselves preferred trading with the Iberian powers.[78] (This as the Dutch attacked Chinese shipping). The Dutch had a growing network of fortified trading towns in Asia, replete with twenty forts and ninety large ships – a projection of power other European

[73] See, especially, P. C. Emmer, *The Dutch Slave Trade, 1500–1850* (New York: Berghan Books, 2006), 109, 128; and Johannes Postma, "The Dimension of the Dutch Slave Trade from Western Africa," *The Journal of African History* 13, no. 2 (1972), 237–248, 248.

[74] den Heijer, "Public and Private Dutch West India Interest," 161.

[75] Onnekink and Rommelse, *Dutch in the Early Modern World*, 122.

[76] For a comprehensive overview of the Dutch footprint in the 1600s, see the illustration in Israel, *Dutch Primacy in World Trade*, 182.

[77] Ibid., 181.

[78] Spain and Portugal were in dynastic union under the Hapsburgs between 1580 and 1640.

empires could not equal.[79] The VOC was listed on the Amsterdam Exchange – the first modern stock market – with its share price rising and falling with the vicissitudes of its conflicts.[80] The nascent company was heavily capitalized by 1,800 investors back in Amsterdam, reflecting its value to the urban economy. The 200 largest investors comprised half of the company's capitalization, indicative of inequality in the seventeenth century that stood only to grow.[81]

*****

Dutch settlements throughout Asia were always along coasts, utilizing rationalist grid layouts where possible. The most important of which was Batavia (later Jakarta). Both in form and function it reflected the ambitions never realized in Recife.[82] This was the site of the VOC's overseas headquarters, the nerve center of its Asian operations. If investors in Europe's alpha city could sit back and follow reports of profit and loss from a safe distance, Batavia's VOC leaders were in the thick of the storm. It was the VOC governor, Jan Pietersz Coen (1587–1629), who founded the city in Java in 1619 as part of a broader blueprint of expansion. "The vast trading system stretching from the Persian Gulf to Japan was focused exclusively on Batavia," according to an extensive study of the Dutch economy.[83] Though the governing structure at the Amsterdam headquarters was famously decentralized, Coen's design for the company's field presence fit the strongman motif.[84] The dyadic relationship between these cities formed twin nerve centers for Asian trade. Batavia was the administrative site, with the governor and council making decisions over war, peace, and the management of resources heading west. Amsterdam infused the massive capital needed to keep the company expanding and accrued the returns from trade within Asia.[85] The influx of goods not otherwise available in Europe was critical to Amsterdam's place as a world *entrepôt*. Pepper and various spices constituted the bulk of the early trade. Put in perspective, these goods could sell for triple their original cost when they reached Europe.[86] Amsterdam merchants relayed orders to Batavia for such goods with each departing flotilla.

These were violent undertakings. The East India Company engaged in the slave trade, albeit on a smaller scale than the WIC. Population transfers were central to its work. Batavia and other urban centers came to dominate their hinterlands, trafficking captives abducted from rural areas across the Indian Ocean to Southern Africa.[87] The VOC's conflict with the Bandanese was

[79] Israel, *Dutch Primacy in World Trade*, 175. [80] Ibid., 186.
[81] Investment figures cited in de Vries and van der Woude, *First Modern Economy*, 384.
[82] van Groesen, "Global Trade," 177.
[83] de Vries and van der Woude, *First Modern Economy*, 386. [84] Ibid., 387. [85] Ibid.
[86] Ibid., 433, 442. [87] van Groesen, "Global Trade," 179.

particularly sordid. It eradicated most of the population and left a nutmeg plantation economy in their place on the Banda Islands that mirrored the plantations in the Atlantic.[88] High death rates among sickly laborers forced to toil under harsh conditions meant that the under-populated network saw the need to manage its numbers carefully.[89] The most important mission of the East India Company was to consolidate control over the storied Moluccan Islands, a source of coveted spices. This was a long, brutal process entailing years of warfare against the local polities that had engaged in clove, nutmeg, and mace production on their own terms.[90] The Dutch clove monopoly dating from 1600 was a relentless effort to concentrate, monitor, and regulate its outflow, thereby controlling price levels.[91] This meant keeping supply down in order to bolster margins in Europe. To do so, the Dutch utilized highly subordinate *corvée* labor bound to the land in continuation of older feudal practices in the region.[92] To maintain strict order – and prevent overproduction – the Dutch armed militias among the local populations to "inspect the surrounding islands, attack villages with smugglers, and destroy the clove trees there."[93]

This recalls the darker facets of the city networks we have explored in the previous chapters. Core cities force the migration needed to address population deficits or surpluses, or to hold labor in place, not simply to transport material goods. The Dutch trading companies did this ferociously, as the most recent estimates on their slave trading operations by historians show. Slaves were a ubiquitous sight in all Dutch-controlled towns in the east, there because of capture by slave raiders or as prisoners of war, criminal convictions, or unpaid debts.[94] In fact, slaves may well have been the first workers travelers would see upon disembarking, as they commonly worked the wharves. The VOC slave trade transported as many as 55,000 forced laborers. In addition, nearly a quarter-million abductees were transported on the company's ships as its officers' property. European and Asian merchants shipped scores more slaves to VOC territories. Remember, the Dutch were the world's premier carriers during the seventeenth and eighteenth centuries. Estimates are rough, but there could have been well over 1.1 million slaves transported by the East India Company. Scholars now hold that the volume of the slave trade in the East actually exceeded that of the WIC, whose name is primarily associated with slavery.[95] The WIC was one of the central drivers of the brutal transatlantic trade linking forced labor from West Africa, with Elmina and Luanda as key

[88] J. L. van Zanden, *The Rise and Decline of Holland's Economy: Merchant Capitalism and the Labor Market* (Manchester: Manchester University Press, 1993), 77.
[89] Ibid. [90] Ibid., 72. [91] Ibid., 71. [92] Ibid., 73. [93] Ibid.
[94] Onnekink and Rommelse, *Dutch in the Early Modern World*, 135.
[95] Statistics and comparisons are based on an overview of the latest research, cited in ibid., 132.

junctures, to the Caribbean and Americas. Dutch vessels shipped an estimated 608,849 slaves along this route, based on available records. Only 509,849 disembarked. The missing 99,000 prisoners perished in transit.[96] It is also important to note that desertion was a primary form of resistance to Dutch population politics. Escaped slaves, known as maroons, established communities in the hinterlands. This tested the reach of urban administration over the periphery. "On every island, stealing canoes and boats was harshly punished," one study noted. "All sorts of regulations were issued regarding the security of ferries, canoes, boats and ships."[97] There was an existential threat of slave rebellions.[98]

Dutch West Africa displayed a litany of territorial political interactions and overlapping sovereignties. In the Netherlands, as we have seen, national identity had scarcely formed. The ink had barely dried on the milestone Westphalia treaties of 1648, the formal birthdate of the independent Dutch Republic. The nation-state as a social construct had yet to fully form even in Europe. The Dutch directly controlled only slivers of African coastline, crucial towns such as Elmina and Luanda. The interiors were controlled by tribal entities, a delicate balance of territorial authorities that allowed the Dutch presence by agreement. These lands were heavily destabilized by the European outposts funneling weapons inland, while extracting key resources. "Gold Coast" is a literal name Europeans gave this region, along with "Slave Coast" and "Ivory Coast" nearby. The Portuguese named Elmina after the mining operations that extracted an estimated $1.6 billion worth of gold from present-day Ghana to Europe.[99] Large amounts of gold flowed from Elmina to Lisbon, an important trading dyad severed by the Dutch.[100]

This was enriching Europe at Africa's expense, as crucial changes were underway that brought on one of human history's worst tragedies. There was a yawning labor gap in the Americas that created a market for the slave trade.[101] The Spanish Empire, beginning with Columbus, enslaved local populations for work in plantations and lucrative silver mines.[102] These regions depopulated rapidly, perhaps killing 95 percent of some indigenous populations from conquest and disease. The Dutch, for their part, struggled to find settlers for their small urban colonies. There were longstanding misgivings about

[96] Statistics compiled in ibid., 131.

[97] Kwame Nimako and Glenn Willemsen, *The Dutch Atlantic: Slavery, Abolition, and Emancipation* (New York: Palgrave, 2011), 83.

[98] Ibid., 82. [99] Page, *Dutch Triangle*, 45. [100] Ibid., 40.

[101] Postma, *Dutch in the Atlantic Slave Trade*, 5.

[102] The transfer of silver from Latin America to Europe adds up to $165 trillion in today's dollars, by one widely cited estimate much discussed in the popular literature by the anthropologist Jason Hickel and others. See Suketu Mehta, *This Land Is Our Land: An Immigrant's Manifesto* (New York: Farrar, Straus, and Giroux, 2019), 75.

enslaving the indigenous tribes among some outspoken Spanish clergymen, most famously Bartolomé de las Casas, calling instead for the importation of slaves from Africa in their place.[103] In sum, the stars were aligned for an expansion in transatlantic human trafficking by the time of Dutch ascendency. "When the gold trade gave way to the slave trade, the need for peace among Africans was no longer an asset," argued a scholar whose research brought welcome focus on the African side of the trade.[104] Since war captives sold to European merchants were the most important source of the slave supply, traders began encouraging conflict.[105] Tribes in West Africa pursued cooperation with the slave trading powers, because to do otherwise could result in their own captivity.[106] The European empires feared the African kingdoms would initiate their own systems of commodity production and refinement, cooperating to stifle local initiative.[107]

Instead, the Dutch retained the key cities of Paramaribo in Suriname and Willemstad on the island of Curaçao. The latter is still part of the Dutch Kingdom.[108] Willemstad was an important market in its own right. The island's port was capable of harboring 300 ships.[109] Its disastrous inability to feed itself made conditions harsh for all of its residents, subjecting them to shortages in basic provisions. This was a common problem in Dutch trading colonies, which endured periodic famines. It was a critical juncture in the slave trade, connecting the Dutch West African colonies to the lucrative Spanish slave market. Most of the 70,000 slaves transferred along this route ended up in the Spanish Main.[110] Suriname was the largest Dutch plantation colony a producer of a variety of products from sugar to coffee to cacao.[111] This was a venture for which Amsterdam placed massive investments, including direct capital infusions and the deployment of soldiers for protracted struggles against the indigenous inhabitants.[112] What began as a heavily protectionist enterprise evolved into a pan-European project as other colonial merchants invested there. This involved ever increasing numbers of European slave ships arriving at Paramaribo from the seventeenth through the eighteenth centuries.[113]

103 Kwame and Willemsen, *Dutch Atlantic*, 16. 104 Page, *Dutch Triangle*, 62. 105 Ibid.
106 Ibid., xxvi. 107 Nimako and Willemsen, *Dutch Atlantic*, 57.
108 It currently has "constituent country" status.
109 Wim Klooster, "Curaçao as a Transit Center to the Spanish Main and the French West Indies," in Gert Oostindie and Jessica V. Roitman (eds.), *Dutch Atlantic Connections, 1680–1800: Linking Empires, Bridging Borders* (Leiden: Brill, 2014), 25–51, 25.
110 Ibid., 28.
111 Karwan Fatah-Black, "Paramaribo as Dutch and Atlantic Nodal Point, 1650–1795," in Gert Oostindie and Jessica V. Roitman (eds.), *Dutch Atlantic Connections, 1680–1800: Linking Empires, Bridging Borders* (Leiden: Brill, 2014), 52–71, 70.
112 Ibid., 69. 113 Ibid., 56.

This merits a brief reflection in a world systems context. Wallerstein concluded that this "triangular trade" was seminal in the emergence of the modern world economy. This occurred even if Dutch hegemony according to his strict operationalized definition was brief, lasting only "from 1648 to the 1660s."[114] Drawing raw materials from the rest of the world, even European rivals, the Netherlands accrued preponderance in high value industry clusters such as textiles, shipbuilding, seaborne carrying, and sugar refining.[115] For starters, he asserts that "the Dutch conducted the first serious slave trade in order to furnish the manpower for the sugar plantations."[116] The Dutch trading companies, in his estimation, "pioneered" the triangular trade, "which provided Europe with its cotton, sugar, and tobacco, all grown of course with African slave labor plus the silver Europe used to obtain the spices and tea from the East Indies."[117]

In other words, the cities in the urban core did not evolve in a vacuum.

Life in the Core Network

Amsterdam's population quadrupled in the period of imperial expansion, from roughly 50,000 in 1600 to 200,000 by 1650.[118] The colonial network had clear impacts on the economy, creating new opportunities for migration. In 1607, there were three sugar refineries in the Netherlands. By 1650 there were forty refineries, nearly all located in the port cities of Amsterdam, Rotterdam, and Dordrecht where raw sugar was imported.[119] Enormous amounts of coffee, cotton, and cocoa reached the port cities for refining, a flow that continued long after Dutch hegemony.[120] Just as importantly to the local economy, refined goods were re-exported, mainly to other parts of Europe. Amsterdam was a giant in tobacco products, for example, exporting them across the Baltics as far as Russia. The industry employed thousands of people in Dutch cities.[121] Overseas slavery played a major role in the city's changed employment base. A case in point, about two-thirds of the African slaves who survived the trip to the European colonies in the Americas ended up in sugar plantations – ensuring the flow of raw goods into the world's leading port cities.[122]

114 Wallerstein, *Modern World System II*, xxiii. 115 Ibid., 43. 116 Ibid., 52.

117 Ibid., 51.

118 Ibid., 45. For a meta-analysis of its population estimates, see Hubert Nusteling, "The Population of Amsterdam and the Golden Age," in Peter van Kessel and Elisja Schulte (eds.), *Rome/Amsterdam: Two Growing Cities in Seventeenth Century Europe* (Amsterdam: Amsterdam University Press, 1997), 71–84.

119 Nimako and Willemsen, *Dutch Atlantic*, 73. 120 Ibid., 72.

121 Simon Schama, *The Embarrassment of Riches: An Interpretation of Dutch Culture in the Golden Age* (New York: Vintage, 1997), 193.

122 Nimako and Willemsen, *Dutch Atlantic*, 64.

The coastal cities in the Netherlands were resultantly magnets for migration. New opportunities in this global division of labor contributed to lasting wage differentials in Europe, with the Dutch city network in a strong position. Amsterdam's complex economy supported 2,000 different professions, the bulk of them tied to trade and seafaring.[123] Nearly a quarter of the city's workforce was employed by either the VOC or WIC.[124] These cities were, nevertheless, population sinks where death rates greatly exceeded birthrates. Cities were still places where barely half of children reached the age of ten, as in Amsterdam.[125] This required an inflow of 4,000 to 5,000 people per year, totaling 425,000 migrants to Amsterdam alone in the sixteenth century.[126] In fact, only a minority of the city's population were citizens, and 40 percent of its population was foreign born. Haarlem and Leiden were each 55 percent foreign born. The VOC and WIC together represented a second population sink. During that same timespan, 300,000 people set sail for the VOC, with only 100,000 returning.[127] It is worth reiterating that the Dutch maintained a mercenary military locked in permanent warfare.[128] The vast majority of its recruits came from elsewhere in Europe, with the ranks routinely depleted by death in battle and the attendant public health nightmares of seafaring.

Simply put, the urban labor market was highly dependent on migration for nearly every function of Dutch statecraft.[129] An estimated 600,000 foreigners migrated to the Republic during its imperial high period. This is an astonishing figure for a polity that was relatively small, with about two-million inhabitants. Personal slaves were common sights in cities. They were not recorded as migrants because they were the "property" of merchants returning from the colonies.[130] Much of both the merchant marine and the home labor force came from Germany and Scandinavia. The major cities attracted migration from across Europe, especially France and the Spanish-controlled Low Countries. Amsterdam had a global mercantile presence at its exchanges.[131] Overall migration concentrated in the wealthier maritime cities, particularly in Holland. Between 1600 and 1672, Rotterdam grew from a population of 12,000 to 45,000. Leiden grew from 36,000 to 72,000. Haarlem grew from

123 Derek Phillips, *Well-Being in Amsterdam's Golden Age* (Amsterdam: Amsterdam University Press, 2008), 35.
124 Ibid. 125 Ibid., 64. 126 Ibid., 33. 127 Ibid.
128 This was literally the case. See Pepijn Brandon, "The Armed Forces," in Helmer J. Helmers and Geert H. Janssen (eds.), *The Cambridge Companion to the Dutch Golden Age* (Cambridge: Cambridge University Press, 2018), 69–85, 74.
129 See the data in van Zanden, *Rise and Decline of Holland's Economy*, 47, 53.
130 Nor were they always freed when arriving in the Netherlands, as they had been in some famous cases. Nimako and Willemsen, *Dutch Atlantic*, 33.
131 van Zanden, *Rise and Decline of Holland's Economy*, 53.

30,000 to 50,000 and The Hague, as administrative center, trebled to 30,000.[132]

Increasingly severe inequality marked the seventeenth century. The prosperity of workers, never quite befitting the term "golden age," gradually declined. Economic order mirrored that of the hereditary civic order, with culturally contemptuous ruling regents monopolizing important government and mercantile positions. The richest 10 percent of households in Amsterdam controlled nearly all the city's wealth. The richest 1 percent alone controlled 45 percent of the city's wealth.[133] The richest few families held fortunes in excess of 100,000 guilders, while three-quarters of the city did not have incomes of 600 guilders, the minimum amount that could be taxed.[134] The typical laborers in the city earned less than half this amount, the minimum survival wage. This entailed thirteen-hour days with few days off, with docked wages if hours declined.[135] In bad times, three-quarters of the population relied on food assistance. "Thousands woke hungry every morning and went to bed hungry every night," according to a study of daily life in Amsterdam. Mirroring the world city theories of today, the more powerful Amsterdam became, the more unequal its distribution of wealth, with palpable consequences. Real wages declined after 1650 in the leading edge coastal cities.[136] They seem to have stagnated in Amsterdam after 1633 following a half-century of remarkable growth.[137] If we factor in the greater costs of key staples like grain, Holland's lead over the rest of Europe in terms of living standards declined from this point.[138]

The mood among the lower classes was volatile, with "cheese and bread games" – aka riots – breaking out during food shortages.[139] Most households were on the brink, just able to afford shelter, fuel, and food until they couldn't. Women who fell on hard times had few options beyond correctional facilities or sex work. Socioeconomic factors certainly underpinned what visitor (male) scribes readily recorded as "loose morals" as they visited the *musicos* (music halls) popular with international tourists.[140] Desperate men were scammed into

132 Population figures cited in Geert H. Janssen, "Migration," in Helmer J. Helmers and Geert H. Janssen (eds.), *The Cambridge Companion to the Dutch Golden Age* (Cambridge: Cambridge University Press, 2018), 49–66, 52.

133 Phillips, *Well-Being in Amsterdam's Golden Age*, 44. 134 Ibid. 135 Ibid., 53.

136 van Zanden, *Rise and Decline of Holland's Economy*, 127.

137 Jan Lucassen, "Labour and Early Modern Economic Development," in Karel Davids and Jan Lucassen (eds.), *A Miracle Mirrored: The Dutch Republic in European Perspective* (Cambridge: Cambridge University Press, 1995), 367–409, 372.

138 Leo Noordegraaf and Jan Luiten van Zanden, "Early Modern Economic Growth and the Standard of Living: Did Labor Benefit from Holland's Golden Age," in Karel Davids and Jan Lucassen (eds.), *A Miracle Mirrored: The Dutch Republic in European Perspective* (Cambridge: Cambridge University Press, 1995), 410–437, 424.

139 Geert Mak, *Amsterdam* (Cambridge, MA: Harvard University Press, 2000), 63.

140 Ibid., 162; Schama, *Embarrassment of Riches*, 467.

the merchant marine – as we have seen, a veritable death sentence – by "soul sellers" who provided the poor with food and shelter until VOC recruiters could browbeat them into service.[141] There they received scant wages, but much debt. The majority died from mast accidents, diseases, combat wounds, malnutrition when supplies dwindled, and shipwrecks.[142] Desertion was common.

In contrast, the mercantile elite, flush with returns from abroad, acquired more land. The interest in land as an investment grew as the richest urban merchants shifted focus from risky trading ventures to more secure investments in land. The infusion of capital drove up rents in the cities, essentially converting wealth accumulated from abroad into the local property market. As is the case in the modern world city, real estate became an increasingly ethereal resource. As one contemporary observer lamented in 1652, "the regents were not merchants . . . they did not take risks on the seas but derived their income from houses, lands, and securities."[143] Rising real estate prices extended to the hinterlands. Urban land masters acquired rural spaces, making leasing costs untenable for the peasantry, driving urban migration among displaced farmers.[144] Increased costs led to reductions in parcel sizes, reconfiguring urban and rural activities alike.[145] The Beemster polder north of Amsterdam is so vast that it is now a UNESCO heritage site renowned for its precise, orderly planning. The system of dykes and rationalist gridded parcels put vast new territory on the market, some of it for country estates. Spearheaded by the VOC, backed by a small circle of elite burgomasters, it is the apotheosis of growing urban control over land.[146]

As with the alpha cities we have explored in previous chapters, Amsterdam engaged in unprecedented city building, taking the urban form we are familiar with today: The market square expanded, the canal system grew, and planners created new neighborhoods along class lines. The city was at the forefront of the classical international styles developing in urban Europe. The emphasis on globalism conveyed the city's power (and that of its ruling regent classes) to the lay public. This justified its steep social hierarchy as a natural order of things. It conveyed the city's might to a steady stream of foreign delegations

141 Mak, *Amsterdam*, 160. 142 Ibid., 161.

143 Cited in Peter Burke, *Venice and Amsterdam: A Study of Seventeenth Century Elites* (Cambridge: Polity, 1994), 129.

144 A. T. van Deursen, *Plain Lives in a Golden Age: Popular Culture, Religion and Society in Seventeenth Century Holland* (Cambridge: Cambridge University Press, 1991), 13.

145 Onnekink and Rommelse, *Dutch in the Early Modern World*, 24.

146 Charles van den Heuvel, "Multilayered Grids and Dutch Town Planning. Flexibility and Temporality in the Design of Settlements in the Low Countries and Overseas," in Piet Lombaerde and Charles van den Heuvel (eds.), *Early Modern Urbanism and the Grid: Town Planning in the Low Countries in International Context, Exchanges in Theory and Practice 1550–1800* (Turnhout: Brepols, 2011), 27–44, 33.

from all corners of the globe. Maria de' Medici's visit to the East India Company headquarters in 1638 was choreographed to include maps of its territories, along with artifacts such as Asian porcelains, cuisines, and spices.[147]

Amsterdam's town hall was for a time the world's eighth wonder. The WIC and VOC's headquarters each radiated a just globalism, making no apologies for the extreme abuses they oversaw at home and abroad. Their architecture was to convey "a well-ordered mercantile civilization," in one analysis.[148] Major cities employed construction, survey, and design teams that oversaw public projects. For example, the East India Company's Hendrick de Keyser-designed headquarters in Amsterdam was a city project, reflecting the public–private overlap in this urban mercantilist organization. The municipally led system of construction put Amsterdam republican architecture on par with the royalist construction elsewhere. Amsterdam's town hall was as grandiose as the greatest palaces of its time. Soon, Dutch design and building techniques were exported throughout Europe, especially in the Baltics where the Dutch maintained cultural and economic hegemony.[149] This process was rooted in the trading system, importing Baltic construction materials and utilizing the river and canal system to reach far and wide for quarried stone supplies.[150] Amsterdam's visual culture took on a new air, to remind onlookers of "Amsterdam's, and by extension the Dutch Republic's, global presence" and its inherent correctness.[151] As the city's elite grew wealthier, detailed baroque décor overran Calvinist austerity in public and private buildings.

Urban planning in Amsterdam reflected its strict hierarchy, emphasizing separation according to class. Not surprisingly, the city expanded mightily to keep up with increased migratory flows and commercial functions. The famed canal ring plans for Amsterdam, which began on paper in 1585 but were completed in the next century, cemented the city's own core and periphery (see Figure 11.2). The inner rings of canals were the preserve of large if narrow

147 Siegfried Huigen, "Introduction," in Siegfried Huigen, Jan L. de Jong, and Elmer Kolfin (eds.), *Dutch Trading Companies as Knowledge Networks* (Boston: Brill, 2010), 1–15, 1.

148 Konrad Ottenheym and Krista De Jonge, "Civic Prestige. Building the City 1580–1700," in Krista De Jonge and Konrad Ottenheym eds., *Unity and Discontinuity: Architectural Relations between the Southern and Northern Low Countries 1530–1700* (Turnhout: Brepols, 2007), 209–250, 213.

149 See Nils Ahlberg, "Netherlandish Expertise in Swedish Sixteenth and Seventeenth Century Urban Planning," in Piet Lombaerde and Charles van den Heuvel (eds.), *Early Modern Urbanism and the Grid: Town Planning in the Low Countries in International Context, Exchanges in Theory and Practice 1550–1800* (Turnhout: Brepols, 2011), 95–176.

150 Gabri van Tussenbroek, "Building Materials and Trade. Changes in the Organization of the Building Industry between North and South," in Krista De Jonge and Konrad Ottenheym (eds.), *Unity and Discontinuity: Architectural Relations between the Southern and Northern Low Countries 1530–1700* (Turnhout: Brepols, 2007), 301–330, 304.

151 Onnekink and Rommelse, *Dutch in the Early Modern World*, 120.

Figure 11.2 Amsterdam's inner ring canal system connected the houses of the bourgeois elite to the Dutch canal system and broader maritime trading network.
Photo by the author.

mansions.[152] The city's plans prohibited the construction of lanes and alleys between mansions in which the poor could settle. The Dam Square remained the hub of business activity.

Another major extension, the Jordaan, had smaller parcels for working class housing. The new plans, recalling the medieval city, created neighborhoods according to profession. The separation of functions kept dirty industrial activities away from the wealthier inner districts, relegating them to working class areas.[153] Yet much of Amsterdam at this time was *unplanned*, as 3,000 slum houses existed in the city's peripheral zones, alongside animals, barns, and workshops amidst ungoverned spaces.[154] The Jordaan was described by one contemporary as a "great stinking garbage dump."[155] It existed in intentional isolation from the inner districts where the richest 10 percent of the population lived, and were spared from the city's myriad environmental hazards. Life expectancy differed based on class in Europe by this era, with the upper classes living nearly twice as long.[156] In C. R. Boxer's phrasing, this was a city where the poor "were living in squalid back premises, cellars, and basements."[157] Even in towns, wood and clay were common materials for the average, severely overcrowded and vermin-infested housing. Few residents had their own homes, with nine people sharing a typical small dwelling.[158] Inside these dwellings, the burning of peat was a hazardous form of heating, but this is also a place where children were reported frozen to death when families went without heating. Planners working for the elite seemed untroubled by all this. As one study of urban conditions put it:

> Since the rich and the rest were considered different types of creatures, the city's fathers considered it fitting and proper that people should inhabit areas commensurate with their positions in Amsterdam's civic and economic hierarchies. All should be in their proper place.[159]

Conclusions: End of an Era

The Dutch Republic is recognized for its seminal place in economic history. It is the arguable beginning of extractive North–South relations, a colonial era where "Dutch sugar" and "Belgian chocolate" and "Rhodes scholars" and "Spanish silver" omit the southern sources of this wealth. The Dutch state

152 Koen Ottenheym, "The Amsterdam Ring of Canals: City Planning and Architecture," in Peter van Kessel and Elisja Schulte (eds.), *Rome/Amsterdam: Two Growing Cities in Seventeenth Century Europe* (Amsterdam: Amsterdam University Press, 1997), 33–49, 35, 40.

153 Ibid., 38.

154 Mak, *Amsterdam*, 106.

155 Phillips, *Well-Being in Amsterdam's Golden Age*, 67.

156 Ibid., 63.

157 C. R. Boxer, *The Dutch Seaborne Empire 1680–1800* (London: Hutchinson, 1965), 55.

158 Phillips, *Well-Being in Amsterdam's Golden Age*, 72.

159 Ibid., 68.

was prototypical in its role as middleman, utilizing its corporate network rather than direct territorial control to manage resources elsewhere. This had been done before, but arguably never in this form or magnitude – this is the shift Wallerstein sees.

In the history of city networks, however, the Dutch empire is a throwback. Unforeseen changes were on the horizon. These can be encapsulated in one word: Industrialization. Automated mass production, beginning in earnest just as Dutch power crested in the seventeenth century, chipped away at the preponderance of the seafaring city as a source of inordinate power. The Republic, essentially a collection of city-states centered on Amsterdam, looks more like its small polity predecessors (Athens, Venice, Lübeck) than the territorial empires that came to dominate world politics (Britain, France, Germany, Russia, the US) in the age of centralization, industrial-scale bureaucracy, and land-based linkages that help manage large territories.

12 Reflections

Dangers Ahead

The twenty-second century could be Venice's last. Seawater threatens to submerge the city at some point after 2100.[1] More than a millennium's worth of Italian, Greek, and Islamic-influenced art and architecture is at risk. This is among the most adaptable cities in history, recasting itself in changing epochs while retaining its medieval form. Anthropogenic global warming may finally subdue a city that fended off popes, Byzantine emperors, and Ottoman sultans.

At the time of this writing, *Bulletin of the Atomic Scientists* placed its famous doomsday clock closer to midnight than at any time in the journal's half-century history, owing to nuclear modernization and rapidly worsening global warming.[2] Research sponsored by the Organization for Economic Cooperation and Development (OECD) reports that 136 littoral cities are at risk of hemorrhaging a combined one trillion dollars in property loss annually by mid-century, absent successful adaptation.[3] The first seven months of the war in Ukraine added 100 million tons of carbon into the atmosphere.[4] The entire world network of cities will likely be reconfigured in this century if greenhouse emissions continue at this rate. Reflecting the histories of statecraft we have seen in this book, nothing is permanent. Political structures adapt to changing landscapes no less than sea barriers. The survival of the world city is in doubt. Yet, as long as the capitalist system retains its current form, the world city will be at the center of it, performing the command functions of the global economy (see Chapter 1). Like the world cities of the past, they are sustained by long distance linkages. What does doomsday look like for them? In the

[1] Intergovernmental Panel on Climate Change, *Special Report on the Ocean and Cryosphere in a Changing Climate* (New York: United Nations, 2019), 358.

[2] *Bulletin of the Atomic Scientists*, "Doomsday Dashboard," available at https://thebulletin.org/doomsday-clock/doomsday-dashboard/ (last accessed February 15, 2020.

[3] Stephane Hallegate, Colin Green, Robert Nicholls, and Jan Corfee-Morlot, "Future Flood Losses in Major Coastal Cities," *Nature Climate Change* 3 (2013), 802–806.

[4] Oli Brown, "How Russia's War in Ukraine Is Threatening Climate Security," *Chatham House*, available at www.chathamhouse.org/2023/03/how-russias-war-ukraine-threatening-climate-security (last accessed July 7, 2023).

context of these chapters, environmental catastrophe or nuclear war would catalyze planetary deurbanization, reflecting interludes between networks. If humankind survives, cities would exist in shrunken form, with a great deal of knowledge lost.

Today's alpha cities manage unprecedented industrial dispersal, production, and consumption. Like Tikal and Teotihuacan, they face existential environmental risks. Both cores and peripheries face their own pressing threats. Even cities that survive intact may have no peripheries to manage as rural regions face ecological perils of their own, as do urban links in the global trading system. This is not unprecedented. Tomorrow's alpha cities may well perform the tasks of their ancestors from Uruk to Athens to Rome: Managing scarcity and consolidation.

A portion of this book was written in isolation as the COVID-19 pandemic reached every continent, concentrating in large globally connected cities The list of the hardest hit places reads like a global cities index. The patterns of the epidemic closely mirrored what Manuel Castells calls the "space of flows" between cities. As I write this, COVID-19 is approaching its seven-millionth documented fatality.[5] Forty-five thousand people died in New York. Tens of thousands died in London. These are the world's preeminent alpha cities, heirs to the cities we have studied in this book. This is another reminder of how unsustainable the world city network is. Just as the spaces of flows have been ungovernable in pre-modern times, so they remain today. This is a key point raised by Saskia Sassen and other theorists of global cities, emerging in a new way. Global cities are oriented toward flows of financial and human capital (excluding undesirables) but cannot filter pandemics and illicit activity. The struggle to govern outside the city walls remains.

The virus emerged at the urban–rural nexus, likely in so-called wet markets that acquire, torture, and kill endangered animals, repackaging them as products for urban consumers.[6] This is one manifestation of the attempt from within cities to control what is organic and "not urban." This book scrutinized the longstanding chauvinism of city over country, "civilized" over "rustic," as far back as the god builder Enbilulu in the Mesopotamian *Epic of Creation*. Back then, the known world existed to be dammed, rerouted, drained, and exploited. Today's systems of exploitation are no less remarkable and terrifying. A twentieth-century invention, the industrial farm is an urban entity managed from cities along the "space of flows." It achieves previously

5 Johns Hopkins Coronavirus Resource Center, "COVID-19 Map," available at https://coronavirus.jhu.edu/map.html (last accessed August 19, 2020).

6 Kenji Mizumoto, Katsushi Kagaya, and Gerardo Chowell, "Effect of a Wet Market on Coronavirus Disease Transmission, 2019–2020," *International Journal of Infectious Diseases* 97 (2020), 96–101.

inconceivable levels of resource drainage, physical and psychological animal abuse, greenhouse gas emissions, and uncontained toxic waste runoff.[7] The dead zones this creates are collateral damage in an ongoing war against the unseen spaces outside cities. The potential for zoonotic infections emerging from these sites potentially dwarfs COVID-19.[8] Sassen's research shows the immense labor needed to support the burgeoning demands of urban lifestyles.[9] While *The Global City* highlights inequities generated within leading cities, it says little about places impacted by their planetary reach. Inequalities in their spheres of influence happen sight unseen and there is little discussion of what the urban age means for the peripheral zones.[10]

A central lesson from these cases is that scarcity is a driver of globalization, with world cities developing linkages outward as they grow desperate to extract resources. Shifts from concentration to dispersal and back again can be wrenching, as seen throughout history. Control over land and labor remains a violent process. The paradox of scarcity is that it makes localism less viable. Today world cities are the drivers of extractive, ecologically destructive relations with the rest of the planet. First, the majority of the world exists in poverty, which is rising.[11] The world's poor are swelling the ranks of the subaltern precariat who serve as links in global production chains. This is what Sassen sees as a significant shift toward a dispersed economy requiring central management.[12] Second, the vast majority of the Earth's surface is in use by humans.[13] Other species are evaporating in a "sixth extinction," a die-off on a scale not seen since the Cretaceous Period sixty-five million years ago.[14] This mass destruction is the result of conscientious decisions made in a few urban centers. This imbalanced relationship between city and *contado* is nothing new. The alpha cities explored here all rose, declined, and fell on the weight of their hinterlands and networks of secondary cities. What is unique to the twenty-first century is that the whole world from land to ocean is a *contado*. It is under assault by a few management centers occupying at most 1 percent of its land. The *contado* has expanded to include all organic life, plant, animal, and human. The corporate web of Monsanto is a primary example. It utilizes

[7] See, for starters, UN Environmental Programme, "Ten Things You Should Know about Industrial Farming," available at www.unenvironment.org/news-and-stories/story/10-things-you-should-know-about-industrial-farming (last accessed August 19, 2020).

[8] Interagency Group on Antimicrobial Resistance, *No Time to Wait: Securing the Future from Drug Resistant Infections* (New York: United Nations, 2019).

[9] Sassen, *Global City*, 9. [10] Robinson, *Ordinary Cities*, 95.

[11] Phillip Alston, *The Parlous State of Poverty Eradication: Report of the Special Rapporteur of Extreme Poverty and Human Rights* (New York: United Nations, 2020), 4.

[12] Sassen, *Global City*, 92.

[13] The World Bank, Our World In Data, "Land Use," available at https://ourworldindata.org/land-use (last accessed August 14, 2020).

[14] Elizabeth Kolbert, *The Sixth Extinction: An Unnatural History* (New York: Henry Holt, 2014).

producer services across the world urban network to patent and privatize biological materials that were once public goods.[15] The result is an epidemic of "debt suicides" by farmers in rural areas forced to purchase patented seeds.[16] Commodity price drops decided by investors in New York and Chicago and London can set off famines in the Global South.[17]

In historic context, much looks familiar about today's city network. Population politics continue in more subtle forms, with cities playing direct roles. The inverse of the urban age is rural dispossession, just as the rise of Alexandria coincided with the crushing exploitation of the Fayum. Agribusiness today is an urban phenomenon, with land grabs financed mainly from the most powerful global cities.[18] The bulk of land grabs originate from global cities, particularly alpha cities in the Globalization and World Cities Research Network (GaWC)'s index.[19] Mass deportations are commonplace, as is mass incarceration and surveillance. Their brutality worsens in tandem with the ethno-nationalist movements in the economic cores. Digital technology promises to increase the ability of states to monitor and regulate large open spaces, giving governments inroads into human activity once thought private. Leaders of the most despotic walled cities could never have imagined this magnitude of state power and social control.

Recalling Juvenal's laments, life for millions in the world's power centers is becoming unbearable as housing costs and evictions worsen.[20] As Sassen predicted in *The Global City*, luxury housing coexists near neglected housing and warehoused property.[21] The notion of planners functioning (for better and worse) as social engineers toward higher purposes has been subsumed by the advent of "starchitects" for hire by a narrow set of elites tied to finance.[22] This fundamentally altered the political dynamics in cities, as marginalized populations resist their effective expulsions or desert leading cities in their own latter day expressions of *anachôrêsis*.

*****

15 Monsanto, "Monsanto Company Headquarters and Office Locations," available at https://craft.co/monsanto-company/locations (last accessed August 19, 2020).
16 B. B. Mohanty, "'We Are Like the Living Dead': Farmer Suicides in Maharashtra," *Journal of Peasant Studies* 32, no. 2 (2005), 243–276.
17 For example, see Oxfam, *Mugged: Poverty in Your Coffee Cup* (Boston: Oxfam, 2002).
18 Joshua K. Leon, "The Role of Global Cities in Land Grabs," *Third World Quarterly* 36, no. 2 (2015), 257–273, 265.
19 See my survey in ibid., 264.
20 These trends are particularly pronounced in the US. See Matthew Desmond, *Evicted: Poverty and Profit in the American City* (New York: Penguin, 2016).
21 Sassen, *Global City*, 192. 22 Ibid., 193.

World Cities in History connected cities across vast scales of time and place. The global cities scholar Peter J. Taylor recently called such undertakings (approvingly) "city generics."[23] In our urban age, there is a search underway for ties between cities in deep time, drawing on essentialist notions of *cities qua cities*. As the urban age careens forward, we are seeing more such studies recasting past and present in a variety of ways.[24] With urban activities inviting ecological crisis, there will be more reflection. The urban–rural divide is growing, leaving a need to explore urban history on those terms. These chapters sought to balance the striking uniqueness and similarities between city networks in time. They sought to bring the oft-omitted hinterlands into the fold, rectifying a common weakness in city studies. Hopefully this captures in detail what makes primary cities alike without being entirely "generic" about these distinctive life worlds. This book has argued that world cities are a special form of social organization that have existed from the very earliest periods of urbanization. To reiterate, these continuities are missing in the world cities literature, which overemphasizes capitalist flows (see Chapter 1).

When we take a long look back, we see a rich variety of city networks across historical contexts, operating according to their own logics. At their essence, flows are the transference of physical and ideational things across city networks. World cities are a distinctive category of cities dating back at least to Uruk in the fourth millennium BCE. They organize and materialize flows across networks and into their peripheries. The world cities literature led by Friedmann, Taylor, Sassen, and Castells emphasizes the transfer of capital from place to place and its social consequences. Recalling Castells, cities are not static places but processes undergoing changes to accommodate networks. These processes differed in their unique cultural contexts. Historical cases shed light on the many important *variances* of flows across time. What has history told us?

Rather than clean and neat channels for finance, cities are historically something akin to pneumatic tubes. Varieties of things flow through them at different times and at different speeds, according to the imaginations of the city builders managing them. In China, the Mediterranean, Mesoamerica, and Mesopotamia luxury trades shaped class structures, fostering social differentiation. In Rome, the Baltics, and the Netherlands, bulk trades and slave labor reshaped urban lifestyles in the networks. In all of these cases, architectural forms blended local and shared visual cultures. In Rome, even substantial

[23] Taylor, "City Generics."

[24] In addition to the academic works cited in Chapter 1, recent books entering the popular discourse include Annalee Newitz, *Four Lost Cities: A History of the Urban Age* (New York: W.W. Norton, 2021); Monica L. Smith, *Cities: The First 6,000 Years* (New York: Viking, 2019); and Greg Woolf, *The Life and Death of Ancient Cities.*

amounts of building materials came from elsewhere. City planning tactics spread over networks, adapting to place-specific imperatives.

In Alexandria, experimentation with museums presaged a key component of today's alpha cities where cultural production expands with financial power. If cuneiform tablets etched information in clay, then museums and libraries in Alexandria, Baghdad, and Chang'an provided its storage containers. Mesoamerican cities seem to have conceived of both approaches. The metaphysics of flows have proven just as consequential. Islam, Christianity, and Buddhism moved through urban networks. Legal traditions, languages, and art forms demonstrated far-ranging aesthetic implications, creating uniqueness as much as homogeneity.

Patterns of flows varied. Consumer cities – Rome, Chang'an – were terminal destinations for vast luxury trades and rural surplus. Others such as the Silk Road cities and Hanseatic Lübeck were central links processing flows, but not the endpoints. They were critical to processing goods in circular trades, and in the case of Amsterdam orchestrating assemblages of material and financial products. The record shows that these relationships were often highly exploitative. The Hanseatic agricultural trades imposed massive labor demands on the rural hinterlands around Eastern Europe. The network of specialized cities in Holland helped further the groundwork for the North–South divide that the world is still grappling with today. Core–periphery arrangements existed in several of our cases, with Ptolemaic Egypt's harsh laboring system serving as an especially brutal example.

These cities found unique channels to link networks. The conduits of flows differed according to immediate need, available technologies, environmental pathways, and historic contexts. For example, the *sacboeb* (elevated causeways in Mesoamerica) are a unique invention that set paths for what and who could be moved and displayed. Seaborne travel and shipping defined Mediterranean cities, while the Dutch moved to oceanic travel. Camel-based transport in the Middle East reconfigured intercity linkages and changed street systems within cities. Lacking sufficient waterborne travel, Mesoamerican cities developed a vast system of human carriers.

Intercity relations played major roles in facilitating flows, proving a force in power politics during certain periods – for example, the Delian League, Lombard League (Chapter 9), and Swabian League (Chapter 10). Lübeck Law cemented the primacy of traders in city governance in the Hanse. Early on, Rome forged lasting diplomatic arrangements that underpinned its ability to marshal armies in Italy. Down the population scale, Lübeck was at the heart of a social network spanning Northern Europe. This lessened its reliance on the formal economic arrangements that Italy and Holland innovated. Tlacaelel's diplomacy reminds us that the Aztec "Empire" was a series of grudging urban alliances (Chapter 8). This multiplicity of intercity arrangements evoke the emerging roles cities have played in global governance today, such as in UN Habitat and the Climate 40. Systems of overlapping sovereignty shifted over several millennia, but the city has constantly adapted to the menageries of statecraft.

None of this is meant to glorify these periods, several of which have attracted the hardly neutral moniker "golden age" by modern historians. Consistent with today's world city network, these cases show rising inequality during their high periods – not to mention slave trafficking, forced population transfers, and so on. Looking at city networks enables scrutiny of these underlying power structures. The history of city networks shows the control of flows to be a primary source of conflict across time, contra the "peace through trade" narrative popular in International Relations. Seaborne and land-based links between cities, and rural spheres of influence, have been the rationales for generations-long wars. Moreover, Tikal, Chang'an, and Baghdad all featured unique forms of movement within cities. They found unique ways to exclude access to important zones in the city, through gates, walls, and canal regulations. As with today's city network, openness to flows has also entailed zones of exclusion.

*****

History bequeaths us a variety of cities with unique geopolitical contexts to unpack. Case omissions are inevitable. The cities explored here were world shaping, but the absence of historic networks from this book in no way signals a lack of importance. This book is not an attempt to capture all networks that existed over time, or to numerically quantify the history of city networks from Uruk to Amsterdam. Readers interested in those undertakings should follow Taylor's Globalization and World Cities Research Network (GaWC), and see the Copenhagen Polis Centre's multidisciplinary research into city-state cultures. Instead, this book adds to this discussion by situating urban aesthetics and experiences within political-economic realities. It seeks to add geopolitical flesh to the bones of so many excellent large studies.

New urbanists may read this volume as anti-urban. It has tried to remain neutral on the question of whether or not quality of life was materially better during urban ages versus periods of deurbanization derided by the sources as "dark ages." This book has sought to avoid this value judgment, more appropriate to professional urban planning literature. It has also avoided statements of the obvious, that public health advances have made concentration more palatable, that a dense, small walkable footprint carries environmental advantages. Elaborations on these points exist in abundance.[25] This book was

[25] See the voluminous works of Andres Duany, Richard Florida, Jeff Speck, and Emily Talen.

concerned with *concentrated power*. Hence its application of the Global Cities literature, which in its purest form scrutinizes not just linkages with other places, but coercive influences over them.

More simply, this book may unintentionally convey a negative tilt because of its emphasis on the urban and rural poor. City building in urban networks entailed pushing these figures all over the map or holding them in place. This is the unfree labor, as St. Croix put it, who made great cities possible. City networks encompass their stories as well as those of the creative classes. The lower strata deserve recognition for their creativity in making cities work, leaving aside that many were artisans themselves. A takeaway of the book is that city networks shaped life worlds. Not just for the mobile elite but those existing on the peripheries. Egyptian farmers who produced grains for the magnetized urban colossi of Rome and Alexandria met distant demand coordinated through urban networks. In this way their lives were global.

Norms have changed in this relatively new era of human rights. *Synoikisms* and unfree labor systems would be considered repugnant today. Yet there are disturbing rhythms to history. Migrants and laborers across the world live in constant danger from stagnant wages, depleting environments, and a migration system that places asylum seekers in prisons. This history of world cities contextualized those darker rhythms echoing from the fourth millennium BCE. The invention of urban-led zones of extraction was a cardinal event in labor history.

Cities are too complex to be considered "good" things or "bad" things. The cities under study here made immeasurable contributions to art, architecture astronomy, the sciences, philosophy, religion, engineering, political thought, and much more. True, we should not judge the rightness or wrongness of a given society on the basis of its recorded contributions in these areas. It is also true that the world we have today would be infinitely more impoverished without them. Cities have been sites of severe repression but have embodied rigorous thinking about how to construct better societies. In this age of economized and neoliberal education systems, modern cities could stand to emulate the intellectual values of Baghdad, Athens, Alexandria, Chang'an, Aachen, and Samarkand. Greek and Roman experiments in democracy, land reform, and debt forgiveness even appear radical in a modern society that glorifies private accumulation.

On the same token, this book does not argue that premodern cities were sites of stagnation until the onset of industrialization. Cultural and scientific flowerings evince numerous positive cycles of creativity that would not be possible without the critical masses available in cities. This extended to economic spheres. E. A. Wrigley's *Continuity, Chance and Change* contends that preindustrial "organic" economies produced economic advancements prior to the advent of fossil fuel powered automation.[26] He points out that early modern cities overcame predictions of land scarcity and falling wages led by doomsayers Thomas Malthus and David Ricardo (although they did so with the benefit of unfree labor and materials in the colonies).[27] As we saw in Chapter 3, recent research shows that the classical Greek economy produced palpable levels of growth with increases in living standards. Peter Hall's *Cities and Civilization* explores *belle époque* periods where creativity "burst forth" spasmodically.[28] This book complements that undertaking, emphasizing political forces underpinning the coalescence of urbanity.

At the same time, Athens, Rome, and cities in the early caliphates dealt seriously with questions of redistribution. Cities are endlessly self-reflective and adaptive. Although cities are traditionally assemblages of concentrated power, this is fluid and dialectical. Solon, the Gracchi, and Julius Caesar stand out as figures posing real threats to their social orders. Thinkers of all stripes likewise share admiration for the physical and metaphysical productivity of cities. Max Weber casts medieval cities as resilient harbingers for what became Western civilization.[29] Engels' vivid *Condition of the Working Class in England* showed the potential for exploitation in cities as well as their promise of reinvention.[30] It is a timeless contradiction. Cities are where leaders organize their most impactful policies and denizens make infinite micro-decisions about how to produce, consume, and act collectively. Their destructive power and creative potency are both immense. They are where answers to the world's compounding crises may be discovered.

In closing, the study of cities must entail a holistic exploration of power in all of its forms, from the apocalyptic to the everyday. The stakes are too high, the finality is all too real not to. No one understood this better than the architecture critic and urban historian Lewis Mumford. A self-described generalist, he knew that the many dimensions of urban power were impossible to compartmentalize. As cities concentrated global knowledge and housed information in ever-greater volumes, technological progress rocketed forward along with destructive power. A warning from his 1961 classic *The City in History* remains as relevant as ever:

> [C]onsider Sennacherib's inscription on the total annihilation of Babylon: "The city and its houses, from its foundations to its top, I destroyed, I devastated, I burned with fire. The wall and outer wall, temples and gods, temple towers of brick and earth, as many as

26 E. A. Wrigley, *Continuity, Chance and Change: The Character of the Industrial Revolution in England* (Cambridge: Cambridge University Press, 1988), 29.

27 Ibid., 47.

28 Peter Hall, *Cities in Civilization* (New York: Pantheon, 1998), 21.

29 Though he is all too quick to discount developments in Chinese and Islamic cities. Weber, *City*, 99.

30 Friedrich Engels, *Condition of the Working Class in England* (Moscow: Institute of Marxism-Leninism, 1969), 53, 55.

there were, I razed and dumped them into the Arakhtu Canal. Through the midst of that city I dug canals, I flooded the site with water, and the very foundations thereof I destroyed. I made this destruction more complete than that by a flood." Both the act and the morals anticipated the ferocious extravagances of our own nuclear age. Sennacherib lacked only our swift scientific dexterity and our massive hypocrisy in disguising our intentions even from ourselves.[31]

[31] This famous inscription describes the Akkadian king's conquest of Babylon in 689 BCE, which we discussed in Chapter 2. Lewis Mumford, *The City in History: Its Origins, Its Transformations, and Its Prospects* (New York: Harcourt, Brace and World, 1961), 54.

References

Abrams, Elliot M. *How the Maya Built Their World: Energetics and Ancient Architecture*. Austin: University of Texas Press, 1994.

Abu-Lughod, Janet L. *Before Western Hegemony: The World System A.D. 1250–1350*. Oxford: Oxford University Press, 1989.

Cairo: 1001 Years of the City Victorious. Princeton: Princeton University Press, 1971.

"The Islamic City: Historic Myth, Islamic Essence, and Contemporary Relevance." *International Journal of Middle East Studies* 19, no. 2 (1987), 155–176.

Adams, R. E. W., and Richard C. Jones. "Spatial Patterns and Regional Growth among Classic Maya Cities." *American Antiquity* 46, no. 2 (1981), 301–322.

Adshead, S. A. M. *China in World History*. New York: Palgrave, 1988.

T'ang China: The Rise of the East in World History. New York: Palgrave, 2004.

Aguilar-Moreno, Manuel. *Handbook to Life in the Aztec World*. New York: Facts of File, 2006.

Ahlberg, Nils. "Netherlandish Expertise in Swedish Sixteenth and Seventeenth Century Urban Planning." In *Early Modern Urbanism and the Grid: Town Planning in the Low Countries in International Context, Exchanges in Theory and Practice 1550–1800*, edited by Piet Lombaerde and Charles van den Heuvel, 95–176. Turnhout: Brepols, 2011.

Akkach, Samer. *Cosmology and Architecture in Premodern Islam*. Albany: State University of New York Press, 2005.

Al Tabari. *The History of Al Tabari XXXI: War between Brothers*. Albany: State University of New York Press, 1992.

Aldrete, Gregory S. *Daily Life in the Roman City: Rome, Pompeii, and Ostia*. Norman: University of Oklahoma Press, 2008.

Algaze, Guillermo. *Ancient Mesopotamia at the Dawn of Civilization: The Evolution of an Urban Landscape*. Chicago: University of Chicago Press, 2008.

The Uruk World System: The Dynamics of Expansion of Early Mesopotamian Civilization, 2nd ed. Chicago: University of Chicago Press, 2005.

Alston, Phillip. *The Parlous State of Poverty Eradication: Report of the Special Rapporteur of Extreme Poverty and Human Rights*. New York: United Nations, 2020.

"Ancient History Sourcebook: Thucydides, Pericles Funeral Oration from the Peloponnesian War." Fordham University. Available at https://sourcebooks.fordham.edu/ancient/pericles-funeralspeech.asp, last accessed August 26, 2018.

Andrews, A. "The Growth of the City-State." In *The Greek World*, edited by Hugh Lloyd Jones, 26–65. Middlesex: Penguin, 1962.
Anthony, David, W. *The Horse, the Wheel, and Language: How Bronze-Age Riders from the Eurasian Steppes Shaped the Modern World*. Princeton: Princeton University Press, 2010.
Apuleius, *The Golden Ass*. New York: Farrar, Straus, and Giroux, 1979.
Arbel, Benjamin. "Venice's Maritime Empire in the Early Modern Period." In *A Companion to Venetian History*, edited by Eric R. Dursteler, 125–254. Boston: Brill, 2013.
Arblaster, Paul. *A History of the Low Countries*. London: Red Globe Press, 2019.
Archibald, Zofia, John Davies, Vincent Gabrielsen, and G. J. Oliver (eds.). *Hellenistic Economies*. New York: Routledge, 2001.
Ardren, Traci, Scott R. Hutson, David R. Hixson, and Justin Lowry. "Connections beyond Chunchucmil." In *Ancient Maya Commerce*, edited by Scott Hutson, 273–297. Louisville: University of Colorado Press, 2017.
Ardren, Traci, and Justin Lowry. "The Travels of Maya Merchants in the Ninth and Tenth Centuries AD: Investigations at Xuenkal and the Greater Cupul Province, Yucatan, Mexico." *World Archeology* 43, no. 3 (2011), 428–443.
Aristophanes. *Frogs and Other Plays*. Oxford: Oxford University Press, 2015.
Aristotle. *Politics*. Oxford: Oxford University Press, 1995.
Arnold III, Phillip J. "Not Carved in Stone: Building the Gulf Olmec from the Bottom Up." In *The Oxford Handbook of Mesoamerican Archeology*, edited by Deborah L. Nichols, 188–199. Oxford: Oxford University Press, 2012.
Arrian. *Anabasis of Alexander*. London: Hodder and Stoughton, 1884. Available at https://en.wikisource.org/wiki/The_Anabasis_of_Alexander, last accessed February 15, 2024.
"Art Humanities: Primary Source Reader, The Parthenon." Columbia University. Available at https://arthum.college.columbia.edu/sites/default/files/PDFs/arthum_parthenon_reader.pdf, last accessed August 26, 2018.
Ashtor, E. *A Social and Economic History of the Near East in the Middle Ages*. Berkeley: University of California Press, 1976.
Augustus. *Res Gestae Divi Augusti*. Cambridge: Loeb Classical Library, 1924.
Austin, M. M., and P. Vidal-Naquet. *Economic and Social History of Ancient Greece: An Introduction*. Berkeley: University of California Press, 1977.
Bagley, Robert. "Shang Archeology." In *The Cambridge History of Ancient China: From the Origins of Civilization to 221 B.C.*, edited by Michael Loewe and Edward L Shaughnessy, 124–231. Cambridge: Cambridge University Press, 1999.
Bagnall, Roger S., and Peter Derow. *The Hellenistic Period: Historical Sources in Translation*. Oxford: Blackwell, 2004.
Bairoch, Paul. *Cities and Economic Development: From the Dawn of History to the Present*. Chicago: University of Chicago Press, 1988.
Baker, Heather D. "From Street Alter to Palace: Reading the Built Environment of Early Babylonia." In *The Oxford Handbook of Cuneiform Culture*, edited by Karen Radner and Eleanor Robson, 533–552. Oxford: Oxford University Press, 2011.
"Urban Form in the First Millennium BC." In *The Babylonian World*, edited by Gwendolyn Leick, 66–77. New York: Routledge, 2007.
Barber, Benjamin. *If Mayors Ruled the World: Dysfunctional Nations, Rising Cities*. New Haven: Yale University Press, 2014.

Barton, John H., Judith L. Goldstein, Timothy E. Josling, and Richard E. Steinberg. *The Evolution of the Trade Regime: Politics, Law, and Economics of the GATT and WTO*. Princeton: Princeton University Press, 2006.

Beard, Mary. *SPQR: A History of Ancient Rome*. New York: W. W. Norton, 2015.

Becker, Marshall Joseph. "Ancient Maya Markets: Architectural Grammar and Market Identifications." In *The Ancient Maya Marketplace*, edited by Eleanor M. King, 90–110. Tucson: University of Arizona Press, 2015.

Beckwith, Christopher I. *Empires of the Silk Road: A History of Eurasia from the Bronze Age to the Present*. Princeton: Princeton University Press, 2009.

"The Plan of the City of Peace: Central Asian Factors in Early Abbasid Design." *Acta Orientalia Academiae Scientiarum Hungaricae* (1984) 38, no. 1, 143–164.

Bell, David, and Mark Jayne. "Conceptualizing Small Cities." In *Small Cities: Urbanization beyond the Metropolis*, edited by David Bell and Mark Jayne, 3–18. London, Routledge, 2006.

Beneš, Carrie L. "Introduction." In *A Companion to Medieval Genoa*, edited by Carrie L. Beneš, 1–24. Boston: Brill, 2018.

Benn, Charles. *Daily Life in Traditional China: The Tang Dynasty*. London: Greenwood Press, 2002.

Bennison, Amira K. *The Great Caliphs: The Golden Age of the Abbasid Empire*. New Haven: Yale University Press, 2009.

Berdan, Frances. "Late Postclassic Mesoamerican Trade Networks and Imperial Expansion." *Journal of Globalization Studies* 8, no. 1 (2017), 14–29.

Berkey, Jonathan P. *The Formation of Islam: Religion and Society in the Near East, 600–1800*. Cambridge: Cambridge University Press, 2003.

Bertman, Steven. *Handbook to Life in Ancient Mesopotamia*. New York: Facts on File, 2003.

Bianca, Stefano. *Urban Form in the Arab World: Past and Present*. New York: Thames and Hudson, 2000.

Bielenstein, Hans. *The Bureaucracy of Han Times*. Cambridge: Cambridge University Press, 1980.

Bilde, Per, Troels Engberg-Pedersen, Lise Hannestad, Jan Zahle, and Klavs Randsborg (eds.). *Centre and Periphery in the Hellenistic World*. Aarhus: Aarhus University Press, 1993.

Billen, Claire, and Chloé Deligne. "Urban Space: Infrastructure, Technology and Power." In *City and Society in the Low Countries, 1100–1600*, edited by Bruno Blondé, Marc Boone, and Anne-Laure Van Bruaene, 162–191. Cambridge: Cambridge University Press, 2018.

Billows, Richard. "Cities." In *A Companion to the Hellenistic World*, edited by Andrew Erskine, 196–215. Oxford: Blackwell Publishing, 2003.

Birnbaum, Henrik. "Kiev, Novgorod, Moscow: Three Varieties of Urban Society in East Slavic Territory." In *Urban Society of Eastern Europe in Premodern Times*, edited by Bariša Krekić, 1–62. Berkeley: University of California Press, 1987.

Blanton, Richard E. *Houses and Households: A Comparative Study*. New York: Springer, 1994.

Blanton, Richard E., Gary Feinman, Stephen A. Kowalski, and Linda M. Nicholas. *Ancient Oaxaca: The Monte Albán State*. Cambridge: Cambridge University Press, 1999.

Blanton, Richard E., Stephen A. Kowalewski, and Gary M. Feinman. "The Mesoamerican World System." *Review: Fernand Braudel Center* 15, no. 3 (1992), 419–426

Bleicken, Jochen. *Augustus: The Biography*. New York: Penguin, 2016.

Blockmans, W. P. "The Formation of a Political Union, 1300–1588." In *History of the Low Countries*, edited by J. C. H. Blom and E. Lamberts, 54–140. New York: Berghan Books, 2015.

Blockmans, Wim, Mikhail Krom, and Justyna Wubs-Mrozewicz. "Maritime Trade Around Europe 1300–1600: Commercial Networks and Urban Autonomy." In *The Routledge Handbook of Maritime Trade around Europe 1300–1600*, edited by Wim Blockman, Mikhail Krom, and Justyna Wubs-Mrozewicz, 1–35. New York: Routledge, 2017.

Blomkvist, Nils. *The Discovery of the Baltic: The Reception of Catholic World-System in the European North*. Boston: Brill, 2005.

Bloom, Jonathan. "Paper and Printing." In *Silk Roads: People, Cultures, Landscapes*, edited by Susan Whitfield, 331–338. Oakland: University of California Press, 2019.

Bloom, Jonathan, and Sheila A. Blair. *Islam: A Thousand Years of Faith and Power*. New Haven: Yale University Press, 2002.

Boardman, John. "Greek Art and Architecture." In *The Oxford History of Greece and the Hellenistic World*, edited by John Boardman, Jasper Griffin, and Oswyn Murray, 330–360. Oxford: Oxford University Press, 2001.

Boatwright, Mary T. *Hadrian and the Cities of the Roman Empire*. Princeton: Princeton University Press, 2000.

Bobrick, Benson. *The Caliphs' Splendor: Islam and the West in the Golden Age of Baghdad*. New York: Simon and Schuster, 2012.

Bockmann, Ralph. "African Rome: The City of Carthage from Its Roman Re-foundation to the End of the Byzantine Period." In *A Companion to North Africa in Antiquity*, edited by R. Bruce Hitchner, 119–141. Hoboken: Wiley Blackwell, 2022.

Bodde, Derk. "The State and Empire of Ch'in." In *The Cambridge History of China: Volume I, The Ch'in and Han Empires*, edited by Denis Twitchett and John K. Fairbank, 20–102. Cambridge: Cambridge University Press, 1986.

Boehm, Ryan. *City and Empire in the Age of Successors: Urbanization and Social Response in the Making of Hellenistic Kingdoms*. Oakland: University of California Press, 2018.

Bogucka, Maria. "Amsterdam and the Baltic in the First Half of the Seventeenth Century." In *Baltic Commerce and Urban Society, 1500–1700*, edited by Maria Bogucka, 433–447. Brookfield: Ashgate, 2003.

"Dutch Merchants' Activities in Gdansk in the First Half of the 17th Century." in *Baltic Commerce and Urban Society, 1500–1700*, edited by Maria Bogucka, 19–32. Brookfield: Ashgate, 2003.

Boltz, William G. "Language and Writing." In *The Cambridge History of Ancient China: From the Origins of Civilization to 221 B.C.*, edited by Michael Loewe and Edward L. Shaughnessy, 74–123. Cambridge: Cambridge University Press, 1999.

Bonner, Michael. "The Waning of Empire, 861–945." In *The New Cambridge History of Islam: The Formation of the Islamic World, Sixth to Eleventh Centuries*, edited by Chase F. Robinson, 305–359. Cambridge: Cambridge University Press, 2010.

Boone, Marc, and Maarten Prak. "Rulers, Patricians and Burghers: The Great and Little Traditions of Urban Revolt in the Low Countries." In *A Miracle Mirrored: The Dutch Republic in European Perspective*, edited by Karel Davids and Jan Lucassen, 99–134. Cambridge: Cambridge University Press, 1995.

Bosman, Lex. "Government Buildings in the Dutch Colonies (Seventeenth and Eighteenth Centuries)." In *Public Buildings in Early Modern Europe*, edited by Konrad Ottenheym, Krista de Jonge, and Monique Chatenet, 119–130. Turnhout: Brepols, 2010.

Bossuyt, Audrey, Laurence Broze, and Victor Ginsburgh. "On Invisible Trade Relations between Mesopotamian Cities during the Third Millennium B.C." *The Professional Geographer* 53, no. 3 (2001), 374–383.

Bowman, Alan, and Andrew Wilson. "Introduction." In *Settlement, Urbanization, and Population*, edited by Alan Bowman and Andrew Wilson, 1–14. Oxford: Oxford University Press, 2012.

Boxer, C. R. *The Dutch Seaborne Empire 1680–1800*. London: Hutchinson, 1965.

Bracey, Robert. "Money and Mints." in *Silk Roads: People, Cultures, Landscapes*, edited by Susan Whitfield, 303–309. Oakland: University of California Press, 2019.

Brandon, Pepijn. "The Armed Forces." In *The Cambridge Companion to the Dutch Golden Age*, edited by Helmer J. Helmers and Geert H. Janssen, 69–85. Cambridge: Cambridge University Press, 2018.

Braswell, Geoffrey E. "Introduction: Reinterpreting Early Classic Interaction." In *The Maya and Teotihuacan: Reinterpreting Early Classic Interaction*, edited by Geoffrey E. Braswell, 1–43. Austin: University of Texas Press, 2004.

Braudel, Fernand. *The Mediterranean: And the Mediterranean World in the Age of Phillip II Volume I*. Berkeley: University of California Press, 1995.

The Mediterranean: And the Mediterranean World in the Age of Phillip II Volume II. Berkeley: University of California Press, 1995.

The Wheels of Commerce. Berkeley: University of California Press, 1992.

Brenner, Neil, and Christian Schmid. "Planetary Urbanization." In *Urban Constellations*, edited by Mathew Gandy, 10–13. Berlin: Jovis, 2012.

Bresson, Alain. *The Making of the Ancient Greek Economy: Institutions, Markets, and Growth in the City-States*. Princeton: Princeton University Press, 2016.

Brown, Oli. "How Russia's War in Ukraine Is Threatening Climate Security," Chatham House. Available at www.chathamhouse.org/2023/03/how-russias-war-ukraine-threatening-climate-security, last accessed July 7, 2023.

Bruijin, Jaap R. "Productivity, Profitability, and Costs of Private and Corporate Dutch Ship Owning in the Seventeenth and Eighteenth Centuries." In *The Rise of Merchant Empires: Long Distance Trade in the Early Modern World, 1350–1750*, edited by James D. Tracy, 174–194. Cambridge: Cambridge University Press, 1990.

Bulliet, Richard W. *The Camel and the Wheel*. New York: Columbia University Press, 1990.

Burckhardt, Jacob. *The Civilization of the Renaissance in Italy*. New York: Penguin, 1990.

Burke, Peter. *The Italian Renaissance: Culture and Society in Italy*. Princeton: Princeton University Press, 2014.

Venice and Amsterdam: A Study of Seventeenth Century Elites. Cambridge: Polity, 1994.

Burke III, Edmund. "Islam at the Center: Technological Complexes and the Roots of Modernity." *Journal of World History* 20, no. 2 (2009), 165–185.

Burkhardt, Mike. "*Kontors* and Outposts." In *A Companion to the Hanseatic League*, edited by Donald J. Harreld, 127–161. Boston: Brill, 2015.

"Networks as Social Structures in Late Medieval and Early Modern Towns: A Theoretical Approach to Historical Network Analysis." In *Commercial Networks and European Cities, 1400–1800*, edited by Andrea Caracausi and Christof Jeggle, 13–44. London: Pickering and Chatto, 2014.

Burns, Thomas S. *Rome and the Barbarians: 100 BC–AD 400*. Baltimore: The Johns Hopkins University Press, 2003.

Caesar, Julius. *The War for Gaul*. Princeton: Princeton University Press, 2019.

Calabi, Donatella, and Derek Keene. "Merchants' Lodgings and Cultural Exchange." In *Cultural Exchange in Early Modern Europe, Volume II: Cities and Cultural Exchange in Europe 1400–1700*, edited by Donatella Calabi and Stephen Turk Christensen, 315–348. Cambridge: Cambridge University Press, 2007.

Campopiano, Michael. "State, Land Tax and Agriculture in Iraq from the Arab Conquest to the Crisis on the Abbasid Caliphate." *Studia Islamica* 3 (2012), 5–50.

Capponi, Livia. "The *Oikos* of Alexandria." In *Ancient Alexandria between Egypt and Greece*, edited by W. V. Harris and Giovanni Ruffini, 115–124. Boston: Brill, 2004.

Caracausi, Andrea, and Christof Jeggle (eds.). *Commercial Networks and European Cities, 1400–1800*. London: Pickering and Chatto, 2014.

Carrasco, David. *The Aztecs: A Very Short Introduction*. Oxford: Oxford University Press, 2012.

Cassis, Youssef. *Capitals of Capital: A History of International Financial Centers, 1780–2005*. Cambridge: Cambridge University Press, 2006.

Castells, Manuel. "Nothing New under the Sun?" In *Connectivity in Antiquity: Globalization as a Long-Term Historical Process*, edited by Øystein S. LaBianca and Arnold Scham, 158–167. London: Equinox, 2006.

The Rise of the Network Society (Oxford: Blackwell, 2000).

"The Space of Flows." In *The Castells Reader on Cities and Social Theory*, edited by Ida Susser, 314–366. Oxford: Blackwell, 2002.

Castells, Manuel, and Pekka Himanen. "Models of Development in the Global Information Age: Constructing an Analytical Framework." In *Reconceptualizing Development in the Global Information Age*, edited by Manuel Castells and Pekka Himanen, 7–25. Oxford: Oxford University Press, 2014.

Chambers, David, and Brian Pullan (eds.). *Venice: A Documentary History, 1450–1630*. Toronto: University of Toronto Press, 2001.

Chaudhuri, K. N. *Trade and Civilisation in the Indian Ocean: An Economic History from the Rise of Islam to 1750*. Cambridge: Cambridge University Press, 1985.

Chavalas, Mark W. (ed.). *The Ancient Near East: Historic Sources in Translation*. Oxford: Blackwell Publishing, 2006.

Chávez, Sergio Gómez, and Michael W. Spence. "Interaction among the Complex Societies of Pre Classic Period Mesoamerica." In *The Oxford Handbook of the Aztecs*, edited by Deborah L. Nichols and Enrique Rodriguez-Alegría, 283–297. Oxford: Oxford University Press, 2017.

Cherry, David. *Frontier and Society in Roman North Africa*. Oxford: Oxford University Press, 1998.

Childe, V. Gordon. "The Urban Revolution." *Town Planning Review* 12, no. 1 (1950), 3–17.

Chittolini, Giorgio. "Cities, 'City-States,' and Regional States in North-Central Italy." *Theory and Society* 18, no. 5 (1989), 689–706.

Christensen, Aksel E. *Dutch Trade to the Baltic about 1600*. Copenhagen: Munksgaard, 1941.

Ch'ü, T'ung-tsu. *Han Social Structure*. Seattle: University of Washington Press, 1972.

Clancy, Flora Simmons. "Public Spaces in the Ancient Maya City." In *Maya Imagery, Architecture, and Activity*, edited by Maline D. Werness-Rude and Kaylee R. Spencer, 210–220. Albuquerque: University of New Mexico Press, 2015.

Clark, Greg. *Global Cities: A Short History*. Washington, DC: Brookings Institute, 2016.

Cobb, Paul M. "The Empire in Syria, 705–763." In *The New Cambridge History of Islam: The Formation of the Islamic World, Sixth to Eleventh Centuries*, edited by Chase F. Robinson, 226–267. Cambridge: Cambridge University Press, 2010.

Cohen, Raymond, and Raymond Westbrook. "Introduction: The Amarna System." In *Amarna Diplomacy: The Beginnings of International Relations*, edited by Raymond Cohen and Raymond Westbrook, 1–14. Baltimore: The Johns Hopkins University Press, 1992.

Coleman, Edward. "Cities and Communes." In *Italy in the Central Middle Ages 1000–1300*, edited by David Abulafia, 27–57. Oxford: Oxford University Press, 2004.

Confucius. *The Analects*. Oxford: Oxford University Press, 2008.

Cornell, Tim J. "The City-States in Latium." In *A Comparative Study of Thirty City-State Cultures*, edited by Mogens Herman Hansen, 207–228. Copenhagen: The Royal Danish Academy of Arts and Letters, 2000.

Cortés, Hernán. *Letters from Mexico*. New York: Grossman Publishers, 1971.

Cosmo, Nicola di. *Ancient China and Its Enemies: The Rise of Nomadic Power in East Asian History*. Cambridge: Cambridge University Press, 2004.

Cotterell, Arthur. *The Imperial Capitals of China: A Dynastic History of the Celestial Empire*. New York: Overlook Press, 2008.

Cowgill, George L. *Ancient Teotihuacan: Early Urbanism in Central Mexico*. Cambridge: Cambridge University Press, 2015.

"State and Society at Teotihuacan, Mexico." *Annual Review of Anthropology* 26 (1997), 129–161.

de Crispigny, Rafe. *Fire over Luoyang: A History of the Later Han Dynasty 23–220 AD*. Boston: Brill, 2016.

Crone, Patricia. *God's Rule: Government and Islam*. New York: Columbia University Press, 2004.

Meccan Trade and the Rise of Islam. Princeton: Princeton University Press, 1987.

Crouzet-Pavan, Elisabeth. "Venice and Its Surroundings." In *A Companion to Venetian History*, edited by Eric R. Dursteler, 25–84. Boston: Brill, 2013.

Crowley, Roger. *City of Fortune: How Venice Ruled the Seas*. New York: Random House, 2011.

Culham, Phyllis. "Woman in the Roman Republic." In *The Cambridge Companion to the Roman Republic*, edited by Harriet I. Flower, 127–148. Cambridge: Cambridge University Press, 2004.
Cunliffe, Barry. *Greeks, Romans, and Barbarians: Spheres of Interaction*. London: Batsford, 1988.
Curtin, Philip D. *Cross Cultural Trade in World History*. Cambridge: Cambridge University Press, 1984.
Cyphers, Ann. "The Early Preclassic Olmec: An Overview." In *The Origins of Maya States*, edited by Loa P. Traxler and Robert J. Sharer, 83–120. Philadelphia: University of Pennsylvania Press, 2016.
Dalley, Stephanie (ed.). *Myths from Mesopotamia*. Oxford: Oxford University Press, 2008.
Daniel, Elton L. *The Political and Social History of Khurasan under Abbasid Rule*. Chicago: Bibliotheca Islamica, 1979.
Daryaee, Touraj. "Great Empires of the Silk Roads." In *Silk Roads: People, Cultures, Landscapes*, edited by Susan Whitfield, 294–301. Oakland: University of California Press, 2019.
Davids, Karel, and Jan Lucassen. "Introduction." In *A Miracle Mirrored: The Dutch Republic in European Perspective*, edited by Karel Davids and Jan Lucassen, 1–25. Cambridge: Cambridge University Press, 1995.
Davies, John K. "Hellenistic Economies in the Post-Finley Era." In *Hellenistic Economies*, edited by Zofia Archibald, John Davies, Vincent Gabrielsen, and G. J. Oliver, 11–62. New York: Routledge, 2001.
Davis, Robert, C. *Shipbuilders of the Venetian Arsenal: Workers and Workplace in the Pre-Industrial City*. Baltimore: Johns Hopkins University Press, 2007.
Demarest, Arthur. *Ancient Maya: The Rise and Fall of a Rainforest Civilization*. Cambridge: Cambridge University Press, 2004.
"The Collapse of the Classic Maya Kingdoms of the Southwestern Petén: Implications for the End of Classic Maya Civilization." In *Millenary Maya Societies: Past Crises and Resilience*, edited by Charlotte Arnauld and Alain Breton, 22–48. Electronic document. Available at www.mesoweb.com/publications/MMS/2_Demarest.pdf, last accessed Janaury 2, 2024.
Deng, Gang. *The Premodern Chinese Economy: Structural Equilibrium and Capitalist Sterility*. New York: Routledge, 1999.
Denoix, Sylvie. "Founded Cities of the Arab World from the Seventh to the Eleventh Centuries." In *The City in the Islamic World*, edited by Salma K. Jayyusi, 115–139. Boston: Brill, 2008.
Desmond, Matthew. *Evicted: Poverty and Profit in the American City*. New York: Penguin, 2016.
van Deursen, A. T. *Plain Lives in a Golden Age: Popular Culture, Religion and Society in Seventeenth Century Holland*. Cambridge: Cambridge University Press, 1991.
Diamond, Jared. *Collapse: How Societies Choose to Fail or Succeed*. New York: Penguin, 2011.
Díaz del Castillo, Bernal. *The History of the Conquest of New Spain*. Albuquerque: University of New Mexico Press, 2008.
Dillon, Brian Dervin. "Aquí Nació El Mundo: Takalik Abaj and Early Mesoamerican Civilization." In *Fanning the Sacred Flame: Mesoamerican Studies in Honor of H. B. Nicholson*, edited by Matthew A. Boxt, Brian B. Dillon, and David Carrasco, 93–136. Louisville: University of Colorado Press, 2012.

Dinsmoor, William Bell. *The Architecture of Ancient Greece*. New York: W. W. Norton, 1975.
Dio, Cassius. *Roman History*. London: Loeb Classical Library, 1917.
Diodorus, *The Library of History*. Cambridge: Loeb Classical Library, 1947.
Dollinger, Phillipe. *The German Hanse*. New York: Routledge, 1999.
Donner, Fred M. "Muhammad and the Caliphate: Political History of the Islamic Empire up to the Mongol Conquest." In *The Oxford History of Islam*, edited by John L. Esposito, 1–61. Oxford: Oxford University Press, 1999.
Drennan, Robert D. "Long Distance Transport Costs in Pre-Hispanic Mesoamerica." *American Anthropologist* 86, no. 1 (1984), 105–112.
Dufton, J. Andrew, and Elizabeth Fentress. "Roman North African Urbanism." In *A Companion to North Africa in Antiquity*, edited by R. Bruce Hitchner, 173–201. Hoboken: Wiley Blackwell, 2022.
Edensor, Tim, and Mark Jayne. "Urban Theory beyond the West." In *Urban Theory beyond the West: A World of Cities*, edited by Tim Edensor and Mark Jayne, 1–27. London: Routledge, 2012.
Egger, Vernon O. *A History of the Muslim World to 1750*. New York: Routledge, 2018.
El Cheikh, Nadia Maria. *Women, Islam, and Abbasid Identity*. Cambridge: Harvard University Press, 2015.
Elson, Christina. "Cultural Evolution in the Southern Highlands of Mexico: From the Emergence of Social Inequality and Urban Society to the Decline of Classic-Period States." In *The Oxford Handbook of Mesoamerican Archeology*, edited by Deborah L. Nichols, 231–244. Oxford: Oxford University Press, 2012.
Emmer, P. C. *The Dutch Slave Trade, 1500–1850*. New York: Berghan Books, 2006.
"The Rise and Decline of the Dutch Atlantic." In *Dutch Atlantic Connections, 1680–1800: Linking Empires, Bridging Borders*, edited by Gert Oostindie and Jessica V. Roitman, 339–356. Leiden: Brill, 2014.
Engels, Friedrich. *Condition of the Working Class in England*. Moscow: Institute of Marxism-Leninism, 1969.
Origins of the Family, Private Property, and the State, chap. V. Available at www.marxists.org/archive/marx/works/1884/origin-family/, last accessed February 13, 2024.
Englehardt, Joshua D., and Michael D. Carrasco. "New Perspectives on Interregional Interaction in Ancient Mesoamerica." In *New Perspectives on Interregional Interaction in Ancient Mesoamerica*, edited by Joshua D. Englehardt, 3–33. Louisville: University of Colorado Press, 2019.
Epstein, Steven A. *Genoa and the Genoese, 958–1528*. Chapel Hill: University of North Carolina Press, 1996.
Epstein, S. R. "Introduction: Town and Country in Europe, 1300–1800." In *Town and Country in Europe, 1300–1800*, edited by S. R. Epstein, 1–29. Cambridge: Cambridge University Press, 2001.
"The Rise and Fall of Italian City-States." In *A Comparative Study of Thirty City-State Cultures*, edited by Mogens Herman Hansen, 277–293. Copenhagen: The Royal Danish Academy of Arts and Letters, 2000.
"Town and Country: Economy and Institutions in Late Medieval Italy." *Economic History Review* 46, no. 3 (1993), 453–477.

Erdkamp, Paul. "Seasonal Labour and Rural–Urban Migration in Roman Italy." In *Migration and Mobility in the Early Roman Empire*, edited by Luuk de Ligt and Laurens E. Tacoma, 33–49. Boston: Brill, 2016.

Errington, R. Malcolm. *A History of the Hellenistic World: 323–30 BC*. Oxford: Blackwell Publishing, 2008.

Ersland, Geir Atle. "Bergen 1300–1600: A Trading Hub between the North and the Baltic Sea." In *The Routledge Handbook of Maritime Trade around Europe 1300–1600*, edited by Wim Blockmans, Mikhail Krom, and Justyna Wubs-Mrozewicz, 428–445. New York: Routledge, 2017.

Estrada-Belli, Francisco. "Regional and Interregional Interactions and the Preclassic Maya." In *The Origins of Maya States*, edited by Loa P. Traxler and Robert J. Sharer, 225–269. Philadelphia: University of Pennsylvania Press, 2016.

Ettinghausen, Richard, Oleg Grabar, and Marilyn Jenkins-Madina. *Islamic Art and Architecture: 650–1250*. New York: Penguin, 2001.

Ewert, Ulf Christian, and Stephan Selzer. *Institutions of Hanseatic Trade: Studies on the Political Economy of a Medieval Network Organization*. Frankfurt: Peter Lang, 2016.

"Social Networks." In *Companion to the Hanseatic League*, edited by Donald J. Harreld, 162–193. Boston: Brill, 2015.

Fargher, Lane F., Richard E. Blanton, and Verenice Heredia Espinoza. "Aztec State-Making, Politics, and Empires: The Triple Alliance." In *The Oxford Handbook of the Aztecs*, edited by Deborah L. Nichols and Enrique Rodriguez-Alegría, 143–160. Oxford: Oxford University Press, 2017.

Fatah-Black, Karwan. "Paramaribo as Dutch and Atlantic Nodal Point, 1650–1795." In *Dutch Atlantic Connections, 1680–1800: Linking Empires, Bridging Borders*, edited by Gert Oostindie and Jessica V. Roitman, 52–71. Leiden: Brill, 2014.

Favro, Diane. "Making Rome a World City." In *The Cambridge Companion to the Age of Augustus*, edited by Karl Galinsky, 234–263. Cambridge: Cambridge University Press, 2005.

The Urban Image of Augustan Rome. Cambridge: Cambridge University Press, 1996.

Feng, Jiren. *Chinese Architecture and Metaphor: Song Culture in the Yingzao Fashi Building Manual*. Honolulu: University of Hawaii Press, 2012.

Feng, Linda Rui. *City of Marvel and Transformation*. Honolulu: University of Hawaii Press, 2015.

Finlay, Robert. "Crisis and Crusade in the Mediterranean: Venice, Portugal, and the Cape Route to India (1498–1509)." *Studi Veniziani* 28 (1994), 45–90.

Finley, M. I. "The Ancient City: From Fustel de Coulanges to Max Weber and Beyond." In *Economy and Society in Ancient Greece*, edited by Brian D. Shaw and Richard P. Saller, 2–23. London: Chatto and Windus, 1981.

The Ancient Economy. Berkeley: University of California Press, 1999.

Firth, Richard, and Mary-Louise Nosch. "Spinning and Weaving Wool in Ur III Administrative Texts." *Journal of Cuneiform Studies* 64 (2012), 65–82.

Fiscal Policy Institute. *Working for a Better Life: A Profile of Immigrants in the New York State Economy*. New York: Fiscal Policy Institute, 2007.

Foias, Antonia E., and Kitty F. Emery. "Politics and Economics: Theoretical Perspectives of the Motul de San José Project." In *Motul de San José: Politics,*

History, and Economy in a Classic Maya Polity, edited by Antonia E. Foias and Kitty F. Emery, 1–29. Gainesville: University of Florida Press, 2012.
Forrest, George. "Greece: The History of the Archaic Period." In *The Oxford History of Greece and the Hellenistic World*, edited by John Boardman, Jasper Griffin, and Oswyn Murray, 13–46. Oxford: Oxford University Press, 2001.
Foster, Lynn V. *Handbook to Life in the Ancient Maya World.* New York: Facts on File, 2002.
Francovich, Riccardo. "Changing Structures of Settlements." In *Italy in the Early Middle Ages 476–1000*, edited by Christina La Rocca, 144–167. Oxford: Oxford University Press, 2002.
Frankfort, Henri. *The Birth of Civilization in the Near East.* London: Ernest Benn, 1951.
Frankopan, Peter. *The Silk Roads: A New History of the World.* New York: Vintage, 2015.
Fraser, P. M. *The Cities of Alexander the Great.* Oxford: Oxford University Press, 1996.
Ptolemaic Alexandria: I. Oxford: Oxford University Press, 1972.
Friedmann, John. *Planning in the Public Domain: From Knowledge to Action.* Princeton: Princeton University Press, 1987.
The Prospect of Cities. Minneapolis: University of Minnesota Press, 2002.
"The World City Hypothesis." *Development and Change* 17, no. 1 (1986), 69–83.
Friedmann, John, and Goetz Wolff. "World City Formation: An Agenda for Research and Action." *International Journal for Urban and Regional Research* 6, no. 3 (1982), 309–344.
Frontinus. *Complete Works of Frontinus.* Hastings: Delphi, 2015.
Gabriele, Matthew, and David M. Perry. *The Bright Ages: A New History of Medieval Europe.* New York: Harper Collins, 2021.
Gabrielsen, Vincent. "Piracy and the Slave Trade." In *A Companion to the Hellenistic World*, edited by Andrew Erskine, 389–404. Oxford: Blackwell Publishing, 2003.
"The Rhodian Associations and Economic Activity." In *Hellenistic Economies*, edited by Zofia Archibald, John Davies, Vincent Gabrielsen, and G. J. Oliver, 215–244. New York: Routledge, 2001.
Gaimster, David. "A Parallel History: The Archeology of Hanseatic Urban Culture in the Baltic c. 1200–1600." *World Archeology* 37, no. 3 (2005), 408–423.
Garland, Robert. *Daily Life of the Ancient Greeks.* Indianapolis: Hackett, 1998.
Garnsey, Peter, and Richard Saller. *The Roman Empire: Economy, Society, and Culture*, 2nd ed. Oakland: University of California Press, 2015.
Gaspari, Stefano. "The Aristocracy." In *Italy in the Early Middle Ages 476–1000*, edited by Christina La Rocca, 59–84. Oxford: Oxford University Press, 2002.
Gasparini, Mariachiara. *Transcending Patterns: Silk Road Cultural and Artistic Interactions through Central Asian Textile Images.* Honolulu: University of Hawaii Press, 2020.
Gelderblom, Oscar. *Cities of Commerce: The Institutional Foundations of the Low Countries, 1250–1650.* Princeton: Princeton University Press, 2013.
Gelichi, Sauro. "The Cities." In *Italy in the Early Middle Ages 476–1000*, edited by Christina La Rocca, 168–188. Oxford: Oxford University Press, 2002.
Gibbons, David. "Shipwrecks and Hellenistic Trade." In *Hellenistic Economies*, edited by Zofia Archibald, John Davies, Vincent Gabrielsen, and G. J. Oliver, 273–312. New York: Routledge, 2001.

Glassman, Ronald, M. *The Origins of Democracy in Tribes, City States and Nation-States*. Cham, Switzerland: Springer, 2017.
Globalization and World Cities Research Network. "The World According to GaWC" (November 13, 2018). Available at www.lboro.ac.uk/gawc/world2018t.html, last accessed February 12, 2020.
Gorse, George L. "Architecture and Urban Topography." In *A Companion to Medieval Genoa*, edited by Carrie L. Beneš, 218–292. Boston: Brill, 2018.
Grainger, John D. *Great Power Diplomacy in the Hellenistic World*. New York: Routledge, 2017.
The Greek Alexander Romance. New York: Penguin, 1991.
Green, Peter. *Alexander to Actium: The Historic Evolution of the Hellenistic Age*. Berkeley: University of California Press, 1990.
The Hellenistic Age: A Short History. New York: Modern Library, 2008.
Griffin, Jasper. "Introduction." In *The Oxford History of Greece and the Hellenistic World*, edited by John Boardman, Jasper Griffin, and Oswyn Murray, 1–12. Oxford: Oxford University Press, 2001.
van Groesen, Michiel. "Global Trade." In *The Cambridge Companion to the Dutch Golden Age*, edited by Helmer J. Helmers and Geert H. Janssen, 168–185. Cambridge: Cambridge University Press, 2018.
Grube, Nikolai. "The City-States of the Maya." In *A Comparative Study of Thirty City-State Cultures*, edited by Mogens Herman Hansen, 547–565. Copenhagen: The Royal Danish Academy of Arts and Letters, 2000.
von Grunebaum, G. E. *Classical Islam: A History 600–1258*. New York: Barnes and Noble, 1996.
Guo, Qinghua. "Yingzao Fashi: Twelfth Century Chinese Building Manual." *Architectural History* 41, no. 1 (1998), 1–13.
Haddon, Rosalind Wade. "Ceramics from Mesopotamia to China." In *Silk Roads: People, Cultures, Landscapes*, edited by Susan Whitfield, 338–346. Oakland: University of California Press, 2019.
Hall, Peter. *Cities in Civilization*. New York: Pantheon, 1998.
"The Metropolitan Explosion." In *The Global Cities Reader*, edited by Neil Brenner and Roger Keil, 23–24. London: Routledge, 2006.
Hallegate, Stephane, Colin Green, Robert Nicholls, and Jan Corfee-Morlot. "Future Flood Losses in Major Coastal Cities." *Nature Climate Change* 3 (2013), 802–806.
Hammel-Kiesow, Rolf. "The Early Hanses." In *A Companion to the Hanseatic League*, edited by Donald J. Harreld, 15–63. Boston: Brill, 2015.
Hammurabi, *The Code of Hammurabi*, trans. L. W. King (1915).
Hansen, Mogens Herman. "Attika." In *A Comparative Study of Thirty City-State Cultures*, edited by Mogens Herman Hansen, 624–639. Copenhagen: The Royal Danish Academy of Arts and Letters, 2000.
"The Concepts of City-State and City-State Culture." In *A Comparative Study of Thirty City-State Cultures*, edited by Mogens Herman Hansen, 11–34. Copenhagen: The Royal Danish Academy of Arts and Letters, 2000.
"The Hellenistic *Polis*." In *A Comparative Study of Thirty City-State Cultures*, edited by Mogens Herman Hansen, 141–187. Copenhagen: The Royal Danish Academy of Arts and Letters, 2000.

"The Impact of City-State Cultures in World History." In *A Comparative Study of Thirty City-State Cultures*, edited by Mogens Herman Hansen, 597–623. Copenhagen: The Royal Danish Academy of Arts and Letters, 2000.

"Introduction." In *A Comparative Study of Six City-State Cultures*, edited by Mogens Herman Hansen, 7–21. Copenhagen: The Royal Danish Academy of Arts and Letters, 2002.

Hansen, Mogens Herman, and Thomas Heine Nielsen. *An Inventory of Archaic and Classical Poleis*. Oxford: Oxford University Press, 2004.

Hansen, Valerie. *The Silk Road: A New History*. Oxford: Oxford University Press, 2012.

Harrison, Peter D. *The Lords of Tikal: Rulers of an Ancient Maya City*. New York: Thames, 1999.

Hartnett, Jeremy. *The Roman Street: Urban Life and Society in Pompeii, Herculaneum, and Rome*. Cambridge: Cambridge University Press, 2017.

Hassan, Mona. *Longing for the Lost Caliphate*. Princeton: Princeton University Press, 2016.

den Heijer, Henk. "A Public and Private Dutch West India Interest." In *Dutch Atlantic Connections, 1680–1800: Linking Empires, Bridging Borders*, edited by Gert Oostindie and Jessica V. Roitman, 159–182. Leiden: Brill, 2014.

Held, David, Anthony McGrew, David Goldblatt, and Jonathan Perraton. *Global Transformations: Politics, Economics, and Culture*. Stanford: Stanford University Press, 1999.

Helmold of Bosau. *Chronica Slavorum*, Book I. Ann Arbor: University of Michigan Press, 1935.

Herodotus. *The Histories*. New York: Penguin, 2003.

van den Heuvel, Charles. "Multilayered Grids and Dutch Town Planning. Flexibility and Temporality in the Design of Settlements in the Low Countries and Overseas." In *Early Modern Urbanism and the Grid: Town Planning in the Low Countries in International Context, Exchanges in Theory and Practice 1550–1800*, edited by Piet Lombaerde and Charles van den Heuvel, 27–44. Turnhout: Brepols, 2011.

van den Heuvel, Danielle. "A Market Economy." In *The Cambridge Companion to the Dutch Golden Age*, edited by Helmer J. Helmers and Geert H. Janssen, 149–165. Cambridge: Cambridge University Press, 2018.

Hillenbrand, Robert. *Islamic Art and Architecture*. New York: Thames and Hudson, 1999.

Hin, Saskia. "Population." In *The Cambridge Companion to the Roman Republic*, edited by Harriet I. Flower, 149–166. Cambridge: Cambridge University Press, 2004.

Hinge, George. "Language and Race: Theocritus and the Koine Identity of Ptolemaic Egypt." In *Alexandria: A Cultural and Religious Melting Pot*, edited by George Hinge and Jens A. Krasilnikoff, 66–79. Aarhus: Aarhus University Press, 2009.

Hirth, Kenneth G. *The Aztec Economic World: Merchants and Markets in Ancient Mesoamerica*. Cambridge: Cambridge University Press, 2016.

Hitti, Philip. *Capital Cities of Arab Islam*. Minneapolis: University of Minnesota Press, 1973.

Ho, Ping-ti. "The Loess and the Origin of Chinese Agriculture." *American Historical Review* 75, no. 1 (1969), 1–36.

Hodge, Mary G. *Aztec City-States*. Ann Arbor: University of Michigan Press, 1984.

Hodgson, Marshall G. S. *The Venture of Islam I: Conscience and History in a World Civilization, The Classical Age of Islam*. Chicago: University of Chicago Press, 1974.

The Venture of Islam II: The Expansion of Islam in the Middle Periods. Chicago: University of Chicago Press, 1974.
Hölkeskamp, Karl-Joachim. "Under Roman Roofs: Family, House, and Household." In *The Cambridge Companion to the Roman Republic*, edited by Harriet I. Flower, 101–126. Cambridge: Cambridge University Press, 2004.
Homer. *The Odyssey*. New York: Penguin, 1996.
Hopkins, A. G. "Globalization: An Agenda for Historians." In *Globalization in World History*, edited by A. G. Hopkins, 1–10. London: Pimlico, 2002.
Hopkins, Keith. *Conqueror and Slaves*. Cambridge: Cambridge University Press, 1978.
Hoppenbrouwers, Peter C. M. "Town and Country in Holland, 1300–1550." In *Town and Country in Europe, 1300–1800*, edited by S. R. Epstein, 54–79. Cambridge: Cambridge University Press, 2001.
Horden, Peregrine, and Nicholas Purcell. *The Corrupting Sea: A Study of Mediterranean History*. Oxford: Blackwell, 2000.
Howard, Deborah. *The Architectural History of Venice*. New Haven: Yale University Press, 2002.
Venice & the East: The Impact of the Islamic World on Venetian Architecture 1100–1500. New Haven: Yale University Press, 2000.
Hsu, Cho-yun. *Han Agriculture: The Formation of the Early Chinese Agrarian Economy*. Seattle: University of Washington Press, 1980.
Huigen, Siegfried. "Introduction." In *Dutch Trading Companies as Knowledge Networks*, edited by Siegfried Huigen, Jan L. de Jong, and Elmer Kolfin, 1–15. Boston: Brill, 2010.
Hung, Wu. "The Art and Architecture of the Warring States Period." In *The Cambridge History of Ancient China: From the Origins of Civilization to 221 B.C.*, edited by Michael Loewe and Edward L. Shaughnessy, 651–744. Cambridge: Cambridge University Press, 1999.
Hunt, Edwin S., and James M. Murray. *A History of Business in Medieval Europe, 1200–1550*. Cambridge: Cambridge University Press, 1999.
Infelise, Mario. "Book Publishing and the Circulation of Information." In *A Companion to Venetian History*, edited by Eric R. Dursteler, 652–674. Boston: Brill, 2013.
Interagency Group on Antimicrobial Resistance. *No Time to Wait: Securing the Future from Drug Resistant Infections*. New York: United Nations, 2019.
Intergovernmental Panel on Climate Change. *Special Report on the Ocean and Cryosphere in a Changing Climate*. New York: United Nations, 2019.
Isocrates. *The Panegyricus of Isocrates*. New Haven: Storer and Morehouse, 1851.
Israel, Jonathan I. *Dutch Primacy in World Trade*. Oxford: Oxford University Press, 1989.
The Dutch Republic: Its Rise, Greatness, and Fall 1477–1806. Oxford: Oxford University Press, 1995.
Jacobs, Jane. *The Economy of Cities*. New York: Vintage Books, 1969.
Jacobs, Martin. *Reorienting the East: Jewish Travelers to the Medieval Muslim World*. Philadelphia: University of Pennsylvania Press, 2014.
Jacobsen, Thorkild. "Primitive Democracy in Ancient Mesopotamia." *Journal of Near Eastern Studies* 2, no. 3 (1943), 159–172.
Jahnke, Carsten. "The Baltic Trade." In *A Companion to the Hanseatic League*, edited by Donald J. Harreld, 194–240. Boston: Brill, 2015.

"The City of Lübeck and the Internationality of Early Hanseatic Trade." In *The Hanse in Medieval and Early Modern Europe*, edited by Justyna Wubs-Mrozewicz and Stuart Jenks, 37–58. Boston: Brill, 2013.

"Lübeck and the Hanse: A Queen without Its Body." In *The Routledge Handbook of Maritime Trade around Europe 1300–1600*, edited by Wim Blockmans, Mikhail Krom, and Justyna Wubs-Mrozewicz, 231–247. New York: Routledge, 2017.

Janssen, Geert H. "Migration." In *The Cambridge Companion to the Dutch Golden Age*, edited by Helmer J. Helmers and Geert H. Janssen, 49–66. Cambridge: Cambridge University Press, 2018.

Jensen, Minna Skafte. "Homeric Scholarship in Alexandria." In *Alexandria: A Cultural and Religious Melting Pot*, edited by George Hinge and Jens A. Krasilnikoff, 80–93. Aarhus: Aarhus University Press, 2009.

Johanek, Peter. "Imperial and Free Towns of the Holy Roman Empire: City-States in Pre-Modern Germany?" In *A Comparative Study of Thirty City-State Cultures*, edited by Mogens Herman Hansen, 295–319. Copenhagen: The Royal Danish Academy of Arts and Letters, 2000.

Johns Hopkins Coronavirus Resource Center. "COVID-19 Map." Available at https://coronavirus.jhu.edu/map.html, last accessed August 19, 2020.

Jones, A. H. M. *The Greek City: From Alexander to Justinian*. Oxford: Oxford University Press, 1940.

Jones, Philip. *The Italian City-State: From Commune to Signoria*. Oxford: Oxford University Press, 1997.

Josephus, Flavius. *The Antiquities of the Jews*, book xii. Available at www.gutenberg.org/ebooks/2848, last accessed January 2, 2024.

Kasekamp, Andres. *A History of the Baltic States*. London: Palgrave, 2018.

Kay, Philip. *Rome's Economic Revolution*. Oxford: Oxford University Press, 2014.

Keay, John. *China: A History*. New York: Harper Collins, 2009.

Kehoe, Dennis P. "The Early Roman Empire: Production." In *The Cambridge Economic History of the Greco-Roman World*, edited by Walter Scheidel, Ian Morris, and Richard Saller, 543–591. Cambridge: Cambridge University Press, 2007.

Keightley, David N. "The Environment of Ancient China." In *The Cambridge History of Ancient China: From the Origins of Civilization to 221 B.C.*, edited by Michael Loewe and Edward L. Shaughnessy, 30–36. Cambridge: Cambridge University Press, 1999.

"The Late Shang State: When, Where, and What?" In *The Origins of Chinese Civilization*, edited by David N. Keightley, 523–564. Berkeley: University of California Press, 1983.

"The Shang: China's First Historical Dynasty." In *The Cambridge History of Ancient China: From the Origins of Civilization to 221 B.C.*, edited by Michael Loewe and Edward L. Shaughnessy, 232–291. Cambridge: Cambridge University Press, 1999.

Kellogg, Susan. "The Woman's Room: Some Aspects of Gender Relations in Tenochtitlan in the Late Pre-Hispanic Period." *Ethnohistory* 42, no. 4 (1995), 563–576.

Kennedy, Hugh. *Caliphate: The History of an Idea*. New York: Basic Books, 2016.

"Elite Incomes in the Early Islamic State." In *The Byzantine and Early Islamic Near East*, edited by John Haldon and Lawrence I. Conrad, 13–28. Berlin: Gerlach Press, 2021.

Kennedy, James C. *A Concise History of the Netherlands*. Cambridge: Cambridge University Press, 2017.
Keohane, Robert O., and Joseph S. Nye. *Power and Interdependence*. New York: Longman, 2011.
Khaldun, Ibn. *The Muqaddimah: An Introduction to History*. Princeton: Princeton University Press, 2015.
Kirby, David. *Northern Europe in the Early Modern Period: The Baltic World 1492–1772*. New York: Longman, 1990.
Kirby, David, and Merja-Liisa Hinkkanen. *The Baltic and the North Seas*. New York: Routledge, 2000.
Kleingärtner, Sunhild, and Gabriel Zeilinger (eds.). *Raumbildung Durch Netzwerke?* Bonn: Habelt, 2012.
Klooster, Wim. "Curaçao as a Transit Center to the Spanish Main and the French West Indies." In *Dutch Atlantic Connections, 1680–1800: Linking Empires, Bridging Borders*, edited by Gert Oostindie and Jessica V. Roitman, 25–51. Leiden: Brill, 2014.
Knapton, Michael. "The *Terraferma* State" In *A Companion to Venetian History*, edited by Eric R. Dursteler, 85–124. Boston: Brill, 2013.
Kolbert, Elizabeth. *The Sixth Extinction: An Unnatural History*. New York: Henry Holt, 2014.
Kron, Geoffrey. "Comparative Evidence and the Reconstruction of the Ancient Economy: Greco-Roman Housing and the Level and Distribution of Wealth and Income." In *Quantifying the Greco Roman Economy and Beyond*, edited by François de Callataÿ, 123–146. Bari: Edipuglia, 2014.
Krul, Matthijs. "Markets in Ancient Greece: The Challenge of the New Institutionalism." In *Reconstructing Karl Polanyi: Excavation and Critique*, edited by Gareth Dale, 178–201. London: Pluto Press, 2016.
Kuhrt, Amélie. *The Ancient Near East c. 3000–330 BC Vol. I*. New York: Routledge, 1995.
Labalme, Patricia H., and Laura Sanguineti White (eds.). *Venice, Cítà Excelentissima: Selections from the Renaissance Diaries of Marin Sanudo*. Baltimore: Johns Hopkins University Press, 2008.
Lambourne, Elizabeth. "Slavery and Servitude in the Indian Ocean." In *Silk Roads: People, Cultures, Landscapes*, edited by Susan Whitfield, 408–413. Oakland: University of California Press, 2019.
Lane, Fredric C. *Venice: A Maritime Republic*. Baltimore: Johns Hopkins University Press, 1973.
Lapidus, Ira M. *A History of Islamic Societies*. Cambridge: Cambridge University Press, 1988.
Muslim Cities in the Later Middle Ages. Cambridge: Cambridge University Press, 1967.
Laporte, Juan Pedro. "Architectural Aspects of Interaction between Tikal and Teotihuacan during the Early Classic Period." In *The Maya and Teotihuacan: Reinterpreting Early Classic Interaction*, edited by Geoffrey E. Braswell, 199–216. Austin: University of Texas Press, 2004.
Lassner, Jacob. *The Topography of Baghdad in the Early Middle Ages: Texts and Studies*. Detroit: Wayne University Press, 1970.

Lattimore, Owen. *Studies in Frontier History: Collected Papers 1928–1958*. Oxford: Oxford University Press, 1962.
Laurence, Ray, Simon Esmonde Cleary, and Gareth Sears. *The City in the Roman West c. 250 BC–c. AD 250*. Cambridge: Cambridge University Press, 2011.
Lavery, Jason. *Germany's Northern Challenge: The Holy Roman Empire and the Scandinavian Struggle for the Baltic, 1563–1576*. Boston: Brill, 2002.
Leick, Gwendolyn. *Mesopotamia: The Invention of the City*. New York: Penguin, 2001.
Leimus, Ivar, and Anu Mänd. "Reval (Tallinn): A City Emerging from Maritime Trade." In *The Routledge Handbook of Maritime Trade around Europe 1300–1600*, edited by Wim Blockmans, Mikhail Krom, and Justyna Wubs-Mrozewicz, 273–291. New York: Routledge, 2017.
Leon, Joshua K. "Global Cities at Any Cost: Resisting Municipal Mercantilism." *City* 21, no. 1 (2017), 1–21.
"The Role of Global Cities in Land Grabs." *Third World Quarterly* 36, no. 2 (2015), 257–273.
Lévi-Strauss, Claude. *Tristes Tropiques*. New York: Atheneum, 1964.
Levy, Thomas E. "Grand Narratives, Technological Revolutions and the Past: Deep Time Studies of Metallurgy and Social Evolution in the Eastern Mediterranean." In *Connectivity in Antiquity: Globalization as a Long-Term Historical Process*, edited by Øystein S. LaBianca and Arnold Scham, 10–25. London: Equinox, 2006.
Lewis, Mark Edward. *China's Cosmopolitan Empire: The Tang Dynasty*. Cambridge, MA: Harvard University Press, 2009.
"The City-State in Spring and Autumn China." In *A Comparative Study of Thirty City-State Cultures*, edited by Mogens Herman Hansen, 359–373. Copenhagen: The Royal Danish Academy of Arts and Letters, 2000.
The Construction of Space in Early China. Albany: State University of New York Press, 2006.
The Early Chinese Empires: Qin and Han. Cambridge, MA: Harvard University Press, 2007.
"Warring States in Political History." In *The Cambridge History of Ancient China: From the Origins of Civilization to 221 B.C.*, edited by Michael Loewe and Edward L. Shaughnessy, 587–650. Cambridge: Cambridge University Press, 1999.
Lindsay, James M. *Daily Life in the Medieval Islamic World*. Indianapolis: Hackett, 2008.
Liu, Xinru. *The Silk Road in World History*. Oxford: Oxford University Press, 2010.
Livy. *The History of Rome*. Cambridge: Harvard University Press, 1924.
Lloyd, T. H. *England and the German Hanse, 1157–1611*. Cambridge: Cambridge University Press, 1991.
Loewe, Michael. "The Former Han Dynasty." In *The Cambridge History of China: Volume I, The Ch'in and Han Empires*, edited by Denis Twitchett and John K. Fairbank, 103–222. Cambridge: Cambridge University Press, 1986.
"The Tombs Built for Han Chengdi and Migrations of the Population." In *Chang'an 26 BCE: An Augustan Age in China*, edited by Michael Nylan and Griet Vankeerberghen, 201–217. Seattle: University of Washington Press, 2015.
Lopez, Robert S. *The Commercial Revolution of the Middle Ages 950 to 1350*. Cambridge: Cambridge University Press, 1976.

Lopez, Robert S., and Irving W. Raymond. *Medieval Trade in the Mediterranean World: Illustrative Documents Translated with Introductions and Notes*. New York: Columbia University Press, 1967.
Love, Michael. "Early States in the Southern Maya Region." In *The Origins of Maya States*, edited by Loa P. Traxler and Robert J. Sharer, 271–327. Philadelphia: University of Pennsylvania Press, 2016.
Lu, Yang. "Managing Locality in Early Medieval China: Evidence from Changsha." In *Early Medieval China: A Sourcebook*, edited by Wendy Swartz, Robert Ford Campany, Yang Lu, and Jessey J. C. Choo, 95–107. New York: Columbia University Press, 2014.
Lucassen, Jan. "Labour and Early Modern Economic Development." In *A Miracle Mirrored: The Dutch Republic in European Perspective*, edited by Karel Davids and Jan Lucassen, 367–409. Cambridge: Cambridge University Press, 1995.
Mackintosh-Smith, Tim. *Arabs: A 3,000-Year History of People, Tribes and Empires*. New Haven: Yale University Press, 2019.
Madden, Thomas F. *Enrico Dandolo and the Rise of Venice*. Baltimore: Johns Hopkins University Press, 2003.
Venice: A New History. New York: Penguin, 2013.
Maglaque, Erin. *Venice's Intimate Empire: Family Life and Scholarship in the Renaissance Mediterranean*. Ithaca: Cornell University Press, 2018.
Mak, Geert. *Amsterdam*. Cambridge: Harvard University Press, 2000.
Malanima, Paolo. "The Italian Renaissance Economy (1250–1600)." International Conference at Villa La Pietra, Florence (May 2008).
"Italy in the Renaissance: A Leading Economy in the European Context, 1350–1550." *The Economic History Review* 71, no. 1 (2018), 3–30.
Mänd, Anu. *Urban Carnival: Festive Culture in the Hanseatic Cities of the Eastern Baltic*. Brepols: Turnhout, 2005.
Manning, Joseph G. "Hellenistic Egypt." In *The Cambridge Economic History of the Greco-Roman World*, edited by Walter Scheidel, Ian Morris, and Richard Saller, 434–483. Cambridge: Cambridge University Press, 2007.
Manzanilla, Linda R. "Neighborhoods and Elite 'Houses' at Teotihuacan, Central Mexico." In *The Neighborhood as a Social and Spatial Unit in Mesoamerican Cities*, edited by M. Charlotte Arnauld, Linda R. Manzanilla, and Michael E. Smith, 55–66. Tucson: University of Arizona Press, 2012.
Marcus, Joyce. "The Maya and Teotihuacan." In *The Maya and Teotihuacan: Reinterpreting Early Classic Interaction*, edited by Geoffrey E. Braswell, 337–355. Austin: University of Texas Press, 2004.
Marozzi, Justin. *Baghdad: City of Peace, City of Blood*. Boston: Da Capo, 2014.
Islamic Empires: The Cities that Shaped Civilizations from Mecca to Dubai. New York: Pegasus, 2019.
Marsh, James G., and Johann P. Olsen. "The Institutional Dynamics of International Political Orders." *International Organization* 52, no. 4 (1998), 943–969.
Martin, John, and Dennis Romano. *Venice Reconsidered: The History and Civilization of an Italian City-State 1297–1797*. Baltimore: Johns Hopkins University Press, 2000.
Martin, Thomas R. *Ancient Greece: From Prehistoric to Hellenistic Times*. New Haven: Yale University Press, 2000.

Martines, Lauro. *Power and Imagination: City-States in Renaissance Italy*. New York: Knopf, 1979.

McCormick, Michael. *Origins of the European Economy: Communications and Commerce, A.D. 300–900*. Cambridge: Cambridge University Press, 2001.

McCormick Adams, Robert. *Land behind Baghdad: A History of Settlement on the Diyala Plains*. Chicago: University of Chicago Press, 1965.

"Old Babylonian Networks of Urban Notables." *Cuneiform Digital Library Journal* 7 (2009), 1–14.

McKenzie, Judith. *The Architecture of Alexandria and Egypt, c. 300 BC to AD 700*. New Haven: Yale University Press, 2007.

McNeill, William H. *Venice: The Hinge of Europe 1081–1797*. Chicago: University of Chicago Press, 1974.

van Meeteren, Michiel, Ben Derudder, and David Bassens. "Can the Straw Man Speak? An Engagement with Postcolonial Critiques of 'Global Cities Research'." *Dialogues in Human Geography* 6, no. 3 (2016), 247–267.

Meeus, Alexander. "The Career of Sostratos of Knidos: Politics, Diplomacy and the Alexandrian Building Programme in the Early Hellenistic Period." In *Greece, Macedon, and Persia*, edited by Timothy Howe, E. Edward Garvin, and Graham Wrightson, 143–171. Oxford: Oxbow Books, 2015.

Mehta, Suketu. *This Land Is Our Land: An Immigrant's Manifesto*. New York: Farrar, Straus, and Giroux, 2019.

Micheau, François. "Baghdad in the Abbasid Era: A Cosmopolitan and Multi-confessional Capital." In *The City in the Islamic World*, edited by Salma K. Jayyusi, 221–245. Boston: Brill, 2008.

van de Mieroop, Marc. *The Ancient Mesopotamian City*. Oxford: Oxford University Press, 1999.

"Reading Babylon." *American Journal of Archeology* 107, no. 2 (2003), 257–275.

Miller, Mary Ellen. *Maya Art and Architecture*. New York: Thames and Hudson, 1999.

Miner, Jeffrey, and Stefan Stantchev. "The Genoese Economy." In *A Companion to Medieval Genoa*, edited by Carrie L. Beneš, 397–426. Boston: Brill, 2018.

Mithen, Steven. *Thirst: Water and Power in the Ancient World*. Cambridge: Harvard University Press, 2012.

Mizumoto, Kenji, Katsushi Kagaya, and Gerardo Chowell. "Effect of a Wet Market on Coronavirus Disease Transmission, 2019–2020." *International Journal of Infectious Diseases* 97 (2020), 96–101.

Mohanty, B. B. "'We Are Like the Living Dead': Farmer Suicides in Maharashtra." *Journal of Peasant Studies* 32, no. 2 (2005), 243–276.

Moholy-Nagy, Hattula. *Historical Archeology at Tikal, Guatemala*. Philadelphia: University of Pennsylvania Press, 2012.

Mollat, Michel, and Phillippe Wolff. *The Popular Revolutions of the Late Middle Ages*. London: George Allen & Unwin, 1973.

Mommsen, Theodore E. "Petrarch's Conception of the Dark Ages." *Speculum* 17, no. 2 (1942), 226–242.

Monsanto. "Monsanto Company Headquarters and Office Locations." Available at https://craft.co/monsanto-company/locations, last accessed August 19, 2020.

Montemezzo, Stefania. "Galley Routes and Merchant Networks between Venice and the North Sea in the Fifteenth Century." In *Commercial Networks and European Cities, 1400–1800*, edited by Andrea Caracausi and Christof Jeggle, 153–159. London: Pickering and Chatto, 2014.
Moraw, Peter. "Cities and Citizenry as Factors of State Formation in the Roman German Empire of the Late Middle Ages." In *Cities and the Rise of States in Europe, A.D. 1000 to 1800*, edited by Charles Tilly and Wim P. Blockmans, 100–127. Boulder: Westview Press, 1994.
Morley, Neville. "The Early Roman Empire: Distribution." In *The Cambridge Economic History of the Greco-Roman World*, edited by Walter Scheidel, Ian Morris, and Richard Saller, 570–591. Cambridge: Cambridge University Press, 2007.
"Globalization and the Roman Economy." In *Globalisation and the Roman World: World History, Connectivity, and Material Culture*, edited by Martin Pitts and Miguel John Versluys, 49–68. Cambridge: Cambridge University Press, 2015.
Mozejko, Beata. "Late Medieval Gdańsk as a Bridge between Regions." In *The Medieval Networks in East Central Europe: Commerce, Contacts, Communication*, edited by Balázs Nagy, Felicitas Schmieder, and András Vadas, 227–235. New York: Routledge, 2019.
Müller, Ulrich. "Network of Towns, Networks of Periphery?" In *Raumbildung Durch Netzwerke?* edited by Sunhild Kleingärtner and Gabriel Zeilinger, 55–77. Bonn: Habelt, 2012.
Mumford, Lewis. *The City in History: Its Origins, Its Transformations, and Its Prospects*. New York: Harcourt, Brace and World, 1961.
Mundy, Barbara. *The Death of Aztec Tenochtitlan, The Life of Mexico City*. Austin: University of Texas Press, 2015.
Muqaddasi. *The Best Divisions for Knowledge of the Regions*. Reading, UK: Centre for Muslim Contributions to Civilization, 1994.
Murray, James M. *Bruges, Cradle of Capitalism, 1280–1390*. Cambridge: Cambridge University Press, 2015.
"That Well-Grounded Error: Bruges as *Hansestadt*." In *The Hanse in Medieval and Early Modern Europe*, edited by Justyna Wubs-Mrozewicz and Stuart Jenks, 181–190. Boston: Brill, 2013.
Naegle, Gisela. "Revolts and Wars, Corporations, and Leagues." In *Routledge History Handbook of Medieval Revolt*, edited by Justine Firnhaber-Baker and Dirk Schoenaers, 236–264. New York: Routledge, 2017.
Nedkvitne, Arnved. *The German Hanse and Bergen 1100–1600*. Köln: Böhlau Verlag, 2014.
Nemet-Nejat, Karen Rhea. *Daily Life in Ancient Mesopotamia*. Westport, CT: Greenwood, 1998.
Newitz, Annalee. *Four Lost Cities: A History of the Urban Age*. New York: W. W. Norton, 2021.
Newton, Lynne S., and Juris Zarins. *Dhofar through the Ages: An Ecological, Archeological and Historical Landscape*. Oxford: Archeopress, 2019.
Nicholas, David. *The Growth of the Medieval City: From Late Antiquity to the Early Fourteenth Century*. New York: Longman, 1997.
The Northern Lands: Germanic Europe, c. 1270–c. 1500. Oxford: Wiley-Blackwell, 2009.

Nicolet, Claude. *Space, Geography, and Politics in the Early Roman Empire*. Ann Arbor: University of Michigan Press, 1991.

van Nierop, Henk. "Similar Problems, Different Outcomes: The Revolt of the Netherlands and the Wars of Religion in France." In *A Miracle Mirrored: The Dutch Republic in European Perspective*, edited by Karel Davids and Jan Lucassen, 26–56. Cambridge: Cambridge University Press, 1995.

Nimako, Kwame, and Glenn Willemsen. *The Dutch Atlantic: Slavery, Abolition, and Emancipation*. New York: Palgrave, 2011.

Nissen, Hans J. "Cultural and Political Networks in the Ancient Near East during the Fourth and Third Millennia B.C." In *Uruk Mesopotamia & Its Neighbors: Cross Cultural Interactions in the Era of State Formation*, edited by Mitchell S. Rothman, 149–180. Santa Fe: School of American Research Press, 2001.

Noordegraaf, Leo, and Jan Luiten van Zanden. "Early Modern Economic Growth and the Standard of Living: Did Labor Benefit from Holland's Golden Age." In *A Miracle Mirrored: The Dutch Republic in European Perspective*, edited by Karel Davids and Jan Lucassen, 410–437. Cambridge: Cambridge University Press, 1995.

Noreña, Carlos F. "Chang'an and Rome: Structural Parallels and Logics of Urban Form." In *State Power in Ancient China and Rome*, edited by Walter Scheidel, 75–98. Oxford: Oxford University Press, 2015.

"Urban Systems in the Han and Roman Empires: State Power and Social Control." In *State Power in Ancient China and Rome*, edited by Walter Scheidel, 181–202. Oxford: Oxford University Press, 2015.

North, Michael. *The Baltic: A History*. Cambridge, MA: Harvard University Press, 2015.

The Expansion of Europe, 1250–1500. Manchester: Manchester University Press, 2007.

North, Michael, and Frits Snapper. "The Baltic Trade and the Decline of the Dutch Economy in the 18th Century." In *From the North Sea to the Baltic: Essays in Commercial, Monetary and Agrarian History*, edited by Michael North, 263–286. Brookfield: Ashgate, 1996.

Norwich, John Julius. *A History of Venice*. New York: Vintage: 1989.

Nusteling, Hubert. "The Population of Amsterdam and the Golden Age." In *Rome/Amsterdam: Two Growing Cities in Seventeenth Century Europe*, edited by Peter van Kessel and Elisja Schulte, 71–84. Amsterdam: Amsterdam University Press, 1997.

Nutini, Hugo G., and Barry L. Isaac. *Social Stratification in Central Mexico, 1500–2000*. Austin: University of Texas Press, 2009.

Nylan, Michael. "Introduction." In *Chang'an 26 BCE: An Augustan Age in China*, edited by Michael Nylan and Griet Vankeerberghen, 3–54. Seattle: University of Washington Press, 2015.

"Supplying the Capital With Water and Food." In *Chang'an 26 BCE: An Augustan Age in China*, edited by Michael Nylan and Griet Vankeerberghen, 99–130. Seattle: University of Washington Press, 2015.

Ober, Josiah. "Greek Economic Performance, 800–300 BCE: A Comparison Case." In *Quantifying the Greco Roman Economy and beyond*, edited by François de Callataÿ, 103–122. Bari: Edipuglia, 2014.

The Rise and Fall of Classical Greece. Princeton: Princeton University Press, 2015.
"Wealthy Hellas." *Transactions of the American Philological Association*, 140 no. 2 (2010), 241–286.

Oertel, Christian. "Road Networks, Communications, and the Teutonic Order." In *Journeying along Medieval Routes in Europe and the Middle East*, edited by Alison L. Gascoigne, Leonie V. Hicks, and Marianne O'Doherty, 205–230. Turnhout: Brepols, 2016.

Ohnersorgen, Michael, and Marcie L. Venter. "Aztec Boundary Interactions." In *The Oxford Handbook of the Aztecs*, edited by Deborah L. Nichols and Enrique Rodriguez-Alegría, 525–536. Oxford: Oxford University Press, 2017.

Olton, Elizabeth Drake. "Spaces of Transformation at Temple 1, Tikal, Guatemala." In *Maya Imagery, Architecture, and Activity*, edited by Maline D. Werness-Rude and Kaylee R. Spencer, 271–307. Albuquerque: University of New Mexico Press, 2015.

Onnekink, David, and Gijs Rommelse. *The Dutch in the Early Modern World: A History of a Global Power*. Cambridge: Cambridge University Press, 2019.

Osborn, Robin. "Urban Landscape and Architecture." In *The Oxford Handbook of Hellenic Studies*, edited by George Boys-Stones, Barbara Graziosi, and Phiroze Vasunia, 238–246. Oxford: Oxford University Press, 2009.

Osheim, Duane. "Rural Italy." In *Italy in the Central Middle Ages 1000–1300*, edited by David Abulafia, 161–182. Oxford: Oxford University Press, 2004.

Ottenheym, Koen. "The Amsterdam Ring of Canals: City Planning and Architecture." In *Rome/Amsterdam: Two Growing Cities in Seventeenth Century Europe*, edited by Peter van Kessel and Elisja Schulte, 33–49. Amsterdam: Amsterdam University Press, 1997.

Ottenheym, Konrad, and Krista De Jonge. "Civic Prestige. Building the City 1580–1700." In *Unity and Discontinuity: Architectural Relations between the Southern and Northern Low Countries 1530–1700*, edited by Krista De Jonge and Konrad Ottenheym, 209–250. Turnhout: Brepols, 2007.

Otto of Freising. *The Deeds of Fredrick Barbarossa*. New York: Columbia University Press, 2004.

Oxfam. *Mugged: Poverty in Your Coffee Cup*. Boston: Oxfam, 2002.

Page, Willie F. *The Dutch Triangle: The Netherlands and the Atlantic Slave Trade, 1621–1664*. New York: Garland, 1997.

Parsons, Jeffrey R. "The Development of a Prehistoric Complex Society: A Regional Perspective from the Valley of Mexico." *Journal of Field Archeology* 1, no. 1 (1974), 81–108.

Patterson, John R. "The City of Rome." In *A Companion to the Roman Republic*, edited by Nathan Rosenstein and Robert Morstein-Marx, 345–361. Oxford: Blackwell Publishing, 2006.

Pennock, Caroline Dodds. "Gender and Aztec Life Cycles." In *The Oxford Handbook of the Aztecs*, edited by Deborah L. Nichols and Enrique Rodriguez-Alegría, 387–398. Oxford: Oxford University Press, 2017.

Pezzolo, Luciano. "The Venetian Economy." In *A Companion to Venetian History*, edited by Eric R. Dursteler, 255–318. Boston: Brill, 2013.

Phillips, Derek. *Well-Being in Amsterdam's Golden Age*. Amsterdam: Amsterdam University Press, 2008.

Pirenne, Henri. *Medieval Cities: Their Origins and the Revival of Trade*. Princeton: Princeton University Press, 1939.

Plato. *Phaedo*. Oxford: Oxford University Press, 2009.

Republic. Oxford: Oxford University Press, 1993.

Pliny the Elder. *Natural History*. New York: Penguin, 1991.

Plutarch. "The Life of Solon," in *The Parallel Lives*. Available at http://penelope.uchicago.edu/Thayer/E/Roman/Texts/Plutarch/Lives/Solon*.html, last accessed February 13, 2024.

Parallel Lives. Cambridge: Loeb Classical Library, 1921.

Pollack, Susan. *Ancient Mesopotamia: The Eden That Never Was*. Cambridge: Cambridge University Press, 1999.

Polybius. *The Histories*. Cambridge: Loeb Classical Library, 1922.

Poo, Mu-Chou. *Daily Life in Ancient China*. Cambridge: Cambridge University Press, 2018.

Pool, Christopher A. "The Formation of Complex Societies in Mesoamerica." In *The Oxford Handbook of Mesoamerican Archeology*, edited by Deborah L. Nichols, 169–187. Oxford: Oxford University Press, 2012.

Postgate, J. N. *Early Mesopotamia: Society and Economy at the Dawn of History*. New York: Routledge, 1994.

Postma, Johannes. "The Dimension of the Dutch Slave Trade from Western Africa." *The Journal of African History* 13, no. 2 (1972), 237–248.

The Dutch in the Atlantic Slave Trade 1600–1815. Cambridge: Cambridge University Press, 2008.

Powell, Anton. *Athens and Sparta: Constructing Greek Political and Social History From 478 B.C.*, 2nd ed. New York: Routledge, 2001.

Prak, Maarten. "Burghers into Citizens: Urban and National Citizenship in the Netherlands during the Revolutionary Era." *Theory and Society* 26, no. 4 (1997), 403–420.

"The Dutch Republic's City-State Culture." In *A Comparative Study of Thirty City-State Cultures*, edited by Mogens Herman Hansen, 343–358. Copenhagen: The Royal Danish Academy of Arts and Letters, 2000.

Prashad, Vijay. *The Poorer Nations: A Possible History of the Global South*. London: Verso, 2013.

Price, J. L. "Water and Land." In *The Cambridge Companion to the Dutch Golden Age*, edited by Helmer J. Helmers and Geert H. Janssen, 32–48. Cambridge: Cambridge University Press, 2018.

Price, Simon. "The History of the Hellenistic Period." In *The Oxford History of Greece and the Hellenistic World*, edited by John Boardman, Jasper Griffin, and Oswyn Murray, 364–389. Oxford: Oxford University Press, 2001.

Puga, Diego, and Daniel Trefler. "International Trade and Institutional Change: Medieval Venice's Response to Globalization." National Bureau of Economic Research, Working Paper 18288 (August 2012).

Pullan, Brian. *Rich and Poor in Renaissance Venice: The Social Institutions of a Catholic State, to 1620*. Oxford: Oxford University Press, 1971.

Purcell, Nicholas. "Mobility and the Polis." In *The Greek City: From Homer to Alexander*, edited by Oswyn Murray and Simon Price, 29–58. Oxford: Clarendon Press, 1990.

"Urbanism." In *The Oxford Handbook of Roman Studies*, edited by Alessandro Barchiesi and Walter Scheidel, 579–591. Oxford: Oxford University Press, 2010.

Pye, Michael. *The Edge of the World: A Cultural History of the North Sea and the Transformation of Europe*. New York, Pegasus, 2015.

Qian, Sima. *Records of the Grand Historian: Han Dynasty II*. New York: Columbia University Press, 1961.

Queller, Donald E. *The Venetian Patriciate: Reality Versus Myth*. Chicago: University of Illinois Press, 1986.

Raccagni, Gianluca. *The Lombard League, 1167–1225*. Oxford: Oxford University Press, 2010.

Radner, Karen, and Eleanor Robson. "Introduction." In *The Oxford Handbook of Cuneiform Culture*, edited by Karen Radner and Eleanor Robson, xvii–xxxii. Oxford: Oxford University Press, 2011.

Raymond, André. "The Economy of the Traditional City." In *The City in the Islamic World*, edited by Salma K. Jayyusi, 731–751. Boston: Brill, 2008.

"Islamic City, Arab City: Orientalist Myths and Recent Views." *British Journal of Middle Eastern Studies* 21, no. 1 (1994), 3–18.

"The Spatial Organization of the City." In *The City in the Islamic World*, edited by Salma K. Jayyusi, 48–70. Boston: Brill, 2008.

Reger, Gary. "The Economy." In *A Companion to the Hellenistic World*, edited by Andrew Erskine, 331–353. Oxford: Blackwell Publishing, 2003.

"Hellenistic Greece and Western Asia Minor." In *The Cambridge Economic History of the Greco-Roman World*, edited by Walter Scheidel, Ian Morris, and Richard Saller, 460–483. Cambridge: Cambridge University Press, 2007.

Rhodes, P. J. *The Greek City States: A Source Book*, 2nd ed. Cambridge: Cambridge University Press, 2007.

Rice, Don S. "Late Classic Maya Population: Characteristics and Implications." In *Urbanism in the Preindustrial World*, edited by Glenn Storey, Rebecca Storey, Li Liu, Sarah M. Nelson, and Roger S. Bagnall, 252–276. Tuscaloosa: University of Alabama Press, 2006.

Richardson, Seth. "Early Mesopotamia: The Presumptive State." *Past and Present* no. 215 (2012), 3–49.

Roberts, Alexandre M. "Al Mansur and the Critical Ambassador." *Bulletin d'Études Orientales* 60, no. 1 (2012), 145–160.

Robinson, Chase F. "The Rise of Islam, 600–705." In *The New Cambridge History of Islam: The Formation of the Islamic World, Sixth to Eleventh Centuries*, edited by Chase F. Robinson, 173–224. Cambridge: Cambridge University Press, 2010.

Robinson, Jennifer. *Ordinary Cities: Between Modernity and Development*. London: Routledge, 2006.

Robinson, O. F. *Ancient Rome: City Planning and Administration*. New York: Routledge, 1992.

de Rojas, José Luis. "Tenochtitlan." In *The Oxford Handbook of the Aztecs*, edited by Deborah L. Nichols and Enrique Rodriguez-Alegría, 219–228. Oxford: Oxford University Press, 2017.

Tenochtitlan: Capital of the Aztec Empire. Gainesville: University of Florida, 2012.

Romano, Dennis. *Patricians and Popolani: The Social Foundations of the Venetian Renaissance State*. Baltimore: Johns Hopkins University Press, 1987.

Ropp, Paul S. *China in World History*. Oxford: Oxford University Press, 2010.

Rörig, Fritz. *The Medieval Town*. Berkeley: University of California Press, 1967.

Roselaar, Saskia T. "State-Organized Mobility in the Roman Empire: Legionaries and Auxiliaries." In *Migration and Mobility in the Early Roman Empire*, edited by Luuk de Ligt and Laurens E. Tacoma, 138–157. Boston: Brill, 2016.

Rosenswig, Robert M. *The Beginnings of Mesoamerican Civilization*. Cambridge: Cambridge University Press, 2010.

Rostovtzeff, M. *The Social & Economic History of the Hellenistic World*. Oxford: Oxford University Press, 1941.

The Social and Economic History of the Roman Empire, 2nd ed. Oxford: Oxford University Press, 1957.

Rotz, Rhiman A. "The Lübeck Uprising of 1408 and the Decline of the Hanseatic League." *Proceedings of the American Philosophical Society* 121, no. 1 (1977), 1–45.

Rowlandson, Jane. "Town and Country in Ptolemaic Egypt." In *A Companion to the Hellenistic World*, edited by Andrew Erskine, 249–263. Oxford: Blackwell Publishing, 2003.

Rozman, Gilbert. *Urban Networks in Ch'ing China and Tokugawa Japan*. Princeton: Princeton University Press, 2015.

Sallares, Robert. "Ecology." In *The Cambridge Economic History of the Greco-Roman World*, edited by Walter Scheidel, Ian Morris, and Richard Saller, 15–37. Cambridge: Cambridge University Press, 2007.

Sarnowsky, Jürgen. "The 'Golden Age' of the Hanseatic League." In *A Companion to the Hanseatic League*, edited by Donald J. Harreld, 64–100. Boston: Brill, 2015.

Sassen, Saskia. *Cities in a World Economy*. Thousand Oaks, CA: Sage, 2018.

"Deciphering the Global." In *Deciphering the Global: Its Scales, Spaces and Subjects*, edited by Saskia Sassen, 1–18. New York: Routledge, 2007.

"Electronic Space and Power." In *Globalization and Its Discontents: Essays on the New Mobility of People and Money*, edited by Saskia Sassen, 177–194. New York: New Press, 1998.

Expulsions: Brutality and Complexity in the Global Economy. Cambridge, MA: Harvard University Press, 2014.

The Global City: New York, London, Tokyo. Princeton: Princeton University Press, 2001.

"Locating Cities on Global Circuits." In *Global Network, Linked Cities*, edited by Saskia Sassen, 1–33. London: Routledge, 2002.

Losing Control? Sovereignty in an Age of Globalization. New York: Columbia University Press, 1996.

Territory, Authority, Rights: From Medieval to Global Assemblages. Princeton: Princeton University Press, 2008.

The Embarrassment of Riches: An Interpretation of Dutch Culture in the Golden Age. New York: Vintage, 1997.

Scheidel, Walter. "Creating a Metropolis: A Comparative Demographic Perspective." In *Ancient Alexandria Between Egypt and Greece*, edited by W. V. Harris and Giovanni Ruffini, 1–32. Boston: Brill, 2004.

"Demography." In *The Cambridge Economic History of the Greco-Roman World*, edited by Walter Scheidel, Ian Morris, and Richard Saller, 38–86. Cambridge: Cambridge University Press, 2007.

"Human Mobility in Italy, II: The Slave Population." *The Journal of Roman Studies* 95 (2005), 64–79.

"Human Mobility in Roman Italy, I: The Free Population." *The Journal of Roman Studies* 94 (2004), 1–26.

Schildhauer, Johannes. *The Hansa: History and Culture*. Leipzig: Edition Leipzig, 1985.

Schneider, Jens, and Damien Janos. "Baghdad: Political Metropolis and Intellectual Center." In *The Place to Go: Contexts of Learning in Baghdad, 750–1000 CE*, edited by Jens Schneider and Damien Janos, 1–45. Berlin: Gerlach Press, 2014.

Schottenhammer, Angela. "Pirates and Slaves on the South China Sea." In *Silk Roads: People, Cultures, Landscapes*, edited by Susan Whitfield, 415–419. Oakland: University of California Press, 2019.

Schutte, Anne Jacobson. "Society and the Sexes in the Venetian Republic." In *A Companion to Venetian History*, edited by Eric R. Dursteler, 354–377. Boston: Brill, 2013.

Scott, James C. *Against the Grain: A Deep History of the Earliest States*. New Haven: Yale University Press, 2017.

Scott, Tom. *The City-State in Europe, 1000–1600: Hinterland, Territory, Region*. Oxford: Oxford University Press, 2012.

"Town and Country in Germany, 1350–1600." In *Town and Country in Europe, 1300–1800*, edited by S. R. Epstein, 202–228. Cambridge: Cambridge University Press, 2001.

Sears, Gareth. *The Cities of Roman Africa*. Gloucestershire: The History Press, 2011

Sharer, Robert J. "Founding Events and Teotihuacan Connections at Copán Honduras." In *The Maya and Teotihuacan: Reinterpreting Early Classic Interaction*, edited by Geoffrey E. Braswell, 143–165. Austin: University of Texas Press, 2004.

Sharon, Moshe. *Revolt: The Social and Military Aspects of the Abbasid Revolution*. Jerusalem: Hebrew University, 1990.

Shelton, Jo-Ann (ed.). *As the Romans Did: A Sourcebook in Roman Social History*, 2nd ed. Oxford: Oxford University Press, 1998.

Shen, Chen. "Compromises and Conflicts: Production and Commerce in the Royal Cities of Eastern Zhou, China." In *The Social Construction of Ancient Cities*, edited by M. L. Smith, 290–310. Washington DC: Smithsonian Institution Press, 1990.

Shepperson, Mary. "Planning for the Sun: Urban Forms as a Mesopotamian Response to the Sun." *World Archeology* 41, no. 3 (2009), 363–378.

Shipley, Graham. "Distance, Development and Decline? World Systems Analysis and the 'Hellenistic' World." In *Centre and Periphery in the Hellenistic World*, edited by Per Bilde, Troels Engberg-Pedersen, Lise Hannestad, Jan Zahle, and Klavs Randsborg, 271–284. Aarhus: Aarhus University Press, 1993.

The Greek World After Alexander: 323-330 BC. New York: Routledge, 2000.

Simonsen, Jørgen Baek. "Mecca and Medina: Arab City-States or Arab Caravan Cities?" In *A Comparative Study of Thirty City-State Cultures*, edited by Mogens Herman Hansen, 242–249. Copenhagen: The Royal Danish Academy of Arts and Letters, 2000.

Skaff, Jonathan Karam. *Sui-Tang China and Its Turko-Mongol Neighbors: Culture, Power, and Connections, 580–800*. Oxford: Oxford University Press, 2012.

Skinner, G. William. "Cities and the Hierarchy of Local Systems." In *The City in Late Imperial China*, edited by G. William Skinner, 275–352. Palo Alto: Stanford University Press, 1977.

Skinner, Patricia. "Material Life." In *Italy in the Central Middle Ages 1000–1300*, edited by David Abulafia, 147–160. Oxford: Oxford University Press, 2004.

Smith, Michael E. "Aztec City-States." In *A Comparative Study of Thirty City-State Cultures*, edited by Mogens Herman Hansen, 581–595. Copenhagen: The Royal Danish Academy of Arts and Letters, 2000.

"Aztec Urbanism: Cities and Towns." In *The Oxford Handbook of the Aztecs*, edited by Deborah L. Nichols and Enrique Rodriguez-Alegría, 201–218. Oxford: Oxford University Press, 2017.

"City Size in Late Postclassic Mesoamerica." *Journal of Urban History* 31, no. 4 (2005), 403–434.

Smith, Michael E., and Frederic Hicks. "Inequality and Social Class in Aztec Society." In *The Oxford Handbook of the Aztecs*, edited by Deborah L. Nichols and Enrique Rodriguez-Alegría, 423–437. Oxford: Oxford University Press, 2017.

Smith, Monica L. *Cities: The First 6,000 Years*. New York: Viking, 2019.

Soja, Edward W. *Postmetropolis: Critical Studies of Cities and Regions*. Oxford: Blackwell, 2000.

Spruyt, Hendrik. *The Sovereign State and Its Competitors: An Analysis of Systems Change*. Princeton: Princeton University Press, 1994.

Stambaugh, John E. *The Ancient Roman City*. Baltimore: Johns Hopkins University Press, 1988.

Starr, S. Fredrick. *Lost Enlightenment: Central Asia's Golden Age from the Arab Conquests to Tamerlane*. Princeton: Princeton University Press, 2013.

de Ste. Croix, G. E. M. *The Class Struggle in the Ancient Greek World: From the Archaic Age to the Arab Conquests*. Ithaca: Cornell University Press, 1981.

Stearns, Peter N. *Globalization in World History*. New York: Routledge, 2017.

Steinhardt, Nancy Shatzman. *Chinese Architecture: A History*. Princeton: Princeton University Press, 2019.

Stoddart, Simon. "The Physical Geography of Republican Italy." In *A Companion to the Roman Republic*, edited by Nathan Rosenstein and Robert Morstein-Marx, 102–119. Oxford: Blackwell Publishing, 2006.

Storey, Rebecca. "Mortality through Time in an Impoverished Residence of the Precolumbian City of Teotihuacan." In *Urbanism in the Preindustrial World*, edited by Glenn Storey, Rebecca Storey, Li Liu, Sarah M. Nelson, and Roger S. Bagnall, 277–294. Tuscaloosa: University of Alabama Press, 2006.

Storey, Rebecca, Lourdes Márquez-Morfín, and Luis F. Núñez. "Teotihuacan Neighborhoods and the Health of the Residents: The Risks of Preindustrial Urban Living." In *The Neighborhood as a Social and Spatial Unit in Mesoamerican Cities*, edited by M. Charlotte Arnauld, Linda R. Manzanilla, and Michael E. Smith, 117–129. Tucson: University of Arizona Press, 2012.

Strabo. *Geography*. Cambridge: Loeb Classical Library, 1932.

Sugiyama, Saburo. "Ideology, Polity, and Social History of the Teotihuacan State." In *The Oxford Handbook of Mesoamerican Archeology*, edited by Deborah L. Nichols, 215–229. Oxford: Oxford University Press, 2012.

Tangheroni, Marco. "Trade and Navigation." In *Italy in the Central Middle Ages 1000–1300*, edited by David Abulafia, 127–146. Oxford: Oxford University Press, 2004.

Taube, Karl A. "Tetitla and the Maya Presence at Teotihuacan." In *The Maya and Teotihuacan: Reinterpreting Early Classic Interaction*, edited by Geoffrey E. Braswell, 273–314. Austin: University of Texas Press, 2004.

Taylor, Peter J. "Advanced Producer Service Centres in the World Economy." In *Global Urban Analysis: A Survey of Cities in Globalization*, edited by Peter J. Taylor, Pengfei Ni, Ben Derudder, Michael Hoyler, Jin Huang, and Frank Witlox, 22–55. London: Earthscan, 2011.

"City Generics: External Urban Relations in Ancient Mesopotamian and Modern Global City Networks." *Urban Geography* 40, no. 8 (2019), 2010–2030.

Extraordinary Cities: Millennia of Moral Syndromes, World-Systems and City-State Relations. Northampton: Edward Elgar, 2013.

"The GUCP/GaWC Project." In *Global Urban Analysis: A Survey of Cities in Globalization*, edited by Peter J. Taylor, Pengfei Ni, Ben Derudder, Michael Hoyler, Jin Huang, and Frank Witlox, 1–11. London: Earthscan, 2011.

"Historical World City Networks." In *International Handbook of Globalization and World Cities*, edited by Ben Derudder, Michael Hoyler, Peter J. Taylor, and Frank Witlox, 9–21. Northampton: Edward Elgar, 2011.

"The Interlocking Network Model." In *International Handbook of Globalization and World Cities*, edited by Ben Derudder, Michael Hoyler, Peter J. Taylor, and Frank Witlox, 51–62. Northampton: Edward Elgar, 2011.

"Problematizing City/State Relations: Towards a Geohistorical Understanding of Contemporary Globalization." *Transactions of the Institute of British Geographers* 32, no. 2 (2007), 133–150.

"Urbanization." In *The Oxford Handbook of Global Studies*, edited by Mark Juergensmeyer, Saskia Sassen, Manfred B. Steger, and Victor Faessel, 513–527. Oxford: Oxford University Press, 2018.

World City Network: A Global Urban Analysis. London: Routledge, 2004.

"Homo Geographicus: A Geohistorical Manifesto for Cities." GaWC Research Bulletin 107. (October 18, 2014). Available at www.lboro.ac.uk/gawc/rb/rb107.html, last accessed January 27, 2020.

Tembhekar, Chittaranjan. "Mumbaikars Die Younger Than Other Indians." *Times of India* (November 3, 2009).

Temin, Peter. *The Roman Market Economy*. Princeton: Princeton University Press, 2012.

Temple, William. "Observations upon the United Provinces of the Netherlands." University of Michigan. Available at https://quod.lib.umich.edu/e/eebo/A64324.0001.001/1:6?rgn=div1;view=fulltext, last accessed October 6, 2019.

't Hart, Marjolein. "The Dutch Republic: The Urban Impact Upon Politics." In *A Miracle Mirrored: The Dutch Republic in European Perspective*, edited by Karel Davids and Jan Lucassen, 57–98. Cambridge: Cambridge University Press, 1995.

"Intercity Rivalries and the Making of the Dutch State." In *Cities and the Rise of States in Europe, A.D. 1000 to 1800*, edited by Charles Tilly and Wim P. Blockmans, 196–217. Boulder: Westview Press, 1994.

The Making of the Bourgeois State: War, Politics and Finance during the Dutch Revolt. Manchester: Manchester University Press, 1993.

Thomas, Edmund. "Architecture." In *The Oxford Handbook of Roman Studies*, edited by Alessandro Barchiesi and Walter Scheidel, 838–854. Oxford: Oxford University Press, 2010.

Thompson, Dorothy J. "The Ptolemies and Egypt." In *A Companion to the Hellenistic World*, edited by Andrew Erskine, 105–120. Oxford: Blackwell Publishing, 2003.

Thompson, William R. "Trade Pulsations, Collapse and Reorientation in the Ancient World." In *Connectivity in Antiquity: Globalization as a Long-Term Historical Process*, edited by Øystein S. LaBianca and Arnold Scham, 32–58. London: Equinox, 2006.

Thonemann, Peter. *The Hellenistic Age: A Very Short Introduction*. Oxford: Oxford University Press, 2018.

The Hellenistic World: Using Coins as Sources. Cambridge: Cambridge University Press, 2015.

Thucydides. *The Peloponnesian War*. Oxford: Oxford University Press, 2009.

Thys-Şenocak, Lucienne. "The Gendered City." In *The City in the Islamic World*, edited by Salma K. Jayyusi, 877–893. Boston: Brill, 2008.

Tiberg, Erik. *Moscow, Livonia and the Hanseatic League 1487–1550*. Stockholm: Almqvist & Wiksell International, 1995.

Tilly, Charles. "Entanglements of European Cities and States." In *Cities and the Rise of States in Europe, A.D. 1000 to 1800*, edited by Charles Tilly and Wim P. Blockmans, 1–27. Boulder: Westview Press, 1994.

Tor, D. G. "The Political Revival of the Abbasid Caliphate: Al Muqtafi and the Seljuks." *Journal of the American Oriental Society* 137, no. 2 (2017), 301–314.

van Tussenbroek, Gabri. "Building Materials and Trade. Changes in the Organization of the Building Industry between North and South." In *Unity and Discontinuity: Architectural Relations Between the Southern and Northern Low Countries 1530–1700*, edited by Krista De Jonge and Konrad Ottenheym, 301–330. Turnhout: Brepols, 2007.

Twitchett, Denis. *Land Tenure and the Social Order in T'ang and Sung China*. Oxford: Oxford University Press, 1962.

UN Environmental Programme. "Ten Things You Should Know About Industrial Farming." Available at www.unenvironment.org/news-and-stories/story/10-things-you-should-know-about-industrial-farming, last accessed August 19, 2020.

Unger, Richard W. "Ships and Sailing Routes in Trade around 1300–1600." In *The Routledge Handbook of Maritime Trade around Europe 1300–1600*, edited by Wim Blockmans, Mikhail Krom, and Justyna Wubs-Mrozewicz, 17–35. New York: Routledge, 2017.

Versluys, Miguel John. *Visual Style and Constructing Identity in the Hellenistic World: Nemrud Dağ and Commagene Under Antiochos I*. Cambridge: Cambridge University Press, 2017.

Victor, Jennifer Nicholl, Alexander H. Montgomery, and Mark Lubell. "The Emergence of the Study of Networks in Politics." In *The Oxford Handbook of Political Networks*, edited by Jennifer Nicholl Victor, Alexander H. Montgomery, and Mark Lubell, 3–58. Oxford: Oxford University Press, 2017.

de Villehardouin, Geoffroi. "Memoirs or Chronicle of the Fourth Crusade and the Conquest of Constantinople." Project Gutenberg. Available at www.gutenberg.org/files/6032/6032-h/6032-h.htm, last accessed May 23, 2019.

Vitruvius. *The Ten Books on Architecture*. New York: Dover, 1960.

de Vries, Jan. *The Dutch Rural Economy in the Golden Age, 1500–1700*. New Haven: Yale University Press, 1974.

European Urbanization 1500–1800. Cambridge: Harvard University Press, 1984.

de Vries, Jan, and Ad van der Woude. *The First Modern Economy: Success, Failure, and Perseverance of the Dutch Economy, 1500–1815*. Cambridge: Cambridge University Press, 1997.

Vrettos, Theodore. *Alexandria: City of the Western Mind*. New York: The Free Press, 2001.

Wade, Robert. "What Strategies Are Viable for Developing Countries Today? The World Trade Organization and the Shrinking of 'Development Space'." *Review of International Political Economy* 10, no. 4 (2003): 621–644.

Walbank, F. W. *The Hellenistic World*. Sussex: The Harvester Press, 1981.

Waley, Daniel. *The Italian City-Republics*. New York: Longman, 1988.

Wallerstein, Immanuel. *The Modern World System I: Capitalist Agriculture and the Origins of the European World Economy in the Sixteenth Century*. Berkeley: University of California Press, 2011.

The Modern World System II: Mercantilism and the Consolidation of the European World Economy. Berkeley: University of California Press, 2011.

World Systems Analysis: An Introduction. Durham, NC: Duke University Press, 2004.

Watson, Allan, and Jonathan V. Beaverstock. "World City Network Research at a Theoretical Impasse: On the Need to Reestablish Qualitative Approaches to Understanding Agency in World City Networks." *Tijdschrift Voor Economische en Sociale Geographie* 105, no. 4 (2014), 412–426.

Webb, Peter. "Islam: A New Faith along the Silk Roads." In *Silk Roads: People, Cultures, Landscapes,* edited by Susan Whitfield, 256–268. Oakland: University of California Press, 2019.

Weber, Max. *The City*. Toronto: Free Press, 1966.

Webster, David. "The Classic Maya Collapse." In *The Oxford Handbook of the Aztecs*, edited by Deborah L. Nichols and Enrique Rodriguez-Alegría, 325–334. Oxford: Oxford University Press, 2017.

The Population of Tikal: Implications for Maya Demography. Oxford: Archeopress, 2018.

Wechsler, Howard J. "T'ai-tsung (Reign 626–49) the Consolidator." In *The Cambridge History of China: Sui and Tang China, 589–906*, edited by Denis Twitchett and John K. Fairbank 188–241. Cambridge: Cambridge University Press, 1979.

Wendell, Charles. "Baghdad: Imago Mundi, and Other Foundation Lore." *International Journal of Middle East Studies* 2, no. 2 (1971), 99–128.

Wengrow, David. *What Makes Civilization? The Ancient Near East and the Future of the West*. Oxford: Oxford University Press, 2010.

Westenholz, Aage. "The Sumerian City-State." In *A Comparative Study of Six City-State Cultures*, edited by Mogens Herman Hansen, 23–42. Copenhagen: The Royal Danish Academy of Arts and Letters, 2002.

Westrate, Job. "The Organization of Trade and Transport on the Lower Rhine and Waal Rivers around 1550." In *Trade, Diplomacy and Cultural Exchange: Continuity and Change in the North Sea Area and the Baltic c. 1350–1750*, edited by Hanno Brand, 95–112. Hilversum: Uitgeverij Verloren, 2005.

Whitcomb, Donald. "An Urban Structure for the Early Islamic City." In *Cities in the Pre-Modern Islamic World: The Urban Impact of Religion, State and Society*, edited by Amira K. Bennison and Alison L. Gascoigne, 15–26. New York: Routledge, 2007.

Whitfield, Peter. "Mapping the Silk Roads." In *Silk Roads: People, Cultures, Landscapes*, edited by Susan Whitfield, 20–39. Oakland: University of California Press, 2019.

Whitfield, Susan. *Life along the Silk Road*. Oakland: University of California Press, 2015.

Whitfield, Susan. (ed.). *Silk Roads: People, Cultures, Landscapes*. Oakland: University of California Press, 2019.

Whyte, Robert Orr. "The Evolution of the Chinese Environment." In *The Origins of Chinese Civilization*, edited by David N. Keightley, 3–20. Berkeley: University of California Press, 1983.

Wickham, Chris. *Framing the Early Middle Ages: Europe and the Mediterranean, 400–800* Oxford: Oxford University Press, 2005.

Land and Power: Studies in Italian and European Social History. London: British School at Rome, 1994.

The Mountains and the City: The Tuscan Appennines in the Early Middle Ages. Oxford: Oxford University Press, 1988.

Sleepwalking into a New World: The Emergence of Italian City Communes in the Twelfth Century. Princeton: Princeton University Press, 2015.

Widmer, Randolph J., and Rebecca Storey. "The 'Tlajinga Barrio': A Distinctive Cluster of Neighborhoods in Teotihuacan." In *The Neighborhood as a Social and Spatial Unit in Mesoamerican Cities*, edited by M. Charlotte Arnauld, Linda R. Manzanilla, and Michael E. Smith, 102–129. Tucson: University of Arizona Press, 2012.

Williams, Tim. "Arteries of the Silk Roads." In *Silk Roads: People, Cultures, Landscapes*, edited by Susan Whitfield, 282–289. Oakland: University of California Press, 2019.

Wilson, Andrew. "City Sizes and Urbanization in the Roman Empire." In *Settlement, Urbanization, and Population*, edited by Alan Bowman and Andrew Wilson, 161–195. Oxford: Oxford University Press, 2012.

Woolf, Greg. *The Life and Death of Ancient Cities: A Natural History*. Oxford: Oxford University Press, 2020.

"Movers and Stayers." in *Migration and Mobility in the Early Roman Empire*, edited by Luuk de Ligt and Laurens E. Tacoma, 439–461. Boston: Brill, 2016.

"World Systems Analysis and the Roman Empire." *Journal of Roman Archeology* 3 (1990), 44–58.

The World Bank, Our World in Data. "Land Use." Available at https://ourworldindata.org/land-use, last accessed August 14, 2020.

van der Woude, Ad, Jan de Vries, and Akira Hayami. "The Hierarchies, Provisioning, and Demographic Patterns of Cities." In *Urbanization in History: A Process of*

Dynamic Interactions, edited by Ad van der Woude, Jan de Vries, and Akira Hayami, 1–19. Oxford: Oxford University Press, 1990.

Wright, Arthur F. "The Sui Dynasty: 581–617." In *The Cambridge History of China: Sui and Tang China, 589–906*, edited by Denis Twitchett and John K. Fairbank, 48–149. Cambridge: Cambridge University Press, 1979.

Wrigley, E. A. *Continuity, Chance and Change: The Character of the Industrial Revolution in England*. Cambridge: Cambridge University Press, 1988.

Wubs-Mrozewicz, Justyna. "Danzig (Gdańsk): Seeking Stability and Autonomy." in *The Routledge Handbook of Maritime Trade around Europe 1300–1600,* edited by Wim Blockmans, Mikhail Krom, and Justyna Wubs-Mrozewicz, 248–272. New York: Routledge, 2017.

"The Hanse in Medieval and Early Modern Europe: An Introduction." In *The Hanse in Medieval and Early Modern Europe*, edited by Justyna Wubs-Mrozewicz and Stuart Jenks, 1–25. Boston: Brill, 2013.

"Rules of Inclusion, Rules of Exclusion: The Hanseatic *Kontor* in Bergen in the Late Middle Ages and Its Normative Boundaries." *German History* 29, no. 1, (2011), 1–22.

Traders, Ties and Tensions: The Interactions of Lübeckers, Overijsslers and Hollanders in Late Medieval Bergen. Hilversum: Uitgeverij Verloren, 2008.

Wycherley, R. E. *How the Greeks Built Cities*. London: Macmillan, 1962.

Xenophon. *The Economist: A Treatise on the Science of the Household in the Form of a Dialogue*. Adelaide: University of Adelaide, 2014, Book I. Available at www.gutenberg.org/files/1173/1173-h/1173-h.htm, last accessed February 24, 2024.

Xiaofeng, Tang. "The Evolution of Imperial Urban Form in Western Han Chang'an." In *Chang'an 26 BCE: An Augustan Age in China*, edited by Michael Nylan and Griet Vankeerberghen, 55–74. Seattle: University of Washington Press 2015.

Xinian, Fu. *Traditional Chinese Architecture: Twelve Essays*. Princeton: Princeton University Press, 2017.

Xinru, Liu. "Buddhism and Trade: Moving Eastwards from Gandhāra to China." In *Silk Roads: People, Cultures, Landscapes*, edited by Susan Whitfield, 152–167. Oakland: University of California Press, 2019.

Xiong, Victor Cunrui. *Sui-Tang Chang'an: A Study in the Urban History of Medieval China*. Ann Arbor: University of Michigan Press, 2000.

Yang, Shao-Yun. *The Way of the Barbarians: Redrawing Ethnic Boundaries in Tang and Song China*. Seattle: University of Washington Press, 2019.

Yates, Robin S. "Body, Space, Time, and Bureaucracy: Boundary Creation and Control Mechanisms in Early China." In *Boundaries in China*, edited by John Hay, 56–80. Chicago: University of Chicago Press, 1997.

"The City-State in Ancient China." In *The Archeology of City-States: Cross Cultural Approaches*, edited Deborah L. Nichols and Thomas H. Charlton, 71–90. Washington, DC: Smithsonian Institution Press, 1997.

Zaccagnini, Carlo. "The Interdependence of Great Powers." In *Amarna Diplomacy: The Beginnings of International Relations*, edited by Raymond Cohen and Raymond Westbrook, 141–153. Baltimore: The Johns Hopkins University Press.

van Zanden, J. L. *The Rise and Decline of Holland's Economy: Merchant Capitalism and the Labor Market*. Manchester: Manchester University Press, 1993.

Zhao, Dingxin. "The Han Bureaucracy: Its Origin, Nature, and Development." In *State Power in Ancient China and Rome*, edited by Walter Scheidel, 56–89. Oxford: Oxford University Press, 2015.
Zhao, Zhongwei. "Long-term Mortality Patterns in Chinese History: Evidence from Mortality Patterns in Chinese History." *Population Studies* 51 (1997), 117–127.
Zhenping, Wang. *Tang China in Multi-Polar Asia*. Honolulu: University of Hawaii Press, 2013.
Zuiderhoek, Arjan. *The Ancient City*. Cambridge: Cambridge University Press, 2017.

Index

www.ingramcontent.com/pod-product-compliance
Ingram Content Group UK Ltd.
Pitfield, Milton Keynes, MK11 3LW, UK
UKHW022002110125
453302UK00021B/115

9 781009 444996